HOMILETICS;

OR,

THE THEORY OF PREACHING.

BY A. VINET, D.D.

TRANSLATED AND EDITED

BY THOMAS H. SKINNER, D.D.,
PROFESSOR OF SACRED RHETORIC AND PASTORAL THEOLOGY, IN THE UNION THEOLOGICAL SEMINARY OF NEW YORK.

Πῶς δὲ ἀκούσουσι χωρὶς κηρυσσοντος;

SECOND EDITION.

NEW YORK:
IVISON & PHINNEY, 178 FULTON STREET.
(SUCCESSORS OF NEWMAN & IVISON, AND MARK H. NEWMAN & CO.)
CHICAGO: S. C. GRIGGS & CO. BUFFALO: PHINNEY & CO.
AUBURN: J. C. IVISON & CO. DETROIT: A. M'FARREN.
CINCINNATI: MOORE, ANDERSON & CO.

1855.

STEREOTYPED BY
THOMAS B. SMITH,
216 William St., N. Y.

PREFACE

BY THE TRANSLATOR.

As the form of preaching should be perfectly adapted to times and places,* it ought to be very different now from what it has ever been; for the peculiarity of these times is, in many respects, radical, and its bearings on all divine and human interests are very decided and general. The mode of preaching which prevailed at the beginning of the nineteenth century could not have been retained entirely unchanged; the renovating power, which has been changing all things in science, in art, in the physical, social and civil life of man, has, of necessity, been felt by the pulpit, the central instrumentality in human history. Preaching, on the whole, has consequently been advancing, together with the general progress of society. It must, however, be admitted, that in the career of improvement, it has not been in advance of the other instruments of change

* See 1 Corinthians, ix. 19–23. Compare, also, Saint Paul's address to the philosophers of Athens (Acts, xvii. 22–31) with that which he delivered to his countrymen at Antioch in Pisidia, (Acts, xiii. 16–41.)

which are exerting themselves with such astonishing efficiency in every sphere of human life; it is doubtless behind the most of them; nor is there any object of deeper interest to every true philanthropist, every one who identifies the progress of humanity with the success of the gospel, than that preaching should receive a new and healthful impulse, which shall give it the precedence to which it is entitled—a just adaptation to humanity in its present excited and over-active state, and a controlling power over all the changes which, with such unparalleled rapidity, are coming to pass everywhere in the world.

It was the chief reason why the translator of this work desired its circulation, that its author insists so earnestly and forcibly on the necessity of modifying preaching, so as to suit it to the character of the age; that a mind so richly endowed by nature, so furnished with every kind of knowledge, so highly disciplined, and so pre-eminent in spirituality and devotion to the cause of christian truth, has, in this work, given its whole strength to the exposition of a theory which embraces this necessity as one of its fundamental and most prominent ideas.* Careful study of the product of its labor has very much increased his desire.

* See chap. vi., part ii., and especially the installation discourse at the end of the book, pages 491–505.

On a subject of the greatest importance and difficulty, and which many eminent men have treated, the author has given to the world an original book; and we venture to say that among all the productions of his powerful pen, it is destined to be regarded universally, as in the first rank of scholarship, learning, intellectual affluence and power, grace and beauty, order and perfection of execution. He confines himself throughout to preaching as his chief subject; but as the theory of preaching and that of secular oratory coincide in their essential elements, (eloquence being in principle the same in every sphere,) he enters freely into the domain of the latter. He shows himself master of it, and avails himself fully of the treasures of wisdom, learning, thought and expression with which the labors of his predecessors have filled it; but he does this only that he may present his work as a more worthy offering at the shrine of sacred eloquence. In return, however, he has laid all kinds of oratory under obligations to him. His book is a directory for all public speakers and all who would excel in argumentative, oratorical and elegant writing. There is scarcely a question pertaining to the philosophy of rhetoric and belles lettres, to the laws of language and reasoning, to the mode of influencing the mind by persuasive discourse, which does not find a place in this book, which is not here treated with the charm of diction, the strength and beauty of style the clearness of statement and method, by which this great author is so eminently distinguished. It is a book for the man of taste, of general literature and philosophy; for the student who desires to furnish his mind as richly as possible with sentiment, with thought, with precise and comprehensive views, with the secret of vigorous thinking and writing; for every one, in short, who aims to bring all the powers of his nature under the highest form of mental discipline. Nevertheless, it is strictly an offering to the pulpit; first and last it is a work whose great purpose is the improvement of sacred oratory, the increase of strength, of skill, of wisdom, and efficiency in preaching.

The reader cannot fail to remark that the illustrative examples, which are very abundant, are taken almost exclusively from French and German authors. The Editor was inclined at first to add others from the productions of English, Scotch and American preachers; but he found that the size of the book would be increased too much if any degree of justice were done to these preachers, who, in number, power and excellence of every kind, stand altogether unrivalled; and when he considered that in this country these authors are comparatively well known, while those of the French and German churches are strangers, except to a few, he had less regret that no additional examples could be well admitted.

The translator's work has been merely one of translation. Certain passages seemed to require paraphrase or commentary, which the Editor was tempted to give, but as he perceived, invariably, that closer application to the author's thought, made comment superfluous, he determined simply to render the French into English. In a few cases, he has made brief remarks at the bottom of the page; but the text is strict translation, with no variations from the manner of the author, which were not required by fidelity to his meaning.

The author generally renders into French the examples which he cites from works in other languages; the awkwardness of translating these translations has been, in most cases, avoided by making or adopting translations from the originals. In two instances a friend has favored the Editor with translations from the German.*

The Editor has added an index, in order to assist the reader in referring to the very numerous and various subjects which are contained in the book.

* These are the citations from Theremin and Herder, at the con clusion of CHAP. VI., PART II.

CONTENTS.

INTRODUCTION.

PART FIRST.

INVENTION.

SECTION FIRST.

SUBJECT OF PULPIT DISCOURSE.

CHAPTER I.

UNITY OF THE SUBJECT.

CHAPTER II.

INTEREST OF THE SUBJECT.

CHAPTER III.

OF THE TEXT.

CHAPTER IV.

SECTION SECOND.

CHAPTER I.

CHAPTER II.

PART SECOND.

DISPOSITION.

CHAPTER I.

CHAPTER II.

OF THE EXORDIUM.

CHAPTER III.

CHAPTER IV.

OF TRANSITIONS.

CHAPTER V.

OF THE PERORATION.

CHAPTER VI.

CHAPTER VII.

PART THIRD.

ELOCUTION.

CHAPTER I.

OF ELOCUTION IN GENERAL.

CHAPTER II.

CHAPTER III.

SUPERIOR QUALITIES OR VIRTUES OF STYLE.

CHAPTER IV.

APPENDIX.

ADVERTISEMENT OF THE EDITORS.

THE remarks we prefixed to the *Pastoral Theology* are yet more particularly applicable to the course on *Homiletics*, and we refer the reader to them.

The original manuscripts, which in some parts of the course are numerous and various, have been compared with one another, and that which we have taken as the basis of our labor, has often been enriched by ideas borrowed from the others. On points, on which M. Vinet left only short and imperfect notes, we had recourse to the note-books of his hearers, and, as in the *Pastoral Theology*, we have indicated the passages borrowed from their note-books, and those in which the original text has been somewhat modified, either by completing imperfect sentences or by combining detached fragments, by enclosing them in brackets.[*] We have omitted this caution only in matters of detail, too unimportant to be noticed.

The work we publish, especially in respect to form, would certainly have been more perfect, if the author himself had revised it; still the last form, which, after

* These are omitted in the translation.

successive revisions, he gave to many extended portions of his course, is doubtless very nearly that which he would finally have adopted, and may be considered as definitive. In every particular this volume, in all its parts, gives with scrupulous fidelity the thoughts of M. Vinet on one of the most important branches of his teaching; nor can we doubt, that while it will be eagerly received by the portion of the public, for whom it is directly designed, it will be also read by others with lively interest and great advantage.

HOMILETICS.

INTRODUCTION.

The office of the Evangelical Ministry consists of different elements, among which The Word has the predominance. The Christian religion, the religion of liberty and persuasion, is a word. Jesus Christ, who is at once the Author and the Object of Christianity, is called The Word.* Even before his advent in the flesh, he spoke internally to the conscience of every man; for the word is not only that series of articulate sounds which conveys ideas to the mind; the word is the thought itself. The thought is a word, as the word is a thought. But this Word, which spoke out of time and internally, has spoken in time and externally. Jesus Christ spoke by facts; he spoke by his life, and by his death; but he spoke also in the ordinary sense of the term. He preached.† We are called to repeat his words; but he sends us, as he himself was sent; that is to say, as he

* John i. 1-4, 14.

† "Summus ecclesiastes Dei filius, qui est imago patris absolutissima, qui virtus et sapientia genitoris est æterna, per quem Patri visum est humanæ gentis largiri quidquid bonorum mortalium generi dare decreverat, nullo alio cognomine magnificentius significantiusve denotatur in sacris literis, quam quum *dicitur verbum sive sermo Dei.*" Erasmus *Ecclesiastes*, lib i., cap ii.

is united in thought to his Father, he would have us unite ourselves to him in thought; that we should be one with him as he is one with his Father. He strikes upon our mind as on sounding brass, which does not resound without vibrating; it is his pleasure, that as we are the offspring of his thought, our brethren should become the offspring of ours. God has purposed that man should be the channel of truth to man. Natural paternity is the symbol of our spiritual relationships; we mutually engender one another.* Not only are words to be transmitted and repeated; a life is to be communicated. The truths of which the Gospel consists must become living and personal in living persons. The Word did not speak once for all (unless we take the letter for the Word); the Word speaks without ceasing, and the letter of the Gospel is only the necessary means through which this Word speaks to all. This is the only just idea of the institution of the ministry. The minister is a minister of the Word of God. Christianity, a religion of thought, should be *spoken.*†

We are authorized to call men ministers of the gospel or pastors who do not exercise the ministry of the word. In doing so, we do but follow the apostles and the primitive church; but still we cannot understand them otherwise than as giving instruction, that is to say, the word, the preeminence among all the labors of the ministry. "Let the pastors who fulfil their functions well, be accounted worthy of a double honor, especially those" (there were then pastors whose office was not speaking) "who labor in preaching the word, and in instruction." 1 Timothy, v. 17, comp. with 1 Corinthians, xiv. 1-4.

* See *l'Essai sur la manifestation des Convictions Religieuses,* pp. 111, 112.

† See *Pastoral Theology,* page 24 of our translation, and the beginning of *the Résumè of the first part of Homiletics.*

The Word is the pastor's great instrument. It varies according to its different uses; it breaks the bread of life now into smaller, now into larger pieces; if need be, it reduces it to to crumbs.

The minister speaks either on the part of man to God, or on the part of God to man; in doing the first he prays, in doing the second he preaches. It is of the second only that we are now to treat.

He preaches to individuals—to the community dispersed, to the community assembled in one place. We are to speak of the latter kind of preaching.

He must preach to the assembled community, in order to reach those who cannot be otherwise reached, in order to prepare in the temple the invisible church which no temple can contain, and which, in its pure state, exists in none; in order to give to the word all the distinction and efficacy of which it is susceptible. A community may be addressed by writing, but the written word cannot hold the place of the other, or render it superfluous.

This predominance of the word in Christian worship, gives the latter a distinct character. It gives reality to the notion of the church. There is no Mahometan, no Brahminical church, and certainly there is not a church in the religion of Homer. With the Jews, instruction was separated from worship, (we say *the Jewish people*, rather than *the Jewish church;*) if there was a Jewish church, instruction, not worship, formed it, and that church had no centre. It is only among Christians that worship and instruction, which are coördinate one to the other, which are interpreted one by the other, form a whole.

With the Catholics, preaching has little place; on the contrary, it is almost everything with us. Except at certain seasons of worship and on certain days of the year, the temple is an auditory. It seems to have no other purpose than to gather hearers around a man who speaks to them. Thus we say of the Catholic, he goes to *mass*, of the Protestant, he goes to *sermon*. We thus unconsciously give perhaps too exclusive predominance to preaching in Protestant worship. Among other inconveniences, this system has that of attributing too much to the individual.

This is not inconsistent with what we said of the transmission of truth from one individual to another. Nevertheless, is it not possible that the habit of going to the temple only to hear discourses, and making little of all the rest, has the effect of displaying only a person and an occasion, a preacher and preaching? And is it not important that the efficacy of worship should be more independent of the person of the preacher.*

Be this as it may, in both the forms of worship which have suggested these observations, the word is of high importance. In the one as in the other, a minister is essentially a man who speaks the word of God. Now, may the word of preaching, which is a word of reconciliation or of sanctification, "according to the oracles of God," (1 Peter, iv. 11,) be reduced to an art?

Eloquence, certainly, is always the same; it is not one thing in the pulpit and another in the senate or at the bar. There are not two rhetorics any more than two logics. Still, the nature of ecclesiastical discourse involves differences, adds rules, which constitute a particular art under the name of *Homiletics*.

We will consider first what is common to Rhetoric and Homiletics, then what is special to the latter. Rhetoric is the genus, Homiletics the species.

The subject matter of Rhetoric corresponds to the object of *public eloquence*. What is eloquence in general?

La Bruyère tells us: "It is a gift of the soul which makes us masters of the mind and heart of others, which enables us to inspire them as we will, or persuade them to whatever we please."†

* See Pastoral Theology, pp. 25, 28, of our translation.

† La Bruyère Les Caractéres, chap. i. *Des ouvrages de l'esprit.*

I would say, it is the gift of acquiring the mastery by language, for a gesture, a look, may be eloquent. It relates, too, to continued discourse, and not to one word only. La Bruyère points out to us the source and effect of eloquence rather than its nature; there is still, however, something of importance in his definition. Eloquence is a *gift*, and *a gift* of the soul. It is the gift of thinking and feeling with others as they think and feel, and of suiting to their thought the words and the movement of our discourse, of speaking the thoughts of others.

Eloquence rests on sympathy. One can never be eloquent except as he can speak or write under an influence from those to whom he addresses himself; they must inspire him, and unless this condition is met, he may be profound and interesting, but he cannot be eloquent. In order to be eloquent, he must feel the necessity of communicating his life to others, and of comprehending intimately what chords must be made to vibrate within them.

Pascal, penetrating farther into the secret of eloquence than La Bruyère, says: "Eloquence consists in a correspondence which we endeavor to establish between the mind and heart of those to whom we speak, on the one hand, and the thought and expressions which we employ on the other. And this supposes that we have carefully studied the human heart, to know all its recesses, and then how we may be able to adapt to them justly-arranged discourse. We must put ourselves in the place of those who are to hear us, and try on our own heart the train of thought which we give to our discourse, to ascertain if one be suited to the other, and whether we may confidently expect that the hearer will be obliged to yield to us."*

What with La Bruyère was a gift, with Pascal was a *method*. But it is at once a gift and a method. And the same

* PASCAL, *Pensées*, Partie ii., Art. xvii., § 105.

idea meets us under each point of view, namely, the vital and inward penetration of the hearer's soul by that of the orator. We find yet another element—that of persuasion—the determinate direction of the soul and the will. Eloquence in the sense of La Bruyère and Pascal is an exercise of real life, an effort against a resistance, a *compulsion*,* a drama we may say, in which only one person appears, but in which there are two, and which has its plot, its incidents, and its catastrophe. The catastrophe may be, in some cases, a determination, a voluntary act of him to whom we speak; in others, a feeling which is also an act, and in a religious and philosophical point of view, is an act *par excellence.*

Thus, without denying the epithet eloquent to language suited to convey light and conviction to the mind, we apply it more particularly to that whose purpose and effect is to determine the will in a certain way, or to a certain act, immediate or eventual.

But is there only the subjective, is there nothing objective in the notion of eloquence? According to Pascal and La Bruyère, it is a power which lends itself indifferently to evil and to good, to error and to truth. If it be so, must we not utterly repel both eloquence and rhetoric which is its theory or method?

I adopt the principle and deny the consequence. It is not to be doubted that there is in eloquence a power of persuasion to evil as well as to good, and that the principle of this power in both cases, is the gift of finding and giving vibration to certain chords in the heart. We may, if we will, refuse to apply the word eloquence to both results, but what do we gain? A word. It were better, I think, while we acknowledge that bad men may be eloquent, and that one may be eloquent in advocating what is evil, to add on the other side—

* *Compelle intrare.*

1. That however man may be inclined to evil, evil has no witness or representative in his conscience; that truth, on the contrary, has its witness in the depths of his soul; that he acknowledges her when she shows herself, and that "if the flesh be weak the spirit is willing."* It hence results that eloquence is more strictly allied to truth than to error, to good than to evil. Truth is in itself eloquent; we do not make it eloquent, we only disclose it; truth, in whatever sense we take the word, is the condition and substance itself of eloquence. In order to persuade to evil, we must give it the appearance of good.

2. What is not perhaps the definition of eloquence, is its rule; or if you will, the rule of eloquence shall be our definition of it. Eloquence, we say, is a deliverer, who comes to the aid of good principle against bad, of truth against error. Yet more we say, that although the object or the life which eloquence has in view is always drawn immediately from *affection*, and although the orator's object consequently, is to create or develop affection, he cannot but make it conformable to eternal and divine ideas, and that in this sense only, eloquence is a power for liberty and not a power for tyranny.

3. The just inference from the fact we have affirmed is, that the more eloquence is used in the service of error, the more should it be used in the service of truth, and that truth should be defended with the weapons of truth. Its best advocates too often dissemble; and that because faith in truth, which alone gives us courage, is rare. It is treachery to a holy cause, to employ in its defence means which are not suitable to it. Indeed, to be eloquent is to be true; to be eloquent is not to add anything to truth, it is to remove one after another the veils that cover it; and this process is not negative, for truth lies in facts. In this sense, Pascal is an orator *par excellence*, because he is as nakedly true as pos-

* Gospel according to St. Matthew, xxvi., 41.

sible. But truth lies not in facts alone; it lies also in the sense of truth. To unite one's self to truth, to be sympathetic with one's subject, is to be true a second time. Truth spoken with love, will it be less truth? No, doubtless, but what is truth within us, when separated from us is no longer truth.

These requisites to eloquence in general are complicated with those which are peculiar to public discourse. And all taken together, constitute the art of oratory.

An oratorical discourse is a discourse delivered to an assembly with the view of inculcating on it certain ideas, impressing it with certain sentiments, or inducing certain resolves, or of doing these three things at once. The last, however, is the final purpose; that in relation to which the other two are means, instruments. The orator should address the heart as well as the understanding, since his desire is to reach the will, and our will is under the control of our affections.*

Oratorical discourse thus appears as a contest, a combat; this idea is essential to it. At one time, the orator combats an error by a truth; at another, he opposes one sentiment to another sentiment. In its just use, oratory is a combat waged against errors of the mind and heart, with the weapon of speech. The orator seeks to make himself master of our will. His attempt is a bold aggression; he lays siege to the soul as though it were a fort; a fort, however, which he can never take unless he keeps himself informed of the interior of the place; for eloquence is but an appeal to sympathy. Its secret consists in disengaging and arresting properties in others which correspond to what is in us, and in every one; its object is to lay hold of a hand which, unknown to ourselves, we are ever extending to it. It arms it-

* On the province of emotion in eloquence, see Part i., Section ii Chapter ii., § 2.

self against us from ourselves; it fortifies itself by our admissions; it supplies itself from our gifts; with our confessions it overwhelms us. In other words, the orator invokes intellectual and moral principles, which we hold in common with him, and does but enforce conclusions from these premises. He proves to us that we agree with him, and causes us to feel and like this agreement. In a word, as has been said, in a bold form of speech, we are only convinced of what we believed before.*

We must distinguish oratorical discourse from didactic discourse, which concludes with an idea, and from poetry which has no conclusion, and of which the purpose is not out of itself, but in itself. Oratorical discourse is ultimately an appeal to the will.

All that we have just said is essentially embraced in Homiletics, the object of which is to furnish the preacher with rules and instructions drawn from the purpose of all eloquence, and from the special purpose of Christian discourse, including the circumstances in which it is pronounced.

What is that religious oratorical discourse which is commonly called the *sermon?*

We have to define what, apart from our idea, has no real existence, what is not, independently of the idea we form of it, since it is our idea itself which makes it what it is. As the object has not been given, the definition becomes a rule or a declaration of principles.

What has been given, is, the purpose, the necessity, the general and unchangeable object of preaching and of worship. Our definition, of course, is to be neither wider nor more contracted than this object, and must allow the preacher, within the limits of Christian truth, all the space which

* Vinet, *Chrestomathie Française*, tome iii., Reflexion sur l'eloquence, à la suite du *Discours de Royer Collard, sur le project de loi relatif au sacrilége.*

the variety of places, times, and circumstances, and his own individuality, demand.

We now define the sermon. It is a discourse incorporated with public worship, and designed, concurrently or alternatively, to conduct to Christian truth one who has not yet believed in it, and to explain and apply it to those who admit it. The Apostles Paul and Peter give the same idea of preaching. "A bishop," says the first, "should be able, by sound doctrine, both to exhort and to convince the gainsayers." (Titus, i. 9.) "I will not be negligent," says the second, "to put you always in remembrance of these things, though ye know them and be established in the present truth." (2 Peter, i. 12.)

We distinguish two classes of hearers, which we designate by the names *believers* and *non-believers*, (the latter substituted for *unbelievers*, which is too often employed, but which has quite a different meaning.) Into which of these two divisions should we put the auditory, which the preacher finds in the temple? According to the definition, we are to distribute them into both. We cannot do this consistently with the idea of a religious assembly. The temple is supposed to be filled with *believers*, met for a common worship. But the reality, the evidence is against this idea, and in the actual state of things, the supposition of the existence of both classes is reasonable. The minister, however, is not to alternate between the two classes, and to apportion among them his discourse or discourses. The two objects of preaching are not separated in so definitive a manner. What is addressed to infidels may be profitable to believers; what is addressed to believers may be profitable to infidels. As to the latter, everything in Christian preaching is adapted to convert them; as to believers, do they not, in one sense, always need to be converted? Not that special sermons are to be excluded, but that there is no part of evangelical truth which is not applicable to all. Although the changes of the spiritual life should be distinguished by different names, they are always but changes of the same work. The work of God in conversion and then in sanctification, is indeed one continuous and indivisible work. The sermons, therefore, of sanctification and of appeal, so called, suit both classes. They are the fat pastures, the green folds of the prophet, the grass of which nourishes the healthy sheep, and heals those which are sick, (Ezekiel, xxxiv. 13–16.) Very often we are better taught by preaching which is addressed to a class to which we are not thought to belong.* It is a fact of experience that men are often led to the Gospel by preaching, which regarding the hearer as on the highest summits of the spiritual life, was not addressed to them, and that, on the other hand, sermons of pure appeal which might well be addressed to pagans, have produced the deepest compunction in advanced Christians. "All scripture is given by inspiration of God, and is profitable for doctrine, for reproof, for correction in righteousness," (2 Timothy, iii. 16.) Why should not esoteric preaching have power to convert those who are without, since it is found that the simple contemplation of the Christian life gains many souls to the gospel? They are at first surprised; many things indeed appear inconceivable to them, but they are struck at the same time with the beauty of their bearings, of their harmony, and they are led to inquire more attentively into their explanation. Preaching of this character exerts an irresistible attraction.

The object of pulpit eloquence, we are aware, as indeed that of all eloquence, is to determine the will; but this object is closely combined with that of instruction. Eloquence is but the form, the edge so to speak of instruction. The preacher is a teacher under the form of an orator. These

* Let the affectation of unconcern and indifference in certain persons at certain times be remembered.

two objects may, indeed, if one so chooses, be combined in all eloquence; but in preaching, instruction is more prominent, exists more for itself than in other kinds of eloquence. "I have often said to myself," says Reinhard, "that, after all, the Christian preacher is more an instructor than an orator."*

Two things distinguish other kinds of oratory from that of the pulpit. 1. A particular circumstance, an interest peculiar to a certain exigence, is the occasion of discourse in the senate or at the bar. 2. The political or judicial orator contemplates, as the result of his effort, an act which is to take place at the rising of the assembly. The preacher, on the contrary, does not seek an immediate and visible result; but, in general, only hopes to produce a certain disposition of soul, with reference to such or such an object. This internal act, this invisible result, is all that the preacher aims at.

The preacher's chief business is instruction; this is the basis of his work; exhortation, reproof, sharpens his teaching, but it is always teaching. Teaching may be eloquent; much more exhortation, even when it does not respect a particular act which is immediate and palpable; but regard to such an act gives rise to differences which seem to be in favor of the other kinds of discourse, differences for which the preacher can have no compensation without violating the nature of pulpit discourse. The orator of the senate or the bar is more naturally eloquent; he has to do with actuality; his auditory is interested, is already excited; it matters little whether for or against him; either is better than the inertia (*plumbea moles*) which the preacher has to encounter, and which he has to remove by abstract truths. Let him not forsake this office; let him solicit from the truth itself, from God, that eloquence which

* "*Ich sagte mir immer, der christliche Prediger sey doch mehr Lehrer als Redner.*"—REINHARD'S *Gestændnisse*, p. 84.

is not to be drawn from his circumstances. He must not make a position for himself like that of the lawyer or the senator. Instruction supposes calmness of which vehemence cannot take the place without putting an end to instruction in the true sense of the word. There is a calm as well as a vehement eloquence; and when we spoke of eloquence as of so much importance, we meant by it, not a particular means, but the assemblage of the means, which are suited to enlighten the understanding and determine the will. This does not imply that preaching is to be without vivacity and earnestness; which it cannot but have, if the preacher does but remember that he perhaps speaks to souls who are hearing the message of peace, for the first and the last time. But this thought must not cause him to neglect instruction. Explication is slow work, and we are tempted to desist from it and to preach to the nerves of our hearers. God, on the contrary, commands us to preach to their souls, their conscience. Let us not be too eager for results, let us not be more urgent than God, who alone knows the time for everything. There is no inconsistency in instructing at once with calmness and affectionate earnestness.

Besides, the pulpit orator has to choose, and in one sense, invent his subjects; circumstances seldom exempt him from this necessity. His ministry, comprehensively, is a matter of business, but not each particular instance of his preaching.

Not only does teaching predominate in the eloquence of the pulpit; the preacher, we add, has a document as the basis of his eloquence. As we have before said, he speaks the Word of God. Alternately he adverts to this document and makes it his point of departure. By turns he is a lawyer and a magistrate; a lawyer, when he pleads before the conscience for the adoption of the document; a magistrate, when he demands man's obedience to the document as adopted. The orator at the bar has a document also, the law; but he does not plead like the preacher in favor of the law; and in the application of his subjects he is very far from contemplating the scenes which lie before the preacher's eyes.

Finally, while the oratorical process is always a *combat*, the combat in preaching is waged against an idea, not a personal adversary; so that. this among all kinds of oratory is alone in not presenting the spectacle of a debate. Yet it is in truth a debate, but the same orator has to perform two parts, so to speak, of which but one is his *own;* he reproduces in order to refute them, the arguments of the adverse party, who is an unregenerate man. Each hearer includes in himself more or less the two contending parties.

We subjoin, that a great part of the preacher's task consists in winning the stage of the conflict. The preacher is an advocate who pleads the cause of God before a bench of corrupt judges, whom it is his first business to render just.

We conclude by removing two errors: one relating to too small, the other to too great expectations from Homiletics, or rather (for under an appearance of moderation, they are truly absolute opinions that we encounter,) some see all in the art, others see nothing. In each case we can only discuss the absolute opinion. The degree, the shadow of the other escapes us. We begin with the last.

They send us back from art to nature. And their opinion is condensed in these two words: Nature is a sufficient guide; nature is a surer guide.

What first strikes us in this argument, is an opposition between nature and art which is imaginary; for, very far from being opposed to each other, the distinction itself between nature and art, it is not easy to establish. Language is often obliged (as the moral sciences abundantly show us) to present, as two different things, under two distinct names, what are truly two changes, two degrees, or two relations of the same thing. Thus, in another sphere, nature is opposed to civilization, or *the art of living in society*, as if civilization were not natural, as if the spontaneous development of a germ were less natural than the germ itself, as if the oak were less natural than the acorn! With as little reason is nature opposed to art. What, in truth, is art but nature still? Art, from the first moment, is present in every creation; if then you would exclude art, where will you begin the exclusion? You see at once that you can never ascend high enough. What we call nature, or talent, is, unconsciously to itself, only a more consummate, more spontaneous art. What we call art, is but prolonged or perfected instinct, which, in all cases, is only a more elementary and more rapid process of reasoning. If instinct removes the first difficulties that present themselves, will it also remove the next? That is the question. And it presents itself again under another form. Does Looking hinder us from seeing? Does not Looking aid us in seeing?

Art, in effect, which we must not confound with artifice, is, in all cases, but the serious search for means suited to an end; so that, to renounce art, we must first prove that, at the first attempt, the whole and the best possible is found. Till this be done, we ask what harm can art do,—what harm especially requiring adherence to the terms of the objection, art is hostile to nature? Laying aside certain privileged geniuses, whom Providence has reduced to pure emotion, or with whom art has all the spontaneity of instinct, I am sure, that inspiration being assumed, (which it is agreed is the first requisite,) the work of art is always essentially one with truth and nature. I am yet to be informed in what particular, works in which art is neglected, on system, have the advantage, so far as they are natural, over those in which the principles and instruments of art have been applied. Much more than this, we may say that generally and in every sphere, art sends us back to nature. We are not naturally so natural as we are thought to be. The barbarian is not simple. Civilization seeks, with more or less of success, to reconnect our life and our manners with manifestations of nature, which she incessantly retraces with her skilful chisel. The triumph of Christianity is the reintegration of nature; for nothing is less according to nature than sin, and nothing more than sin estranges us from nature. In religion, in civilization, the progress of humanity is essentially a restoration. We do not advance, we retrograde, because we have to do so. It will be very strange if the work of the writer forms an exception to this universal law. This law, in fact, prevails in spite of him; and these despisers of art, in regard to eloquence, apply to their productions, without suspecting it, the art of all, in default of art in themselves. To a certain degree, they are artists in spite of themselves.

We must be careful as to consequences. To exclude art, that is to say, reflection, from one of the gravest spheres of human activity, is to proscribe reading, observation, and method, in all spheres, which is to renounce perfection. Nothing that may be said of the necessity of conversion, and the power concerned in conversion, forbids us to think that there is an art and a method of living well for the convert; this all readily consent to. I inquire, then, why there should not be an art and a method of speaking well. Conversion is but a *talent*, which art cultivates and makes productive.

May not genius, it will be asked, dispense with it? If genius may have a dispensation, we do not think it should be in haste to avail itself of it. Genius has a method for itself, but yet it is a method; and if poverty so readily leads to prodigality, why then we must be rich in order to be economical. This great word *genius* is imposing, we would make of it I know not what sort of magic; but as genius is only the most excellent of instincts, the most favorable of starting-points, it will not oppose itself to that law, which does everything by weight, number and measure, that is done in the world, and which permits wisdom of no kind to be a superfluity. Moreover, possess genius and we shall observe your course; possess by all means a club, but tie to it your bundle of rods; possess wings and fly, but while you are waiting, learn to walk.

We concede only this, and we do it very willingly, that as instinct by depending on itself becomes art, art by exercising itself becomes instinct. Art is nothing more than an intelligent instinct. It involuntarily follows rules; it becomes in its sphere what habit is in the moral life, a second nature. It is as natural and as easy to those who have cultivated their instinct to write well and to do well, as it is to those who have left it uncultivated to write badly or do badly; they are no longer able to refrain from it. There is nature in the termination as well as in the outset.

Others would make religion a substitute for study and art. They rely on the general spirit of Christianity, which, say they, illustrates strength in weakness, and demonstrates the power of truth in the absence and to the exclusion of purely human means.

So far from denying this general spirit of Christianity, we rejoice to proclaim it. But how shall we abide faithful to it? Undoubtedly not by giving the flesh as an aid to the spirit; which would be giving the spirit its mortal enemy as an aid, calling death to the support of life, taking an obstacle for an instrument. Now the question is, whether art applied to preaching is a carnal auxiliary, an instrument whose tendency is opposed to the end we have in view. But this art, call it by what name you please, is nothing else than observation, reflection, experience applied to the explication of truth. Are all these to be condemned? On the contrary, are they not the natural auxiliaries of truth, and in employing them in its service, are we not simply giving it its own? Is it not by these means that we have learned, that we have understood the truth? If under a divine direction we have applied them in convincing ourselves, are we to be prohibited from the use of them in convincing others? Sooner might it be said (if it could be proved), that man in the work of the ministry is to pass for nothing; that he must restrict himself to the mere repetition of inspired words; in other terms, that preaching should be suppressed. But if it be admitted that the preacher is a man, it is well assuredly that he applies himself to his work; that he infuses himself entirely into it; that in the full force of the expression he speaks the word of God; this itself is sanctioning the study and the practice of an art, which is nothing but the rational and thoughtful use of all the natural means which are at the preacher's command.

It is undoubtedly God who converts, but he converts man by means of man: We here have a principle and a fact. I speak of man as personal, living, moral. To admit the fact, is to admit of art in preaching; otherwise should we not have a man without his thought, or shall he have thought and be forbid the exercise of reason in what he does? And if he is permitted to reason, shall he reason by halves? If the Holy Spirit does not hold the pen, the preacher must needs hold it himself; if he is not inspired, he must reflect. Laying aside inspiration, I cannot see why he should trust his first impulse rather than reflection, chance rather than art. Does the first thought come from the Holy Spirit, and the second from the man? Is not the first thought from the man as well as the second? and in each case, has not the man recourse to himself? Is there more faithfulness on the first system than on the second? On the contrary, let it be once admitted that the man is to have recourse to himself, and faithfulness consists in drawing from himself the best and the most perfect of whatever he has, in joining to the first emotion which perhaps was involuntary, a second which is not; in a word, in joining to natural force that which is acquired, and which does not seem opposed to it. Is it not forgotten that our real virtues are acquired ones,—works of art? We cannot trust ourselves to our first impressions; we must correct these by those which follow. It is in this, not in indolence of thought, that faithfulness consists, and that the blessing is found. It is with talent and with art as with riches, of which it has been said, "make to yourselves friends of the unrighteous mammon." (Luke, xvi. 9.)

In vain do we despise means; indeed, in despising we use them: whatever of ourselves we put into our ministry, little as it may be, belongs to the category of means. The first means is ourselves; if we must use this means, we should do it as completely and perfectly as possible. "Let all that is in us, the spirit, the soul and the body, be preserved blameless unto the coming of our Lord Jesus Christ." (1 Thessalonians, v. 23.)

Man is the medium through which God has purposed that truth shall come to man. Truth alone is luminous, the medium is only transparent. But let it be indeed transparent, and as far as we are concerned, let not the rays of truth be obscured and broken by fault in the medium.

We concede to Bossuet, that God condescends to employ means, and that between himself and man, his principal means is man, without comprehending perhaps the full extent of this admission. If God uses means, we surely may use them; our faculties are not more unworthy of us than we are of God; and if it is certain that God consents to make man his instrument, let us employ the whole of the instrument, that is to say, the whole of man in God's service.

Now man comprises art; man essentially is an artist; remove art, and man is no more man.

What, moreover, would we accomplish by means of art? Would we add something to truth? We have said that nothing is to be added to truth. All that is to be done, is to remove, one after another, the veils which hide truth from the view of man. This is the purpose and effect of eloquence. And this, indeed, shows the difference between false art and true. For nothing could be more arbitrary and less philosophical than to say that true art is that which despises detail, since art in detail is only truth in detail.

True art is that which has truth for its object; false art is that which promotes error and falsehood. We should, moreover, if possible, be perfect, be thorough in art of every kind. It is, however, true that each kind has its proprieties which art teaches us to distinguish, and the beautiful excludes the *pretty.**

We oppose, then, to the principle which is objected to us, the fact, the institution itself of God. If there is inconsistency between the principle and the fact, not ours, but God's is the responsibility. But in truth, neither on us nor on God is there any responsibility; the inconsistency does not exist. When it is said that truth should be self-sufficient, is it meant that truth is not to be spoken, or that those who speak it are not to speak it as men who understand and feel what they say? Is it meant that they are not to unite themselves to it? Is truth spoken with love, something more than truth? Why, then, should truth spoken with intelligence, be something more than truth? Is not the adherence of our intellect, as well as of our heart, to truth, its natural *right?* And has not truth a full right of possession to everything which witnesses to this adherence, and which is suited to beget it in other minds and hearts? On what principle, or

* *Le beau exclut le joli.*

what experience do they rely, who think that something immethodic and unstudied in the discourse of a preacher, best agrees with his purpose, or that the abuse of an art is art *par excellence?* We confess ourselves entirely ignorant.

It may be surprising to some that we take so much pains in combatting an opinion which has so little weight. But there is not one of our arguments which does not meet a prevalent prejudice, an often-expressed opinion. And therefore, without fearing to be somewhat repetitious, we shall discuss the passages which have been commonly objected to us.

"Take no thought how or what ye shall speak: for it shall be given you in that same hour, what ye shall speak." (Matthew, x. 19.) This direction seems to be connected with a promise of extraordinary assistance. When no such assistance is promised, must there not be a substitute for it?

We doubt not, indeed, that the promise of this assistance remains to us in all cases in which working is impossible, and in which the assistance is needed.

These two cases excepted, unless the assistance in question be in its principle and nature unlike all the aid which the Holy Spirit grants the believer, we say that the promise of this assistance is not against the use of human means; or that if the human means implies a want of faith in this case, it does the same in all cases. We should not supply ourselves with clothes or food, because it is written, "Take no thought what ye shall eat, or what ye shall drink, or wherewithal ye shall be clothed, for your Heavenly Father knoweth that ye have need of all these things." (Matthew, vi. 25, 32.)

But further, we give a much loftier direction to the reproach of inconsistency, though the reproach in truth is without any object: The use of human means excludes neither the necessity of aid from above, nor the sense of that necessity. With the hammer and trowel in hand, the workman says to God, "Except the Lord build the house, they labor in vain who build it." (Psalm cxxvii. 1.) The hammer and the trowel are the first gifts of God, the first testimonials of his goodness, the first causes for our gratitude. Strength and the will to act, are a first advance of the Divine Lender. We do not say, "Work, *although* God works within you to will and to do;" but with the apostle, "Work, *because* God works in you to will and to do." (Philippians, ii. 12, 13.)

It has been said, that Christian wisdom is to be tranquil as if God did everything, and to act as if he did nothing. Let us rather say: God does all; he has made us,—us who work; he has wrought in us the will to work; he has wrought by us all that we accomplish; but he has done it by us, and wills not to do it otherwise. After having worked however abundantly, we are not the less required on that account to say with Paul, "We are not sufficient of ourselves even to think anything as of ourselves." (2 Corinthians, iii. 5.) Where is the inconsistency?

Another citation: "Christ sent me to preach the gospel; not with wisdom of words, lest the cross of Christ should be made of none effect." (1 Cor., i. 17.)

The discourse or reasoning of human wisdom, renounced by Saint Paul, ought to be renounced by every preacher, whose business is to proclaim Jesus Christ; for worldly wisdom, drawing from its own depths, does not find Jesus Christ. To begin with human wisdom, to which the cross is foolishness, is to renounce this foolishness, which nevertheless is the doctrine of salvation. But reflection, method, in one word, art, has nothing in common with that human wisdom which is here in question. The most skilful of preachers, the *wisest* as to art, may abound in the doctrine of the foolishness of God, while the greatest stranger to this divine foolishness may be absolutely wanting in art.

"Our religion," says Pascal, "is foolish, when regard is had to its effective cause; and wise, when we regard the wisdom which is shown in the presentation of it to men."* It may then be wise as to the part which is confided to us in presenting it. It is really foolish in no respect, except to fools, of whom, it is true, the number is great. Why may we not on this account call the least exercise of charity *foolishness;* since this also is above or beyond reason, which by all its efforts is not competent to explain it?

Saint Paul who excepts against human wisdom, still does not abjure art, and though his rhetoric may not be proposed as a model universally, in how many respects is it at all times appropriate? Be it so that the Holy Spirit taught it to him; yet He did teach it to him. We who have not the same Master, may not neglect an art which he taught to Saint Paul.

But another passage is objected to us: "And I," says Saint Paul to the Corinthians, "when I came to you, came not with excellency of speech or of wisdom,† declaring to you the testimony of God, for I determined to know nothing among you, save Jesus Christ and him crucified." (1 Corinthians, ii. 1, 2.)

Every preacher ought to adopt these words of Paul; they are the Christian preacher's motto; he is to know nothing but Jesus Christ. The meaning is that to him "there is no other name given among men, whereby they can be saved." (Acts, iv. 12.) This is the meaning; for, in any other sense, Saint Paul *knew* many other things.‡ As to eloquence and

* Pascal, *Pensées*, Edition Faugère, tome ii., p. 354.

† French Version.—"Avec des discours éloquents ou avec une sagesse humaine."

‡ On the idioms of Saint Paul, see Chrysostom De *Sacerdotio*. Cap. vi.

philosophy he did not pride himself on brilliancy here ; but he used his abilities to the uttermost to be clear, persuasive, convincing. We find in him every essential of the orator. If he is sometimes unpolished while yet powerful, shall we hence infer that he is powerful because he is unpolished ? Is it not enough to say that whatever there is of want of polish in him, is, as far as it extends, an addition to his power ? Be as unpolished as he was, not however of premeditated design, (for nothing were more absurd than premeditation here,) be as unpolished as he was, but press argument as he did, and we shall be content. But if to imitate, or rather to parody him, you make yourself a barbarian, you need do nothing more to show that there is no necessary connection between barbarism and power. The matter is to be powerful; attain to this in whatever way you please. If mere instinct makes you eloquent, (I mean an eloquence coherent, sustained, instructive,) we will excuse you from art; we do not pursue the longer road for the sake of the length ; we shall be content if you reach the end of the road ; but will you reach it ? That is a question, or rather it is not one. Will you do as well, working at hazard with scattered forces, as in concentrating them ? Will the fire be as warm if you have taken no care to collect into the brazier the scattered coals which, apart from each other, are extinguished and dark ? Will you do as well without meditation as with it, without purpose as with it, without combination as with it ? Now, all this is art, and art is nothing else.*

* See Fénélon, *Dialogues sur l'Eloquence. Dialogue* iii. We here reproduce from a preceding manuscript, the first form which M. Vinet gave to his reply to the objection drawn from 1 Corinthians, ii. 1, 2.

"To know Jesus Christ crucified, is indeed the knowledge of the preacher, and truly as regards religion, his only knowledge. As regards religion we say ; for, in any other view, Paul was not igno-

Separated from art, that is to say, separated from itself, in a measure, truth may produce great effects; words proceeding from the heart, may occasionally avail more than the best-prepared sermon. But if we take the great majority of cases, if we take preaching as a whole, and its essential characteristic, which is instruction, we shall find that it cannot make progress by either impulse or *inspiration*, and that it demands the aid of art.

There is, on this subject, a great and dangerous mistake. Art is denied for the sake of religion; the preacher, it is supposed, is to be remanded to religion; but what is the real fact? In remanding him to his first impression, he is sent back to nature! For who assures him that his first impressions will be the most religious, or that they will even be religious? I am bold to say, that Christian analogy condemns this

rant, does not care to appear so; he makes an abundant use of his knowledge. The Apostle carefully explains himself on this point, in the following verses, where he opposes *that mystery* which God only could reveal, to the imaginations of human wisdom, which cannot attain to the secret of God. Thus, as to knowledge: in regard to eloquence, he denies to it as eloquence, the power of creating faith (verse 5). The great work of conversion can have its ground and its reason only in the nature of the fact which the Apostle announces, Jesus Christ crucified. And to gain reception for this truth belongs only to the Divine Power, (Ibid.) But as this fact is suited to inspire eloquence, why should not the preacher endeavor to give back to it all he has received from it? Why not strive to give additional views of it, to commend it to the conscience of all, to appeal to human nature in order to produce a sense of the necessity of it? May he do this without meditation? May he attain to the utmost force of argument without combination. May he find combinations without having observed human nature, and discovered the most direct and sure way to the centre of the soul? If you deny the name of art to all this, you are masters of it, and we shall not dispute about a thing so small. Adopt the means, and give them what name you please."—Editors.

method; for religion itself is a work of art, and in its highest sphere it consecrates the prerogatives and the dignity of art; religion does not confine itself to our first emotion, to our first glance; it continually appeals to thought, to reflection; it is not content with instinct. In despising art then, we act in the spirit and under the influence of nature rather than in the spirit and under the influence of religion.

A generous enthusiasm may have given circulation to the maxims we oppose; but indolence has intercepted them; this it is which makes the most use of them. Who will dare deny it? Zeal also, I am very willing to admit, takes advantage of, and applies them. Is it right in this? Has it need of these maxims? We shall have occasion to examine this question.*

We now turn to those who are disposed to expect too much from *Homiletics;* and first to those who expect too much from the teaching of Homiletics. For even if Homiletics, or the theory of ecclesiastical eloquence, were able to create eloquence, it would not follow that a Homiletical course though the best that could be heard and though listened to in the best manner, might of itself alone make a preacher eloquent.

A course, or a regular indoctrination in Homiletics, is necessary, since it gathers and arranges under the eyes of the student a quantity of ideas and facts, which, in general, the student cannot gather. This course will give an idea of the subject matter of the art, and the art itself, in its extent, which it is necessary to have in advance, since practice, from which we afterwards learn the necessity of principles, does not give a full notion, and cannot be a substitute for the study of them. A very rare organization, and circumstances no less rare, are necessary, in order to our learning art well

* See part iii., chap i., of *Elocution in general.*

from practice alone. When facts react much upon ideas, the ideas throw their light in advance of the facts. Now, these ideas, in the present case, are Homiletics.

But the professor is not one of those roads which move and bear us on to the place whither we are to go.* He is not a river, he is only a road.

Any course whatever, but especially a course of the latter kind, is truly given only when it has been received; and to receive it is to be more than passive, it is an act of the will: to learn is to take.†

Strictly, what does the professor give? Not science, but directions to us for making ourselves scientific. You do not here learn; you here only learn to learn.

Remark, moreover, that if in one sense art is one, it is not so in all senses; it multiplies itself in individuals, it individualizes itself in each. The question which will one day present itself before you, will be, not what ought to be done, but, what ought I to do? In this preparatory period, oratorical discourse may appear to you as an end; but in ministerial activity, it will be only as a means of attaining an actual end, on some occasion which will resemble exactly no other. The professor responds to the question, what ought to be done? He does not respond to the question, what ought I to do? He is obliged to abstract his individuality from himself; he teaches every one's art, not his own.

The professor whom you hear, the rhetorician you read, cannot give you a rhetoric of your own; each one has always to do this for himself.

But if we must not rest too exclusively on the course we attend upon, no more must we put too much confidence in

* PASCAL, *Pensèes*, Partie i., Art. x., § xxxviii. "Les rivières sont les chemins qui marchent, et qui portent ou l'on veut aller." I. 206, lxxxvi.—Tr.

* *Apprendre c'est prendre.*

Homiletics themselves, that is to say, in the abstract ideas of art. I call them abstract, because they are isolated from the subject, the circumstance, and the concrete ideas of the very substance itself of the discourse.

I might oppose here talent to art; to art which is talent acquired or developed, talent which is art, native, spontaneous, intuitive; art in germ; and say, that no theory can either give or be a substitute for talent. But this concerns me less. I think it more important to oppose the theory or the abstract ideas of art, to the substance itself of that eloquence which art would control. Let it not be forgotten that eloquence primarily is in things; in one sense, it is wholly in things, from which we only detach it. Eloquence has no existence by itself, independently of things; after putting aside the truth, the beauty of the objects, and the sentiments which correspond to them in the orator's soul, what, I ask, remains, except the logic and the psychology, of which eloquence is but a more or less happy use? The essential eloquence is neither psychology nor logic; it is the truth, it is the soul.

This is a chief point. Eloquence is substantial; it is on that account an affair of reality, for though an abstraction, is of no time or place, substance belongs to time and space: it is a reality. Hence, as things are of the first importance, the season and the place are to be reckoned something; the orator has something to learn from them. He would be ill prepared if he should take art for anything terminating in itself, absolute and independent of circumstances, as a form prescribed once for all, or an unchangeable programme; if he should not remind himself that each time and for each one the task is to be renewed, and that as that there is a general art for making discourse in general, (discourse which has no existence,) there is an art for making the discourse of to-day, an art for making that of to-morrow. The homiletics of the closet should leave a place for those of the temple and of the parish.

Eloquence has the character of business. Now business is not learnt by abstraction; commerce only understands commerce; politics are learnt in the management of State affairs, and life in living.

Rules are the summary, the generalization of particular experiences. A rule does not qualify us fully for acting; it has no active force; it inspires not; it communicates nothing; it prompts to action. Rules, however, are not on this account, of small use; they aid our views, they keep us from false views; they shorten the time and the uncertainty of walking in the dark. They are, if you please, anticipated experience formed from the experience of others, and from certain *à priori* reasonings. We live by their help, as the child lives on his father's goods, until we are able to gain our living, and they put us in a condition for gaining it; that is to say, rules teach us to make rules for ourselves.

There is indeed reaction; for, as rules (generalizations, abstract ideas) aid our views of facts, these latter, in their turn, give us the true understanding of rules, and measure their extent.

It may be dangerous to give too absolute a value to rules, and to leave the mind in captivity to them; we must, at least, always refer them to the more general principles from which they emanate; we must always keep open and free the communication between principles and rules, as also between rules and facts. Principles, facts, these are our light; rules are a *tie* between principles and facts, but it is necessary that the tie be a living one. A rule whose two extremities are not constantly in contact with principles and facts, is an empty formula.*

* See REINHARD'S *Gestændnisse*, p. 51, and p. 45 of the translation published in 1816, by M. John Monard, under the title: *Lettres*

As for models, in what spirit must we study them?* It is with beauty as with virtue, neither the one nor the other are to be copied; they impress themselves, the one on the taste, the other on the conscience; they have only to show themselves; by contemplation of their forms we become like them.† This excludes neither reflection nor analysis; looking does not hinder us from seeing. But beauty does not transport itself ready-made; and we less resemble models the more we wish to resemble them. It is simply or chiefly a contagion, to which we must expose ourselves. Admiration is fruitful.

And what are models? Not only sermons, but all oratorical discourses; not all these only, but eloquence wherever it is to be found; eloquence, not oratory; the eloquence of narration as well as that of reasoning; eloquence of kinds the most diverse, that we may have the most comprehensive, the most pure, the least conventional idea of it; not only eloquence prepared to hand, but that which makes itself eloquence. Ready-made eloquence may put your own out of doors.

de F. V. Reinhard sur ses études et la carrière de prédicateur. Paris, 1816.

* Barante, *Melanges*, tome ii., p. 874, and Herder's *Briefe*, etc., Letter XLI.

† "We shall be like him, for we shall see him as he is." (1 John, iii., 2.)

PART I

INVENTION.

The division of a course upon the art of Oratory, has always been, as it ever must be, *Invention*, *Disposition*, *Elocution.*

Invention, strictly speaking, expands itself over the whole field of Rhetoric. We invent our plan, we invent our language. The same faculty is applied to everything ; it is the whole talent, it is the whole art.

But if we consider here, not the faculty, the exercise of which is unlimited, but the object, which is special, we shall find a real difference and distinction between these three things ; the matter or ground, (which is to be invented,) the order, (which is to be invented,) and the style, (which is to be invented,) a division which corresponds to the ancient one, and which, perhaps, we may use to advantage.*

While, however, we retain the terms, we premise that by the word invention, we understand only the invention of the ideas, or the matter, of which the disposition and expression are afterwards to be invented.

Invention here, then, is taken in the narrower sense, (the invention of the matter of the discourse,) for, in the absolute sense, it presents itself at every point in the art. It is true, nevertheless, that the invention of the principal ideas of the discourse is invention in the highest sense of the term.

* Pascal, *Pensèe*, Edition Faugère, tome i., p. 254, § xxiv.

It is difficult to explain invention, taken as an active spring, as an energy of the mind. At whatever point we place it in the art, invention, in its principle, is a mystery. Talent may explain its methods, not itself. The development of the germ is human, the germ is divine. To say that invention is not something *sui generis*, were to say that imagination is not a distinct faculty, a primitive force. And if nothing but mere method were here to be recognized, yet must it be admitted that this method is, in certain minds, innate, that it is a talent. This instinctive, enchantress-like method is, perhaps, talent itself. Invention is a kind of divining-rod.* It is impossible to give it to ourselves, absolutely ; it is even impossible when one has one kind of invention to give himself another kind. We may be inventive in philosophy without having the least measure of historical invention. Invention, however, is an element in every mind ; but minds in this respect are very unequal and very different. Where there is no invention, art loses its perogatives; but it never loses them, for there is always some measure of it. No one can do everything, but no one does all he can do. To know our wealth we must make it available. An inventive mind may become more so by the use of certain means which are not talent ; and a mind in which invention is feeble, but not entirely wanting, may, by the use of the same means, develop this power in itself. The means of turning to account and developing what we have of invention, are the following:

1. *Knowledge.* The more we know the greater is our advantage for inventing ; an original mind does not lose, it

* "The generality of writers pass and repass over mines of gold, a thousand times, without suspecting their existence. Genius alone has the instinct which gives notice of the riches of the mine, as it alone has the power of penetrating into its bowels and drawing thence its treasures."—MARMONTEL.

gains in originality by knowledge.* The mutual intercourse of mind with mind, of thought with thought, is not unfriendly to individuality ; in this sphere, also, it is not good for man to be alone. Every kind of knowledge does not promote originality, but an original mind has an original erudition; knowledge, an element as it seems wholly objective, becomes in it a subjective element. However this may be, it is given to no man to draw something from nothing ; the most exalted imagination must have a point of departure or a point of rest. Talent is a lever, but a lever only. "The human mind can create nothing, it can produce only after it has been made fertile by experience, (its own or another's,) or by meditation. Its knowledge is the germ of its productions."

2. The second means is *Meditation*, a species of incubation which warms and fructifies the germ. It is the concentration of the thought, nay even of the life, upon a point with which we seek to identify ourselves. Meditation is aided by analysis, but meditation is not analysis. If we are not mistaken as to the etymology of the word, meditation introduces us into the midst of the object. We seek to obtain by means of it, not a simple idea or a formula, but a direct perception. There is analysis, logic in it also, but it is rather that of the object than of the subject, rather that of sentiment than of thought, it is a continued and deep impression of the thing, a sort of consubstantiation. It implies a force, a peculiar aptitude; but as will has much to do here, we put meditation among the means of invention; we do not make it the principle of invention. Meditation is to talent what conscience is to the moral sense.

* "He (Petrarch) proved that knowledge contributes much to invention, and his genius was the more original, as like eternal forces, it could be always present.—MADAME DE STAEL, *Corinne*, Sec. ii., Chap. iii.

3. *Analysis*, a different thing from meditation, strives to ascend to the remote idea of the object, as to a summit where we may command all the declivities, and where we may see, in proportion to our elevation, a more extended horizon. It incessantly climbs toward the most simple and lofty principle, always meeting as it mounts, elements less contingent, less accidental. When guided by sound logic and profound metaphysics, it arrives at surprising results, surprising, I mean, to itself; it makes new and striking discoveries. We must not confound with this process, the methods of a trivial logic which is always sure to produce something, always sure to fill a certain space, but which never moves anything beyond the uppermost layer of the soil.

4. *Exercise.* The more we exact of the soil, the more it produces. It does not exhaust itself. *Nihil feracius ingeniis;* we shall get the more from it the more it has given us. We may not here apply the passage, "Your strength is to sit still," (Isaiah, xxx. 7,) for sitting still will enfeeble and kill us. It is rust and not use that tarnishes the lustre of steel.

Under the head of invention, the rhetoricians, we may observe, neither treat of the talent of invention nor of the means of developing it. They would rather prescribe certain laws to it; they attempt to regulate it. In the ancient systems of rhetoric, invention is less the faculty of finding, than the art of choosing among things found. "The orator must use discernment. He must not only find ideas to express, he must examine them. Nothing is more prolific than the mind, especially when it has been cultivated by study; but as a rich, productive soil, not only produces wheat, but all kinds of weeds that injure the good seed, the mind, in like manner, sometimes produces frivolous thoughts, or thoughts foreign to the object it has in view, and of no utility, and the orator must carefully select the ideas which are to have a place in his work.*"

* CICERO, *Orator.*

It should be observed that the ancient orators, having in view only judicial and deliberative eloquence, have nothing to say on invention of the subject, which was always prescribed to the orator. It is otherwise with the eloquence of the pulpit. The preacher, it is true, might be compelled to choose a text, but he cannot be forbidden to choose his subject first, and his text for his subject; and then, as to the text itself, after it has been chosen, he has often to find or create a subject for it. Besides, we do not admit that the use of a text is essential to pulpit eloquence. We may then say, that the preacher is often required to choose his subject. And when we say choose, we do not mean take it ready prepared from the midst of a table of contents, all arranged in order, of a list of heads with their subdivisions. The number of subjects is incalculable; each following the relation, the combination which has been preconceived, multiplies itself; it is as the five loaves and two fishes of the gospel. No one in this matter is obliged to walk in the steps of his predecessors. Without seeking novelty, we may be new. A simple impression received from our text, or a view furnished by life, may contribute to novelty. But the most reliable means of invention, as to the subject of discourse, is a truly philosophical culture. Under this conviction, we cannot too earnestly recommend to candidates for the pulpit, the study of philosophy, which will be constantly giving them new aspects of the same truth.

But this, strictly speaking, is not in the sphere of Homiletics; it belongs to a previous preparation. We restrict ourselves to Cicero's point of view; under the name of invention, we treat of the choice of materials, and with this limitation, we shall speak first of the *Subject*, and then of the *Substance* of Pulpit Discourse.

SECTION FIRST.

SUBJECT OF PULPIT DISCOURSE.

THE subject of judicial and of political discourse is a question of fact, justice, or experience, arising out of an actual and contingent fact. Discourse of these kinds, treats its subject, whether genus or species, only in an indirect or occasional way, having an ulterior end; pulpit oratory abides in the category of genus or species. In this eloquence, an individual and even an actual question is not wanting; but it remains concealed. The process as to this, is conducted in the dark, in the secresy of every man's conscience. What appears is the generic and the permanent.

Moreover, it is always a question, whatever may be its nature, which is to be subject to the laws of discourse. We here advance the first rule or the first condition of pulpit discourse: ITS SUBJECT IS ONE.

CHAPTER I.

UNITY OF THE SUBJECT.

THE human mind inherently demands unity. Apart from unity, we can recognize neither truth, goodness, nor happiness.

In morality, we want a principle to move and direct us; in life, a purpose; in institutions, harmony; in poetry, an idea; in history, a point of view; in the universe, one final cause of all effects.

We are not pursuing identity under the name of unity. Where there is identity, the very idea of unity disappears; plurality is necessary to give unity a place; systems of identity spring from our impatience to find unity, and our repugnance to regard things as disconnected.

Unity is essential to every work of art, art itself having as its chief aim to make one whole by combining scattered elements.* In defining art, the assemblage of the means for making a thing, we return to the same idea; for *making* is *uniting*, as *unmaking* is *separating*.

Every work of art is a work of subordination and of coordination. The first includes the second. All elements subordinated to one and the same principle, are thereby coordinated with one another.

Unity in works of art, requires not only the exclusion from one and the same whole, one assemblage, elements which are incompatible with one another; but the bringing all the parts into relation to one and the same centre, one and the same end. There are two degrees in it. We may call the first *negative unity*, and the second *positive unity*.

Oratorical discourse demands unity yet more imperatively.

Not being read, but heard, it would very quickly weary our attention, if it were required to transfer itself successively from one side to another.

Its duration being short, compared with that of other productions, it is less at liberty to entertain the hearer with a variety of subjects.

Having to act upon the will, it gains on this account by concentrating itself on a single thought. It is when it does this, as different from discourse, which, however full, is inco-

* *Ars* formed *artus.* Ἄρω, *to adapt; αρα, then, consequently; ἀρι,* a particle of corroboration; Ἄρης, *the God of power; ἀρετή, virtue; ἀρτιος, accomplished. Harmony* has the same etymology

herent, without definite aim, or confused, as an army is from a rabble. The strongest thoughts, which are not interconnected, injure one another, and the more in proportion to their strength. Only very powerful minds can obtain profit from that which is without unity, or from that which is inconsistent with itself. Attacked by a crowd of mutually self-neutralizing impressions, we are made captive by none, and are fixed to nothing.

Mark, when you have opportunity, the effect of such discourse on its seriously-minded hearers, taking them as you find them. Each hearer of this class, unconsciously to himself, will endeavor to give unity to a discourse to which the preacher has not given it; or will attach himself to one of the preacher's ideas, and adhere to that; or will perhaps force all these ideas to take the direction which pleases his own thought.

The very solemnity of preaching requires unity. The solemnity would be less if the discourse, instead of being a procession, were a promenade.

Evidently all this applies without abatement to the discourse of the pulpit, and we were right in saying that the first requisite in the subject of this discourse is that it be one; or, which comes to the same, that the first requisite in this discourse is to have one subject; for, when there are many subjects, there is none. If you tell a man that you have been hearing a discourse, his first question is, what was its subject? He never asks you what were its subjects?

Unity of subject, in order to be real and to be felt, involves, unquestionably, a convergence or a gravitation of all the parts, even the minutest, towards the centre. But this has regard to execution, of which we are to speak hereafter. Here we consider only the choice of the subject.

To obtain a clear idea of oratorical unity let us distinguish it from purely historic, and purely didactic unity.

It is different from historic unity in this, that it embraces at once the *subject* and the *attribute*, that is to say, both terms of the proposition,* while history places unity in the subject only. For example—

The Greeks { were united,
conquered;
were divided,
were overcome.

It is true, that in this example even, we see how many attributes may be reduced to but one: The Greeks were stronger in proportion as they were united. But yet this attribute is but one of those of which Grecian history is composed, the unity of which, under the purely historic point of view, resides wholly in the *subject*, or material of history. Between the historic and didactic elements there is the difference which exists between the contingent and the necessary, the individual and the general, fact and law which is a great primitive and unchangable fact. That "union is strength," is a general truth which results from many facts like that which has been above indicated respecting the Greeks. And yet this maxim may have two meanings, one *à priori*, the other *à posteriori.*

Oratorical unity is different from didactic in this, that all the elements it combines have for their last term a practical application or conclusion. The truth or idea which has been obtained is not left to expatiate and wander in the mind; out of all the conduits into which it flows, imagination, reason, sentiment, it is gathered and confined in one conduit into which all the others issue, that of the will; and thus it receives a course towards action, more or less rapid.†

* I say this because all discourse, though it were a book, may be reduced to one proposition.

† We may indeed assemble the hearers in a public place, in order

In a word, the subject of oratorical discourse is a simple imperative proposition: "Do this," "Do not that." It is absolutely so at the bar or in the senate: "Release this prisoner," "Vote this law."

The pulpit orator is in a position somewhat different. Strictly oratorical unity resides in his preaching, rather as a whole than in each one of his discourses. The reason is, that he is not only an orator, like the lawyer or the politician, he is also and essentially a teacher, an instructor. But let us remark first, that there is in religion no didactic subject which has not practical bearings direct or indirect; nothing is level, all is inclined; nothing still water, all is a river or a torrent. Next, let us not forget that we are to treat these subjects as the best preachers do, in an oratorical spirit, and that charity gives this spirit:—Truth commands; fact becomes law.

I conclude with Schott, "Although it enters into the essential notion of oratorical discourse to make the determination of the will its supreme and ultimate end, we do not refuse the name of oratorical discourse to a composition in which this practical direction, without appearing in the announcement of the principal proposition, reveals itself clearly and unequivocally in the spirit and substance of the entire performance. . . . But a theme which has no relation to a subject practically important, or which cannot be made so, without painful effort, is not a proper basis for an oratorical discourse."*

All subjects drawn from the Christian religion, are, as having this character, more or less suitable for the pulpit; still I think, that ordinarily the preacher should not be content to

to expound to them, merely, certain truths; this is instruction, but not an oratorical discourse, although the instruction may not be without oratorical characteristics.

* *Schott's Entwurf einer Theorie der Beredsamkeit*, p. 31.

leave the people to make the inference, but should himself do this, and, at least, infuse a practical spirit into every part of his discourse.

Saurin has given a highly and directly practical bearing to many subjects of a very speculative aspect. Thus, in the sermon on *the Beatific Vision of the Deity*,* "We shall see God as he is, and we shall thus be made like him :" The plan of God is to render man like God ; it is the plan of the devil to make man like the devil ; into which of these two plans do you propose to enter? Subjects of this class may be compared to an arrow which though unarmed with a point, pierces the object by mere projectile force. In the sermon on *the Ministry of the Angels*,† he demands of us an imitation of those blessed spirits who execute the divine commands with the swiftness of the winds and the activity of fire. In that on *the Equality of Man*,‡ after having established the essential equality of man, he remarks that he would hence infer nothing in favor of either anarchy or fanaticism ; his inferences are these : Moderation ; submission to providential allotments ; watchfulness (to know the duties of your position) ; zeal and fervor ; all the mortifications of inequality are to have an end.

On the whole, I conclude that to have unity in a sermon, it must be reducible to a doctrinal proposition, which is readily transformed, and is in fact transformed into a practical proposition.

Assuming this, we shall now present some of the principal forms under which this unity may exist.

We omit the consideration of practical or parenetic unity, because it is to be henceforth understood that this characteristic should appear in all subjects ; and farther, that the pulpit is essentially didactic. Thus, the *impulsive* character of

* SAURIN, tome iii., p. 95, Nouvelle Edition

† Ibid., tome vi., p. 447. ‡ Ibid., tome iii., p. 309.

pulpit discourse is assumed in all the examples we are about to consider.

1. There is unity in a simple proposition, whether doctrinal or practical ; I mean a *unique* proposition consisting of a single subject and a single attribute Examples:

"There is no peace to the wicked." (Isaiah lvii. 24.)

"God is not in all the thoughts of the wicked." (Psalm x. 4.)

"I am with you always, even to the end of the world." (Matthew, xxviii. 20.)

"Bless those who curse you." (Matthew, v. 44; Luke, vi. 28.)

"Prove what is acceptable to the Lord." (Ephes. v. 10.)

"To him that knoweth to do good, and doeth it not, to him it is sin." (James, iv. 17.)

"The wicked worketh a deceitful work." (Prov. xi. 18.)

"That which is highly esteemed among men is abomination in the sight of God." (Luke, xvi. 15.)

"The work of righteousness shall be peace," (Isaiah, xxxii. 17.)

"He who is not with me is against me." (Matthew, xii. 30.)

It need not be said that the development of the thesis or the exegesis of the text which contains it, together with its proof, forms no duplicity. It is not against unity to explain fully the subject or attribute, or both. As well might we proscribe definition. Both the conviction and the determination of the will are often the result of exhibiting the sense in detail; as in 1 Timothy, i. 5: "The end of the commandment is charity, out of a pure heart, a good conscience, and faith unfeigned." What this charity is was meant to be determined. In some cases the subject or attribute may need no elucidation, but these cases are uncommon, and it is useful to regard them so and to determine well what is to be proved. The mere announcement which suffices for the preacher, does not suffice for the generality. And thus the preacher, even if the hearers be not ignorant of his subject, should give it vitality, that they may have a strong perception of the point which he is to prove and enforce in his sermon.

2. The proposition retains simplicity, even though it have many subjects or attributes, provided these subjects or attributes form a whole. "In this the children of God are manifest and the children of the devil: Whosoever *doeth not righteousness, and loveth not his brethren, is not of God.*" (1 John, iii. 10.) "Follow peace with all men, and holiness, without which no one shall see the Lord." (Hebrews, xii. 14.)

Thus a discourse which exhibits the different qualities of a thing, may have unity, provided these qualities are such that they may be combined in one and the same attribute. There is no oratorical unity in the description of a machine, of a place, of a man. A place may be beautiful, celebrated, difficult of access, uninhabited; these characteristics of it are not such as may be combined in one and the same attribute. But when there is an idea common to many different or even opposite attributes, it may be expressed. Thus when Massillon says of ambition, that it is *restless*, *scornful*, *unjust*, he does not violate unity. In like manner there is unity in this passage: "Christ was made unto us of God, wisdom, righteousness, sanctification and redemption." (1 Corinthians, i. 30.)

3. The qualities of a thing may be subjoined, not only when they have a common affinity or tendency, but when they mutually counterbalance or modify or limit one another. "Nevertheless the foundation of God standeth sure, having this seal: *The Lord knoweth them that are his:* and, *Let him that nameth the name of Christ, depart from iniquity.*" (2 Timothy, ii. 19.) The seal of the foundation laid by God is of two parts, but they are inseparable;—a twofold char-

acteristic of the true faith, a characteristic which is genuine only as being twofold.

As each of the peculiar truths of Christianity consists of two truths,* even as the axis has necessarily two poles,† christian preaching may often introduce subjects of this character As a religion which reconciles all antitheses, should begin by putting them in relief, it is well that our discourses are antithetic. Thus Bossuet says: "The spirit of Christianity is the spirit of firmness and resistance, the spirit of charity and gentleness."‡ Bourdaloue, in like manner: "*On the severity and mildness of the Christian law.*"

4. On the same principle, consequently, there is unity in a complex proposition, when the propositions of which it consists are integrant parts of the same truth. Thus: "There is no perfect bond among men; but charity is a bond of perfectness." (See Colossians, iii. 14.) "Things which have not entered into the heart of man, God hath prepared for them that love him." (1 Corinthians ii., 9.) There is a fine example in Saurin's sermon on the *Repentance of the Unchaste Woman.*§ Here a seeming triplicity is reduced to perfect unity.‖

5. I find unity also in two perfectly independent but con-

* Observe, for example, the opposition of these two propositions: "Answer a fool according to his folly: Answer not a fool according his folly," (Proverbs, xxvi. 4, 5;) and between these two: "He who is not with me is against me," (Luke, xi. 23;) and "He who is not against us is for us," (Luke, ix. 50.)

† It is the distinction of Christianity, that it has restored the broken axis and reunited the two poles.

‡ Troisème sermon pour le jour de la Pentecôte.

§ Saurin, tome ii., p. 303, Nouvelle edition. See the same author, tome iv., p. 87.

‖ "This instructive history presents *three* very different objects to our meditation, the conduct of the incontinent woman, that of the Pharisee, and that of Jesus Christ"—Tr.

trasted propositions; for contrast is a kind of unity. Examples: "Render unto Cæsar the things which are Cæsar's, and unto God the things which are God's." (Matthew, xxii. 21.) "The wicked shall go away into everlasting punishment, but the righteous into life eternal." (Matthew, xxv. 46.) Massillon's sermon *on the death of the sinner and the death of the righteous*, makes this contrast very prominent.*

6. There is unity where there is a successive exposition of a general truth and a particular truth, of which the first serves as the basis of the second, or of which the second completes the sense of the first. "Now abideth faith, hope, charity, these three, but the greatest of these is charity." (1 Corinthians, xii. 13.)

But I think that, in order to maintain strict unity, the orator must make the particular truth his object and his end.

We cannot preserve unity if we treat successively of genus and species.†

7. There is unity in a discourse which exposes successively a principle and its consequences; for the principle has its interest only in the consequences, and these have their solidity only from the principle. Thus, "God is a Spirit, and they who worship Him must worship Him in spirit and in truth." (John, iv. 24.)

Plurality of consequences does not break unity. When we speak of the consequences, however numerous they may be, we speak of the principle; we express what it contains; we make known its influence and its extent; we measure it; we give the principle its whole character; we declare at what price it is to be accepted. Example: The Characteristics of Charity. (1 Corinthians, xiii.)

8. There is unity in a discourse which after expounding a

* Sermon pour l'Avent.

† See for example, *la Solitude recommandée au pasteur*, in the Nouvelles études evangeliques, p. 265.

duty indicates the motives to its performance. But then there is here one part which is auxiliary or instrumental to the other, and we must not give this the same place which we give the other. If we have to exhibit a duty which has not been known, then we insist but little on the motives, we may put them before or after; if we have to enforce a duty which is well known, we give our care to the forcible presentation of the motives. It is difficult to conceive of a discourse which confines itself to the exposition of motives without ascertaining the nature of the duty; it is scarcely easier to conceive of one which speaks of duty without occupying itself with motives. Didactic unity doubtless may pass them by, but not oratorical unity. In every case, one of the parts, now one, now the other, must be made prominent and constitute the unity of the subject.

9. Unity may have place in a discourse which in treating of a fact notes its different circumstances. Thus in the example before given, Christ is made unto us, *on the part of God*, wisdom, righteousness, sanctification and redemption. (1 Corinthians, i. 30.) I mean not merely that a proposition in which the subject is complex, or in which the attribute is complex, (complicated, I would say, with an adventitious circumstance,) is, on that account, less one: Thus, "a double-minded man is unstable *in all his ways*:" (James, i. 8.) That need not be said. I speak of circumstances which may be omitted, but which illustrate, or at least do not subtract from the main object. "As you have always obeyed in my presence, much more in my absence, work out your salvation." (Philippians, ii. 12.) Let it be understood that we assume that what we here sanction, is to be performed in a proper manner.

There are cases in which what appears as a circumstance, is the leading idea. "Judas, betrayest thou thus the Son of Man with a kiss?" (Luke, xxii. 48.) *To betray*, (the action,) *the Son of Man*, (the object of the action,) *the kiss*, (the mode of the action;) three things which are concurrent, but yet of which one, for example *the kiss*, may be considered separately, and form the theme of the discourse. Another example, "Do good unto all men, *especially unto the household of faith*." (Galatians, vi. 10.) See, also, Hebrews, xii. 14, "Follow peace *with all men*," and Ephesians, ii. 10, "created *in Christ Jesus*, unto good works, etc." Thus we obtain many plans in perspective, and that which now has precedence, may at another time give place to another.

10. Unity in discourse in the same manner, may be maintained by presenting the same truth in several relations and bearings. These relations or bearings are accessories which offer no violence to unity. "Glory, honor and peace to every man who doeth good; to the Jew first and also to the Gentile." (Romans, ii. 10.) "I exercise myself to have always a conscience void of offence toward God and toward man." (Acts, xxiv. 16.) In a case like the last, however, it is difficult to prevent one of the relations indicated, from becoming the principal object of the discourse.

11. There is no inconsistency with unity in the exhibition and application of the same proposition to different classes of hearers, on whom it should make different impressions. If the truth in its principle is the same to all, yet the impressions which some receive from it tend to confirm the impressions of others. The returning confirms the salient angle, and this confirms that: Sadness and joy, fear and hope, correspond reciprocally to each other.

12. One and the same discourse may treat of a fact and its mode, of a duty and the means of performing it, without violating the law of unity.*

* See the sermon *sur la Sanctification* in the Meditations evangéliques.

ADDITIONAL REMARKS ON UNITY OF SUBJECT.

1. Although a factitious, verbal unity, the result of an artifice of language, is real unity only in the view of inattentive minds, the sports of appearances,* I cannot object to the process by which two objects in themselves not forming unity, are placed under a common point of view, covered by a common idea, which allows of their presentation as a whole. In fact, there is nothing here factitious or false; it is a unity, not fabricated, but discovered; it existed before; it was only necessary, to set in relief the side on which it was perceptible. Thus Bourdaloue, *Carême*, tome i., p. 198, col. 2, édition Lefèvre.

2. After having laid down the principles of rigid oratorical unity, and maintained it in each of the forms which I have indicated, I will add, that in presenting the ideal of oratorical composition, I do not exclude all preaching which is not strictly conformed to it.

The French preachers of the Catholic communion adhere to this ideal more closely than others. A sermon of theirs generally forms a bundle more compact, a sheaf better prepared to be put into the garner. This accords with the character of the nation, which demands in all respects the satisfaction of the æsthetic sentiment, which perhaps has the predominant influence in art.

It is wise to be restricted, as these preachers were, to the most severe method, and to reserve liberties for the age of experience and maturity; and the maxim of Fénelon, taken to the letter, is a good one at the beginning: "All discourse which has unity, may be reduced to a single proposition:

* Thus, speaking of spiritual and political liberty in a sermon on "The truth shall make you free." (John, viii. 32.) Thus, again, on the text, "My commandment is exceeding broad," (Psalm xix. 96,) a preacher under warrant of the word *broad*, proved successively that the law of God embraced many things, and then that it extended itself over the whole earth.

The discourse is the proposition developed; the proposition is the discourse abridged."*

It is useful to subject each of your discourses to this test. Let it not be enough to be able to give them a title; endeavor to condense them into one proposition; and distrust your work when you cannot succeed.† Could Reinhard ever have reduced to one proposition the sermon he has entitled, *Uber die Freudigkeit des Glaubens* (on the joy of faith)?

The scheme of it is this:

1. Conditions of this joy:
   a. Seriousness; *b.* Docility; *c.* Impartiality.
2. Grounds of this joy:
   a. Scripture; *b.* Excellence of the gospel; *c.* Experience.
3. Effects of this joy:
   a. Firmness; *b.* Frank confession; *c.* Zeal for the propagation of the gospel.
4. The value of this joy:
   a. The certitude which it gives; *b.* Courage in misfortune; *c.* Hope of heaven.

To make the didactic character of pulpit eloquence an apology for such a discourse, would be to cut up the substance of morality and theology into chapters. Now we do not think that a sermon is a chapter; in all cases a chapter is too long, I mean intellectually. It is easy to fall into this error after contenting ourselves with a title, such as Rheinhard has given to his discourse.

Even in the other case, that in which the sermon has a proposition for a title, may not the subject have too much

* Fénelon, Lettre écrite à l'Academie Française, iv. The first of these two phrases, is not a textual citation, but a summary; the second, on the contrary, is wholly from Fénelon.—[Editors.]

† Théremin has a sermon on Hebrews, xii. 11, which he does not entitle, Die Leiden (suffering), but *Alles Leiden ist Strafe* (all suffering is chastisement).

breadth? Not in itself. It may embrace too particular subjects; we cannot think it can be too broad. Extent is not multiplicity; it does not therefore exclude unity, which may be as much wanting in a discourse on a very particular subject, as in one on a very general subject. Everything depends on the execution. It is proper and useful to present to an auditory sometimes a subject of a very vast extent; but then we must not introduce into it all the ideas which we would introduce into each of its parts, taken separately, as the subject of an entire sermon. There are, it is true, very intellectual auditories, and perhaps a very intellectual orator might be able, without violating the laws of unity, to keep their attention quite to the close of a sermon equal to two common ones.* Particular subjects are more useful at first; they oblige us to examine thoroughly, to search out ideas which, in vast subjects, present themselves in a crowd. We should, on this account, study with caution the great models of the seventeenth century. Their majesty, with which we are so impressed, proceeds in part from the breadth of the subjects of which they treat. Bourdaloue, nevertheless, was very popular during the thirty-four years to which his career as a preacher extended, because, in his *vast* sermons, he observed the rules we have mentioned. But, in general, we should prefer a few ideas thoroughly examined, or well illustrated, to a great number of ideas lightly touched upon.

As a summary of our complementary remarks, we add in conclusion, that there are two tests of unity; one logical, which consists in reducing the whole discourse to a single proposition; the other psychological or sentimental, which consists in consulting our own impression and that of the auditory, on this twofold question: Has the course been finished? Has the limit been passed? The soul, the life, still better than the understanding, knows what unity of the subject consists in.

* Bourdaloue *sur la Passion.*

CHAPTER II.

INTEREST OF THE SUBJECT.

It may be thought that this chapter should have been the first; this is not our opinion. We must present the subject itself of pulpit discourse, before inquiring in what consists the interest of the subject.

It is not necessary to prove that preaching should treat of only interesting subjects, but what, in a pulpit-point of view, is an interesting subject, is the question before us.

Interest, a word which expresses both the subjective and the objective, denotes, in the second sense, the property of an object to draw our thought and soul to itself, so that our happiness, in some measure, depends on it. The etymology (*inter-esse*) defines the word, as it does ordinarily. In a subjective sense, interest consists in identifying ourselves more or less profoundly and permanently with an object which is out of us.

Didactic interest manifests itself when our thought or our reason perceives an agreement between itself and the object which is proposed to it. Purely oratorical interest reveals itself in a sense of the manifest importance of our taking such or such a proposed determination. When no determination is to be taken, oratorical interest has no place.

But we may express little or much in requiring that a sermon should be interesting. Remark attentively (for this observation advances us toward our object) that in the view of artists, the principal end and triumph of art is not interest. They endeavor to affect parts of our being in which interest, in the ordinary sense of the term, has little place ; they aspire to a region above those in which our ordinary affections move. The interest here is indeed greater, but it is not commonly called by this name.

The artist herein, is guided, if not by a holy purpose, at least by a superior instinct, and it is in this truly that the dignity of art resides. But while he addresses himself to the contemplative faculty, the preacher addresses a faculty yet loftier, that which Saint Paul calls *spirit*, by which we rise to invisible and celestial things, that better *self*, of which Saint Paul also speaks, which even in sin, perceives itself distinct, separates itself from the other *self* and disavows it. It is then an ideal hearer that the preacher would interest ; but he must first evoke, first create him, so to speak. The poet has not this disadvantage ; he finds man as he needs him, ready-made ; at least, he has not the trouble which the preacher has in awakening him. Man, by contemplation, voluntarily raises himself to ideas ; but man does not raise himself naturally to spiritual things, or to God. In his estate of sin, he thinks he cannot raise himself to God without forsaking himself ; in other terms, God is not his happiness ; his happiness is out of God. It is not merely an illusion of his corrupt nature, it is rather a revelation of his better nature, which, while it presents God to him as a dreadful judge, does not permit him to combine two ideas originally inseparable, God and happiness. Christianity has removed this difficulty ; Christianity, alone, among all religion, does not separate us from ourselves ; it shows us a reconciled God, and permits us or rather obliges us to combine the two ideas which have been violently separated. In exhibiting this truth, the preacher becomes conscious of the presence of that ideal auditor, which he does not find already prepared for him in each of us; then after he has obtained him, he goes on to speak to him; he speaks to this man of that which this man henceforth loves. This is his task, this his object. This is the interest of preaching—to invite to God, (a matter of interest to the natural man,) to preach holiness to the ideal or spiritual man, henceforth existent. According to this standard, or under this twofold form, we are to regard a sermon as interesting.

Such is the general principle as to interest in preaching. Now, is it possible to give rules more particular and more precise than the principle? We must indeed always bear in mind the meaning and scope of the principle. Are those subjects, which announce a dogma or a duty of Christianity, the only ones which are proper in the pulpit? If so, must we not exclude from the pulpit such a subject as this—which was treated by Reinhard: *Distinguished men are an enigma to the multitude?** According to this position, since the Bible surely should be no less christian than our sermon, what am I to do with this passage of Proverbs (treated by Irving): "Iron sharpeneth iron; so a man sharpeneth the countenance of his friend?"—(Proverbs, xxvii. 17.)

To resolve these and similar questions, we must possess ourselves of another principle. Every truth is a part of truth. Christianity embraces all; it shows the sovereignty of its principle, not by destroying anything whatever, but by assimilating all things to itself. To the Christian, everything becomes christian; nothing is absolutely foreign to the province of the Gospel; it saves the whole of man, it saves the whole of life. Whence it is, that when once Christianity controls the life, a great liberty is enjoyed, and to this liberty a slight previous servitude is the apprenticeship. Nothing

* "*Wie raethslehaft ausgezeichnete Menschen der grossen Menge Sind.*" See Reinhard, *Sermons for* 1809, tome ii., p. 228, on Acts, xxviii., 1–10.

except sin is profane ; life is not divided ; there is no point at which Christianity stops abruptly; as well forbid the atmosphere of two countries to intermix above the mountains which form a boundary between them. On the contrary, the truth frees us from conventional distinctions or separations, as well as from all others; our liberty is proportioned to our submission ; our latitude to our precision.

What has disparaged certain subjects is nothing in their own nature, it is, that they have not been treated in a christian manner: By Christians, they would have been made christian. Let them be treated in a different spirit, but let them be treated.

Whatever of a voluntary and moral nature belongs to human life, the Bible, it must be admitted, accepts and expresses. I do not say that every verse in the Bible which has this character, is a proper text for a sermon,* but what it embraces may have place in a sermon, as it may in life, in religion.

This is not saying that because everything is regarded by a Christian in a christian manner,† everything may become a subject for a sermon. The pulpit has not been erected to treat all things in a christian manner; it has a special purpose, which is to introduce the christian idea into life. It draws from the mine the precious metal, out of which each one may make vessels and instruments for his own private use. In its principles, and in its particular applications, it is properly Christianity which it teaches: Christianity is uppermost; Christianity is its object; all else is but example, illustration, etc.

Under the negative form, then, the only one which can be given to this precept, I would say: whatever does not tend to edification, (to form Christ within us)—whatever an ordinary hearer cannot of himself convert into the bread of life,

* Thus, Ecclesiastes, v. 9. The profit of the earth is for all, the king himself is served of the field. See, also, Proverbs, xxvii. 22-27.

† *Omnia pura puris.* (Titus, i. 15,) comp. Luke, xi. 41.

or at least, whatever in the preacher's own apprehension has not this character, is not to be made the subject of preaching.

We are to exclude, of course, every theme which has worldly interest directly for its object. We are to present religion as favoring this, only so far as may be necessary to evince the universal goodness of God, and the truth of religion itself.* Never should the Christian pulpit be sold to the interests of this passing life. There was a time when the pulpit had to do with subjects of worldly interest almost exclusively. When the church, undermined by infidelity, undermined especially by the corruption of her ministers, had to ask compassion for what remained to her of existence, she gave herself, as if she had been a mercenary, to the circulation of whatever ideas she was furnished with, in order to gain a miserable subsistence. Dr. Ammon tells us: "Schlez, in his sermons on Rural Economy, (Nuremberg, 1788,) has undertaken to speak of fallow-grounds; before his time, homiletical instruction was given on silk-worms. Another preacher pourtrayed, in a touching manner, the duties of Christians at the appearance of a murrain; this preacher was highly praised, even for the choice of his subject. The distance thence was not far, to substitutes for sugar and coffee, in times when these commodities are scarce, to the Christian mode of cultivating red beets, and the truly pious method of making tobacco. Did not Luther announce that the time was not distant when there would be preaching on blue ducks? That time will come soon.†" So wrote Dr. Ammon, in 1812.

Shall we exclude also, objects which respect social good? No: still, we will say that whatever aims to advance society

* Perversion of this passage: "Godliness is profitable unto all things." (1 Timothy, iv. 8.)

† AMMON'S *Anleitung zur Kanzelberedsaukeit,* tome ii., at the beginning.

without doing this through the individual, (through the individual's christian advancement,) is external to the object of preaching.

Whatever has science for its direct object, and religion only as incidental to this, forms no part of the subject matter of pulpit discourse.

I add again, assuming the observance of all these rules, that the interest of pulpit discourse is not only of a religious, but of a Christian character. To the true minister, the true Christian, there is but one religion. No subject is to be treated, which does not re-produce without effort, the characteristic traits of the gospel, its peculiar physiognomy, everything which prevents not only the confounding, but even the comparing of it with any other system. It must have this distinctiveness. I do not say in form only, or in form always, but so palpably in spirit, that a man who hears it for the first time, will be struck with something new and absolutely peculiar, and have a pungent sensation of something divine penetrating into some part of his soul. What should we say of a political discourse, and especially of a series of political discourses, which would not give a stranger who has just arrived, some impression of the general form of government under which the orator and his hearers live?

Having explained all these points, and assured to preaching all the liberty and space which its principle allows it, which its mission presents to it, we return to the formula, the adoption of which we have been holding in suspense: Christian doctrine and Christian morality form the proper and peculiar matter of pulpit discourse. But we give precision to this formula by subjoining that of Schott: "Doctrine, so far as it has a practical bearing; and morality, in its immediate and natural relation to doctrine."*

* SCHOTT, *Die Theorie der Beredsamkeit, mit besonderer Anwendung auf die geistliche Beredsamkeit*, tome ii., at the beginning.

Decomposing with him this general idea, we find as proper to the pulpit the five classes of subjects which he indicates:

1. Doctrinal subjects properly so called.
2. Moral subjects properly so called.
3. Historical subjects.
4. Subjects drawn from the contemplation and study of nature.
5. Psychological subjects.

§ 1. *Doctrinal Subjects.*

Subjects of this class are such as are suited to give the Christian life a solid foundation, in all times and places. Of course, they are never to be exhibited in the purely scientific method.

It is not everything in doctrine that forms this kind of subject matter; it is the most substantial part, the heart of each truth. Not that the rest is indifferent, or unworthy of attention; but it has its use elsewhere, and what is not proper for the pulpit, may be employed in fortifying the outworks of that truth which is very suitable to the pulpit.

Excellent teachers have sermons which may be called *theological.* Perhaps they were sometimes wrong in treating of such subjects; perhaps there is more wrong on our part that we do not treat of them. Theology, as a discussion of the text, or a comparison of systems, is not suited to the pulpit; but as a thorough consideration of saving truth, it has its place in preaching. Some theological sermons may be compared to the celebrated tragedies of Corneille: they pertain not to a genus, if you will, but are an exception, which requires execution to justify it. But still the exception is admitted. The contemplation of sublime things is not without its effect on the heart and the will. It is useful, as we have said, to elevate all the human powers; the soul purifies itself in these lofty regions.

Moreover, it is not easy to say what is theology and what is not. We must not refer to the title to decide. Tillotson has a theological sermon on sin; that of Chalmers on the same subject is not theological. Saurin, in treating of *the beatific vision of God*, (1 John, iii. 2,) need not have been theological, and he is not so everywhere; but he is too often so. He demonstrates that this vision produces a communication of ideas, of love, of virtue, of happiness.*

If we should transform theology into religion, with stronger reason should we not transform religion into theology, as Saurin has done in the sermon we have cited; and as we always do when we analyze and dissect too much. Every dissection of a moral fact is supposititious and hypothetical. We separate that which is not separated, which cannot be, which, if separated, would lose its nature; there is therefore in analysis, performed in the best manner, something false, were it only in giving successiveness to simultaneous facts. Against this, perhaps God would guard us, by giving to all truths, or leaving on them the synthetic and complex form. To express them, undoubtedly, is already to analyze them, as little analytical as the expression may be; but we may say, the Spirit who dictated the Scriptures has avoided the rigour of scientific formulas, and preserved to the ideas the most synthetic character of which they were susceptible, seeing that it was his design to announce them. With this, we have not been content, and have analyzed what was not, taking as strict classifications what were but apparent ones. The abuse has advanced even to puerility. With the same seriousness with which we should distinguish with Saint Paul, the spirit, the soul and the body, a preacher of a certain class distinguishes between honor, glory and immortality; what is in the heavens, on the earth and

* See SAURIN, tome iii., page 103, nouvelle édition, sur les *idées* de Dieu, et page 114, sur les *sentiments* de Dieu.

under the earth; the sheep and the lambs which Saint Peter was to feed; not only does he give each word a meaning, to which I consent, but he erects into scientific classifications, oratorical repetitions, the accumulation of emphasis, figures of speech, Hebrew parallelisms, &c. Exegesis has rendered so much service that we should not be unwilling to forgive it much, but truly in this matter it has much to be forgiven.

Let us beware of this cruel anatomy practised on the living, and always murderous. In treating the passage, Hebrew iv., 12, "The word of God pierces even to the soul and spirit, the joints and the marrow;" let us not undertake to distinguish nicely the elements of a passage, the confusion of which forms its beauty. What would be the astonishment of Saint Paul if he should see a discourse founded, or a system built on distinctions of which he never thought!

Purely intellectual sermons, such as those of Dwight on the Sabbath, of Clark on the Existence of God, do not appear to me to be sermons; not that I would deny that there are times and places, in which such discourses may be preached.

Apologetical subjects may be introduced into the pulpit. In one sense all preaching is apologetical; but taking the word in the ordinary sense, the thing which it expresses is not to have place in preaching except with much discretion. The nature of the auditory, the small extent of the discourse, scarcely comports with it. In seeking to edify, let us fear giving scandal. Let us not forget that in Christianity, to show is to demonstrate.* *Virtutem videant.*†

There is a general *apologetique*, which in every country, may supply subjects for the pulpit. Saurin, (*sufficiency of revlation,*) Bourdaloue, (*the wisdom and mildness of the Christian law,*) Tillotson, (*the tranquillity which religion*

* "Montrer c'est demontrer."

† PERSEUS, Satire iii. v. 38.

gives, and the utility of religion in relation to societies) have not shunned them.

The sermons on Boyle's Foundation, those of Chalmers' *on Astronomy*, are not to be condemned, but they appear to require a special auditory. It is to be wished there were auditories to which sermons of this kind might be properly addressed. Perhaps there is too much timidity in introducing such subjects.

After apologetical subjects it is proper to mention *controversial* ones. The proper controversy of the pulpit is controversy with sin, which is the great heresy. That of symbol with symbol, of Church with Church, is, in general, unseemly. It may be said that sin is at the bottom of every heresy, or easily attaches itself to it; that in religion no error is inactive. This is true; but then either this heresy does not present itself to the notice of your church, and then why speak of it? or, it is under its observation, and then, in general, it is better to overcome evil with good, to absorb error in truth. Here again we say, *Virtutem videant.*

We may not, however, always avoid controversy. We must observe the errors which appear in the places where we preach; those at least which have footing therein; but we must not do them the service of publishing them, and propagate while we oppose them.

The Apostles who protested against vain disputes, engaged in controversy. But they did this after the manner of Saint Paul, who hastened to the end, passed swiftly on to edification, never permitting any question to remain in a purely speculative state.*

May the truths of natural religion have place in a sermon?

*Examples: Romans, xi. 32, 36; Galatians, iv. 19, 20; Romans, v. (See what precedes;) Hebrews, x. 19-25. We may read the sermon on *Transubstantiation* in the *Theological sermons of Tillotson*, vol. iii., p. 317, 371; and in vol. ii., that on *The Uncertainty of Salvation in the Romish Church.*

The first difficulty presents itself in the announcement of the question. What are we to understand by the truths of natural religion? Where is the limit? These truths have received a new aspect from Christianity, a new form apart from which the Christian preacher is not at liberty to regard them. As he cannot abstract Christianity from them, he can place himself at the stand-point of purely natural religion only by a fiction which is neither proper nor profitable. There are natural truths in Christianity, but they are transformed, completed. And what advantage is there of depriving them of the complement which they received from Christianity? By the same means by which we preach Christianity we also preach natural religion, and there is no necessity for sermons distinctively on the latter. In the pulpit, indeed, it is much better to consider the truths which religion embraces as internal moral facts, than as objective verities.

It is doubtless always well to show that we carry within us truths which Christianity has come to confirm—a germ which it has made fruitful. There are arguments of more or less strength in favor of certain verities on which religion rests and which it implies, and in favor also of the duties of morality. These arguments the Bible itself uses, especially in enforcing morality. As to the doctrines of natural religion, we only give a sketch of the demonstration which Christianity completes. I would not make these arguments seem more strong, nor yet more feeble than they are. Let us not forget, moreover, that the preachers who by complaisance or by an ill-considered method have sought to conduct their hearers to revealed religion through natural, have had little success. Revealed religion leads better to the natural than the latter to the former. This is not a paradoxical assertion. In truth, natural religion, as it is called, assumes the reality, and deserves the name of religion only after it has received the seal of revelation. For *natural religion*, in the strict sense, there is none. Revelation gives a certainty, a new perception to truths, which though presupposed, have as yet no vitality, no influence on the conscience. Evangelical preachers, generally, make no trial of this false method; it is rationalism which prefers treating these subjects. If its object were the display of eloquence, it would be greatly mistaken; even, oratorically, the truths of natural religion left to themselves, are nothing; and the oratorical advantage of the Christian over the rationalistic preacher, is beyond estimation.

§ 2. *Subjects of Morality.*

Moral subjects, and the word moral itself, are at this day very unjustly disparaged. Though this word is not to be found in the gospel, we must not conclude, on this account, that the use of it is improper. The Bible uses the language not of science, but of life, and constantly inculcates morality, without supposing it necessary or useful to tell us what morality is. It uses the word virtue scarcely more, and yet we constantly speak of the Christian virtues, without the least impropriety. What has discredited moral subjects, is the manner in which they are often treated; by separating morality from the doctrine from which it derives its authority and its efficacy, rendering it distasteful and insipid. We may then, without impropriety, restore the word. Morality is the doctrine of manners, or of practical life, considered in its relations to law and grace. We have little hesitation in obtaining from it subjects for the pulpit, when we attend to the following considerations:

1. Morality abounds in the discourses of Jesus Christ, and in the writings of the apostles. Jesus Christ was a preacher of morality. His discourses indeed include more of morality than of doctrine, as it was entirely natural that they should.

He himself was Doctrine; the grand fact with which all others were connected. When he said, "I am he who should come," he gave rules of life. Neither are the apostles wanting in morality, even in a morality very special.

2. It is an excellent schoolmaster to lead us to Jesus Christ. Let us not despise morality, as though conversion were everything. We must be led to conversion, and nothing enforces its necessity better than expounding the rules of practical life. Has not God himself purposed that the law should serve as a precursor to Christianity?

3. Morality throws much light on doctrinal teaching.

4. It has intimate relations to individual and social happiness.

We must distinguish as to subjects of moral preaching:

1. *Descriptive* morality, which, as its designation indicates, employs itself in studying and painting the phenomena of moral life, after the manner of La Bruyère and Rochefoucauld; and *preceptive* morality, which is occupied with rules of conduct. The first is very useful for the pulpit; facts preach. It furnishes material and a ground for the second: preceptive morality, only, furnishes *subjects* for preaching.

2. *General* and *particular* morality. We must not confine ourselves to the first, nor borrow from the second subjects too particular.

3. The same subjects, with different designs, according to the impressions we wish to make: consolation, encouragement, humiliation, fear.

4. Finally, general and particular circumstances. It is useful to dwell on the last, provided we do this in order to connect strongly that which passes with that which does not pass away. Let us recur to these distinctions when they have respect to preceptive morality, that which supplies subjects for preaching.

General duties are those from which all others flow, those which are the first effluence of doctrinal truths towards practice, duties intermediate between doctrine and the details of life, the duties of piety and Christian methodology. These duties may be considered as essential subject matter for preaching. It is astonishing to see the affluence of general morality, which Christianity offers us. The preacher, of course, is to be much occupied with it; here, as in all things, he is to enforce principles. The task here has become easier from the fact, that the field of general morality has been much more cultivated, and is consequently more accessible. But this consideration itself should show us the necessity of not confining ourselves to general facts. The preacher must illustrate the power of Christianity, which opens a way to itself even into the details and to the extreme parts of life. We must see it thus in operation, in order to possess a thorough sense of its excellence. Error or half-error is not infinite; truth alone penetrates to the very bottom of things. It is moreover very necessary to combat or correct received ideas on certain points of morality. The gravest errors are accredited even in the bosom of the most cultivated classes of society. And in descending lower, yet worse ones will be found. The Christian preacher should, in this respect, extend aid to the people, give them, as far as possible, elevated ideas of morality, and direct his endeavors most particularly to the points where danger lies.

Still, though it is interesting to show that the minutest details of life are under the protection of Christianity, which has a hand as delicate as it is powerful; though it is also necessary to give juster ideas on parts of morality which have been too much obscured; it is not less true that we must avoid subjects which are too particular. If you separate a very small drop from a colored or sapid liquid, it will have in its isolation neither color nor taste. At the last extremity of a branch, it is difficult to retain a view of the stem. Represent to yourself, for example, sermons on neatness, politeness, etc. Some topics of this sort, doubtless, may be approached, but it must be done incidentally; they should never furnish the subject of a sermon. Particular morality is not to be excluded, but such details of it may have their place in more general matters, or in historical subjects.

There are some subjects closely related to those treated by the gospel, which it has not even mentioned, as suicide, slavery, etc. These last, so far from deserving to be excluded, are sometimes among the most interesting and most evangelical. The silence of the gospel on these points has been complained of, but we ought rather to be pleased that it has not said everything. Besides circumstantial reasons, we must consider in general that the gospel would put us under the necessity of finishing, of completing things for ourselves. The church is the continued revealer of truth; it can add nothing to principle, but as developing, applying, inferring principle, it has always to be active, always advancing. If the gospel had said everything there would be no need of preaching.

Ought morality as applicable to the different classes of the auditory, to parents, to children, to magistrates, to be preached? We think so; men are seldom as much touched with general as with particular truths. We must take every one on his own ground, apply the truth to individuals. Saurin has a sermon on the *Life of Courtiers*.* Let us not fear that that which is specially spoken with reference to certain hearers, will touch them only. What does not concern us directly may furnish us useful instruction, and indirect lessons sometimes move us more than those which are addressed to us immediately. It is moreover well for us to be instructed in the duties of a position we are never to occupy;

* SAURIN, tome iii., nouvelle edition.

we thus acquire a more complete knowledge of Christian morality as a whole.

Particular sins, can be the sins only of certain persons. But, as the virtues are sisters, even so are the vices brothers. There is a consolidation of all the parts of evil, as there is of those of good. We must show our hearer that if he is exempt from certain vices which offend him, he is so often from the effect of circumstances. There is then a philosophy of evil, the knowledge of which is inseparable from that of Christianity. And as it is not enough to speak of duties without connecting them with *one* duty, neither is it enough to speak of sins without showing their organism. The believer should know not only life but all life. And the Bible here is not sparing. It is a natural, perfect picture of elementary human life: so should be preaching.

Cases of conscience, like the morality of certain positions and the sins of certain classes, are to be approached with caution, under the sanction of general and manifest utility; but they are not to be absolutely excluded. We must treat them neither in special discourses, nor even in one discourse, separately; but show them as absorbed in a great principle, which, when it penetrates the soul, explains the difficulties of practical life. If our unity with our Head were perfect, we should be strangers to cases of conscience. As the fact is, every one meets with them; some of which are very difficult, very perplexing, even with all the aid of prayer. But in general, the pulpit is not the place for casuistry, the multiplied subtilities of which have subjected the gospel to reproach. One who is tormented with scruples of this sort, should have recourse to the pastor rather than the preacher, whose task is not so much the resolution of questions of this kind as the dissipation of them. Love is the best casuist.

We may also class sermons on morality, as we have said before, according to the nature of the impression we wish to produce. Regarding the auditory as a single man, having different moral wants, we exhort, we encourage, we console, we rebuke or correct. This kind of preaching, sermons of reprehension, (in German, *Strafpredigten*,) which were formerly much more frequent, seems now to be confined to a single day of the year.* It is useful sometimes to preach in this spirit. The multitude require this agitating strain, and the searching examinations now instituted, are of great utility to the believer also; but there are perils to be avoided. Age, in discourse of this kind, gives an authority that does not belong to youth. There is, however, an authority independent of age, with which the preacher, as such, is invested. It is to young Timothy, that the wise, discreet and staid Paul has said: "Them that sin rebuke before all, that others also may fear." (1 Timothy, v. 20.) "Preach the word: be instant in season, out of season; reprove, rebuke, exhort with all suffering and doctrine." (2 Timothy, iv. 2.) Thus, also, he said to Titus: "These things speak, and exhort and rebuke with all authority." (Titus, ii. 15.) Besides, truth itself rebukes, and it is important that the hearer perceive that it is the word of God and not man, that corrects him. "For the word of God is quick and powerful, and sharper than any two-edged sword, piercing even to the soul and spirit, the joints and the marrow, and is the searcher of the thoughts and intents of the heart." (Hebrews, iv. 12.)

As to the preaching which is opposite to this, the *laudatory* kind, we may find examples of it in the epistles of Saint Paul; but it is scarcely credible that it is applicable to the present church—at least to our churches.

Occasional Sermons. Connecting general truths with certain and known facts is doubtless a means of reanimating general

* The author alludes to the Fast-day, which is annually celebrated in all the Swiss churches.—[EDITORS.]

truth; and on the other hand, it is giving to particular facts which are often misjudged or unobserved, the form of instruction.* If the preacher may say God instructs us by events, (God also preaches occasional sermons,) he should also adopt the absurd inference that he ought never to speak of events. Undoubtedly, indeed, the substance of preaching is not that which is transient, it is that which does not pass away; but this does not imply that we deprive it of this character, by using it to connect with passing events, truths which do not pass away. The hearer brings into the temple all the small money of his particular impressions, that it may be converted into gold. All history, with the Christian, is a sermon; a sermon may become history. He who preaches in this manner, that is to say, in the spirit which generalizes the particular, which eternizes the temporary, may discourse of circumstances: We forbid it to the man who only regards it as a means of stimulating our dull curiosity. The din of the world should die away at the gate of the sanctuary, as in the eternal world, "time is no longer." The temple is a heaven; we enter for a moment into eternity, to come back into time, and of the events which pass without, nothing whatever should have admission here but the truths which they bring.

As to *patriotic* and *political sermons*, they are rather to be avoided, and yet in certain grave circumstances, we may be obliged to touch upon such subjects in the pulpit. On one hand, the human character of Christianity puts it into contact with all the interests of life, gives it a word to speak in all circumstances; on the other hand, it never surrenders its liberty to place and time, and with extreme reserve, mixes itself with everything that does not bear the stamp of eter-

* See the sermon of Saurin sur *les Malheurs de l'Europe*, tome viii., new edition.

nity.* We must beware, lest we inflame on this hearth, the passions of the natural man. How shall we now speak of politics without taking a side? We must remark, also, the utilitarianism which for the most part is concealed in these subjects.† It is better for the preacher, as it is for the navigator, to keep himself on the high sea; it is in the neighborhood of coasts that shipwrecks are most frequent.‡

I believe, indeed, that we cannot wholly avoid discoursing to the public on that which preoccupies and absorbs it; but we must discourse to it only in order to calm or moderate it. Control worldy affairs without touching them; have to do with them only to impress a character on them; show them to your hearers from the heights of heaven.

See the Lord and his apostles. I would not rigorously enforce the example which they have set us on this point. It is, nevertheless remarkable, that loving their nation as they did, they should have approached political subjects with so much reserve. As the apostles have followed their master, they have left, in this matter, but one example.

We must here distinguish the preacher from the religious writer, who may be, if he pleases, a journalist, a pamphleteer. The preacher, moreover, is at the same time one who presides over a worshipping assembly. His discourse itself forms part of the worship. This does not allow him, so it seems to me, to make a sermon whatever he may be tempted to make it. We have, at this day, so many other means.

* The manner in which the *fast* is observed, shows too plainly that the nation is no longer *the church.*

† Saurin has some political sermons, but they are in general restrained within just limits. See, also, the sermon of Ancillon, *Sur le Jubilé de la Monarchie.*

‡ . . . . Nimium premendo
Litus iniquum.
HORACE, *Odes*, lib. ii., ode x.

§ 3. *Historical Subjects.*

What we have said concerning oratorical unity does not seem to lead us to the idea of historical subjects. If, as Quintilian says, we write in order to narrate and not to prove, we speak in order to prove and not to narrate. But in the first place, the first business of a preacher, as we have already said, is to teach or to instruct; and to narrate may be a form of instruction. "We reason," I have somewhere said, "only because we know not how to narrate." Facts well narrated are the most incisive, and, I will say, the most decisive kind of instruction, because the hearer or reader now gives instruction to himself. It is by histories, especially, that God wins our heart. It is by histories, by romances, that ideas are diffused. We are too fond of reasoning, which is only one form of demonstration. Moreover, we have nothing to do with narration, simply and purely; the recital is but the basis, the support of the instruction which is to follow. Narration then agrees entirely with the idea of oratorical discourse; but the orator does not narrate after the manner of a historian.

We add, that nothing so interests the mass of hearers as history. We have truly little regard to the wants of the multitude, if we withhold recitals from them. God has been more condescending.

We seek to transform history into precept; Herder would transform each precept into history.* Both are good; we must accept both. Thus, instead of saying avarice, let us say *miser*, or, better still, *a miser*.

Besides sacred history, properly so called, there are abundant materials for preaching, in the history of the Church, in

**Lehrsatz*, (precept.) See HERDER: *Briefe das Studium der Theologie betreffend*, tome ii., p. 36. Edition de Carlsruhe, 1829.

which the history of the old and new Testament has its continuation ; in the history of religion, and even that of the world, which is, as it were, a history of Providence. What a field, too, is the history of missions and Christian labor, as also that of persecution?* The history of individuals, biographies of holy men, ought also to have place in the pulpit.

Catholic preachers have here an advantage over us, as *panegyrics of the Saints, funeral orations* have regularly a place in their preaching.† These sermons give us all the interest which general truth acquires by being individualized. Why, instead of taking the apostles' words for our texts, should we not take the apostles themselves? Instead of regarding their words in their objective sense simply, why not consider them in a subjective point of view, and endeavor to discern in them the beautiful characteristics of the primitive Church? They are models of moral excellence which it would be of great advantage to study. And as the work of God is identical with itself, let us pass the bounds of apostolic times, and from the immense field of the Church, even of the Catholic Church before the Reformation, and since, let us reap a rich harvest of the finest memorials.

There would be ingratitude in suppressing the lives of our believing fathers. Would we be Christians, and yet have but vague knowledge of Paul, James and Peter; would we ignore, so to speak, a Luther, or a Viret! The history of the work of the Spirit in the Church, and the lives of holy men, are often more edifying than all demonstrations. Let us not fear even anecdotes. Why deprive an auditory of all this, which they will not find elsewhere or not so seasoned? Let us not forget, however, while we freely use these materi-

* See my *Installation Discourse*, (in the appendix.)

† See Bossuet, *Paneygriqué de l'apotre Saint Paul et l'Oraison funebre de la Princesse palatine.*

als, that all things are lawful only to him who is the devoted servant of God, and in proportion as he is his devoted servant. The subjects which we have just mentioned allow of very sufficient oratorical unity, and meet all the proprieties of the pulpit.

§ 4. *Subjects drawn from the contemplation of Nature.*

Subjects of this class have also been abused, and have hence fallen into discredit like that which has happened to morality. There has been a surfeit of romantic sermons, and the fault of the preachers has been transferred to their favorite themes. The disgust doubtless is excusable, but still it is unjust, and it is proper that the subject, we speak of, should have the place which belongs to them. The God of nature is put in opposition to the God of the gospel. This, before conversion is done in one way, after it in another. What we have said of the truths of natural religion is applicable here; for this is nothing else. Grace is not opposed to nature: because the heavens do not declare all the glory of God, it does not follow that they have become silent on this important subject. Shall we say that their speech has lost all value since the gospel has spoken? We cannot think so. No; they speak; let us receive what they say. It is true that nature also speaks of the fall and of sin, and constrains us to desire a new earth and a new heavens; but it is useful to speak of the present world, even in this particular, and to know how everything is calculated for the religious education of man!

Moreover, the correspondence of the physical to the moral world is striking. Nature is an immense parable.

Only let us remark, that what is allowed to the pulpit of this kind of subject matter, is neither science nor poetry, although science in its general results, and poetry by a necessary consequence, have a place here. The contemplation of nature should be essentially religious. It is aided by science. it naturally abounds in poetry; but science is only a means and poetry an accident. It is to be desired that the preacher should not speak of these subjects in a vague and uncertain manner, but with the precision which science gives. Wonders which are hidden are not the least.*

§ 5. *Psychological Subjects.*

That psychology, or the knowledge of the elements, the springs, and the motives of the physical man, is necessary; in a word, that *man* ought to be known by the preacher, no one doubts. Some in contempt of this study, say the Bible is sufficient, forgetting that the psychology which it includes, invites us to the study of that psychology which is a flambeau to aid us in looking into man, and that it is man into whom we are to look. How much is there in Job and Ecclesiastes on the mysteries of the human soul! What points of view are indicated!

He who affirms authoritatively, "man is this, man is that," without having himself seen man, accomplishes little; as well might he allege that there is no other motive to duty than the authority of the Bible. No one thinks himself reduced to that. No one should have it to say, "If the preacher knew us better, he would not speak as he does." A preacher who speaks of man without having studied him, will fall into grievous errors, and will want authority. He should show that he knows, as far as a man can know, "of what we are made." (Psalm iii. 14.) But in general, psychology is better adapted to supply our sermons with substance than with subjects strictly so called; in either case, however, it should be neither scientific nor superficial. The psychology of the

* We may cite as examples of this kind of subjects, some sermons of *Celériêr* and that of *Manuel on Winter.* (*Sermons,* tome ii., see part xviii.)

preacher should be practical and popular. A purely speculative, or a too refined psychology, withdraws the hearer from that which ought wholly to preöccupy him; it supplies his self-love with nutritious food;* it creates within him imaginary impressions; besides, it is an element but little oratorical.

Psychology, as we here understand it, regards not only individal man, but social man also; there is a social psychology as there is a social physiology. It forms part of the domain which we have just opened to the preacher. Nothing is more natural and more easy than to connect all providential institutions with the idea of God; to show, for example, that from the beginning of the Bible and of the world, God was the founder of society and civilization, by the almost simultaneous institution of the *family*, of the *word*, of *law* and of *labor*. These subjects, which are very much neglected, and which, at the same time, give a sort of religious shock to the hearers, are comprehended in the preceding one. In truth, institutions, manners, and with them, industry, arts, civ-

* "A very refined psychology, which busily pries into all the movements of the soul, stealing into its secret places, extorting its confessions, ferreting, if we may so speak, into its darkest corners, and above all, making it conscious of all its evil, and multiplying, by recounting its sorrows,—I think I have some perception of its injurious influence on all the soul's great interests. So far as regeneration necessarily depends on self-knowledge, the difficulty of this work is perhaps augmented by this minuteness of observation. It turns into a study, a matter of curiosity, the mighty impressions which would bring the soul into the sphere of light. It stealthily changes the sorrows of repentance into the pleasures of self-love; the reproaches of conscience become intellectual discoveries. We do not enter into, we rather depart from ourselves. Amused spectators of a serious evil, we cease to identify ourselves with it, we separate ourselves from it, we withdraw ourselves from it while it engages our attention." (VINET, *Etudes, sur la Litterature Française au* xix. *siecle.* Tome iii., pp 28-29.)

ilization, multiform developments, flow from human nature. All truth leads to truth. Christ, without doubt, is the centre of all truth; but to show that Christ is the centre, we must speak of the circle and of the most remote circumference.

We acknowledge, nevertheless, that the word psychology, which we have just used, cannot be understood, without doing a sort of violence to the secret tie which unites the different parts of the world, and the different elements of human life. It is rather philosophy, in which these are embraced. Philosophy in religion, is an instrument, a method; it has less to do with a given philosophy, a philosophical construction than with that philosophical spirit by which we class, generalize, abstract, find the true relation of things, ascend from appearance to reality, from phenomena to principle, comprehend the whole. This spirit aids us in discovering the philosophy of religion, that is to say, the relation to one another and to the centre, of the elements which compose it, and its own relations to the world and to life. It is by the aid of this spirit, that we seize and manifest the secret harmony which exists among all things; between religion and nature or human life, between individual and social existence, between reality and art, between thought and action, between liberty and order, between particular and general affections,* between instincts and duties, between present interest and thought for the future. But all this enters into the class of apologetical sermons, and philosophy appears here, as I have said, not as an object but as an instrument.

May not this almost boundless extension of the sphere of preaching, which at least excludes nothing, be an occasion of offence? We may be asked, whether Jesus Christ came to

* Example: "Weep ye not for the dead, neither bemoan him: but weep sore for him that goeth away; for he shall return no more nor see his native country." (Jeremiah, xxii. 10.)

discourse on all sorts of subjects? No: Jesus Christ spoke of a *good part*, a *one thing needful*, which we must choose, if needs be, to the exclusion of all others. There is, in the evangelical ministry, a character of urgency. The teaching of Jesus Christ and the apostles, is vehement, little resembling the tranquil style of scientific exposition. "Save yourselves from this untoward generation." (Acts, ii. 40.) Save yourselves, though you leave your treasures and remnants of yourselves;—such is the preaching of Jesus Christ—such is evangelical preaching. The Christian pulpit is not an academical chair. Men will not so regard it. Those who regard the pastor as a missionary (as they have reason to do), cannot understand our moderation. Still, let us not forget that to preach is to instruct. If urging the sinner to flee to the foot of the cross were all, there might be some excess even in preaching the gospel. The good news dwells in many subjects. Alarms to the conscience are spread through the gospel, and they abound about us. Doubtless they should have a place virtually in every discourse, but we cannot be excused, on this account, from studying the various aspects of truth. To alarm is not everything; it is indeed a small thing; we must move the heart, and in order to this, we must instruct. There are a great many souls that we can win to Christ only by this means. Let us hasten then to instruct, and to instruct at our ease; God meanwhile will do his own work. Instruction is a matter, not of taste, or of choice, but of necessity. An essential part of the preacher's mission is a course of instruction, in all its parts tending to edification.

Moreover, it must never be out of view, that a great means of perpetuating interest is novelty, and that preaching to retain this quality must be incessantly renewing itself. We desire something new, and generally we are not wrong in this. The necessity for novelty is more serious than we think, and the most earnest hearer is far from being a stranger to it. Every wise preacher "will bring forth from his treasure things new and old." (Matthew, xiii. 52.) That which is not ancient is not true; for it is not ours to make a new gospel. And, on the other hand, that which is not new, that is to say, suited to the mental state, the tendency and necessities of each epoch, is not completely true, any more than the other. The wonderful flexibility of the gospel, its adaptation to the forms of society, to characters, positions, the most diverse mental tendencies, is no feeble indication of its divine origin. Shall preaching lose its resemblance to it? It is too often like itself in one preacher and another, in one epoch and another. There are few things the force of which is entirely independent of form. There are few sermons of past centuries which we could use well without a transformation.

There is then a legitimate novelty—a novelty even of subjects; not of doctrines but of themes. By this means, art, which is an affair of humanity, renovates itself; the gospel is unchangeable, but it is divine. In order to attain the novelty of which we speak, genius is not necessary, the preacher has only to open his eyes and observe. Let him not confine himself to a general and abstract idea of man, but let him study the men who are before him, and to whom he speaks. If he will but take this pains, he will be new. The study is a difficult one, requiring a constant attention; one in which zeal will sustain and direct him, but from which he is not to be excused.

After having thrown down barriers we raise them up again; that is to say, after having opened to preaching in general, five or even six departments, we reduce them for the sake of the young preacher to two: Doctrine and Morality. The three latter classes of subjects suppose the preacher to have a discernment, a tact, which only experience can give him. The young preacher is safer within narrower limits, which yet are not so narrow as to cramp his zeal, and restrict the usefulness of his ministry, and into which also he may easily introduce ideas and facts gathered from the departments from which he does not take the subjects of his preaching.

CHAPTER III.

OF THE TEXT.

§ 1. *Of the Text in General.*

In treating first of the subject, separate from the text, I have decisively shown that I do not regard the use of a text as essential to pulpit discourse.* And in truth it is not. What gives a christian character to a sermon is not the use of a text, but the spirit of the preacher. A sermon may be christian, edifying, instructing, without containing even one passage of holy scripture. It may be very biblical without a text, and with a text not biblical at all. A passage of scripture has a thousand times served as a passport for ideas which were not in it; and we have seen preachers amusing themselves, as it were, by prefixing to their composition very strong biblical texts, for the sake of the pleasure of emasculating them. We have witnessed a formal immolation of the Divine Word. When the text is only a deceptive signal, when a steeple surmounts a play-house, it would doubtless be better to remove the signal and throw down the steeple.

Preachers who love the word of God, will not fall into this abuse; yet even with respect to them how often has the text been the occasion of a painful distortion! So far are the text and the subject from always aiding one another, that there is very often a kind of war between them.

* Origin of texts: See Luke, iv., 16, 21.

That this war may never have place, two things are necessary: one, that every text contain a subject; the other that every subject be sure of finding a text. Neither the one nor the other is invariable.

And first, every text does not contain a subject. Avoiding the homily, which is now out of question, and to which we shall return, the question here relates only to synthetic discourse, in which everything meets in one point. This discourse rests upon a thesis. We must then search for a text which embraces a thesis. Do we always find it? Remark that the thesis results from an abstraction, is a truth carefully detached from an assemblage of truths, as a member from the body to which it belongs, upon which it has grown, in which it forms a distinct and inseparable whole, a unity. The thesis includes in itself whatever forms it, nothing more, nothing less; it has no more excrescences than defects; its extremities are connected with nothing foreign to it, it has nothing of the subjective, the historical, the accidental. Conceived as thesis, thesis by birth, it proceeds to its object without sinuosities, and by following the most direct line. There are doubtless many texts in the Bible which will meet these conditions, but there is a greater number, the contexture, the form, the ground even of which, suppose an occasion, a personal emotion, fortuitous contact with other ideas, in a word, a complication foreign to thesis strictly so called, and which regarded by itself would seem arbitrary. Now, it is often in a passage of this kind that the truth we are to treat is deposited as in a sort of *gangue*,* and the thesis then rises up by the side of the text, throws its roots into it obliquely as in the crevice of a rock; it draws from it a new life, some new interest, far more than it is

* "The earthy, stony, saline, or combustible substance, which contains the ore of metals, or is only mingled with it without being chemically combined, is called the gangue or matrix of the ore."—Tr.

itself substantially drawn from it. And if it seeks to absorb the whole text, it becomes surcharged, it is out of proportion, it is thesis no longer.

Ah, well! says one, let us abandon the theses, and embarrassment will disappear. But I ask whether the preacher in the course of his career, will have no other subjects of preaching presented to him besides passages of the Bible? Experience also is a book; experience also furnishes texts. A proposition which has its precise expression in no passage of the Bible, is suggested altogether by the preacher's own mind, under the influence of circumstances or meditation. In compliance with a usage which has the force of law, he would now obtain a text for this preconceived subject, and he probably finds a text which has some perceptible relation to his subject; but does he always find a text which expresses his subject? We cannot think so. And now he will do one of two things; either he will take from the Bible only what exactly suits his subject, and leave the rest; or he will make the text the mould of his discourse. Is it probable now that his plan will be a truly natural one, which, having been first formed in his mind according to the nature of things and from a particular point of view, has to be afterwards formed anew according to the sinuosities of a text which has not the form of his thesis or of any thesis?

If you tell him to abandon the form of his thesis, or rather his thesis itself, in favor of the text, with what chains would you load the minister of the Word? And know you not that the Bible includes many more truths than it expresses? And that it is one of its excellencies that it suggests, that it excites, a multitude of ideas which it includes virtually, though not actually? If now you prefer that the preacher should appear to have regard only to the text, and should yet treat his proposition, completely and independently, just as he conceived it, that perhaps were much worse. You oblige him to use an artifice unworthy of the pulpit; you prefer that under the appearance of inviolable respect for the letter of the Bible, he should offer it violence, he should wrest it. Is it not evident that he would show more respect for it, by following it not so closely, and not, while pretending to bring his conception into the circle of the divine Word, by forcing that Word to enter into the circle of his conception? To all hearers of the least cultivation or sagacity, this is a feigned respect.

When we are told that preaching ought to be as it was in its origin a simple explanation and application of the inspired Word, we are transferred to an entirely different stage, to another question, which we may discuss without touching, without compromitting in any respect the ideas we have just presented.

Men of characters very different and of very opposite doctrines, unite in the opinion that the use of texts is an abuse. According to Voltaire, whom we must not hastily refuse to hear (for why might he not have fallen in with the truth on this point, which is not precisely a religious question?*): "It were to be wished that Bourdaloue in banishing from the pulpit the bad taste which disgraced it, had also banished the custom of preaching on a text. Indeed, to speak long on a quotation of a line or two, to exhaust oneself in subjecting a whole discourse to the control of this line, seems a trifling labor, little worthy of the dignity of the ministry. The text becomes a sort of motto, or rather enigma, which the discourse develops."†

We must shake off the yoke of custom which at length becomes a second nature; we must place ourselves at the stand-point of a man who has never heard preaching, who knows the end without knowing the usages of preaching, and

* Fas est ab hoste doceri. OVID. *Met.*

† VOLTAIRE *Siecle de Louis XIV.*

think how he would feel to see an entire branch of oratory subjected to this rule, and each discourse developing not an idea of the preacher or an idea which has become his own, but a word taken from the midst of a foreign discourse; I think I may say, he would at least be astonished. And doubtless he would not rest in simple astonishment if the discourse on which he had fallen were a discourse of Bourdaloue's, who seems like other orators of his communion, to have taken a text only to show how skilfully he could disembarrass himself of it: And if the preacher could not have done otherwise, if the text were imposed upon him, the blame in that case has a different direction, but it has its mark; the preacher is innocent but the institution is not. The astonishment would not be less, if, instead of a sermon of Bourdaloue, it should be one of Reinhard's: the one disencumbers himself of his text, the other tortures it to make it speak what it has not spoken, and what it is not willing to speak. But if this stranger, this new-comer should hear one of those sermons, of which the reformed pulpit offers so many examples, in which the text is not a pretext, in which the text is not a defile which one traverses with effort, but truly a text, a divine thought, the meaning of which is to be penetrated, the extent to be measured, the parts to be unfolded, the consequences to be deduced, would he be equally astonished? I think not. He would, perhaps, make no reflection on the usage; and if he should make one, it would very probably be favorable to the usage.

At length, however, and in proportion as he enters into the spirit of preaching and of the ministry, he may also come to doubt the legitimacy of the usage, at least when regarded absolutely. He may make the reflections, which we have presented, on the incompatibility of the text with the subject, taking each of them in the rigor of its notion. He may say with Claus Harms: "May we be permitted to ask, if preaching on texts is founded as much in reason as on custom? May we venture to express the opinion that the theme and the text approach each other only in order to their mutual exclusion of each other? That a theme does not need a text, and that a text does not need a theme? May we dare even to say, that the usage of preaching from a text has done injury, not only to the perfection of preaching as an art, but to Christian knowledge also, and what is yet more serious, to the Christian life."*

There are two things in this passage, one is a strictly true assertion respecting the forced alliance of a subject or a theme conceived beforehand, with a text conceived and committed to writing by another. We have already admitted the force of this objection; the difficulty cannot be denied; we shall see, presently, if it cannot be surmounted. The second part of the passage quoted is a simple remark of which no proof is given, concerning the injury which this usage may have done to preaching itself, to Christian knowledge, to Christian life. I do not think it can be absolutely repelled. The manner in which the usage has been observed, may, to a certain extent, have produced these effects. If the continuous interpretation of the texts of the Bible had been the exclusive form of preaching, it would not have had all these inconveniences; but the use of isolated texts connected with the necessity of never preaching without a text, has, certainly, in a rigorous and absolute view, something false, something serious, which narrows the range, which limits thought, which puts restraint on the

*Harms, *Pastoraltheologie*, tome i., p. 65. See, also, tome ii., p. 153. These opinions of Harms were discussed by Tholuck, *Theologischer Anzeiger*, in the year 1838, Nos. 63 and 64. See on the same subject, Koester, *Lehrbuch*, p. 194, § 35, *de l'Homiletitque*, and Huffeld, *Uber das Wesen und den Beruf das evangelisch-christlichen Geistlichen*, tome i., p. 35.

preacher's individuality. Considering this method as employed without qualification, without allowance, I think we ought to be on our guard in respect to it.

It remains for us now to see whether the opposite method, or simply the liberty of preaching without a text, would not have had yet more inconveniences, whether the abuses which would have resulted from this, might not have been more serious. We see the abuses to which the prevalent method has given place ; and we do not see those which the other method might have produced ; but it is not very difficult to represent them to ourselves, and it is not more difficult to understand that a usage so constant and so universal is not without some solid foundation, and was not, in its principle and simplicity, an abuse or an error. It yet remains to be seen whether the use of texts is not susceptible of modifications, which without making it a mere contemptible formality, would purify it of whatever there may be in it that is false, servile, irrational.

I will, in conclusion, examine this point. But first, taking this method in general, without regard to the application which it may have received, and the abuse which may have been made of it, I make the following observations :

In the first place, this method has received from time and universal consent a sacredness which gives it such force that only time which, introduced, can abolish it, and perhaps time itself cannot abolish it without producing a convulsion in the Church.

In the second place, this method, externally and formally at least, well represents the idea, that the preacher is the minister of the Word of God. It recalls this to others and himself.

Thirdly, it has real advantages. The first is, the moral advantage to the preacher of having his discourse connected with a passage of the Bible. The second is, the impressions of respect which the enunciation of the sacred word makes on the auditors, at the beginning of the sermon. The third is, that generally a text well comprehended and closely followed will produce a discourse more special, striking, spirited than one founded on an abstract conception—a discourse thoroughly original. Finally, to the majority of preachers this method is better suited than the other, to multiply subjects.

Ammon has very well summed up the advantages of using texts in the following words: "The Bible is the source of our external knowledge of religion. It is, especially in its historical parts, very easy to be understood, very interesting, and very dramatic. It supplies abundant materials of the greatest value, for the most various expositions in theology, religion, and practical wisdom. Its passages are very easily remembered, on account of their simple and striking language; they thus facilitate the particular reproduction of truths which have been expounded. The subjective divinity of its origin gives the objective divinity of its contents an authority* which strengthens the religious convictions of cultivated men, and which holds the place of proof with the unlettered."†

Claus Harms himself, after making the objections which we have mentioned against the custom of preaching on a text, is still in favor of retaining this method;‡ he adheres to it from regard to moral utility, and though he admits of sermons without texts, he admits of them as exceptions.

If preaching on texts presents theoretic difficulties, they certainly may be much diminished in practice. We shall make ourselves understood by distinguishing three cases:

The first, which certainly does present itself, and which indeed is not so uncommon, is that in which our text is one

* In German, *Eine Glaubwürdigkeit.*

† AMMON, *Handbuch der Kanzelberedsamkeit,* p. 88 of the third edition.

‡ HARMS, *Pastoral theologie,* tome i., p. 83.

with our subject. The one exactly covering the other, in this case there is no difficulty to be diminished, no obstacle to be removed.

Again, when a preconceived subject has no precise formula in a passage of Scripture. If, notwithstanding this, the subject has a christian character, it may be supported by a text of the Bible, the meaning of which has the relation to the subject of the species to the genus, or the genus to the species; or which expresses the idea of the subject by complicating it with certain accessory or adventitious circumstances, or which encases the idea in an individual fact;—in brief, a text with which, without witticism or subtilty, we may connect the subject of our discourse. We abstract that which is accessory or contingent, or we speak of it and dismiss it. The text, in such a case, will at least be the general announcement or starting point of the truth which we wish to establish. It adorns, it solemnizes the preacher's discourse. There is nothing in this inconsistent with that frankness which is the first essential of pulpit dignity. The text is not a pretext; the sermon is scriptural. Such a manner of connecting ourselves with the Bible, is surely preferable to that imaginary respect which does violence to the text or the thought; and it justifies itself by the necessity, which circumstances may create, of preaching on a subject which has no exact and adequate expression in a passage of Scripture.*

Again, finally, when we have before us from the first and purely, a text. This, I remark, is the most frequent case, the

* As would be the case with a preacher in the United States, who should have to preach on slavery; of him also who should have to preach on the necessity of reforming individuals through the reformation of society; or on order in domestic affairs; or with the purpose of justifying mysteries in religion; or on signs as a means of determination; or on progress in understanding the ways of God.

most natural position of the preacher ; one which, by the force of things, as it were, by a habit which a mind incessantly occupied with the Bible naturally forms, produces a harmony, an interfusion between the text and the subject, of which we cannot conceive *à priori*. We are then at the service of our text, not however in the spirit of servility, of puerile minuteness and exegesis; it is to us, as it were, a mystic fruit, the entire juice of which we would express, the entire perfume would preserve; we seriously develop not the precise words and the accidental details of it, but its ideas. Nevertheless, as the idea and the form are always united, and nowhere so closely as in the Bible, the discourse takes the form of the text, and with what advantage I have already said. It has nothing abstract. It is concrete, like a fact, a history. The assertion of the sacred author, is as a fact of which we give an account.

We would gladly make this method the rule, as, in truth, the case we have supposed is the rule. But then, if we enter fully into this view, we shall abound in the spirit of this procedure, which sees in each assertion of the sacred author, not only an assertion, but a fact; I mean a fact of the author, a fact which has not twice had place in the same manner. We start with the idea that every text is unique and individual, so to speak ; we start with the idea, that in a book, the authors of which have not spoken merely for the sake of speaking, there are as many thoughts as words, that two forms claim two ideas. La Bruyère has justly said, that among all the different expressions which can render a thought, only one is good.* For the same reason, of two meanings which we may give a text, only one of them is good. A word may serve to individualize a text. For example : "*Forget not* to do good." (Hebrews, xiii. 16.) It is impoverishing ourselves and preferring vagueness, to follow a

* LA BRUYERE, Les Caractères, chap. i. *Des Ouvrages de l'esprit.*

different mode. It is to rob ourselves of a great part of the subjects which are indicated in the Bible. It is to forego in many cases that harmony between the text and the subject of which we have said so much. For it is often by means of a word, though a characteristic word, that a text may become the exact or approximate expression of the subject we had in view before seeking or meeting with our text. Very often, in order to produce this harmony, the true way is not to abstract this or that feature of the text, but, on the contrary, to take account of it.

§ 2. *Rules for choosing Texts.*

I.

After explaining these points, we propound the rules which should guide us in choosing texts.

The first is as precise as it is absolute. The text ought to be drawn from the word of God. "If any man speak, let him speak according to the oracles of God." (1 Peter, iv. 11.)

We may appear to be saying an idle thing, but we have not said, "The text ought to be taken from the Bible." This would be idle. But this Bible, translated by Osterwald, Martin, or some other, is the word of God only under restriction.

1. After what we have just said, texts from the *apocryphal* books are not to be chosen.

2. May we take for a text a passage which criticism rejects or renders considerably doubtful? There are passages of this character which are very beautiful, very evangelical, but if they have evidently been interpolated, or are strongly suspected, they must be excluded. The passages of this class are few. John viii. 1–11, and 1 John, v. 7—may be taken as examples.

3. May we take for a text a defective translation of the

Bible? No; otherwise we should exalt translators to the rank of prophets, inspired men. Our texts ought to be taken from the original, and if the version in use has changed the sense, we must correct it. We may create some surprise by doing so, if the passage is very well known; but the scandal is given already by the diversity of the translations in use. It is then, we repeat, very important to study the text in the original. If we doubt, we must abstain, and in all cases use prudence; but while we are not to introduce into the pulpit discussions which should have no place there, we shall be obliged to establish the true sense, in the exordium of the discourse, for example, or in approaching the subject. We will cite here some examples of varying or defective versions.

Isaiah, lii. 15, "He shall make the blood of many nations to gush forth," (*Osterwald,*) or, "he shall bedew, he shall sprinkle," (*English version,*) instead of "he shall startle many people."*

Philippians, ii. 6, "He thought it no robbery to be equal with God," (*Osterwald,*) instead of "He did not glory in," or, "was not vain of it."

Romans, ix. 28, "The Lord is about to make a great diminution in the earth," (*Osterwald,*) instead of "a short work," (*Martin,* English version,) or, "a work which he has determined on."†

Romans, xii. 6, (comp. ver. 3) is often translated: "According to the analogy of faith." Osterwald rightly translates: "According to the measure of faith."

Romans, xiv. 5, "Let each one be abundant in his understanding." (*Fénélon.*) This is an erroneous translation.

* "Also wird er viele Voelker in freudiges Erstaunen setzen.—De Wette.

† Συντέμνω, *decerno, definio, résoudre.* Die beschlossene Sache wird der Herr thun auf Erden.—De Wette.

Osterwald says : "Let every one act according to a full persuasion in his own mind." The text is strictly, "Let each one be persuaded in his mind."

Romans, xiv. 23, "Whatever is not done with faith is a sin," (Osterwald,) instead of," Whatever is not of faith is sin."

John, i. 9, Martin translates, "The light which enlighteneth every man that cometh into the world." It refers, according to this, to conscience, the light which enlighteneth every man. It should be translated, "The true light which enlighteneth all men is come into the world."

Psalm xix. 13, *Et ab alienis*, (from the sins of others,) according to the vulgate and M. de Lamennais,* instead of "absolve me from secret faults," Osterwald says: "Cleanse thou me." (Proverbs, xviii. 3.) This passage, which is used as an epigraph to the book of M. de Lamennais, *Sur l'indifference*, is translated in the vulgate by the words, "*Impius quum in profundum venerit contemnit.*" (The ungodly man is a despiser, even when he has fallen to the bottom of the abyss.") Osterwald translates, "When the wicked cometh, contempt also cometh, and reproach with ignominy."†

"It is truly unpardonable," says De Wette, "that many preachers confine themselves implicitly to the version of Luther, so often erroneous, especially in the Old Testament, and that they preach thus upon a supposed biblical thought to be nowhere found in the original text. A reader of my translation expressed to me one day his astonishment at not finding a text there on which he had just heard a very edifying sermon. He had reference to the passage of Isaiah, xxviii. 19: 'Trials‡ teach us to take heed to the word.' The original text here, we know, includes no thought that has the

* *Imitation de Jesus Christ*, book iii., chap. 14. Reflections.

† Kommt der Frevler kommt auch Verachtung, und mit Schande Schmach—DE WETTE.

‡ In German, Die Anfechtung.

least analogy to this."* De Wette himself translates: "It is a terror even to hear the report." Osterwald says: "After the report shall be heard, there will be only trouble." De Wette corrects Luther also, on John, xiv., which he translates: "Let not your heart be troubled: trust in God; trust also in me;" while in Luther, it is: "If you believe in God, you believe also in me."

4. May we take for a text a word of man contained in the Word of God? Yes, when this word is presented for a fact. The fact is often of very great importance, and very worthy to be searched into by preaching, even though this word may have come from the mouth of an adversary of the truth. God has thought it wise to preserve it in the book of his oracles. If "wisdom is justified of all her children," (Luke, vii. 35,) it is also of some of her adversaries. See some passages of the class which we have in view:

Mark, ii. 7, "Who can forgive sin but God only?"

Mark, ix. 24, "Lord I believe, help thou my unbelief."

Luke, ix. 1, "Lord teach us to pray."

John, vii. 46, "The officers answered, never man spoke like this man."

Luke, vii. 19, "Art thou he that should come, or look we for another?

Luke, xxiii. 47, "The Centurion seeing that which came to pass, glorified God, saying, Truly this was a righteous man."

Luke, xxiv. 32, "Did not our heart burn within us, when he talked to us by the way, and explained to us the Scriptures."

John, vi. 68, "Lord to whom shall we go? Thou hast the words of eternal life."

Acts, v. 38–39, "And now I say unto you, Refrain from these men, and let them alone; for if this purpose or this

* De Wette. Preface to his translation of the Bible.

work be of men, it will destroy itself; but if it be of God, beware lest you be found fighting even against God."

Romans, xv. 4, "These things are written for our learning."

Genesis, xlvii. 9, "The days of the years of my pilgrimage are a hundred and thirty years, few and evil have been the days of the years of my life." This is the complaint of Jacob and of humanity, which we must remember. Our sighs are often prophesies.

II.

We have not yet left the threshold of the question; we must penetrate further. All the rules which we have just given are not a sufficient guaranty; we must add that our text is drawn from the word of God, only when we give it the sense which it has in the intention of the sacred author. We are not concerned with the work of the translator, although we have supposed that every preacher is also a translator: we consider only the preacher. To arrive at a perfect knowledge of the meaning of the passage, we must examine first the text itself then the context.

1. *The text itself.* We have to settle in each passage, the verbal or external sense, and the internal sense. The first is that which is commonly called *the signification*, the idea which signs convey immediately to the mind independently of every ulterior consideration, every consideration foreign to the philological elements of which the passage is composed. The second is the idea, which, by means of the external sense, the author of the passage would communicate to the mind of the reader; so that the first idea regards the second only as the words regarded the first. The key to the first meaning is the knowledge of words, the key to the second is the knowledge of things.

In order to make no mistake as to the sense we call external, we must have a precise idea of the language of the authors; I mean of the import of the signs and forms of this language, when compared with correspondent signs and forms in our own language. In other words, we must know how to appreciate the principal terms which occur most frequently, and which enter into the most important passages.

In the language of the Bible there is a certain number of words which we may call capital, the meaning of which exactly seized, becomes the key of the Bible. If we confine ourselves purely and simply to the usual signification of the terms which the translator uses in rendering such words into our language, we are in great danger of committing serious errors. Thus, as to the words *fear*, *flesh*, *soul*, *heart*, *faith*, *righteousness*, *understanding*, *foolish*, *light*, *just*, *good man*, *wicked*, *virtue*. (2 Peter, 1, 5.) The translator has translated for you the words; you must translate the ideas for yourselves.* The preacher, or more generally the exegete, will

* It is not the part of the translator to explain or comment. He should render the expressions of the original, and retain its harshness, its obscurity, its paradoxical character, without concerning himself with the consequences; he should not be afraid of metaphors which seem strange because they are strange. (" Vinum dat *cornua* pauperi." See the word *horn*, in 1 Samuel, ii. 10, and Psalm cxxii. 9.) There is even here, however, a limit. These metaphors, for example, in the language of the text are lifeless; they are revived in the translation, and thus even exaggerate the thought of the original. This depreciation of the signs of language has place in all idioms, and shows us why we receive in certain respects a more vivid impression from works written in another language, than from those of our own. We are even led into error under the force of the expression. It is some time before the Frenchman who reads English books, can reduce to its just import the adjective *anxious*, which signifies neither *angoissé* nor *anxieux* but simply *desireux* or *curieux*. Then, there are modes of speaking, the exact reproduction of which would produce, without any advantage, a strange effect. What if we should translate literally such a phrase as this: *οὐ παραγγελία παρηγγείλαμεν*. (Acts, v. 28.) We

have to consider here two things, which perhaps are only one, the character, the customs of the language, and the philosophy of the people. Let us speak first of the former point.

The same words, the same forms have one meaning in a language in which the spirit of synthesis predominates, another in a language distinguished by an analytic spirit. Synthetic language is that of pure poetry; analytic that of pure prose. Neither one nor the other exists. Analysis prevails in our language, synthesis in that of the sacred authors.

It appears to be the character of a synthetic language to establish a communication between all communicable ideas, so that the entire language becomes an unbroken line. Analysis classifies and distinguishes with more and more precision; each sign occupies a circumscribed sphere, from which it is not permitted to depart. Words which before the reign of analysis were very elastic, have afterwards to retreat into their shell.* Bossuet hence remarked of the style of Calvin, that it is *triste*, that is to say, *nude*, *austere*. Languages in this way are becoming more and more subject to order; nothing is arbitrary; and if we cannot but observe that our own language in this respect differs from itself as it was two centuries ago, how much more striking must be the difference between the French and the Hebrew!

When we have to do with a book written in poetic language in which synthesis predominates, we ought to have regard to the usages of this language.

should do wrong, nevertheless, not to translate מוֹת תָּמוּת (Moth-tthamoth.) Genesis ii. 17: "Thou shalt die of death." (*Tu mourras de mort.*) Would it be a safe rule always to translate the same word by the same word? It is neither safe nor natural to do so. We must not flatter ourselves that we shall be as much more faithful as we are more literal. Often we shall be less; this is easily understood. We are far from having an exact translation, and if in order to hear the word of God, we must have the *letter* of that word, then we do not possess the word of God.

* *Rentrer dans leur coquille.*

A poetic language, a language I mean spoken by a poetic people, delights alternately to diminish and augment, that the imagination of the reader may be exercising in adding or retrenching.* The Bible is filled with these modes of speaking, and they have been often abused.

It delights by turns to make absolute that which is relative, and relative that which is absolute.†

It generalizes that which is particular, and particularizes that which is general; takes duty sometimes at its summit, sometimes at its base.‡

It does not distinguish nicely the notions which are closely related to each other. *Wicked* and *foolish; to say* and *to do; to know*, and *to prove; to regret* and *to repent; to repent* and *to change a purpose; to forget* and *to betray*, *to judge* and *to condemn*. It takes sentiment for action; and reciprocally. It delights in the consonance of ideas, in synonyms, in symmetry, in parellisms, in advancing in couples or in pairs of ideas.§

* Examples: "Sin by the commandment slew me." (Romans, vii. 11.)

"Whosoever is born of God doth not commit sin." (1 John, iii. 9.)

"That which is highly esteemed among men is abomination in the sight of God." (Luke, xvi. 15.)

"If any man will come after me and hate not his father and his mother, he cannot be my disciple." (Luke, xiv. 26.)

"Against these things there is no law." (Galatians, v. 23.)

"The unfruitful works of darkness." (Ephesians, v. 11.)

"(Onesimus) who was formerly unprofitable to thee." (Philemon, 11.)

† "Invite not thy friends." (Luke, xiv. 12.)

"He went down to his house justified rather than the other" (Luke, xviii. 14.)

‡ "Thou shalt not bear false witness against thy neighbor." (Exodus, xx. 16.)

§ "The turning away of the simple shall slay them, and the prosperity of fools shall destroy them." (Proverbs, i. 32.)

It classifies without scientific purpose. "Create in me a clean heart, and renew a right spirit within me." (Psalm li. 12.) The Old and the New Testament abound in similar examples. We frequently find in the prophets and apostles series of substantives or adjectives, which have been taken very improperly as the base of divisions in discourses.

It likes to play upon words, a character, however, which in some measure obtains in all languages.*

Such is the language of the Bible; and further, each of the epochs which are represented in it, each of the authors who contributed to it, has a peculiar style. We must even go farther, and not only compare the words of the author with another, but those of the same author with themselves. The word *faith* has not always the same signification in the same author. Sometimes it has an abstract sense (Hebrews,

"Thy word is a lamp unto my feet, and a light unto my path." (Psalm, cxix. 105.)

"The Lord is my light and my salvation; whom shall I fear? The Lord is the strength of my life; of whom shall I be afaid?" (Psalm xxvii. 1.)

"Rejoice not when thine enemy falleth, and let not thine heart be glad when he stumbleth." (Proverbs, xxiv. 17.)

"He satisfieth the longing soul, and filleth the hungry soul with goodness." (Psalm cvii. 9.) See also Isaiah, lix. 1–6.

Our modern languages are not strangers to this *usus. Perils and risks; death and martyrdom; fear and trembling; usages and customs; by way and by road; ways and means.* On this character of Biblical language, see Herder, *Hebr. Poesie*, tome i., p. 23, and Petavel, *La fille de Sion*, p. 76.

* The German has: *Schutz und Trutz, leben und weben; schalten und walten; eile mit Weile.* The French: *Ni feu ni lieu; sans foi ni loi; peu et paix.* Kempis says: *via crucis via lucis.* These paronomasia, or chimes, are common in Scripture: תֹהוּ וָבֹהוּ (Genesis, i. 2.) כְּרֵתִי וּפְלֵתִי (2 Samuel, vii. 18.) In Greek: Romans, i. 29; Hebrews, v. 8,—comp. Herder, *Hebraische Poesie*, tome ii., p. 280–287; Gesenius, *Hebraisches Lehrgeboeude*, § 237; and Winer, *Grammatik des Neutestamentlichen Sprachidioms*, § 62.

xi. 1), sometimes a concrete sense; here it has an intellectual, elsewhere a moral sense.* I say nothing of cases in which the word faith has neither of these significations, but means mere *persuasion.*

Not to err as to the external sense of the text which he uses, the preacher must consider, as we have said, together with the custom and character of the language which supplies them, the philosophy of the people who speak it, their habits of thought, the classifications of their different notions. He will be greatly aided in this by the etymology of words. A language is formed out of a multitude of things; the inward thoughts of a people, their beliefs, their religion, their history, their social and political life, the external circumstances in which they are placed, are reflected in it, as in a mirror. The whole external and internal life of a people, is in their language. However profoundly their habits of thought may be modified, their language at once is sensibly affected by them.

Christianity has, in one sense, corrupted the Latin; it has removed it from its sphere; it has obliged it to give expression to a life, from which it was originally foreign. In proportion as men were converted, they converted the language. A Roman, certainly, could not find his langnage in the Latin of the Church, and he could not even understand it except by becoming a Christian. A religion may create a philosophy of language. Our modern languages are christian.

Only by having performed this labor, and fixed the prin-

* Comp. 1 Corinthians, xiii. 2, "faith to remove mountains," and James, ii. 20, "faith without works is dead;" Philippians, ii. 17, "the offering of your faith," and Colossians, ii. 8, "the confirmation of your faith;" James, i. 7, "the trial of your faith," and 1 Thessalonians, iii. 10, "that which is lacking in your faith;" Hebrews, xiii. 7, "whose faith follow," and James, i. 6, "let him ask in faith."

ciples of rendering Biblical language, may we assure ourselves that we have taken a text in its true sense.

The true object, in this matter, is not so much to obtain mere precision, as to guard ourselves against having too much of it. Let it be observed, that it is this precision or literalism which has given place to the dogma of the real presence : " Except you eat the flesh of the Son of man, and drink his blood." (John, vi. 33.) This ill placed rigor of interpretation has given rise to a multitude of heresies, which spring only from literalism. Let us beware lest, while we cry out aginst this rigor, we fall into it.

A language less vague, expressions less fluctuating, will give place, it is said, to fewer doubts and disputes. But where shall we find this perfectly precise language ? for nothing less is needed, when once we lay down this rule. One word is distinct from another which follows it, but how shall we separate them ? Such a language has no existence ; if it did exist, it would not be a human language. It would only express abstractions. It would be the most perfect of philosophies, the philosophy definitive, but it would not be a word.

We well know the extravagancies of which the language of the Bible has been the pretext ; know we that also of which a language wholly different would have been the occasion ?

It is not to be doubted that the language of the Bible, without that ideal precision of which we have spoken, might have been more precise. It might have been so precise as to give, I do not say the understanding, but the heart and conscience, nothing to do ; but this precisely is what God has not desired.

" It has been a cause of scandal that the Bible has not been so written as to render divisions impossible. Doubtless he who made the Bible could have given a symbol, and the most perfect of all symbols in place of it. But why has he not done this? That man might not be obliged to enter into relations with him, immediately and with his whole being? That the most rigorous precision and concentration of religious ideas, might excuse him from making any use of his conscience in this study? That there might be nothing to put his rectitude and his candor to the proof? That he might receive, already prepared, the true sense of the Bible, and that he might not occupy himself in ascertaining it? In a word, that he might remain passive, where it is most important that his activity, his liberty should be displayed, and his responsibility exercised? God be praised that it is not so, and that every man is at the same time able and obliged to find, through all those phases, all those facts, all those personalities, of which the Bible is composed, that general and eternal truth, which is presented to him in the Bible only in a character in some sort occasional, under the form of an application, and always mixed up with some event or some life. God be praised that his book has not the clearness of a symbol, that we are not forced to understand it aright; that many senses may be given to his word! God be praised for having left a part to our own activity, in the acquisition of faith, and that intending that our belief should be an action, he has not added to the Bible, which is sufficient for sincere hearts, the dangerous appendix of a symbol!" *

This is what we had to say on the determination of the verbal sense. He who shall have used all these precautions, doubtless will not be disposed, after closing one source of errors, to open another; that is to say, to fix arbitrarily the *internal* sense of the text—I mean the intention of the author. Nevertheless it is necessary to speak of this also.

* M. Vinet here quotes himself. See *Revue Suisse*, in the year 1839, p. 26, *et seq.*—(EDITORS.)

If we take the Bible as a whole, we shall find in it only one intention, only one purpose, only one sense, which is spiritual —the triumph of the spirit over the flesh, the adoration of God in spirit and in truth.

But as soon as we descend from this height, from this panoramic view, at the first step we take in the details, we meet with two orders of ideas and two orders of texts which correspond to them.

And first, *as to things purely temporal and material, and of texts relating to temporal order.*

Their sense is neither uncertain nor two-fold. If nothing clearly indicates or expressly reveals an allegorical intention, (symbolical, typical, prefigurative,) we must rest in the strict sense.

We do not condemn, on the contrary we approve, the intention of pious men, who have given a more elevated sense to passages concerning temporal order ; arising from a necessity which they felt of spiritualizing everything. Thus, Quesnel, in expounding these words : "The wise men returned to their own country by another way," (Matthew, ii. 12,) observes, that "we never return to heaven except by a different way from that which enstranged us from it." Spiritual men certainly can do nothing better than to make everything a means of awakening spiritual ideas in themselves, but the question here relates to interpretation and teaching, and we can see nothing serious in arbitrary and loose interpretation. It would seem that the Bible has been trifled with in proportion to its sacredness, and that as God has surrendered the world to the vain disputes of men, he has surrendered his Word to the frivolity of their imagination. No human book has in this way been so tortured and sported with, as the holy Scripture. The preacher cannot excuse himself under the pretense that he is not an interpreter, and that he only seeks in the sacred word a starting-point for his teaching ; the excuse avails nothing ; for were he only to announce a text, only to say that he is going to preach on a text, that is always saying that the text is to be explained, or that the truth which it contains is to be proved; in a word, that it is to be taken in a serious sense. Catholic preachers have done much, by the choice or interpretation of their texts, to diminish the respect which is due to the divine Word. When one sees Massillon interpreting with so much lightness a very plain text,* he cannot be astonished at what less serious writers have done in the same way ; that a writer, treating of the abolition of the death-penalty, should take for his epigraph these words of Saint Paul : "Thou art therefore inexcusable, oh man, whosoever thou art that condemnest others." (Romans, ii. 1.)

We must distinguish well between extension (catachresis) and metaphor. There is only a simple extension of the sense when one takes these words: "in quietness shall be your strength," (Isaiah, xxx. 16,) as the text of a sermon, on the duty of waiting in peace, and without useless disquiet for the salvation of the Lord. But would it be equally proper in preaching on the necessity of coming to Jesus Christ in times of trouble and darkness, to take as a text the words: "Abide with us, for it is toward evening, and the day is far spent"? (Luke, xxiv. 29.) I think not; there is here more than extension, there is metaphor and even a play of words.

One abuse gives the signal for another. Those who would see realities in all images, develop the opposite error, which sees nothing but images in realities. Idealism begets realism. In the hands of the last, everything takes body ; everything loses body in the hands of the other. One of them sees types everywhere; the other everywhere finds myths.

* In *l'Homilie sur Lazare,* John, xi. 30, and in *le Sermon sur la Confession,* John, v. 3.

When we abandon the rules of common sense, everything is put in doubt, and no sense has a refuge.

Reason has principles which are common to man, imagination has none; for one has the principle of identity as its basis, the other that of analogy or resemblance.

I speak here of fixing the sense or meaning of a passage; for, otherwise, I know that the germ of allegory is everywhere, and that there is no object which may not be used as an image of some other. The Bible may be as properly so used as the creation, but neither more nor less. It is because the temporal things which are in the Bible, make part of the visible world, that I say of the Bible what M. de Sacy says of the world: "That it was created not only to manifest the power of God, but to depict invisible things by visible." But these things in this view, are the world and not the Bible.

Temporal texts then, at least as to their precise bearing, are to remain in the temporal sense. Allegory puts all at hazard, and those who use it to the advantage of one tendency, form, without knowing it, the contrary tendency.

We now pass to things of the spiritual order, and to the texts which relate to them. There are two sorts of these: one purely spiritual, of which the reality is altogether in the invisible world; the other mixed, which is spiritual also, but which, combined with facts of the temporal order, take place in time and in space.

The second are not spiritual in the way of allegory; they are so essentially or in themselves; they include, they express the same truths with the first, but after all, they are spiritual only in one aspect, with which we must be content. Everything which matter and time connect accidentally with a spiritual fact, remains material and temporal. We must not wish to spiritualize this element. That would be wishing to enchase a diamond in a diamond, without advantage; for it is not with the diamond of truth as it is with other diamonds;

its value depends not upon its size, but upon its purity and its brilliancy. Without reason, then, has it been said that Jacob's crossing his arms over two of his children, signifies that there is no blessing but under the cross; it would follow that the other children of Jacob were not blessed. It has been said, also improperly, that where there is only one victim, it is to remind us that the only victim is Christ, and that where there are two, it is to indicate that Christ behooved to experience sufferings twice—in Gethsemane by night, and on Golgotha by day.*

The government, the education of the Jewish people, are spiritual things. Their history, as a whole, is the most perfect image of the individual and of the Christian, under the direction of God. What we say of the whole, we may also say of the grand incidents. The favorable entrance of Israel into Canaan, is not only the image but the pattern of the obedience and resolution of the Christian who, like the Jew, is called to fight and to suffer. Faith is the soul of both. (See Hebrews, xi.) The manna of the seventh day is an exercise of faith and of confidence. But if we would see in the manna the distribution of the spirit of God to believers, in each of the enemies encountered by the Jews the figure of each obstacle which the soul meets in the way of life, we introduce a sort of amusement into the most serious matters. By seeking to make all certain, we make all uncertain. We must not object to the figures and types indicated in the Bible. They indicate to me, among other things, that all is not type and figure; if all were so, nothing would be.

As to texts which are purely spiritual, which express some idea or some fact of the moral world, we comprehend those in this number which are complicated with a temporal circumstance too insignificant to be taken into consideration.

In these texts we must distinguish different orders or

* G. Monod, *Explication de l'Ecriture*, page 118.

different degrees of spirituality. The text is more or less spiritual, according as the idea is more or less distinct, the object more or less elevated, the sentiment more or less profound.

The faith of the blind men (Matthew, xx. 29–34) who cried : " O Lord, thou son of David, have mercy on us," etc., though real, is it a model of christian faith in its ideal ? There is spirituality here, but an inferior spirituality. All that the christian exercises with respect to Christ, is not to be found here. In the hosannah of the multitude, (Luke, xix. 37–38) there is, if you will, the entire christian system. This multitude had a confused impression that Christ was a blessed being, and that in his coming there was peace for men and glory to God. But that this impression was distinct, clear and complete, is more than doubtful. It would be a mistake to understand these words as we might do, if they had been pronounced by a Paul, a Peter, a John, after the descent of the Holy Spirit. *

This difference as to degree may be found between passages of the same book ; it is found necessarily between the Old and New Testament ; for though the work which these two books, as a whole, exhibit to us, is a unique work, it is also a progressive work. It is unique, since God has never designed more than one thing, the re-establishment of his image in us, the formation of a people which should be his ; unique, since the same principles penetrate all parts of the Bible ; as faith, sanctity and love, in respect of God ; as the law of his life, obedience and faith, in respect of man.

In the first view, we see from the fall everthing prepared, everything concerted with a view to restoration.

In the second, we see forcibly and perpetually inculcated, the principles on which the whole evangelical doctrine is built. Christianity is more ancient than Judaism ; faith, in its princi-

* See as examples of the same kind in the Old Testament, Jeremiah, xiii. 16 and xx. 7.

ple, more ancient than the law. Paul remanded the Hebrews quite through the law, to the faith of Abraham. The law did only then "supervene," (Romans, v. 20,) to *supervene* is not to *interrupt;* but no more is it to *commence.*

But this unity, as I have said, has the form of progress. We advance, at least, to more, whether it be in work or in principle. This progression is that of a germ, which does not increase by superposition from without, but which produces from within a successive development purely of itself.

There are in the Old Testament, principles laid down, an expectation excited, a necessity created; principles which the gospel embodies, an expectation which it realizes, a necessity which it has met. This is saying beforehand, that from the Old Testament to the New, we at least go from less to more. If we do not, in fact, at least go from less to more, we do not comprehend the necessity of delay, nor the reason of the two economies. Of what use is the second, if all is found in the first?

It may be said that all the elements of the New Testament are to be found in the Old, though under cover, wanting in precision, in perfection, and farther, not as powerfully consecrated by facts, as in the New Testament.

But, after all,* they are consecrated by facts, they present themselves at the outset, under this form.

* The passage which commences here, and which terminates at page 125, in these words, "the color and the relief are wanting," is marked in the principal manuscript of the *Homiletical Course*, with a sign which is not explained, but which appears to indicate that M. Vinet intended to review it. He has also thus condensed it in a more recent but much abridged manuscript: "Whatever is elementary in the truth, is expressed in the same manner, and with the same force in both of the books; but beyond this the difference begins and it is considerable. We must not give to Old Testament texts a degree of spirituality which they have not, and which they cannot have."—[EDITORS.]

God consecrates by a fact the idea of his unity, in locating his presence, although his agency is represented as universal, and his nature as spiritual.

He consecrates his providence by the fact of the adoption protection and government of a particular people.

He consecrates his sovereignty by making everything converge in himself, even to the least detail, in the direction of outward things. (Theocrasy, jealous God.)

He consecrates his justice by penalties and rewards.

He consecrates the principle of spiritual obedience, or of "worship in spirit and in truth," (John, iv.) by rejecting a purely outward service, though it were perfectly exact. (Cain.)

He consecrates the principle of justifying faith, by connecting his blessing with it, and making the head and personification of his elect people, a hero of faith. "All the nations of the earth shall be blessed in him."*

He consecrates by the perpetual sacrifice, the defection of man and the necessity of restoration. He announces a Restorer.

Finally, in the bosom of the legal people he created a spiritual people, subject to the perfect law which is the law of liberty.

All these ideas are realized in the Old Testament, but it was necessary that they should be personified. Second degree, *person* after *facts*.

When the gospel says: "The law was given by Moses, *but* grace and truth came by Jesus Christ," (John, i. 17,) it does not establish an opposition between the truth and the law, but it means to say, that the truth was not entirely

† Genesis, xviii. 18. The most spiritual things are the most ancient; they precede the law, and we cannot too well remember that the law only *supervened*, (Romans, v. 20,) "that sin might abound." The end and the beginning are united, over the Mosaic Economy, that grand episode.

known, distinctly seen, except by means of the grace which embraced it all. (Baptism of water, baptism of fire; voice from the earth, voice from heaven; the water and the spirit.)

Now this grace was not revealed to the people of the Old Testament as distinctly as it was by Jesus Christ to that of the New. The law contained only the *shadow* of good things to come; (Hebrews, x. 1, viii. 5,) the law is the shadow which grace throws behind itself; every shadow supposes, announces, gives the anticipation of a body; it gives the contour of it, the general form, the outline, but the color and the relief are wanting. We may say of it, as was said of prophecy, "that it is a light which shineth in a dark place," (2 Peter, i. 19,) compared to the sun of righteousness, who conveys healing in his wings. (Malachi, iv. 2.)

Moreover, the spiritual members of this people penetrated with all the principles which we have indicated, were virtually Christians; I mean to say that each of them was such that if Christ had unexpectedly come and manifested himself, he would not have had to change his principles in order to be an actual Christian. He was a Christian because he would have been one; he was a Christian generally, not specially; implicitly, not explicitly; virtually not actually; he was elementally a Christian.

Whenever he expressed these elementary convictions, which, apart from the immediate knowledge of Jesus Christ, would have had to him all their clearness and meaning, this Christian of the Old Testament said a thing identical to that, which the same terms express in the mouth of an "Israelite" of the New Testament;* and we may without restriction or modification, appropriate his words to ourselves, although he did not attach to them all the ideas, or one idea as precise, as distinct, as concrete, as a Christian would attach to them, under the new dispensation. A remarkable thing: even a

* "The Israel of God." Galatians, vi. 16.

spiritual Israelite is not identical with a spiritual Christian; still the spiritual people of the Old Testament is a perfect image of the Christian. Nothing is more spiritual than that which was spoken to this people or of this people in the Old Testament. (Isaiah, lxiii. 14, lxvi. 12; Jeremiah, xxxi.) But there are passages which seem to be intended to show the advantage of the New Testament over the Old; passages in which the idea is not only less precise, but less perfect; passages in which the comparative defect of the Old Testament appears; ideas which require to be completed, purified, by the spirit of the New Testament.

Considering spirituality only, or the obligation of the preacher to keep himself on a level with the spirituality of the gospel, a Christian preacher confining himself to elementary subjects, might preach very long on texts taken from the Old Testament; or at least he might, without altering the sense, and without remaining below the spirit of Christianity, preach very often on texts taken from this portion of Scripture. We will endeavor to give the proof of this.

Condition of Man. Psalm xxxix. 7–13, "Surely every man walketh in a vain show. I am a stranger with thee and a sojourner as all my fathers were."

Moral Condition. Jeremiah, xvii. 9, "The heart is deceitful above all things and desperately wicked."

Moral wants of man. Psalm lxiii. 2, "My soul thirsteth for thee; my flesh longeth for thee in this desert land." Psalm li. 12. "Create in me a clean heart and renew a right spirit within me."

Character of God. Isaiah, lxiii., 9, 10, 11, lxvi. 15, "Behold the Lord will come with fire, and with his chariots like a whirlwind, to render his anger with fury, and his rebukes with flames of fire." Micah, vii. 18, "Who is a God like unto thee that pardoneth iniquity, and passeth by the transgression of the remnant of his heritage? He retaineth not his anger forever, because he delighteth in mercy." Job, xv. 15, "The heavens are not clean in thy sight." Habakkuk, i. 13, "Thou art of purer eyes than to behold evil." Psalm ciii. 12, "As far as the east is from the west so far hath he removed our transgressions from us;" (and the whole Psalm.) Lamentations, iii. 33, "He doth not afflict willingly nor grieve the children of men." Numbers, xiv. 18, "Forgiving iniquity and transgression, and by no means clearing the guilty." Exodus, xx, 5, 6, "I the Lord thy God am a jealous God, visiting the iniquity of the fathers upon the children unto the third and fourth generation of them that hate me; and shewing mercy unto thousands of them that love me and keep my commandments." Jeremiah, iii. 14, "Turn O backsliding children saith the Lord," (He who first loved us.) Ezekiel, xxxiii. 11, "I have no pleasure in the death of the wicked; but that the wicked turn from his way and live." Isaiah, xlviii. 9, "For my name's sake will I defer mine anger," (God is love.) Ezekiel, xx. 22, "I withdrew mine hand for my name's sake." Psalm cviii. 4, "Thy mercy is great above the heavens; and thy truth reacheth into the clouds."

Law of God. Genesis, xvii. 1, "Walk before my face." Deuteronomy, xxvii. 26, "Cursed be he that confirmeth not all the words of this law to do them." Comp. 1 Samuel, ii. 30, "Them that honor me I will honor, and they that despise me shall be lightly esteemed." 1 Samuel, ii. 25, "If one man sin against another the judge shall judge him; but if a man sin against the Lord, who shall entreat for him?"

Conditions of the Covenant.—I. Psalm cxv. 1, "Not unto us, not unto us, O Lord, but unto thy name give glory for thy mercy and thy truth's sake." Psalm xliv. 26, "Redeem us for thy mercies' sake." Jeremiah, xiv. 17, "O Lord, though our iniquities testify against us, do thou it for thy name's sake.

II. Deuteronomy, x. 16, "Circumcise the foreskin of your heart." Deuteronomy, xxx. 6, "The Lord thy God will circumcise thy heart." 1 Samuel, xv. 22, 23, "Hath the Lord as great delight in burnt offerings and sacrifices as in obeying the voice of the Lord? Behold to obey is better than sacrifice, and to hearken than the fat of rams. For rebellion is as the sin of witchcraft, and stubbornness is as iniquity and idolatry."

These are evangelical elements. These are texts which may be prefixed to a sermon without putting any force upon them, without stretching them on the bed of Procrustes. But happy as we may be to discover this unity or ideality, we must not seek it where it is not, and forget the difference which subsists between the two economies, a difference which should edify rather than offend us.

We must not give to texts more of a Christian character than belongs to them; we must not subject men of the Old Covenant to the exact conditions of the Gospel. We present some traits which belong to a preparatory economy.

Sentiment of self righteousness. 2 Samuel, xxii. 21–23, (it is David who speaks,) "The Lord rewarded me according to my righteousness; according to the cleanness of my hands hath he recompensed me. For I have kept the ways of the Lord, and have not wickedly departed from my God. For all his judgments were before me; and as for his statutes I did not depart from them." Whence is it that there is not a passage like this in the New Testament? For what Paul says, (1 Corinthians, iv. 4,) "I am conscious of no blame," is another thing.

Traces of severity. Psalm cxxxix. 21–22, "Do not I hate them O Lord, that hate thee? I hate them with perfect hatred." Nehemiah, iv. 5, "Cover not their iniquity, and let not their sin be blotted out from before thee." Jeremiah, xviii. 23, "Forgive not their iniquity, neither blot out their sin from thy sight." Deuteronomy, xxiii. 6, "Thou shalt not seek their peace nor their prosperity all thy days forever." (Referring to the Ammonite and the Moabite.)

We must remark certain terms, the recurrence of which is frequent, and which are of most important meaning, (*Saviour*, *Redeemer*, *the redeemed*, *just*, *soul*, *wisdom*, *word*,) and recognize what of accordance there is in each of these words with Christian ideas, but not constrain what remains, (*compelle intrare*,) to enter into the Christian system.

We read in Proverbs, viii. 34–35, "Blessed is the man that heareth me, watching daily at my gates, waiting at the posts of my doors. For whoso findeth me, findeth life, and shall obtain favor of the Lord." It is wisdom that speaks. It is a virtual Christian who makes him speak; under a more vague notion, it is what an actual Christian loves, what he adores in Jesus Christ, and under the name of Jesus Christ: the two adore the same object; and the difference between them is, that one knows perfectly, as the other does not, what he adores. (John, iv. 22.) In treating this text, I would not say that the author saw what Saint John expressed under the term *Word* or *Reason*. But this wisdom of the virtual Christian includes elements which the actual Christian does not reject. We have distinguished and enumerated these elements, we have only to translate this passage into the language of the gospel, after having carefully remarked its primitive sense, which differs from ours, not essentially, but only as having less precision.

But, it will be said, why not draw directly and exclusively from the gospel? In order, we answer, to manifest the unity of God's work and thought, the unity of the two economies, the perpetuity of Christianity in two senses, (as remounting into the past, as descending into the future,) the fraternity of the living members of the church in distant times. It is alike interesting to exhibit the agreements and differences between the Old and the New Testament. There are many in our day who know not what to make of the Old Testament, who see in it our origin and nothing else; a chasm in our religious life. We shall be reconciled to the Old Testament only when we shall find the New in it. Preachers must make it necessary, must make it savory, and show that the prophets were "a light which shone in a dark place." (2 Peter, i. 19.)

When the Christian preacher has a Jewish text, let him not abide in it, but let him show that he does not, and at the same time that there is a connection between the Old Testament and the New. Out of many passages relating to the righteous and the wicked, let us take one example: "He who walketh uprightly, walketh surely." (Proverbs, x. 9.) We may say that the converse is true according to the sense of the gospel. But still why reverse the terms? He who has a good conscience, that is to say a conscience which follows evangelical principles, walks surely, even when he sees not whither he is going. We must then treat this passage in the sense in which we find it, not in that which we give to it.

While observing all these cautions we may still come short of the rule by making a false application of the text; for example, by taking as the text of a sermon on the infallible connection of sin and punishment, the passage of Matthew, vii. 16, "Do men gather grapes of thorns or figs of thistles?"

As to the extension or catachresis of the text, that is another thing. In certain circumstances nothing is more legitimate or more necessary.

All that we have now said comes to this: that we must not, in the matter of spirituality, rise above the text. This is consistent with saying, that neither must we remain below it. But though we would not have either ascending or descending extension, we are not opposed to a lateral or horizontal extension.

We have spoken of the internal sense of texts. This internal sense comprehends not only the idea which springs immediately from the words of the text, but an idea which may be implicated with it—such or such a consequence or application, which, though not present to the writer's mind, and from the time and circumstances in which he lived could not perhaps have been present to it, springs spontaneously from the principle which he expresses. It is objected, that we may thus descend or rise beyond the writer's views, since we do not conflict with it. We answer, that there is as to this a simple rule—to inquire if the author would recognize and own his thought, in the development which we give to it. It is characteristic of the method of Jesus Christ, to lead us to argue from the species to the genus, in order to exercise us in moral reasoning, the logic of conscience, spontaneity. Thus, Matthew, xix. 16–23.

The true utility of taking texts is not so much that they present, directly, the truth we wish to develop or prove, as that they offer it in an aspect more salient, more pointed, more accidental, than that of abstract presentation.

Thus it is advantageous to descend, in the choice of the text, from the idea of the genus to that of the species, and even of the individual. We may here apply the word of Fontenelle, (which is not absolutely true,) that we must not introduce "the truth by the large end." It is a psychological remark, which may be easily verified, that a great grief, a great joy, affects us less by the broadest aspect, than by some accessory circumstance, some unsuspected detail. In morality, the oblique rays are the warmest.

Let us cite some examples in support of this remark. Genesis, xxix. 20, "Jacob served seven years for Rachel, which seemed to him only as a few days, because he loved her." We have here the expression of the general idea, that when one loves, sacrifices appear light, and time short. Yet this general idea makes less impression than the particular idea of the text. Acts, xiii. 46, "Then Paul and Barnabas waxed bold, and said: It was necessary that the word of God should first have been spoken to you, but since ye put it from you and judge yourselves unworthy of everlasting life, lo, we turn to the Gentiles." If we would present the idea, which, by the way, cannot be everywhere treated, that besides the Gospel, there is an apocryphal Gospel, a false Messiah, we might take for our text the passage, 'Art thou he that should come?" (Luke, vii. 20.) Or again, that, in the book of Acts where the evil spirit says to the sons of Sceva, "Jesus I know, and Paul I know, but who are ye?" Acts, xix. 15. All makers of new gospels, all self-styled reformers of human nature are overthrown by these singular words. In short, to treat a text is not only to draw from it a truth substantially or formally contained in the expressions of which the text is composed; it is likewise to deduce from it such truth as this text supposes, of which it offers the starting-point, or which it presents in an example or inference, or some other such natural appendage.*

It is only by proceeding in this large method, that we can treat all the subjects which deserve our attention; for, if we follow a narrower way, we shall find ourselves reduced to the alternative either of sacrificing many subjects, or, if we will treat them, to do a cruel violence to texts. We may excuse Tillotson, for finding, in 1 Corinthians, xi. 26–28, the subject of frequent communion, but how can we excuse the preacher who founded a sermon on the reciprocal duties

* Nevertheless, the doctrine of Maury is loose, when it admits that we may be content with an analogy between the text and the subject. *Essay sur l'Eloquence de la Chaire*, vii.

of proprietors and tenants, on Acts, xxviii. 30, "Paul dwelt two whole years in his own hired house."*

2. *The Context.* We may obtain the true sense of a text by having regard to the nexus or context, that is to say, to what precedes or follows the text when it makes part of a connected discourse, in the *place* of the passage.

There is a context of action as well as of words. Life is a book, of which each day is a page and each hour a line. We cannot judge of each of these pages or lines taken by themselves. This rule of morality which we are bound to observe in judging of the conduct of other men, becomes now a rule of interpretation.

There is a general context—the *place* of every text—which is the Bible taken as a whole. We must not fail to compare our text with the general doctrine of Holy Scripture, from which we are permitted to subtract nothing. It is of great importance that we guard ourselves against the suggestions of party spirit, which, in such a matter, may easily warp a judgment otherwise very sound. When Jesus says, for example, "My kingdom is not of this world," (John, xviii. 36,) has he not admonished us that it would be forgetting the spirit of his teachings, to see in Matthew, xx. 25, 26, a proof that democracy is preferable to other forms of government?

There is a particular context, which, in respect to each *passage*, (this word itself conveys instruction,) is the place in which it is found—the words which precede and follow it.

By disregarding the context, we may give to the text a sense contrary to the intention of the author, or to the general sense of revelation. The finest sense is to be rejected

* These impertinences, a long time ago, gave occasion for the remark of Cardinal Hypolitus of Este, cited by Balzac: *Buon per la predica! Riservate questo per la predica!*

when the context is against it. To what extremes would this procedure lead us, applied to such passages as Jeremiah ix. 4: "Take ye heed every one of his neighbor, and trust ye not in any brother;" and Psalms vi. 11, "All men are liars," and others which might be mentioned?

There are texts, which, as isolated, announce interesting truths, which yet we must not draw from them, because the context does not authorize it. Thus:

1 John, iii. 20, "God is greater than our heart."

John, viii. 32, "The truth shall make you free."

2 Corinthians, iii. 17, "Where the spirit of the Lord is, there is liberty."

The study of the nexus has not only a negative importance. We are not simply to avoid a false sense, but to seize the whole truth. The circumstances which surround a text, (an assertion without proof,) surround it with a light, or tinge it with a reflection which must not be neglected. For even if they add no shade, they always individualize the truth.

What, moreover, is an idea without some nexus, and with no appearance of individuality? What man does not mix something of himself with his idea?

We do not, by this, mean to say that an announcement, general in its form, is to be compressed within the circle of the particular circumstances of him who gave it expression.* The nexus never hinders us from generalizing, from understanding the idea of the text according to the principles which we have already laid down.

We must ascend no higher than is necessary to determine well the sense or meaning of the words of the text. Saurin has unquestionably passed beyond just bounds, in his sermon on *True Liberty*.†

* Example: "I can do all things through Christ, who strengtheneth me." Philippians, iv. 13.

† Tome iii., p. 335, Nouvelle Édition.

Let us here introduce an observation which is not without importance. A text has not two senses. Though, according to the tenor of the words of which it is composed, it may present two distinct senses, and these two senses be very fine, we are to give but one of them to our auditory, and above all are we not to give them the discussion which establishes it.*

III.

A text without offering two senses, may not offer a clear sense.

There may be obscurity in the idea, when the object of the text is in a region too high to be reached by our analysis. Thus, as to the passage in 1 Corinthians, xv. 27, 28, on the subjection of all things to God ;† in 1 Peter, iii. 18–20, on

* See Ephesians, i. iv, "Without blame *in* or *by* love."

John, i. 9, "Every man that cometh into the world."

Colossians, iii. 14, "The bond of perfection."

Philippians, ii. 6, "He thought it not robbery," or "did not take a pride in."

Matthew v. 9, "Blessed are the peacemakers."

Luke, vii. 47, "For she hath loved much." Osterwald translates, "It is for this cause that she loved much."

† Quesnel explains this passage thus: "In the estate of innocence, God spake to and communed with men, immediately by himself. Sin has changed everything. In the estate of natural law and the law of Moses, this was done by angels, by men and by various outward means. In the estate of the law of grace, it is done by Jesus Christ, his Son, sent to men in order to bring them again to obedience, and to establish the kingdom of his Father. In heaven, God by himself works all in all. Jesus Christ having finished his work, which is to gather together the elect of God, to direct them on earth, and to conduct them to his Father, there will be no more the mediation or sacrifice of Jesus Christ, no more the ministration of angels, no more the ministry of men, no more need of the Scriptures, no more necessity of external means. God in the trinity of his person, will reign by himself; the entire body of the Church, the head and the members, will subsist and live in him

preaching to the spirits in prison, and in Romans, vii. 17, "It is no more I that do it, but sin that dwelleth in me." The obscurity of such passages is not always invincible; they often contain high and important truths, which we must hold in high esteem; they open a vast field to meditation; but yet we may say in general, that we are not to prefer such subjects or the texts which express them.

In vain would one here apply the word: "These things were written for our instruction," Romans, xv. 41; it is not applicable to everything. Instruction is a whole, which has its remote accessories. We are not to preach on these accessories.

What must be done when the obscurity is in the expression, in which I comprehend also the forms of reasoning? It is said, that the minister is essentially the commentator or interpreter of the word of God, and, as all ought to read it he must make it intelligible to all. I reply, it is not said that the whole is addressed directly to all readers of all times. The plain man, at least, will not comprehend everything, and will not believe everything which may be addressed to him. Undoubtedly, the teaching of the Spirit of God does, in a considerable degree, open the understanding; but it may be that many passages whose form belongs to another age, will always remain obscure to some of the readers of our day. Edification is the instruction of the soul; and it is not incompatible with that of the intellect; but though we must give, in order to edification, a certain measure of aliment to the intellect, too much labor of the intellect is manifestly injurious to edification. A very peculiar talent is necessary to our being permanently edifying on

and of him; he will render them immortal as eternity, will enlighten them, and render them all luminous as himself, will diffuse himself among them, and make them perfect in himself, in love." QUESNEL, *Reflexions morales sur le Nouveau Testament.*

such subjects ; much indeed is necessary to our being as perspicuous as the pulpit demands. "Let every man examine himself," 1 Corinthians, xi. 28.

After all, as to such texts, the whole office of the interpreter, perhaps, is to show that they are obscure, and this sometimes is the best service we can render. Examples :

Galatians, iii. 20, "A mediator is not of one ; but God is one."*

Romans, xii. 20, "Thou shalt heap coals of fire on his head."

1 Timothy, v. 24–25, "Some men's sins are open beforehand, etc."

Romans, vii. 10, "The commandment which was ordained to life I found to be unto death, etc." French version : "The commandment which was given me for life, has given me death, etc."

Moreover, obscure texts are either important ones, which may be replaced by others, or they are not fruitful, and this almost always is the case. We may then, in brief, propose the following rule :

Do not take as a text for your discourse, an obscure, difficult passage, or one, the elucidation of which will require a too extended preliminary discussion. There may be an exception to this rule, when the text which is chosen contains an important truth not elsewhere announced.

IV.

Choose a fruitful text. I call a text fruitful, which, without foreign addition, without the aid of minute details, without discussion, furnishes, when reduced to its just meaning, matter for a development interesting in all its parts, and which leaves with us an important result. Every fruitful text will be also

* See QUESNEL on this passage.

a practical text, for though a preacher may touch upon speculative points, he must always do this with a practical purpose, and not for a purely philosophical purpose.

It is difficult to give examples. That which is sterile with some is productive with others, and *vice versâ*.

Good theological studies, meditation, a philosophical habit of mind, may discover fertility where it did not appear at first. He who seizes the relations of the idea to other ideas, its affinities, its extended bearings; he who knows how to generalize, to ascend to principles, to see distant consequences, makes a soil productive which others would find unfruitful. I assume, moreover, that the preaching is to be textual; for the embarrassment would be small, if the texts were to be treated only after manner of Catholics.

But it will be said, since we are at liberty in the choice of texts, why not go directly to those which are manifestly fruitful? In the first place, we should avoid texts which have their own peculiar merit, a character of their own, and thus should we reduce greatly the latitude of our choice. And then it is very probable that at this rate, there would be very few fruitful texts. The richest are at last rich only to a meditative mind. Let us remark, in passing, that on this account especially, it is very useful to be obliged for some time to treat prescribed texts, and to be at all times willing that they should be prescribed.

But it is nevertheless true that if the majority are impoesd upon by the appearance of sterility, others are deceived by the contrary appearance.

Every striking, attractive, moving word, is not fruitful. Truths at the extremity or the summit, are not as fruitful as those which are at the point of departure or mid-way. They simply excite emotion. Examples—Colossians, i. 16. Psalms lxiii. 25.

Sometimes a salient or piquant idea, which we meet with

in a text, may induce a youthful imagination to treat it; but this text presents that one idea only; all the rest is filled with common-place.

V.

We may, in certain cases, though not without caution, use in the body of our discourse, passages, the terms of which are somewhat repulsive, but we must not take them as texts for our sermons. Example: 2 Peter, ii. 12.

With passages presenting a disagreeable image, I class those which are somewhat odd or too familiar; but in general, these texts relate to subjects which we are not called to treat.

VI.

We have nothing to say on the dimensions or material extent of the text. As to its logical extent, we recommend integrity and unity.

Claude has given the following rule: "The text must contain the complete idea of the writer from whom it is borrowed; for it is his language, they are his sentiments, which we are to explain to our hearers. For example, if we take the words in 2 Corinthians, i. 3, 4, *Blessed be God, the Father of our Lord Jesus Christ, the Father of mercy, and the God of all comfort, who comforteth us in all our afflictions, that we may be able to comfort them who are in any trouble, by the comfort wherewith we ourselves are comforted of God;* and stop after these words, *the God of all comfort*, we have a complete sense, but not the complete sense of the apostle. If we proceed farther and add, *who comforteth us in all our afflictions*, we have not yet the complete sense of Saint Paul; we do not embrace all his thoughts; we must advance to the end of the fourth verse. When the idea of the sacred author is embraced, we may stop, for there are few texts of holy scripture that do not furnish the matter of a sermon, and it is equally bad to embrace too much and to embrace too little; we must avoid both extremes."*

I do not adopt the rule of Claude. I content myself with a sense complete in itself, provided it be conformed to the thoughts of the sacred writer.

The rule of Claude would, on application, defeat itself, by leading us to embrace a sense more than complete, as when, in Saint Paul, for example, many thoughts are linked to one another, not by their broadest side, but by their extremity, by their terminal points.†

Even when it is not so, there would be much disadvantage in not being at liberty to take for separate consideration one of the propositions of which a period is composed.

We may easily find cases in which we should fail to obtain a complete, sufficient sense, if we did even go quite to the conclusion of the author's sentence. The following passages, I think, are of this number: 1 Corinthians, xiii. 13; ii. 9; Philippians, ii. 12, 13; iv. 6, 7.

Is not even the passage cited by Claude one of these? Are not 1 Timothy, iv. 13–16; Ephesians, i. 7–10; Hebrews, xii. 1, 2, and Hebrews, xii. 15, of the same class? The rule would put us at the mercy of an accident of speech, of a conjunction (*for*, *then*, *and*,) of nothing.—See John, xiv 21. It would interdict certain texts which are formed of

* CLAUDE, *Traité de la composition du sermon*, in the first volume of his *Œuvres posthumes*.

† Applied to writers whose style is grammatical, this rule would be unobjectionable; but such are not the writers with which we have to do. Their periods often disregarded the law of rhetorical unity. We say this freely, for we see in it a beauty, inasmuch as it reveals a great fulness of heart. If Paul and Peter have fallen into a fault here through negligence, yet seeing the principle of their irregularity, we admire and are silent. In each of their thoughts their charity would fain have embraced all the thoughts of Christianity, all the interests of their hearers.

few words, suspended in the sentence, and not forming a proposition, as Ephesians, v. 10, " Proving what is acceptable to the Lord," and 1 Peter, v. 7, " Casting your care on him."

An important idea, very suitable as the subject of a sermon, is often included in an appendix to a sentence. Thus, 1 Timothy, i. 15, "To save sinners *of whom I am chief.*" Romans, i. 31, "Without understanding, covenant-breakers, *without natural affection*, implacable, unmerciful." 2 Timothy, iii. 3, " *Without natural affection*, truce-breakers, false accusers, incontinent, fierce, despisers of them that are good."*

The rule of Claude appears to me vague or inapplicable. I think we find a complete sense and consequently a text in every series of words from which an attentive mind can draw out a proposition, and which is adequate in itself; that is to say, which presents a true sense independently of the words preceding or following.

Doubtless we ought to examine carefully whether the more particular ideas, the author's additions to his principal idea, are not the completion of it, do not present it in its fulness of light, do not guard it against ambiguity or prejudice,† etc. We oppose only the rule which would find, in some purely accidental circumstance, the limitation of a text.

As we must not confound texts with phrases and periods, nor logical unity with grammatical unity, neither must we

* I do not reckon in this number the words, " A little while," on which Harms made a sermon, of which he gives the plan thus, "The phrase, *a little while*, (*uber ein Kleines*,) considered in its divine energy, 1. Cheers the afflicted. 2. Maintains joy in joyful hearts. 3. Stimulates dulness. 4. Disturbs indifference. 5. Sustains us in conflict. 6. Strengthens us in death.

† See the examples cited above, 1 Corinthians, ii. 9; xiii. 13. Philippians, ii. 12, 13, iv. 6, 7.

think that the text ends where the grammatical sense ends, or even where logical unity closes. Many logical unities may, together, form a greater unity ; and it is impossible to say beforehand and in an absolute manner, what are the limits of a true text. The same text may furnish ten ; ten texts may make one. The art of cutting up a text, the art of grouping many texts into one, deserves examination.

Thus, in the passage in Matthew, v. 3–10, each *beatitude* forms a particular text; but we may also unite them all in one text. That in John, iv. 31–38, presents three traits in the character of Jesus Christ ; a sublime engagedness, (he forgets to eat,) a sublime impatience, (the fields are white,) a sublime self-denial, (one sows and another reaps.) Of the whole, we may make three distinct subjects.

Doctor Busch treated in a sermon the passage in Luke, x. 23–37.* Here, the first words of Jesus Christ, "Blessed are the eyes which see the things that ye see," are represented as having provoked the Pharisee's question. This man's error was connected with a pure intention. Jesus Christ replied to his question by a new question. To the Pharisee's answer, "Thou shalt love the Lord thy God, etc." Jesus Christ replied, "Thou hast answered well." The orator shows that the Pharisee had indeed *answered well.* But in the presence and under the influence of Jesus Christ, this answer, so tranquillizing in appearance, does not tranquillize him. Though he has *answered well* as to the law, he doubts still, if he has *well kept* the law. Seriously desiring to be justified before God, he would fulfil the precept of love to our neighbor, in the manner and sense required by God.†

* See the collection of sermons by various authors, published by Fleidner and Leopoldt, in favor of the Evangelical Church, of Karlsbuld in the Donamoos, under the title, *Ein Herr, Ein Glaube Barmen*, 1837, p. 352.

† As to the first commandment, he asked no question? Why?

Now comes the story of the Samaritan. The author inquires what impression this story, so beautiful always, and for every one, ought to have made on this man, in these circumstances. Then he passes to the Pharisee's answer, the expressions of which he weighs, and which show, as he thinks, that his heart was touched. To the love of our neighbor, his heart was opened; but this love implies the love of God, such as the first commandment prescribes. As the Pharisee had not yet had experience of such a love of his neighbor as this, our Lord presents it to him in a fact, and ends by recommending him to reproduce it. There is then an application of the subject to ourselves, who have need of being taught the same thing by Jesus Christ; and finally, the answer to this objection: since truly good works are unprofitable to us, since, of course, we cannot be saved by our works, how is this to be reconciled with the replies of Jesus Christ to the Pharisee, "*Thou hast answered well;*" "Go, and do thou likewise."

Doctor Julius Müller's Sermon on Matthew, xvii. 1–18, may be also cited here. "The recital in our text," he says, "begins by the relation of the most sublime and wonderful event in the life of Jesus Christ, his transfiguration on a mountain of Galilee, and the appearance of Moses and Elias, in the glorious light which surrounded him. This recital then conducts us to the three disciples who were witnesses of the event, describing to us their amazement and their fear, and gives us some idea of the holy emotion of their heart when they descended from the mountain. We are, finally, transported into the midst of a multitude which covers the plain, and are present at one of those sad spectacles which human sin and misery afford. Thus our history descends, so to speak, by degrees, from the shining height of Christ's glory, into the dark valley of human debasement. We are to reverse this order in our meditations of to-day. Instead of descending, we shall rise, and we shall contemplate three steps of the Christian life; the first, that of doubt, hesitation, and perplexity; the second, that of the beatific knowledge of Jesus Christ, and of entire surrender to his will; the third, that of perfect communion with Jesus Christ."*

We must not hastily ascribe two meanings to texts which better considered, show a unity that could not fail to have been in the intentions of the sacred writer, who would not unite two things without knowing why. We must seek out this unity. I have cited already 1 Thessalonians, v. 15, and Ephesians, iv. 28. In 1 Timothy, ii. 8, "I will that men pray everywhere, lifting up holy hands, without wrath and doubting," the common thought is, advice given to the persecuted, to oppose prayer to the evils which they suffer. This thought is not expressed directly; but if it was not present to the apostle's mind, he at least wrote under its influence. Tholuck has inquired for the apostle's unity of intention in Hebrews, xii. 14: "Follow peace with all men, and holiness, without which no man shall see the Lord." "There are," he says, "three things in our text. Two exhortations, and a threatening, which may also be understood as a promise, (a threatening to some, a promise to others.) The apostle certainly would not have combined these two exhortations, one to peace, the other to holiness, if he had not regarded holiness as the root of that peace, which he recommends us to maintain with all men."† We may find the unity of the text in another idea: "*Peace without prejudice to holiness.*" According to him, "Peace *by means* of holiness." See also James, i. 17. (Comp. 1 Corinthians, iv. 20.)

* *Ein Herr, ein Glaube*, a collection of sermons by various authors published by FLEIDNER and LEOPOLDT, p. 108.

* THOLUCK, *Akademische Predigten*, 2e Sammung.

VII.

We add some other rules to those which we have already given.

It is proper to vary texts. We are struck at the constant recurrence of certain texts, as if the generality of preachers considered themselves as under obligations to repeat them. Doubtless, there are some which, by their importance, should draw the attention of all; but there is, nevertheless, another thing of importance, and of more serious importance than at first we may suppose, that we do not allow a sort of traditional monotony to have place in the choice of texts. The use of a new text imparts novelty to the same subject. Upon the same subject there are ordinarily texts of three kinds, out of which we may make our choice: didactic, or sententious texts; historical texts; and texts which may be called ejaculatory. We cite some examples of the last.

Psalm xlii. 3, "When shall I come and appear before God!"

Psalm lxxxiv. 4, "Thine altars O Lord of Hosts, my King and my God!"

Psalm xxiv. 9, "Everlasting doors be ye lifted up, and the king of glory shall come in."

Psalm vi. 4, "But thou O Lord how long?"

Psalm lxxiii. 19, "How are they brought into desolation as in a moment!"

Micah, vi. 6, "Wherewith shall I bow myself before the High God!"

Romans, vii. 24, "O wretched man that I am, who shall deliver me from the body of this death!"

1 Corinthians, xv. 55, "O death where is thy sting?"

Another rule, as important as it is neglected, is that texts be individual. All other things being equal, of two texts, that which shall be most in accordance with our individuality is much to be preferred.

May we invert in the sermon the order of the parts of a text? Without doubt we may, and in some cases must. Preachers have frequently done it. Our discourse, however, must not invert the order of the parts of the text, except where it is evidently necessary. "The chief thing in our worship," says Bossuet, "is that we have just sentiments toward God, and that we believe him to be what he is. It is the effect of this belief that we purify our intentions in his presence, and that we order ourselves as he requires. Thus the essence of religion is contained in these two words, (*in spirit and in truth*,) and I pray my Saviour to forgive me, while, in order to aid your understanding, I begin the explanation with that which it pleased him to announce last."*

Finally, to the question whether we may prefix two texts to a sermon, we simply reply that as a rule, we are to preach on one passage of scripture, but that nothing forbids, if need be, that we combine two passages to make one text. This is sometimes done with great advantage and propriety.

CHAPTER IV

OF HOMILY AND PARAPHRASE.

All that we have said thus far, appears to relate only to *Synthetic* discourse, and even to assume that this alone is the legitimate kind.

In truth, all the rules we have given, whether as to subjects or texts, involve the idea that the whole sermon rests on one proposition.

It is of course necessary, when we do not find this propo-

* Bossuet, *Sermon sur le Culte du à Dieu.* Œuvres Edition Lefévre, 1836, tome, iv., p. 162.

sition contained implicitly in the text, to collect in one point the more or less scattered and divergent elements, to condense them so as to form only that one proposition of which we have spoken.

But are not the two kinds of preaching which are known under the name of *Paraphrase* and *Homily*, to follow the contrary method? Is not the method here that of an analysis, instead of a synthesis? To this question I reply as follows:

The method is both analytic and synthetic, and the combination of these two methods is not exclusively proper to the homily. The synthetic sermon, if we examine it closely, analyzes the text, and in this analysis, finds its whole division. This was the almost constant way of the French Reformed preachers before Dubosc. They spelled, if we may so speak, the biblical word. Still, as these analyses were not generally employed on very extended texts, their discourses pass for sermons and not homilies. We may at least say that they mark the transition, or hold the intermediate place between the sermon and the homily. These three forms are but three degrees of the analytic method, which abounds and triumphs in the homily. But in all the three, analysis is but the preliminary and means of synthesis, in which it must always end.

Even paraphrase is admissible only on this condition. In the strictness of its ideas, it is only discourse parallel to that of the sacred author, a continuous explication of the text, an explication to the extent of which there is no precise limit. We find in Massillon more than one example of it.* If we consult the nature of the human mind, I think we shall feel that it demands combination after analysis and the giving of some connexion, the connexion of a common idea, to the elements which we have successively gathered. I know indeed,

* Among others, see tome viii., p. 59, de l' edition Mequignon, 12mo.

that if the connexion is very loose the unity is scarcely more than nominal. The nature of *existence*, is ultimately a uniting bond of the most opposite ideas.

Dismissing paraphrase and confining ourselves to homily, we say, that if it is not as greatly different from the ordinary sermon as we commonly suppose, it yet has a character of its own. This character belongs to it, not only from its having to do most frequently with recitals, or from any familiarity peculiar to this kind of discourse, but rather from this, that its chief business, its principal object, is to set in relief the successive parts of an extended text, subordinating them to its contour, its accidents, its chances, if we may so speak more than can be done in the sermon, properly so called.

Nothing distinguishes, essentially, the homily from the sermon, except the comparative predominance of analysis ; in other terms, the prevalence of *explanation* over *system*. All that we have said of the sermon generally applies, then, to the homily. The difficulty as to unity, presented by this kind of discourse, never amounts to impossibility. We do not at random cut from the general text of the sacred books, the particular text of a homily. The selection is not arbitrary. The limit of the text is pre-determined by reference to unity, which therefore we shall be at no loss to discover in it. * The only danger is that unity of subject will be relinquished, as the thread of a path may be buried and lost beneath an intertwined and tufted vegetation. There is, doubtless, an art of analysing. To analyze is not only to sift, to disjoin, it is at the same time to tie ; to preserve or mark articulations, to respect the life of the text, to develop rather than decompose it. Amidst all the lines which cross, interlace, or shade each other in a recital or a parable, we

* When one takes, like Luther, two recitals, (Matthew, viii. 1–13,) because one follows the other, he can find no unity, because none was aimed at.

must detect and seize the chief line, the mother-idea, cast aside or throw into half-light, in a second plan, that which is less important, that which forms an integrant part of the recital, without forming an integrant part of the instruction which it was intended to afford. We must also proportion the development of each trait to its measure of importance, not allowing ourselves to pursue this or that detail, though attractive, and often of serious interest, which on another occasion it might not be well to resume and treat by itself; we must not course two, much less three hares at once: The more important the ideas which have been gathered, the more wearied and dissipated does the mind become, as each one of them offers it a strong temptation.*

I assume that preachers are left at liberty in the choice of texts; if they are not, and a prescribed pericope does not of itself offer sufficient unity, I should prefer neglecting it altogether, to obtaining it by force. It is however seldom that a common vinculum does not present itself.†

As the preacher appears to be more sustained by his text, in the homily than in the synthetic sermon, the former is thought to be more easy of execution. And it certainly is

* AMMON, *Anleitung zur Kanzelberedsamkeit*, p. 107, cites the example of a homily on Matthew, xiv. 1–10, "Which," he says, "loses part of its interest by the accumulation of the following subjects: 1. Transition from debauchery to cruelty. 2. Of the duty of boldly declaring the truth. 3. Female resentment. 4. The secret terror with which defenceless virtue inspires bad men in power. 5. The inconsistency of bad men. Unity," adds AMMON, "should never be sacrificed even in homily, and it is unjust to this kind of preaching that a want of unity should be made its distinctive mark."

See, as examples of homilies, CELERRIER on 2 Samuel, ii. 1–7, (*Homilies*, tome i., p. 210,) and ROCHET, *les Anges logés chez Abraham, Discourses et Meditations*, p. 223.

† See the example cited by AMMON, *Anleitung zur Kanzelberedsamkeit*, p. 108, note 1.

more easy to make a homily than a sermon, but a good sermon is made with more facility than a good homily. The great masters in the art of preaching, Bourdaloue for example * have not succeeded in homily.

The most excellent judges in the matter of preaching have recommended the homily.

Fénélon. " Would you have a preacher explain the holy Scriptures consecutively and litterally ? Yes, this would be admirable."†

Herder. " After preaching ceased to be what it was in the mouths of the Apostles, a message, properly so called, it became an exposition of the Word of God, of the apostolic writings, of their doctrine, and an application to the silent and assembled flock, of all which had just been read. It was called *homily*, and was in fact, neither a harangue nor a discourse. In my view the exposition of Scripture is the highest and best kind of preaching, especially in our time ; and in particular, I regard it as the best and safest mode for young persons."‡

Dutoit Membrini. " It is much to be desired that this kind of preaching were more general. We would have a consecutive exposition of the Word of God, and not a tissue of human reasonings to which the text is accommodated. The discourses of the Fathers of the Church were homilies. Homilies made in good taste, and by men capable of making them, would be extremely useful. We take a pas-

* Example : Homily on the *man born blind,* (tome ii., p. 239, de l'edition le Fevre ;) of which this is the plan : 1. The blindness of the Pharisees. 2. The sincere, noble, convincing testimony of the blind man. A discourse of this kind is more a sermon than a homily.

† FENELON, *Dialogues sur l'eloquence,* dialogue III., toward the end.

‡ HERDER, *Briefe über das Studium der Theologie,* 43. Brief, tome ii., p. 19–24, de l'edition de Carlsruhe, 1829.

sage of Scripture and explain it in its connexion ; we unfold its interior sense ; a multitude of ideas enter, and come, as it were, in file ; a number of duties are explained in few words.* It is a way of preaching more pithy, more scriptural, more Christian. We thus teach the people how to read the Scripture ; we explain it to them ; we show the connexion between ideas which at first seemed to have little relation to each other. We also adhere more closely to the true Word of God."†

Ammon.—"Homilies are suited to make the Bible understood, which is always little known; they facilitate the application of its principles to private and public life; the simplicity and variety by which they are characterized, give them a more general and lasting effect on the majority of the hearers; they also excite the preacher himself to a more connected and profound study of men and of the documents of our religion. On the other hand, they have the inconvenience of cramping the free course of the preacher's thoughts, of di viding the attention by proposing to it too great a variety of subjects, and by leaving too little space for the development and application of a particular truth."‡

Scholl.—"In the homily, the word of God is more completely the basis and the clue of discourse. This kind of preaching includes naturally and without effort, a greater variety in teaching, and is thus better adapted to the various wants of souls. It is opposed to that uniformity in the choice of subjects, and the exclusive tendencies to which preachers are too much inclined. It is more suited to give the knowledge of holy scripture, both as a whole and in its details—to inspire a taste for meditation in this Divine Word, and to

* An advantage which touches very closely a disadvantage.

† DUTOIT MEMBRINI, *Philosophie chrétienne*, Discours preliminaire, p. 89.

‡ AMMON, *Anleitung zur Kanzelberedsamkeit*, p. 111.

teach those who study it, to read it with understanding, with reflection, and always with direct and personal application."

In short.—This method has not all the advantages of the synthetic method, and it is susceptible of abuse more or less hurtful. Ammon has just shown us this. But the want of certain advantages, and the possibility of certain abuses, are not faults. The other method also has not all the advantages which we may imagine; neither is it a security against all the abuses which we fear. The recommendations of the Homily are these:

1. It explains and honors holy scripture.

2. It is intelligible to a greater number, and gives pleasure to all, by substituting more vivid tints for the sober ones of abstraction.

3. It opposes the exclusive tendency to which preachers are but too much inclined.

4. It secures more variety than the synthetic kind of preaching.

SECTION SECOND.

MATTER OF PULPIT DISCOURSE.

The chapter of our Course on the text, may be considered as a simple appendix to the preceding one on the subject. Thus far, we have treated only of the subject of the sermon. We now enter on the consideration of the matter of the sermon. The matter is to the subject what the edifice is to the foundation. The subject is the proposition, the matter is the development of it, the very substance of the discourse, the pulp of the fruit.

The order we follow in our course is not necessarily that which the thought of the preacher follows. We advance from the subject to the matter. In the preparation of his discourse, he may go from the matter to the subject, that is to say, he may be led to the mention of his subject by the mention of the leading ideas of his sermon; his subject may be the summary, the conclusion of them. And in this case, it would seem that his discourse should be an explanation of the manner in which he arrived at this conclusion.

It is possible that this form, in certain cases, would be the most happy, the most persuasive. It is the form of some of Pascal's pieces.

We should be mistaken, however, if we should think that the sermon may ordinarily be a confession or a disquisition. The road by which the preacher arrives at his personal convictions, may not be necessarily that which he will take with his hearers. Let us regard reality; let us take what, on the whole, is the position of the minister generally.

He has before him a truth which to him is certain, and which it is his business to explain and prove to others; in a word, he pursues the same order that we have done in our course; he goes not from the matter to the subject, but from the subject to the matter.

To accomplish his purpose, he may use not only another order, but other means than those by which he himself was instructed and convinced. The way which leads us to faith is providential. God uses means which we often despise. Having arrived at the end, would we take others through all the turnings and windings by which God has led us?

As preachers, we are to place ourselves in a more general point of view. We ought to consider what in our experience is human. We should use means suited to the majority, even means which have had no effect on ourselves. The definitive secret of conversion always escapes us. Often a man is converted by the most feeble instrumentality. In the conversion of two men, it is impossible that there should have been no means in common; but there may be also great differences.

When we speak of explaining and proving, it is not because we think there should be sermons of explanation, in which there is no proof, and sermons of proof to which there is no explanation. A sermon, whatever may be its kind, resolves itself always into demonstration, and a demonstration never has place without a formal or indirect explanation; I mean to say, that every demonstration rests upon a foregoing explanation.

To give knowledge, to produce faith, is the two-fold task of the preacher in every sermon.

I say more: it is not always easy to distinguish or to separate one of these things from the other. To inform is often to convince; to explain is to prove; to show is to demonstrate.

Formal demonstration has had preference—demonstration, which takes advantage of one of our admissions, in order to wrest others from us. The truth is not presented to us as a thing which we may acknowledge at the first view, and to which the best parts of our being spontaneously subscribe; the address is not made to that spirit of which it is said, (Matthew, xxvi. 41,) that it is willing.* The nature and force of truth is not sufficiently tested.

Demonstration itself, when we choose this way, has a true force of persuasion only in proportion as the demonstrative process presents to us the truth. The vivid representation of objects is the principal force, the life of eloquence.

These two elements, then, must fuse themselves into one another. But in our course, we are obliged to distinguish them. And this, the more, since the preacher is essentially an expounder, interpreter, reporter, and this is a distinct and principal part of his mission.

We distinguish then in the Sermon, *Explication* and *Proof.*

And in each of these, we distinguish again. For explication comprehends *facts* and *ideas.* Facts are either successive, and are related, (*narration,*) or they are simultaneous, and are described, (*description.*) Ideas are defined and expounded.

Thus as to Explication. As to *proof,* it embraces *speculative* truths and *practical* truths, (*doctrines* and *duties.*) With the first it employs *reasons;* with the second, *motives.*

These are all the elements of the sermon. We make here a sort of chemical decomposition of discourse. Hereafter, under the head of *Disposition*, when treating of its parts as in juxtaposition or succession, we shall proceed to its physical decomposition. Now, we speak of combined parts or elements, which have no distinctive places assigned to them in the discourse, any more than have the blood and the flesh in the human body.

* *Prompt.—Fr.*

CHAPTER I.

OF EXPLICATION.

§ 1. *Explication of facts.*

ANTECEDENT to the two kinds of explication which I have indicated, *narration* and *description*, there is another peculiar to pulpit discourse; this is *exegesis*, or the explication of the text, verbal explication with the necessary historical elucidation.

A sermon may, in certain cases, be only an exegesis, enlivened by affecting sentiment and a practical application. But taking the word in its ordinary signification, what place may exegesis hold in the teaching of the pulpit? A place narrower than it had in the practice of Saurin, but more extended, perhaps, than that which it has in the general preaching of the present day. Though discussions of this kind little suit the pulpit, certain results may be indicated there; and it would not be amiss, if preaching gradually imparted to believers such comments as are necessary to their reading the Bible with advantage.*

As to *Explication*, we comprise in it not only the decomposition of facts or the enumeration of their parts, whether in time or in space, but also the indication of the relations which bind their different parts together, the *why* with the *how*. In this, I admit, we touch on the proofs, or rather the proof enters into the explication, but explication is always the object. We have to make known that which has been,

* See SAURIN, *Sermon sur les dévotions passagères*, tome ii., p. 110. Nouvelle edition.

that which is, or that which shall be. Under the name of facts, we include whatever has a determinate place in time and space, facts of the moral order as well as others.

Let us first take *narration.* It forms an essential part of the discoure of the bar.* The advocate has first to present facts, and this is a part of his work in which he may use the most art, and display the most skill. He presents facts which are either little known, or ill known, and which, in all cases, have not been before related. The preacher shows wisdom in reasoning on known facts.

Narration, nevertheless, may become an integrant and even considerable part of the discourse. Witness the discourses of Stephen and the first apostles. (Funeral Oration —Description of an Epoch of the Church.) As to the representation of simultaneous facts, or *description,* it is less frequently the object of the sermon, than the form of certain ideas, which constitute part of the sermon. Still, sometimes it necessarily has its place in pulpit discourse; thus in depicting the manners and customs of a certain epoch, or in the representation of a certain condition of man and of society, recital becomes the fixed character of the discourse.

But still, even where narration and description form an integrant portion of the discourse and appertain to the subject, they perform, most frequently, a subordinate part. Ideas are the ground of pulpit discourse. No relation, no description of contingent facts is admissible, except for the purpose of establishing immutable truths. The same cannot be said of history in an absolute sense. Without applying to it, as M. de Barante has done, the remark of Quintilian, *Scribitur ad narrandum non ad probandum,** we may yet say, that in history, recitation holds the highest place, that

* See les playdoyers de Cochin, de Loyseau de Mauléon.

† QUINTILIAN, lib. x., cap. 1.

the historian's first object is *ad narrandum.* It is not thus with the orator; he writes only to prove. This suggests a remark, which will be presented hereafter, under another aspect. It is that the extent of narration and description is restricted, and their form modified, by the purpose and general character of the sermon. Oratorical force perpetuates itself through all the incidents of the matter, and narration or description is ordinarily only an incident. This axiom governs the whole. We may convince ourselves of this, by observing how the masters of the art have narrated and described.*

Narration and description may be fused into one another; but the second often takes the form of the first, which is more oratorical.†

Narration and description have their respective advantages. One has more of vivacity and movement; the other incorporates all homogeneous elements.

We must not forget, that narration and description, in evangelical discourse, are in general auxiliary or subsidiary. They are only indirectly matter of the sermon. They are elements and materials for demonstration.

§ 2.—*Explication of Ideas.*

Let us be understood, as to the meaning which we attach to the word *idea.* In general, an idea is a *view* of the mind, the view of a very particular fact as well as any thing else. It is the fact reflected in the mind, the object in the subject.

* See Saurin, *Sur les Malheurs de l'Europe,* tome viii., pages 332 et 335, nouvelle edition; Massillon, *Sur le Jugement universel,* tome i., p. 33, èdition Lefèvre, 1823; *Sur la Verité de la Religion,* (la fin.,) tome i., p. 145; *Sur les tentations des grands,* depuis: "Sa gloire Sire," tome i., p. 565.

† See Massillon, *Sur la Divinetè de Jesus Christ,* tome i., page 95, colonne 1, èdition Lefèvre.

It will be seen that we spoke of ideas, thus regarded, in the preceding paragraph, in so far as it is the object of narration and description to give an idea of facts.

But we are henceforth to take the word *idea* in another sense. We have now to do not with an intellectual view of concrete facts; but with purely intellectual elements by means of which we form this idea, or obtain this view for ourselves, and without which we cannot obtain it.

Idea, in this sense, has no definite relation to time and space, although it may have been detached or abstracted from a multitude of similar facts accomplished in time and space; it is their common law, it is a generic fact; it is, in every proposition (for an idea does not exist apart from a proposition), an attribute separated from every subject, an attribute in a substantive form. "The world is great"—"greatness." Time and space are no longer anything.

When we say *The world is great*, or when we apply the epithet *great* to the substantive *world*, must we already have the idea *of greatness?* Undoubtedly. It is true we may say, that this idea is not conceived before the objects, or before their impressions on us. Without these objects, without the impressions which we have received, it could not have been conceived any more than the idea of a quality. A quality, a manner of existence, presupposes existence. But, on the other hand, it is impossible that objects and sensations should beget in the human mind any general idea, if there be not in it something anterior, which we will call not *idea*, but *form* or *category*, which external impressions do not create, but of which they give us the perception. However, it may be in respect to these anterior forms, it remains certain, that in whatever way we acquire general ideas, it is impossible for us without these ideas, without ideas, to draw anything from facts whether for thought or for life. It is by means of ideas, that we judge, measure, apply facts. A fact never has a form or name except by means of an idea previously acquired. It is only in the light of an idea that we can possibly see a fact, and the more general and elevated the idea, the more light does it throw on the fact; great ideas are best adapted to illumine facts or delineate them clearly on the shadow of our ignorance. Moreover, the design and the use of facts is to conduct us to ideas; to elevate us to them; here is all our dignity; and the more general the ideas are, that is to say, the more numerous the groups of facts which they embrace, the more are we elevated. The idea of God is the highest and grandest, because it embraces everything, and beyond it there is nothing.*

Thus, an idea appears by turns as a means, and as an end. In one view an idea is the condition or the means of the knowledge of facts, a lever by the aid of which we raise

* Instead of this paragraph, we read in an earlier manuscript the following passage which we think it may be useful to reproduce. "Let us here remark the importance of ideas. It is perceived by philosophy that in the absolute sense, idea precedes fact. The human mind, before all experience, presents in its interior a certain number of moulds or matrices, without which facts could not penetrate it, or would remain without form, which is the same thing. Reciprocally these moulds or matrices would, apart from the facts, remain eternally unfruitful. These moulds or matrices are primary ideas, primary and fundamental attributes of which all others are composed. These attributes or predicates only wait, so to speak, for subjects; but without them no proposition, no judgment, can have existence in the human mind. Now what we say of primitive and perfectly simple ideas, we say in like manner, other things being equal, of whatever is called an idea; that is to say, of every attribute separated from every subject and rendered substantive. These secondary ideas are not conceived without the aid and concourse of facts; but once conceived, they become the rule or the measure of other facts. A fact never has a form, a name, except by means of an idea antecedently acquired." Here the two manuscripts are connected.—[EDITORS.]

them and detach them from the soil ; or, if we will, the light in which we discern and measure them. In the other view, it is the end itself of the knowledge of facts. Through facts, we seek to attain ideas, which are not only their representation but their law, and which, in respect to God, are the true facts, the supreme facts, of which facts, properly so called, are but the expression or the symbol.

It is evident, that facts have much to do in religion and in preaching. Religion, which is founded in facts, resolves itself into ideas. Preaching is occupied especially with the ideas of religion.

Facts, we have seen, are related or described. Idea, as such, is defined, in other terms is classified.

Definition is defined by the etymology of the word. It marks the limits of an idea. To define definition positively, we say that it teaches of what elements an idea, as a whole, is composed. It consists in bringing together many general ideas, of which one is limited by the others. When the idea, so to speak, is fortified, entrenched, so that on all sides it repels ideas which would mix themselves with it, the object is defined.

We must not confound definition and judgment.

Definition does but verify identity ; judgment expresses a relation. Definition is an analytical proposition ; judgment is a synthetic proposition. Definition only decomposes an object ; judgment composes, or adds to the notion of an object, taken in the whole of its constituent elements, that of some quality.

Definition aims to make us know ; judgment, to appreciate. Very often, however, definition appreciates, and involves judgment ; and judgment is equivalent to a partial definition. We must not however confound with definition, those judgments which give force to a characteristic of an object, and are only designed to excite toward it such or such a sentiment. Examples :

"The existence of man is the dream of a shadow."*

"The history of the Church is the history of truth."

"Rivers are roads that move and carry us whither we would go."

"The beautiful is the splendor of the true."

"Hypocrisy is an homage which vice pays to virtue."

"Envy is the awkward homage which mediocrity pays to merit."

"Man is but a reed, the feeblest of created things ; but he is a thinking reed."

"Life is a combat for a prize which is in heaven."

"Raillery is a discourse in favor of our wit against our good nature."

"Time is the treasure of the poor."

"A courtier is a man who has neither honor nor humor."

"Time, that changeable image of unchangeable eternity."

"A tomb is a monument placed on the boundary between two worlds."

"Nature is the outward throne of the magnificence of God."

"Charity is the fulfilling of the law."

"Vice may be defined, the sacrifice of the future to the present."

"*Historiâ testis temporum, lux veritatis, vita memoriæ, magistra vitæ, nuntia vetustatis.*" (CICERO.)

When the notion of the attribute does not exhaust that of the subject, and one cannot be put indifferently for the other, we have not a definition, we have a judgment. Satire defines after its own manner. Thus Rochefoucald defined moderation, "A fear of falling into envy and contempt,

"* *What shadows* WE ARE, *what shadows* WE PURSUE."

which those deserve who are intoxicated with their good fortune," and La Bruyere defined gravity, " A mystery of the body designed to conceal weakness of mind." According to Diderot," Religious liberty is the right of each one to persecute in his turn." It is evident, that the reference in these examples is to false moderation, false gravity, false liberty.

A definition is indeed a judgment, but a judgment which contains or begets all the judgments which at any time may be pronounced upon an object. And reciprocally, by combining all the judgments which at any time may be pronounced on an object, we have a definition.

We may give this name to the following propositions:

" Skill is the just distribution of one's forces." (*Montesquieu.*)

" Rectitude is a purity of motive and intention, which gives form and perfection to virtue, and which attaches the soul to good for its own sake." (*Fléchier.*)

" An army is a number of armed men, larger or smaller, assembled under a chief, for the purpose of defending their country, or of attacking another country in favor of their own." (*Fléchier.*)

" Gratitude is the memory of the heart," (the sense of benefits received.)

" The universe is a sphere of which the centre is everywhere, the circumference nowhere."

" Faith is the substance of things hoped for, the evidence of things not seen." (Hebrews, xi. 1.)*

A definition may involve a judgment, or contain an explicit judgment. " Death is the termination of an *unquiet dream which is called* life."

Every discourse begins, or is supposed to begin, with a de-

* See examples of definition drawn from Cicero, in Rollins' note on definition, tome i., p. 340, by *Quintilian,* lib. v., cap. x., *de locis argumentorum.*

finition of the object, unless when it is very well known, as is almost never the case. And when it is known, it is not distinctly present to the mind of the greater part of the hearers.

Cicero rejects formal definition, as presenting some danger by the rigor which it requires, as savoring of pedantry, and also as entering with difficulty into the mind of the hearer, who has no time to pause.* "Besides," says Marmontel, "all kinds of eloquence do not require the same care as pleading, in which the plaintiff and defendant have to be constantly on their guard, and to strike and parry almost at the same time. Thus definition . . . . . is less critical, and attended with less danger in eulogy or deliberation."†

But it is always necessary to define the object exactly to one's self.

Definition is not only a means of perspicuity, an element of instruction, the basis of argumentation; it is often the beginning of proof.‡ Demonstration, at least, is firm and sure in proportion to the exactness and clearness of the definition. Thus the definition of the word *good*, in Romans, viii. 28, "All things work together for *good* to them that love God."

Definition is *direct* or *indirect*—direct when it goes straight to the idea; indirect when its course is circuitous.

Direct definition may be precise or free. In the first case, which is that of definition properly so called, it is reduced to what is indispensable, with care to omit nothing. In the second, we repeat, under various forms, the terms of which the definition consists,§ either defining them, or dividing again

* Cicero, *de oratore*, ii. 25.

† Marmontel, *Elêments de littérature*, tome ii., Article *Definition.*

‡ See Quintilian, lib. v. ch. x.

§ Example "The world is the creation taken by itself; it is whatever passes, it is all that is not God.

the matter of each of them, which is enumerating the parts.*

Direct definition is sometimes *simple*, sometimes *combined*. It is combined when it is complicated with another definition, by the accession of an idea either different, or opposed, or similar, or vicinal, or more particular, or more general, etc.†

Finally, direct definition may be either *ascending* or *descending*. The descending is the most ordinary form. The ascending or regressive form consists in constructing the idea, or, if you will, in giving its genesis.

These different forms may again be combined.‡

We present some rules as to the use of direct definition:

1. Not to give the definition too much place in the discourse, lest the movement be interrupted.

2. To avoid too subtile distinctions and classifications, which assume a great habit of abstraction, and an exact knowledge of language on the part of the hearer.

* See BOURDALOUE, *Avent, Sermon sur la recompense des saints*, the beginning of the second part. Edition Lefèvre, tome i., p. 5.

† Combined definition has the form,

a. Either of a *distinction.* A thing is this and not that. Thus the world in the sense of 1 John, ii. 15. is neither the whole of humanity, nor the order of the creation, nor the tumult of society. See the definition of courage in *l'oraison funebre de Turenne*, by FLECHIER.

b. Or of *exclusion.* True zeal defined by the characteristics of the false. (See *le Tartuffe*, Acte i. Scene vi.)

c. Or of *comparison with similar things*, (*assimilation*,) remorse, repentance.

d. Or of *the difference between species and genus.* Republic, democracy; self-love, vanity; justice, equity.

e. Or of *the proof* itself of the existence of the object.

‡ See REINHARD, *sur l'Embarras*, (sermons for 1792), Sermon ii., and MASSILLON, *Carême*, Sermon *sur l'Immutabilitè de la loi de Dieu*, the beginning of the second part. (Tome i., p. 459, Edition Lefèvre.)

3. Not to recur to formal definition without necessity,* but to give it as much as possible the form of the construction or discussion.†

4. Not to seek to define everything; as

a. That which is well known and is alreaay present to the mind of all;

b. Ideas which are too simple, as being the very substance which serves as the common basis of all the ideas, the organic molecules of thought and discourse, something which cannot be defined, because it cannot be decomposed, and which defines itself by the mere view of the object or the fact, and not by words;

c. Ideas, which instantly escape, and refuse definition, on account of the elevated or purely moral sphere to which they belong. Their nature is rather felt, than conceived. We define them by renewing the impression which they have produced. They are known, they are seen, when they are felt.‡ The Bible formally defines but little. Ideas taken above the region of physical or moral observation, borrow names by analogy from the relations of the visible and human world. God is the *father* of Spirits; Jesus Christ is the *husband* of the Church. It is metaphor alone that gives these names.

Finally, though ideas may suffice to make known ideas, they cannot give that vivid intuition of things, which is necessary for most minds. When this is the case, we

* When we examine the works of the masters, we find that they seldom prefer the formal definition. As they prove by defining, they define by proving. Their definitions seldom arrest the discourse; we do not hear them say as Defendant dans *les Plaideurs*—

. . . . Puis donc qu'on nous permet de prendre
Haleine, etc.

† See CHRYSOSTOM on Vain Glory.

‡ The comprehensive and philosophical meaning of the word *know* in the Bible.

must replace, or complete the *direct* method, of which we have given the different forms, by the *indirect*, which consists in translating the idea into facts, so that we may relate or describe the idea, as we relate or describe a fact. Only let us remark, that this, properly speaking, is not to replace definition, but to supplement or lead to it. In regard to ideas, only abstract terms can be exact. We may define an idea,

a. By its external signs or manifestations ;*

b. By individualizing it, or by giving it the concrete form, (*personification,*) avoiding, however, excess of portraiture ;†

c. By historical examples: *Via brevis per exempla.* Perhaps no one of them corresponds precisely to the idea, but by taking that which each of the facts has in common, and leaving the rest, we construct the idea. It is not necessary to cite many ;‡ but those which we do cite, we must define, that the essential elements of the idea may distinctly appear ;

d. By recalling to the hearers a situation or an experience of their own; definition now becomes dramatic ;§

* See the description of pride in BOURDALOUE, *Pensées sur divers sujets de morale et de religion,* (Edition Lefèvre, tome iii., p. 416.)

† See the description of the penitent by MASSILLON, *Carême, sermon sur le petit nombre des élus,* (Edition Lefèvre, tome i., p. 302.

‡ Abraham and Lot.

Alexander and his physician, greatness of soul. The anecdote related by Diderot of a Curate, who, having begged of an officer to contribute to a collection for the poor of his parish, received a blow, insisted still, saying, "this is for myself; but for my poor?" The story of the negro who when questioned as to the motives which induced him to bestow his attentions on an old man, replied, "Massa, he is my enemy." See Hebrews, xi, 4, 5, 7, 8, 11, 17, 20, 21, 22, 24, 29.

§ See BOSSEUT, Premier Sermon *pour la fête de tous les saints,* (Sermons choisis, p. 493 ;) et GERMOND, dans *le Recueil de Sermons de divers Ministres évangeliques du Canton de Vaud,* p. 246.

e. By bringing upon the stage the orator himself who places himself in the position of which he wishes to give an idea. "I do not know," says Pascal, "who has sent me into the world, nor what the world is, nor what I am myself. I am fearfully ignorant of all things. I do not know what my body is, what my senses are, what my soul is, and that very part of me which thinks what I am now speaking, which reflects on everything and on itself, knows itself no more than other things. I see an awful expanse in the universe in which I am included. I find myself confined to a narrow corner of this vast extent, without knowing why I am put in one place rather than another, or why that little time I am to live, has been assigned to this point, rather than to some other in that eternity which has preceded me, or in that which is to come. On all sides I see only infinities, which enclose me as an atom, and as a shadow that remains for an instant and never returns; all that I know is, that I am presently to die; but what I am most ignorant of is that death itself which I know I cannot shun,"* etc.;

f. By a parable. Jesus Christ often used this form of instruction, and this would seem to be one of the best for us also, if we could resist our propensity to conceits. A parable, besides, is but a continued metaphor, which we always use in explaining what is great. While literal language is finite, metaphor is infinite. There are things which we cannot reach but by a stretch of the imagination.†

While we avoid formal definition let us not suppress or mutilate definition; the whole, often, hardly serves to introduce the idea; and when all is done, even when the preacher

* PASCAL, *Pensees*, partie ii., art. ii. of the former editions, tome ii., p. 9; edition Faùgere.

† Parable of Ephrem Syrus, Bridaine, cited by MAURY, Eloquence de la chaire, xx. See, also, in the *discours sur quelques sujets religieux*, the discourse entitled, *Les trois reveils.*

seems least engaged in the labor of defining, he is putting forth all his efforts to give directly or indirectly a distinct notion, a vivid perception of the idea.

Definition as much as possible should excite and stimulate the free and vital forces of the soul. Perfect definition is that which, at the same time, gives knowledge, comprehension, feeling and faith.

CHAPTER II.

OF PROOF.

WE have defined, we have not yet *judged;* for definition adds nothing to the object, it only names it. We are to pass judgment. Every judgment which is not a pure and immediate intuition of the soul, implies or demands a proof.

Proof, as an act, consists in approaching the judgment in question with another judgment already formed, already attained to in our conviction ; one of these judgments implies the other ; this is common to every species of demonstration.

But though in every judgment proof is implied and should be at hand, may not the preacher announce judgments without producing the proofs of them ? May he not, in some cases, restrict himself to simple and direct affirmation ? Without doubt ; and he must even often speak thus to his auditory, proof being understood. But we have nothing to say here, concerning those judgments which explicit proof does not precede. In respect of form, it suffices to apply to them what we have said of the forms of definition.

It is is less of judgment than of *proof* that we now have to speak.

Proof is the intellectual act by which the effect of certitude is realized in us.

Definition terminates relative ignorance, proof puts an end to doubt. By the first we know, by the second we believe.

We must distinguish two orders of truths : *speculative* and *practical.* But both are alike established by proof.

In regard to both of these, proof produces conviction, which is a state in which one can deny neither the fact nor the right, without, in some sort, denying himself. For proof consists, as it were, in opposing a hearer with his own signature ; that is to say, the admission of some more general or previously proved truth, which involves the truth in question, or from which it irresistibly flows.

If the question be one of fact, the arguments (means, instruments of proof) are called *reasons* ; if of right or duty, they are *motives.* To recognize, fact or right, is to admit its conformity, in either case, to *the idea of the true* which is in us, or that it is implied in a truth which we hold already as certain and incontrovertible. This recognition is what the preacher would first of all obtain, in respect not only to fact but to right. The result in both cases is called *conviction.*

Persuasion, which comes afterwards, or the inclination of the will to such or such an act, is necessary, but neither more nor less than conviction ; and if the preacher does not think that he has attained his purpose unless conviction be also persuasion, neither does he suppose he has attained it if he has persuaded without convincing.

We first regard only the means of producing conviction, but let it be remarked carefully, that what we here separate, the orator ordinarily does not separate, and that he endeavors to produce at one and the same time, conviction and persuasion.

§ 1. *Proof, properly so called, or reasons.*

Whether we have to prove that a thing is, or that it ought to be, there are three ways of arriving at certainty : immediate *experience ; testimony*, which is the experience of others, and which is called *authority*, or the assumption that the credibility of the witness is out of doubt; finally, *reasoning*, which is the testimony of reason (of our reason) not of the senses, and which binds together and renders mutually fruitful, the truths acquired by means of experience or authority.*

In preaching, *authority*, or testimony worthy of belief, appears to hold the first rank, although the words "worthy of belief," imply the use of experience and even of reasoning. What gives authority the first rank is, that the doctrine which the preacher teaches is a revealed doctrine. If, however, authority, in the matter of preaching, were all, or nearly all, preaching would be reduced to nothing or nearly nothing.

Experience and reasoning are combined with authority in the pulpit, not in order to prove the authenticity of the document, which is out of question, nor to supplement it, since the certitude, which springs from the testimony, is not a half-certitude; but because, subjectively, and in regard to the last end which is proposed, no proof suffices in this sphere, if the inward witness is not connected with it, and because the declarations of the Bible are often only starting points for reason.

Those whom we vanquish, must become our allies; we gain nothing until they do.

Experience and reasoning have much to do here.

The pulpit does not create experiences, but it renovates while it recalls them.

The object of proof by *experience*, or by facts is, 1, to

* See BOURDELOUE tome i., p. 149, ancienne edition.

prove contingent facts, that which has place, either by anterior facts (*à priori*) or by posterior facts (*à posteriori*); 2, to prove general or generic facts, which are formed by individual facts, more or less numerous, appertaining to the genus or species in question; 3, to prove a principle or an idea (idea is the law of facts), that which has place when, by an action, a personal being, clothed in our view with authority, has consecrated the principle, (this returns to testimony,) or when facts which are not actions, reveal an idea; but this supposes conviction previously established, from the unity of truth, or from the unity of thought which created the universe.

Proof by experience is the most accessible, the most popular, but it is that of which the abuse is the most frequent and the most to be feared.

When it is said, "this is a fact," it is thought that everything has been said; this cuts the matter short; what reply can be made to a fact? Two things: It is not true;—it is not conclusive.

Prejudice in favor of proof by experience may end by degrading the testimony of reason and of conscience. We no longer believe in truth, when we only believe in external facts.

A perpetual dispute here presents itself between men of theory and men of practice, a difference as to which taken in its extremes, there is blame on both sides. It would be equally improper not to be willing to descend to facts and not to be willing to rise to principles. What is a principle but a primordial elementary fact, or perhaps a truth of the conscience? I would distrust facts as much as ideas.

We have spoken of the principal uses of experience in proof. It remains for us to make some citations to show under what principal forms proof by experience is presented.

Massillon, intending to prove that common life cannot be

christian life, says that the saints in all ages have been singular men.* Here experience proves a principle.

Saurin would prove to his hearers, that they give but little. He cites the example of the Jews and first christians.† This proves directly a general fact, and by that general fact it establishes a principle.

Proof from experience may alternately be taken from a distance or at hand, in respect to the hearer; in facts foreign or personal to him;‡ in biblical or in profane history; in what is known to him and what is unknown. It may also, sometimes be better to multiply examples, to raise up "a cloud of witness," as Massillon and Saurin prefer to do; and sometimes to restrict ourselves to a single example and treat it amply and thoroughly.

As to the first point, it seems at first view, that there can be no hesitation, and that we must always take examples near to the hearer rather than seek them at a distance. This rule, however, is not to be invariably followed; the one course or the other is to be preferred, according to cases, according to the character of the auditory, according to the object we have in view. Though facts which occur near the hearer, have a special influence upon him, those which are brought from a distance, may nevertheless strike him more powerfully, by showing him that truth remains the same in all times, in all places, and perhaps in all conditions. Moreover, though it is not the object of religion to enlarge our ideas,

* MASSILLON, *Carême, sermon sur le petit nombre des elus.* (Tome i., p. 306, edition Lefèvre.)

† SAURIN, *Sermon sur l'Aumône,* tome ii., p, 27, nouvelle èdition.

‡ SAURIN, *on the agreement of Religion with Politics,* (tome viii., p. 24, nouvelle èdition,) takes an example in facts near his hearers. In the third sermon on the *Delay of Conversion,* (tome i., p. 109, nouvelle edition,) he begins with Scriptural examples, in order thus to arrive at personal examples.

still it has a tendency to do this, which we must not neglect. Many persons, especially in the lower classes, have narrow and false opinions, because they want the terms of comparison. We add, that facts taken from the neighborhood of the hearer, are seldom viewed with advantage; the contemplative faculty has need of a calmness which is often disturbed when it applies itself to objects too near to us. Contemporary literature is more a matter of real life than of pure literature; it takes this character in after-times. He who, meanwhile, would give himself a literary culture, should ascend to the literature of the ancients. Thus, ancient history, precisely because it is ancient, is more instructive than contemporary history. We may apply the same remarks to examples drawn from facts which are more or less personal to the hearers. The danger here consists in occupying the hearer with himself, with his own personality, or that of some other who is on the stage. We should not, on account of this danger, forego manifest advantages; but it becomes a preacher to be very circumspect in such cases, and to treat matters so delicate, with much tact and gravity. As to examples drawn from profane history, we do not see why they should be banished from preaching. Men only are profane, facts are not, and the example of Regulus may certainly be cited with profit in Christian teaching.

Reasoning.—Proof from authority, or from experience, establishes a fact and does nothing more. That fact, in regard to proof by reasoning, is but a point of departure. By reason, we discover another fact involved in the first. The knowledge obtained by reasoning is not without a connection with faith; it rests, at least, on faith in the principles of reason.

Pure reasoning handles ideas and not facts. It is a sort of geometry of intellectual space. This geometry, however, is less certain than the other, the import of signs here being less invariable. Hence the necessity of not coursing entirely through the void, and of descending often to the earth to set our feet on facts. Otherwise, we run the risk of proving too much, and of losing, at length, the sense of reality. At the end of the most sound reasonings, when the reason of the hearer seems to be overcome, something more intimate than logic, rises up within him, and protests against your conclusions.

There are understandings which logic infuriates; these are no longer souls, they are dialectic machinery. Thought also may be stupefied, having connection no longer with sentiment, with conscience, with testimony. We sometimes receive this impression by contemplating those powerful logicians whom we admire and dread. Let us not trust either in the senses or the intelligence; let us trust in the soul.

To return to the preacher, he also is in danger from this quarter; he may arrive by dialectics at impossible, even absurd results. Bourdeloue, in his admirable sermon on *Impurity*, goes too far when he strives to prove that the voluptuous man is in greater darkness than the devils; he ought only to have said that the sinner, enlightened by hell, will suffer more. Thus a modern preacher, who is moreover very distinguished, passes all bounds, when, after showing that all sins are equal, he endeavors further to prove that little sins are even greater than great ones. There is a very great difference between logical dexterity and the sentiment of reality. We may be rigorously dialectic and be wanting in good sense, and Pascal is right in distinguishing, as he has done in two places, between the method of Geometry and that of common sense.

Even when we run no risk of misleading ourselves, we yet may not always attain our whole object. On the one hand, we may have attained the hearer's submission rather than his adherence; have conquered him, rather than converted him into an ally—the true victory ; on the other, the truth, which, in its very substance, should be united to man, become consubstantial with him, remains apart from him.

Reasoning, moreover, when it is too much prolonged, too dialectic, wearies attention, and goes beyond the bounds within which it is commonly obtained. Nevertheless, the province of reasoning is of great extent, first, because there are many things the knowledge of which is to be gained only in this way ; next, because it is necessary to prove what is known and believed, not precisely to make it known and believed, but to give more presence to the proofs of truth. Even in the cases in which reasoning seems superfluous, it may be greatly useful, since its object is not so much to prove what is not yet believed, as to fill the mind with the evidence, and if we may so speak, to multiply the brightness of truth. *

We must then reason, and even abound in reasoning. But this, however true, does not set aside the following rules :

1. To prefer the shortest road in every argument we use.
2. To prefer the most popular arguments. †

* "Let a man susceptible to the power of eloquence, and familiar with the genius of Demosthenes, read again the fourteenth Provincial, the famous letter on homicide. Pascal first encloses his adversaries between corrupt religion and outraged humanity ; he then advances on them with a slow and irresistible progress, descending always from the loftiest principles, supported by all the sacred authorities, and applying the exactness of the severest logic to the demonstration of the most manifest truths. In defeating his enemies he employs, so to speak, a superabundant force ; and it is evident that he holds them so long under the sword of his eloquence, not to confute but to punish them. Every time he completes an argument, the cause is gained ; but he recommences in order to lead his conquered adversaries through all the humiliations of their error." VILLEMAIN.

† "What is the true ground of eloquence, if it is not *commonplace?* When eloquence is combined with high philosophical considerations,

3. To avoid a too formal way of reasoning.

Argumentation may be affirmative or negative, simple or combined, direct or indirect.

1. *Affirmative and negative argumentation.* Affirmative argumentation establishes truth; negative argumentation refutes error.

In general, refutation does not suffice without proof, and has not the force of proof. We are more inclined to refute than to prove, to destroy than to build up. It is more easy, more flattering to self-love, more in accordance with our natural passions.

Every one is eloquent in anger; love, and peace seldom make men eloquent. In the pulpit, affirmative argumentation is of the highest value. In morality and in religion, it is much more important to give assurance of truth, than to refute error. Whence springs the hatred of evil in the christian soul? From the affirmation of good, as every one knows who has had a divine experience of grace. This is what preaching should aim to secure. It is not enough to clear the ground of error, for christian life is not a vacuum, it is a plenum. What Quintilian says of the greater difficulty of refutation, *difficilius est defendere quam accusare*,* is true of pleading, not of the sermon. Nevertheless, we must abound in proof; when we have proved, refutation is already well advanced. Proof should absorb error. Even in christian conversations, we must endeavor rather to ab-

as it is in many modern examples, we are at first tempted to attribute to philosophy the impression we receive from it; but eloquence is something more popular; it is the power of making the primitive chords of the soul (its purely human elements) vibrate within us—it is in this and nothing else, that we acknowledge the orator." VINET, *Chrestomathie française*, tome iii. Reflections à propos du *Discours de Royer Collard sur le projet de loi relatif au sacrilegé.*

* Quintilian, lib. v., cap. xiii.

sorb than refute error, to conquer without being obliged to pursue fugitives. Strictly, he who has proved, has done everything; he is not obliged to refute objections. But though he may maintain his right, *summum jus*, he must not avail himself of it. It is only light that can swallow up darkness; we are to "overcome evil with good." (Romans, xii. 21.) Yes, but we are to condescend to the weaknesses and necessities of our brethren, which are as our own weaknesses and necessities. God, in restoring us to the truth, had to overthrow within us many idols of our heart, of our understanding; he destroyed much, refuted much, before he proved; he disabused us before he showed us his glory; many souls have acquired a taste of the truth through a distaste of earthly things. What God does, we should do also. Proof often needs refutation as a supplement, and even as a complement. It often happens that a mere refutation becomes proof in the soul of the hearer. There are even cases in which refutation suffices, without proof, when the subject permits of *sous-entendre*. Discourse may very properly consist altogether of refutation.*

In refutation, we recommend above all things perfect sincerity. In morality, in prudence, in art, it is a rule. One may experience surprise and a species of fear in anticipation of an objection, which turns into delight when it is refuted. Confidence in the orator is hereby increased. In this respect, Saurin is a model. He has a courage in exposing objections, which tends to produce a powerful impression.† Accordingly, it is important to determine well the import and extent of objections. We are not as strict with ourselves in the pulpit as we ought to be. We are inclined to

* Such is the sermon of *Massillon* sur *le jeune*, and his conversation sur *le Zele pour le salut des ames.* We find striking examples also, in Bourdaloue and Saurin.

† See the first part of the Sermon *sur le Renvoi de la conversion*, tome i., nouvelle édition.

take with some abatement, certain rules which other kinds of eloquence do not allow to be transgressed. The pulpit enjoys a privilege no less hurtful than advantageous; it is, that debate is excluded from it, that replies are not possible or admissible; yet, taking us as we are, we surely have need of them. As there are none to contradict us in the temple, we should prescribe to ourselves the greater rigor in our argumentation. In this respect, too, Saurin is an excellent model. He may even be thought sometimes to carry his rigor to excess.

In all cases in which it seems necessary, we must divide the difficulty. Refutation ordinarily gains by a division of the objection. It is seldom that one reply alone can demolish directly with a single stroke, all parts of the error. Such orators as Bourdaloue and Massillon* have perhaps pursued this method too far, but used with moderation, it is of great advantage in refutation. The hearer sees you conqueror many times in succession; he perceives that there are many errors on the other side, and many truths on yours. We shall always be feeble, if we have no regard to the contradictor which exists in souls. A discussion is necessary in a sermon.

Finally, we must know how to take the offensive, and, if possible, turn the objection into a proof. Prolonging the defensive, enfeebles us; and to defend ourselves to advantage, we must make the attack. Great preachers have always observed this rule. In the error which we decompose or attack, we should find the very germs of truth.†

2. *Simple and combined, (or graduated,) argumentation.*—We do not distinguish here between the purely external forms

* Bourdaloue, second part of the *Sermon sur l'Aumône,* (Edition Lefèvre, tome ii., p. 80,) and Massillon, *Sermon sur la Verité, d'un Avenir.* Edition Lefèvre, tome i., p. 167.

† See the Sermon of Saurin, *sur l'Aumône; et les conférences de* Massillon.

of reasoning, or figures of logic, such as the syllogism, the enthymeme and the dilemma; the syllogism, the ideal form which very rarely appears; the enthymeme, which is the most frequent; the dilemma, the truly oratorical form. The forms we have in view are less external, and affect more the very foundation of thought. After this statement, we distinguish—

(1.) Proof *à priori*, or descending, which, from a given principle, descends to the consequence, which proves the fact from its cause or its nature; and proof, *à posteriori*, or ascending, which, from a known consequence, strives to ascend to the principle, which proves the fact by its effects. I prove *à priori*, that lying is offensive to God, because He is a God of truth; I prove the same *à posteriori*, by the manifestations which God has given of his abhorrence of lying. I prove *à priori*, that covetousness is idolatry, from the very nature of covetousness, and I prove the same *à posteriori*, from the effects of covetousness, which are the same with those of idolatry, properly so-called. I prove *à priori*, that bad companions are hurtful, because whatever is peculiar to them, tends to evil, and I prove the same *à posteriori*, from examples: "God has helped him, for he asked aid from God," or again, "God has helped him, for he has done what he could not have done without God."

(2.) *Analytical* and *synthetical* argumentation. According to the first form I announce the truth I would prove, and I prove it by decomposing it, either in its parts or in its effects; according to the other method, I gradually form the truth from the elements which enter into its composition.

The latter process is scarcely proper in the pulpit. When we have only to put the understanding under a kind of constraint, when we have only to reduce an adversary to silence, this method to which Socrates has given his name, may certainly be employed with great propriety. We remark it in many of our Lord's discourses; but it is interesting to observe, that he uses it rather to confound his unprincipled adversaries than to instruct well-disposed hearers. As far as it is employed with captiousness and subtlety,* it is perfectly adapted to minds destitute of benevolence and sincerity, and that would set themselves against the truth, if it should be presented to them directly; but as thus employed it is not necessary to the preacher. He must not regard his adversaries as unprincipled hearers, as enemies whom he may entangle in skilfully-prepared nets. Their presence in the temple implies, in respect to the greater part, that they are under some other influence than that of malevolence; and those of them who may seem to have this disposition, cannot be discriminated and taken personally apart in the assembly; cannot be confounded since they have made no attack, cannot be reduced to a silence which they have not disturbed. The preacher's design moreover is revealed or betrayed by his text. And after all, these means are not the best for disarming malevolence. We must exhibit confidence even towards those who do not deserve it. Let us add that this method almost necessarily excludes eloquence.

Under these different forms argumentation is simple or elementary, when, with more or less force, it confines itself to prove the truth of one proposition or the falsity of another. The different moral sentiments or effects which may result from proof, indignation, joy, courage, do not thus enter into consideration. But when the proof is complicated or enforced with another element, when the proof is, so to speak, accentuated, becomes more pointed or more steeled, when truth or error, in their own nature impersonal, becomes a personal fact, when the adversary finds himself placed, less between truth and error than between error and the first

* In saying, *Dolus an virtus quis in hoste requirat,* this is not the case. VIRGIL, Æneid, ii. 390.

principles of good sense or of instinct, then the argumentation, which was elementary, becomes *combined* or *graduated;* it includes an element which it could not include without ceasing to be complete. Perhaps it is scarcely anything more than one of its essential elements put into prominence, in relief; a stone cut in order to render it more brilliant.

The first of the forms of combined argumentation is the *reductio ad absurdum*, reduction to the contradictory or the offensive. All reasoning is impliedly a *reductio ad absurdum*, since, if it is just, it must always reduce the hearer to the alternative of either accepting its conclusions or rejecting some truth of certainty and common sense. It would always lead us to this, it would push us to this extremity. The *reductio ad absurdum* becomes a particular form of argumentation, only when supposing the proposition which is denied to be true, we draw from it whatever it contains, that is to say, its object, or its principle, or its consequences. It compels error to refute itself. It employs the swan to cover the eggs of the vulture or the crow. It leaves the tares to grow till the harvest, that we may see from the ear what seed was sown.

A very simple and short method of reducing to absurdity, is to transfer the idea to its more naked expression; that is, avoiding the illusion of words to name the object by its true name; but what is its true name? There may not be agreement as to this; and the error from this means may be very great. "What is a throne?" said Napoleon. "A piece of velvet stretched upon four pieces of wood." The periphrasis which one opposes to the true name, is often the true name. Voltaire makes a quaker to say: "Our God who has commanded us to love our enemies and to suffer without complaint, doubtless does not desire that we should cross the sea in order to engage in butchering our brethren, because red-coated murderers with a cap two feet high, enlist citizens by making a noise on an ass's skin well-stretched."

The whole artifice of the *Persian Letters*, consists in making persons name and describe things, who are not acquainted with conventional and current notions. The pope appears here under the designation of muphti, the monk under that of dervish.

This means, we must see, is scarcely admissible in the pulpit.

The most regular and least objectionable form consists in showing the characteristics of the object, its principles and its consequences. Diogenes made a *reductio ad absurdum* in action, when he cast an unfeathered cock before Plato. It is often only necessary to deprive the cock of his feathers; that is to say, to deprive the object of all the adventitious ideas which have connected themselves with it by degrees from the effects of time; to translate a case with which custom has familiarized us into another, as to which custom has not yet had this influence; to show the perfect identity of that which we repel with that which we accept.*

The second form of combined or graduated argumentation, is the argument *ad hominem*. We may say, indeed, that all arguments are *ad hominem*, or that the argument *ad hominem* is comprised in every argument, in this sense, that we avail ourselves against the hearer of that in which he tacitly at least agrees with us.

But the argument *ad hominem* consists, especially, in making an appeal to something which the person whom we

* Examples of *reductio ad absurdum:*

a. From the character of the object. The discourse of Mirabeau, *sur la banquerote*, tome i., p. 399.

b. From principles or consequences. Cicero, *Pro Milone*, vii. Massillon, *Sermon sur la Verité d'un avenir*, édition Méquignon, tome ii., p. 249; and *Sermon sur le Respect humain*, édit. Méquignon, tome iii., p. 199. Bourdeloue, *Carême* i. ancienne édition, page 149. Pascal, *Pensées*, partie ii., petite edition de Bure, tome ii., p. 17. Lamennais, *Importance de la Rèligion par rapport à Dieu.* (*Chrestomathie*, tome iii., p. 178, troisième édition.)

wish to convince or confute has done or said, in no connection with the discussion. We commonly name many things the argument *ad hominem*, from which it must be distinguished. Thus, referring to a personal reminiscence of the hearer;* creating in the hearer an interest in conformity with the import of our conclusion,† arguing from the contrariety of the hearer's conduct to his doctrine, opposing his opinion to his character. This last refers us to a general and delicate question. Is a doctrine responsible for the character of those who profess and maintain it? It would be absurd to affirm absolutely and in every case, "This man is dishonest, his opinions are of course false." Though it were true that truth itself is adulterated and corrupted in corrupt hearts, it would be not the less contrary to all good logic to condemn an opinion or principle on account of the dishonorable or questionable character of him who professes it. On the contrary, these two things must be separated. We must indeed say, *Timeo Danaos et dona ferentes;* but we must regard the idea and the man, apart from one another. I would say with Mirabeau: "It has been proposed to you to judge of the question, by comparing the character of the persons who hold the affirmative, with that of those who hold the negative. I cannot follow this example."‡

Still, when we are convinced that a doctrine is false, it is very lawful to judge of the tree by its fruits, and to bring it into antecedent suspicion by the life which it produces, or to confirm the evil we have said of it, by the evil which flows from it. All this however is not the argument *ad hominem*. There are two things to which I give this name:

a. Putting the adversary in direct contradiction with the

* See 2 Corinthians, vii. 9–11.

† The "sans dot" of Harpagon.

‡ MIRABEAU, *Discours sur l'exercise du droit de la paix et de la guerre.*

words he has pronounced or the acts he has performed. Understand us well. We should be dishonest in using this means, if we should make an ill use of it. It does not follow from a man's having been of a different opinion formerly, that he is wrong in thinking as he now does. A man is often reproached for making progress, when reproached with inconsistency. Though he does not dissemble the fact of his having changed, we cannot take advantage of it against him. But we may represent a man's words and actions as a testimony which, in other circumstances, he rendered to the truth which he now discards, assuming that then he was better informed, less prejudiced, in better circumstances for judging rightly. We may often thus recall to him an honorable memorial, which encourages and reproves without mortifying him. *

b. Showing the hearer, that an opinion such as he does hold, draws after it necessarily that which he does not hold ; thus seizing, in order to turn it against him, a weapon which he himself has unconsiously and involuntarily furnished. But may we do this, whether we partake or do not partake with him in this opinion ? Or whether we hold or do not hold it in the sense in which he holds it ?

If, when we do not hold it, the use we make of it implies that we do, we assuredly are in the wrong. But then it will be asked, what use may we make in argumentation of an opinion which we neither hold, nor admit to be true ? This :

* Examples: Iphigénie to Agamemnon, "Mon père etc." RACINE, *Iphigenie*, acte iv., scene iv.

Burrhus to Nero: "Ah ! de vos premiers ans etc." RACINE, *Britannicus*, acte iv., scene iii.

CICERO, *Pro Ligario*, Ch. xi. Flavien to Theodosius : "Mais, est-il besoin de rappeler etc." See VILLEMAIN, *Melanges*, tome iii.

PELISSON to Louis XIV. Peroration of the second discourse to the King for M. Fouquet. (See the fragment in the *Chrestomathie française*, tome ii., p. 254, troisième édition.)

to show the dishonesty of the adversary, that his opinion, true or false, would lead to the end to which we bring him, but that he does not fully admit the consequences of his principle, or applies it in a wrong sense, or does not seriously hold his own opinion, and does not allow to it its natural consequences.* As to the use of this means in the pulpit, it may be remarked, that a church possesses few facts or words distinctively peculiar to it, which may be urged against it; human nature is the adversary to be confounded.

Again, the use of this means, everywhere dangerous, is specially so in the pulpit.

We may regard the parable as a form of the argument *ad hominem.*†

3. *Direct and indirect Argumentation.* Argumentation is direct when we draw the proof either from the nature of the object, or from its causes, or from its effects, or finally from experience and authority. We have, until now, had regard to this only. It is indirect or lateral, when we seek some fact which is neither the object itself nor the cause, nor the effect, but which, notwithstanding, cannot be admitted without admitting also the fact which is in question.

The human mind is so formed that it often prefers the reflection of light to light itself, the echo of the voice to the voice. By examining ourselves, we find that in almost all discussions we tend rapidly and imperceptibly towards indirect proof. Man in everything submits more readily to indirect constraint. The final judgment that springs from a syllogism is a kind of judgment by constraint. I do not think we should indulge

* Thus may be explained: Matthew, xii. 27, "If I cast out, etc." Luke, xix. 22, "Those wicked servants, etc." 1 Corinthians, xv. 29, "What then shall they do who are baptized for the dead, if, etc." Acts, xvii. 23, "For as I passed by, etc." and 28, 29, "For to him, etc." John, vii. 22, 23, "Moses commanded you, etc."

† A beautiful example furnished by Bridaine, after that of the prophet Nathan. See MAURY, *Eloquence de la Chaire*, xx.

freely an inclination which is not always without weakness. I think we should accustom the mind to look truth in the face, to seek truth at her own home and not at another's; but it is also important that we see (and we do this peculiarly through indirect or lateral argumentation) from how many directions the light comes to us at the same moment, that all things concur in proving what is true, that truth is connected with everything, that "all things answer to one another." (Proverbs, xvi. 4.) It is to this, as to impressions from surprise, that the peculiar virtue of indirect argumentation is to be ascribed. We add that there are some subjects in which, whether it be from the evidence or too great simplicity of the object, direct argumentation is almost impossible; there are others, on the contrary, in which it is very possible, and much in place.*

If we would see how much the indirect proof is to be preferred before the other on certain subjects, we may compare the two sermons of Saurin and Massillon, on the *Divinity of Jesus Christ.* In the discourse of Massillon the proof of the doctrine is drawn from the lustre of Christ's ministry and the spirit of that ministry, on this ground, that all that lustre is without meaning and a contradiction, and thus, all that spirit falsifies itself, if Jesus Christ is not God. The plan of Saurin is this: 1. Jesus Christ supremely adorable and supremely adored, according to Scripture. 2. Contradiction between the idea and the fact that Jesus Christ is not God, since it is only to God that all the foregoing things are applicable. (This should have been, not a second part, but the conclusion of the first; Saurin moreover has completed it only by an incidental discussion.) 3. Our ideas on this point are conformed perfectly to those of the times, the orthodoxy of which is least to be suspected. For the reasons which I have expressed I think indirect argumentation more oratorical and popular than the other; for the

* As on the subject of the *Recompense des saints.* BOURDALOUE.

same reasons, he who excels in direct argumentation appears to me the greater genius. In some cases no argumentation is so easy as the indirect, and this consideration exalts, in my view, the merit of the orators who excel in direct argumentation, power in which ought to be especially aimed at. Bourdaloue in this kind is distinguished by a *virtuosité*,* by a courage which nothing intimidates.

(1.) Among the forms of indirect argumentation the chief place belongs to *apagogic* argumentation, or argumentation by *ablation*. In this which is the inverse way, or proof by retrenchment, the orator, undertakes to show the nature of one thing by the nature of another which is opposed to it, or by the effects of its absence; as the utility of science from the consequences of ignorance, the beauty of virtue from the deformity of vice, the tranquillity of faith from the perturbations of unbelief. Just as we ascertain the capacity of a vessel alike by filling and by emptying it, and prove addition by subtraction. This method is very natural to the human mind, and very agreeable to the hearers, to whom very often the nature of a thing is best made known by the effects of its absence. And in particular, it may doubtless be said with truth, that nothing makes the majority of men so sensible to the goodness of conduct which is conformed to the law, as a view of conduct which is diametrically opposed to it. It was doubtless this fact which led Massillon, when preaching to ecclesiastics on the necessity of a good example, to dwell chiefly on the consequences of a bad example. He shows in this discourse, that without a good example, all the functions of the priest are unprofitable and are even an occasion of falling and of scandal to the poople whom God has entrusted to him.† Good example, undoubtedly, has positive and appreciable advantages which Massillon might have enumer-

* This is a new word, which I can find in no Lexicon.—Tr.

† MASSILLON, *conferences*, édition Méquignon, tome xiii., p. 2

ated; but he judged correctly, we think, that his auditory would be more impressed by the evil consequences of bad example, which are more manifest and, so to speak, more palpable. It is certain that as *good*, or conformity to law, and happiness, or conformity with interest, are just what should be and what order requires, they are less striking than their contraries, and are very often in our view, but the mere absence of evil and misery; so that *good* which is essentially positive, appears negative to us, and *evil* which is essentially negative, appears positive.

(2.) Next to apagogic argument or argument from ablation, we may name *refutation*, which under another point of view we have already contemplated. This indeed is also a form of indirect argumentation, whether from its constraining the mind by the removal of all objections, to embrace truth, even without knowing it,* as if in despair of the cause; or because refutation, when it is all that it may be, becomes a proof, which perhaps should always have place, when the principle which is alleged is true. We may not be able to resist the offence of the cross without revealing the glory of the cross. When there is no possible medium between two opposed propositions, the exclusion of one establishes the other, and even renders it conspicuous.†

(3.) We name, thirdly, the argument *ex adverso*, which consists in opposing one fact to another contrary fact, which occurred in exactly parallel circumstances. This is not so much an argument as the means of giving more point to an argument. *Quaedam argumenta*, says Quintilian, *ponere satis*

* As examples, we cite the plan of a sermon of Massillon on *le Pardon des offenses.* (Edition Lefèvre, i. 146; and his Sermon sur la Prière, ibid., i. 198.

† See REGUIS, ii. 119; *sur le support du prochain;* BOURDALOUE i. 560, édition Lefèvre, *sur le scandale de la croix;* MANUEL, Sermons, i., *Paul devant Festus;* SAURIN, tome i. 39, et tome i. 107, même sujet.

*non est, adjuvanda sunt.** This is a most powerful means, when the circumstances are strictly parallel, and the comparison of course legitimate. Pascal's fine opposition of the maxims of the Jesuits on homicide to the rules which legal justice follows,† assumes the anterior demonstration of a truth; this opposition, of itself, proves nothing.

We see the same in the following passage from the sermon of Bourdaloue, on the *Scandal of the Cross*, "Behold the marvellous fruits of grace, which this thought has produced in the saints, the miracles of virtue, the heroic conversions, the renunciations of the world, the fervors of penitence, the noble zeal of martyrdom. What produced all this? The view of a Godman and a God sacrificed for the salvation of man. This it was that won their hearts, that filled them with rapture, with transport; and yet, christians, it is this which gives us offence, offence which keeps us in a loose, impure, irregular life, that is to say, in a life in which we do nothing for God, and in which we keep ourselves constantly estranged from Him.‡

Let us hear again Voltaire, in the *Henriade*, when he makes President Potier say—

Infidèles pasteurs, indignes citoyens,
Que vous ressemblez mal à ces premiers chrétiens
Qui, bravant tous les dieux de métal ou de plâtre,
Marchaient sans murmurer sous un maître idolâtre,
Expirant sans se plaindre, et sur les échafauds
Sanglants, percées de coups, bénissaient leurs bourreaux!
Eux seuls étaient Chrétiens, je n'en connais point d'autres.
Ils mouraient pour leurs rois, vous massacrez les vôtres.

---

* QUINTILIAN, lib. v., cap. xii., "Some arguments, it is not enough merely to propose, they are to be set off to advantage."—Tr.

† PASCAL, *Quatorzième Provinciale.*

‡ BOURDALOUE, Edition Lefèvre, tome i., p. 563, col. 1. See, also, MASSILLON, *Avent*, Sermon *sur la Divinité de Jesus Christ*, first part. "Mais ici, mes frères, etc." (Edition Lefèvre, tome i., p. 87.)

Et Dieu, que vous plaignez implacable et jaloux,
S'il aime à se venger, barbares, c'est de vous!*

The contrast is a complete argument, when of the two facts which are opposed, one is authoritative, the citing of which is citing the rule.

With *contrast* we unite *difference*. When the hearer may be inclined to apply to one case the rules of another; when an accidental or accessory resemblance may hinder him from seeing an essential or important difference, and from deciding according to that difference, it is useful, with a view to proof, to make the difference very prominent.

. . . "The glory of his ministry," says Massillon, in the Sermon on *the Divinity of Jesus Christ*, "is the most firm foundation of our faith, the spirit of his ministry is the only rule of our conduct. Now, if he were but a man sent from God, the glory of his ministry would become the certain occasion of our superstition and our idolatry, the spirit of his ministry would be the fatal snare of our innocence. Thus, whether we consider the glory or the spirit of his ministry, the glory of his divinity remains alike and irresistibly established.†

* VOLTAIRE, *La Henriade*, Chant vi.

Unfaithful pastors, worthless citizens,
What likeness do ye bear to those first saints
Who, braving all gods of metal and of plaster,
Meekly submissive to their pagan lords,
Without complaining, yielded up their life,
And on the scaffold, bleeding, pierced with wounds,
God's blessing on their cruel murderers sought.
They, they alone the Christian name deserve,
Others may claim it not. They, for their kings
Poured out their blood, yours you massacre,
And God whom you describe implacable
And jealous, will, if to avenge himself, he purpose,
Make you, barbarians! victims."—Tr.

† Edition Lefèvre, tome i., p. 88, col. 1. See, also, the Sermon, *sur*

It is the same as to *resemblance*, where we would see nothing but difference. Thus Bourdaloue:

"Ah! Christians, permit me to make a reflection here, very painful both to you and myself, but which will seem to you very touching and very edifying. We deplore the fate of the Jews, who, though they had the advantage of seeing Christ born among them and for them, had nevertheless the misery of losing that inestimable benefit, and of being, among all the nations of the earth, the least profited by this happy birth. We commiserate, and while we commiserate, condemn them, but we do not consider that in this very respect their condition, or rather their misery, and ours, are nearly the same. For in what consisted the reprobation of the Jews? In this, that instead of the true Messiah, whom their God had appointed, and who was so essential to them, they imagined another accordant with their gross conceptions and with the desires of their heart; in this, that they despised Him who came to be the deliverer of their souls, and thought only of one from whom they might expect the imaginary restoration of their worldly prosperity; in this, that having confounded the two kinds of salvation, or to speak more properly, having rejected the one, and vainly flattered themselves with the hope of the other, they were at once disappointed as to both, for them there was no redemption." See, says St. Augustine, the source of their ruin: *Temporalia amittere metuerunt, et æterna non cogitaverunt, ac sic utrumque amiserunt.* Now, my dear hearers, is it not identically this which is destroying us every day? For though we are not like the Jews looking for another Messiah, though we adhere to Him whom Heaven has sent us, is it not true (let us confess it to our shame) that judging from our conduct, we are in regard to the Saviour sent of God, in

les Communions indignes, édition Méquignon, tome vi. p. 255, and SAURIN, tome ii., pp. 384, 385, nouvelle édition.

the same blindness in which the Jews were, and in which they remain in regard to the Messiah, whom they look for, and in whom they hope?"*

To conclude, we remark in general, that most persons judge only by comparison, or by the aid of comparison. How far should we accommodate ourselves to this disposition?

4. To this class of arguments belongs that which is called *à fortiori*, or *à majore ad minus*, (argument progressive.) It consists in proving that a thing being true in certain circumstances is more evidently so in others, which have the same influence with the first, and with augmented weight. It is strengthening the conclusion by strengthening the premises:

1. The true Christian is wise;
2. But wisdom includes prudence, or prudence is a part of wisdom;
3. And the whole implies the part;
4. Therefore Christians are prudent.

There is in this argument a surplus, or superabundance; it consists in showing this; it establishes a proof as more than complete, by bringing from far or from near, a fact suited to make this superabundance prominent. It is founded on the simple idea, that the greater includes the less.

This argument has great force provided the difference between the two cases is indeed real, and that there is no essential difference between them of which one may avail himself to annul or impair the conclusion. The orator must also show strongly the difference which is in favor of his conclusion. The two cases should be similar and unequal.

The argument *à fortiori* is, perhaps, of all arguments, that

* BOURDALOUE, Edition Lefèvre, tome i., p. 122, col. 2, *sur la Nativitè de Jesus Christ.* See, also, the sermon *sur la Resurrection de Jesus Christ.* Edition Lefèvre, tome i., p. 453. "Car, pour developper. . . . ."

which orators most prefer. Cicero makes skilful and frequent use of it. Thus, in the discourse *pro lege Manilia :*

"Your forefathers often engaged in war to revenge the insults offered to their merchants and seamen. How then ought you to be fired when you call to mind that in consequence of a single express so many thousand Roman citizens were butchered in one day ? Corinth, the pride and ornament of Greece, was, by your ancestors, doomed to utter destruction because of the insolent behavior of the citizens to their ambassadors ; and will you suffer the tyrant to escape with impunity by whom a Consular Senator of the Roman people was condemned to be bound, scourged and put to death with most cruel torments? Your fathers would not permit the least infringement of their privileges ; and will you tamely overlook the murder of Roman citizens ? These avenged even a verbal insult on the dignity of their ambassador ; and shall the blood of a Roman Senator, shed in the most cruel manner, cry for no vengeance from you ? Beware, citizens, beware, lest as it was glorious for them to transmit so extensive an empire to posterity, your inability to preserve and defend it prove not infamous for you."*

And in the first against Catiline :

"Long since, O Cataline, ought the Consul to have ordered thee for execution, and pointed on thy own head that ruin thou hadst been long meditating against us all. Could that illustrious citizen Publius Scipio, sovereign Pontiff, but invested with no public magistracy, kill Tiberius Gracchus for raising some slight commotion in the commonwealth ; and shall we, Consuls, suffer Catiline to live who aims at laying waste the world with fire and sword ?" †

Let us again hear Mirabeau, in his discourse on the plan of M. Necker : "Well, gentlemen, *you* remember there was a ridiculous excitement at the Palais Royal, a laughable in-

* Duncan's translation. † Duncan's translation.

surrection which never had any importance except in weak imaginations or the perverse designs of certain unprincipled men. You heard, not long since, these furious words : Catiline is at the gates of Rome, and we deliberate ! And certainly there was about us, neither Catiline, nor perils, nor factions, nor Rome. But to day bankruptcy, hideous bankruptcy, is before us ; it threatens to consume you, your property, your honor—and you deliberate !"*

No form of argumentation is more frequent in the Gospel : "If God so clothe the grass of the field which to day is, and to-morrow is cast into the oven, shall he not much more clothe you, O ye of little faith !" (Matthew, xxvi. 30.) "If they have called the master of the house Beelzebub, how much more shall they call them of his household." (Matthew, x. 25.) "If they have done these things in the green tree, what shall be done in the dry ?" (Luke, xxiii. 31.) "The time is come that judgment must begin at the house of God ; and if it first begin at us, what shall the end be of them that obey not the gospel of God ? And if the righteous scarcely be saved, where shall the ungodly and the sinner appear ?" (1 Peter, iv. 17, 18.) "If the word spoken by angels was stedfast, and every transgression and disobedience received a just recompense of reward, how shall we escape if we neglect so great salvation ; which at the first began to be spoken of the Lord, and was confirmed unto us by them that heard him ?" (Hebrews, ii. 2, 3.) "For if the blood of bulls and goats, and the ashes of an heifer sprinkling the unclean, sanctifieth to the purifying of the flesh, how much more shall the blood of Christ, who through the Eternal

* Other examples : SAURIN, tome ii., p, 26, and tome i., p. 89, nouvelle édition ; BOSSUET, *Choix de Sermons*, p. 346 ; BOURDALOUE, *Sermon sur le Jugement dernier*, tome i., p. 13, col. 2, édition Lefèvre ; MASSILLON, tome i., p. 417, tome iv., p. 255, tome xii., p. 244, ancienne édition.

Spirit, offered himself without spot to God, purge your consciences from dead works to serve the living God." (Hebrews, ix. 13, 14.) "See that ye refuse not him that speaketh. For, if they escaped not who refused him that spake on earth, much more shall not we escape, if we turn away from him that speaketh from heaven." (Hebrews, xii. 25.) "He that spared not his own son, but delivered up for us all, how shall he not, with him also, freely give us all things." (Romans, viii. 32.)

5. Argument by *Analogy*. "We reason by analogy," says Condillac, "when we judge of the relation which effects should have to one another from that of their causes; or when we judge of the relation which causes should have to one another from that of their effects."* Reasoning by analogy is as good, as strict, as any other, when the relation between the effects or causes is real; when there is identity and not resemblance. The relation between the two terms of which a metaphor is composed, cannot be the ground of a conclusion. It however has currency both in the world and in the pulpit,† and perhaps more in the latter than in the former, under the usurped name of argument by analogy. It is in itself so difficult to establish real resemblance or essential identity, that argument by analogy is almost always to be accepted with caution; but it is not only to be received with caution, it is wholly illusory when it rests on a metaphorical relation, which is a relation only in appearance. The people have even already testified their distrust in it, by the known proverb, "Comparison is not reason." And yet, how many men, how many preachers are there, who act as if a comparison were a reason! How often is a fortuitous coincidence given and received as proof! Nothing is more to the taste or the fancy of orators who are wanting in logic or con-

* CONDILLAC, Art de Raisonner.

† Buon per la predica! See page 133.

science; it is their chief resource; when these outward resemblances fail them, they are reduced to nothing. "If the lightning had fallen upon low places," says Pascal, "the poets and those who can reason only on things of this nature, would have been destitute of proof."* Nothing is better adapted to deceive superficial and inattentive minds, than those familiar resemblances which express a salient relation, and conceal a greater dissimilitude. It is the favorite weapon of sophistry; it is the snare most frequently set to catch credulity; it is the argument most frequently employed to gain the assent of ignorant and simple men.

One of two things:—either the relation † is only apparent —in which case it is to be used to illustrate, not to prove—its familiar use in the greater part of the parables of the gospel,—or the relation is real between two otherwise different objects, in which case we reason conclusively. We must employ this argument. We cannot dispense with it. In some cases it is almost the only one. The whole form in which our religion is presented, is an analogy. The physical world as a whole, is an analogy of the moral world. Without the aid of analogy, we can neither express nor understand anything. But it is important to be well assured as to relations.‡

* PASCAL, *Pensées*, partie i., art. x., § 18.

† "Analogy ought to be distinguished from direct resemblance, with which it is often confounded. . . . . Analogy being a resemblance of ratios, (*Δόγων ὁμοιότης*,) that should strictly be called an argument from analogy, in which the two things (*viz.:* the one *from* which and the other *to* which we argue) are not necessarily themselves alike, but stand in similar *relations* to some other things; or, in other words, that the common genus which they both fall under, consists in a *relation*." WHATELY'S Rhetoric, seventh edition, London, pp. 90, 91, 92.

‡ "In this kind of argument, one error which is very common, and which is to be sedulously avoided, is that of concluding the *things* in question to be *alike*, because they are *analogous*, to resemble

It is an argument from analogy, (combined with *à fortiori*,) that we find in those words of Jesus Christ, "What man is there of you, whom if his son ask bread will he give him a stone? or if he ask a fish will he give him a serpent? If ye then being evil, know how to give good gifts unto your children, how much more shall your Heavenly Father give good things to them that ask Him?" (Matthews, vii. 9–11.) See, also, Malachi, i. 6–8.

Saint Paul, in our opinion, reasons from analogy, when after stating to the Corinthians this precept of the old law, "Thou shalt not muzzle the ox which treadeth out the corn," he adds, "Doth God take care of oxen?" (the absolute for the relative?) "or saith he it altogether for our sakes?" (1 Corinthians, ix. 9, 10.)

We give another example taken from Pascal: "A man in a dungeon who does not know whether sentence of death has been pronounced against him, and has but one hour to learn what is the fact, and that hour sufficient if he ascertains that the sentence has been passed to procure its restoration, acts unnaturally, if he spends this hour not in informing himself, but in sport and diversion. This is the condition of the persons we speak of with this difference, that the evils with which they are threatened are something beyond the mere loss of life and the transient punishment which awaits the prisoner. Yet they run on without thought to the precipice, after covering their eyes to keep them from seeing it, and deride those who warn them of their danger."* We distin-

each other in themselves, because there is a resemblance in the relations they bear to certain other things, which is manifestly a groundless inference. Another caution—not to consider the resemblance or analogy to extend further, (*i. e.*) to more particulars than it does. WHATELY'S Rhetoric, seventh edition, London, pp. 91, 92.

* PASCAL, *Pensées*, part. ii., art. ii. See, also, XIe. *Provinciale*, p. 263, de l' édition de Didot, 1822; SAURIN, tome i., pages 56 and 90, nouvelle édition; MASSILLON, tome xii., p. 388, édition Méquignon.

guish, in this example, the true elements of identity and resemblance.

6. In conclusion, let us speak of the argument which may be called the argument from *supposition* or *construction*, another form of indirect argumentation. We create, with the hearer's consent, a fact, apart from real and known facts; we make what is called in geometry, *a construction;* we are assisted by this *dotted line*, which we instantly erase, in testing the regularity of the figure which we first traced. We have to show that there is the same relation between the supposed fact and the conclusion we draw from it, that there is between the premises of the reasoning which we institute and the conclusions from these premises. The conclusion which we accept involves that which we reject.

There is always an identical element, a common point between the supposed fact and the real fact. If the identity is not perfect, the argument amounts to nothing.

There are fine examples of this in Cicero:

" Wherefore, if Milo, holding the bloody dagger in his hand, had cried aloud, citizens I beseech you, draw near and attend: I have killed Publius Clodius: with this right hand, with this dagger, I have saved your lives from that fury, which no laws, no government could restrain: to me alone it is owing, that justice, equity, laws, liberty, modesty, and decency have yet a being in Rome; could there be any room for Milo to fear how his country would take it? Who is there now that does not approve and applaud it? Where is the man that does not think and declare it as his opinion, that Milo has done the greatest possible service to his country; that he has spread joy among the inhabitants of Rome, of all Italy, and the whole world; I cannot indeed determine how high the transports of the Roman people may have risen in former times; this present age however, has been witness to many signal victories of the bravest generals; but none of them ever occasioned such real and lasting joy." *

"Form now in your minds, (for our thoughts are free,) form, I say, in your minds the picture of what I shall now describe. Suppose I could persuade you to acquit Milo, on condition that Clodius should revive. Why do your countenances betray those marks of fear? How would he affect you when living, if the bare imagination of him, though he is dead, so powerfully strikes you? What if Pompey himself, a man possessed of that merit and fortune which enables him to effect what no one besides him can; if he, I say, had it in his power either to appoint Clodius's death to be inquired into, or to raise him from the dead, which do you think he would choose? Though from a principle of friendship he might be inclined to raise him from the dead, yet a regard to his country would prevent him. You, therefore, sit as the avengers of that man's death, whom you would not recall to life if you were able; and inquiry is made into his death by a law which would not have passed if it could have brought him to life." †

We find the same form of reasoning in this passage from Voltaire:

CASSIUS.‡
Ecoute: tu connais avec quelle furie
Jadis Catilina menaça sa patrie?

---

* CICERO, *pro Milone*, (Duncan's translation.)

† CICERO, *pro Milone*, (Duncan's translation.)

‡ "CASSIUS.
. . Brutus hear me: thou know'st that erst
The monster Catiline with desperate rage
His country's ruin sought.

BRUTUS.
I do.

CASSIUS.
If, on the day by him assigned to give
The mortal blow to liberty, the traitor,

BRUTUS.

Oui.

CASSIUS.

Si, le même jour que ce grand criminel
Dut à la liberté portér le coup mortel;
Si lorsque le Sénat eut condamné ce traître,
Catilina pour fils t'eut voulu reconnaître,
Entre ce monstre et nous forcé de decider,
Parle: qu'aurais-tu fait?

BRUTUS.

Peux-tu le demander?
Penses-tu qu'un instant ma vertu démentie
Eût mis dans la balance un homme et la patrie

CASSIUS.

Brutus par ce seul mot ton devoir est dictè.*

The supposition or construction, which we here present as a means of argumentation, may become, also, an oratorical figure and one of the greatest boldness.†

By the Senate doomed to death—if he
Thee as his son had wished to recognize,
Forced to decide 'twixt him and us—
Say, what would'st thou have done?

BRUTUS.

How can'st thou ask? Dost thou suppose
That for an instant to my virtue false,
I could in balance put my country and a man?

CASSIUS.

That one word, Brutus, points thee to thy duty."—TR.

* VOLTAIRE, *La mort de César*, acte iii., scene ii. See, also, SAURIN, *sur le prix de l'âme*, tome ii., p. 383, nouvelle édition; BOURDALOUE, *sur la Nativité de Jesus Christ*, tome i., p. 124, col. 1, édition Lefèvre; MANUEL, *sur la Résurrection du fils de la veuve*, premier recueil, p. 22, *et sur Lydie*, deuxième recueil, p. 144.

† See MASSILLON, Carême, *sur le petit nombre des élus;* and l'abbe POULLE, sermon *sur l'Aumône*, tome i., p. 159.

We have enumerated the principal, if not all the forms in which argumentation may be clothed. Experience and authority apart, which in certain cases dispense with argumentation or are an addition or a prelude to it, there are in argumentation, properly so called, proof and refutation, in both, simple analytic and synthetic argument, (too much of finesse in this last,) and combined and enhanced argument, which has place when we introduce a personal element, or when not content with convincing our adversary, we force him into absurdity or odium ; and, in each of these kinds, we have to choose between the direct form, and indirect means. These latter are numerous.

We may proceed in the way of subtraction, of refutation, of contrast, of comparison, of analogy, of supposition, of progression, and each of these forms makes use of some fact, taken from without the sphere of the proper matter of the reasoning, the subject of the argumentation. We may use, by turns, each of these weapons, which taken together form the complete armor, the *panoply* of the orator; but we may also accumulate them on the same subject. It is important to make the attack on many sides, and with many different weapons,

"Le fer, l'onde, le feu, lui declarent la guerre"

for the purpose of reaching different classes of the auditory, and the different parts of the intellectual man, and of showing how great are the resources of the truth.

There is sometimes an advantage in the assemblage of many different arguments.* Only let us not imagine that number may be a substitute for quality. Twenty half-proofs do not make ten proofs. Taken together, they are only one half-proof. One false and questionable reason perhaps does more harm than two decisive proofs do good. The remark

* See MASSILLON, tome iv., pages 24, 25, édition Méquignon.

of Quintilian: *Firmissimis argumentorum singulis instandum; infirmiora congreganda sunt,** is altogether in the insincere spirit of the rhetoric of the ancients, (Aruspices.)

Let us not confound half-proofs, that is to say bad proofs, with *probable evidence.* When we have furnished on a question nothing besides probabilities, we have done something; we repress, by these means, the temerity of contradiction. When we have proofs to advance, probabilities or presumptions happily prepare the way for them; and often by a kind of retroactive effect, proof when administered, gives to presumptions a force which they had not seemed to possess.†

2. *Motives.*

The last end of argumentation is action, or the determination of the will. Now the will is determined only by affection. "All our reasoning," says Pascal, "must resolve itself into yielding to sentiment."‡ We will only what we love; or, at least, we will only because we love.

Always, when the will is to be determined, one of two things is necessary, either we must address an affection already existing, make an appeal to it, excite it by presenting objects to it by which it may be nourished, or create affections which have a just relation to the end we have in view.

But the second case never has place, at least in an absolute sense. We may awaken affections; we do not create them. I say this in reference to good as well as to evil. Propension,§ for this name suits better than affection; propension or

* "If our proofs be strong, let them be proposed and urged separately; if weak, it will be best to collect them into a body."—QUINTILIAN, lib. v., cap. xii.

† See SAURIN, tome iii., p. 265, nouvelle édition. A fine example of compressed and cogent reasoning may be found in Bordaloue's sermon, *sur le Jugement dernier.*

‡ PASCAL, *Pensées*, partie i., art. x., § 4.

§ Or inclination, or susceptibility. The French is *l'attrait,* attraction, by metonomy, the condition, the possibility of being attracted.—*Tr.*

a sense of need exists; if it did not exist, in vain should we evoke it. It is a germ perhaps buried, but not dead. A reprobate is often concealed in an honest man; and this man often needs only circumstances to make him a felon. More than circumstances are necessary to make a natural man a saint. A principle of renovation, out of and above the order of nature, is indispensable. But this extraordinary principle of renovation must have a ground. There must be a soil in the human soul to receive it. If the death of which Saint Paul speaks (Ephesians, ii. 1, 5) were the annihilation of all the sentiments and ideas which have relation to good, it must be as to man an everlasting fact. The germ is overborne, not annihilated.

In all cases, then, we must present to the soul what is suited to attract it, or, as we say, *touch* it. So long as you have only made proof, so long as your proof has only reached the intellect of man, the hearer has not been *touched;* he remains *intact.*

Instead of touching we also say *moving*, *setting in motion.* The simple conviction of the mind *sets nothing into motion.* The soul remains unmoved. The understanding, it is true, is the subject of an impression, has received an impress; but the man, taken as a whole, remains where he was; the point aimed at, however, was to make him change his place. Whatever is suited to make him, in this sense, change his place, is called a *motive.*

As man follows his inclination (*trahit sua quemque cupido*),* and as in our present state, sensible and passing things have very vivid attractions for us, while we are asleep in respect to the things of the unseen state, the result has been, the result always will be, that the will of man is determined by the attractiveness of sensible things and in the direction of

* "Every man is drawn of his own desire." (Epistle of St. James, chapter i. 14.)

those things. Man, of course, is no longer free, not however because he feels an attraction, since, assuredly he must needs feel one, but because that which he feels is from below not from above, because he is attracted not in the properties of his better but of his inferior nature, because he obeys an attraction which is against the promptings of his law, which is God. Now, conformity to the law, is to him liberty.

The liberty of man, who is not an absolute being, consists not in acting without motives, but in acting from good motives. We will present to him only good ones, but then we will present them.

It is a remarkable thing, which shows that all light is not quenched in man, that though he is determined by bad motives, he would fain disguise them to himself. He does not, at least, urge them upon others, above all he does not dare to propose evil explicitly to assembled men, or, to speak more correctly, to present as a motive the pure and simple gratification of lust. Eloquence would not be eloquence, if it did not pretend at least to be in favor of good, if it did not give the appearance of good to the evil which it recommends. It is of course indissolubly connected with the idea of good. Eloquence is detached from its only roots, when it separates itself from justice and truth. Marat, himself, had to pretend that he was defending principle and not interest. Evil is as an azote in which eloquence expires; it expires, likewise, in what may be termed in some sense the too pure or too subtile air of speculation.

Motive, *attraction*, *affection*, the name is of small importance—this is indispensable to the determination of the will, and consequently it is essential to eloquence.

Let us then see what points we may touch; we shall see hereafter how we should touch them. All the motives that we can use as levers may be reduced to these two: *Goodness* and *happiness*. Our reasons will be given hereafter for not excluding the second motive.

In the first motive I distinguish goodness as such, from the author of goodness or of the law. Goodness corresponds to our nature under these different aspects; it is its need, which, in the absence of certain conditions, has insufficient attraction for it; in the presence of these conditions its attraction is all-powerful. We cannot, however, distinguish and separate, absolutely, the author of the law from the law itself. The law cannot be sincerely, fully loved by one who does not love its author. The author of the law is also its object; he is, we may say, the law itself; he is goodness. Duty, properly, has respect to God. The love of God is moral truth itself, and the very principle of life; and the whole gospel is calculated to render us susceptible of this sentiment. Gratitude to God is the substance, the summary of the gospel. "Knowest thou not that the goodness of God leadeth thee to repentance?" (Romans, ii. 4.) We would not however deny or let it be forgotten, that goodness has its reasons in itself, and, though in the absence of the love of God it is in a state of decay, incomplete, and to a certain extent irrational, it is not, nevertheless, chimerical and without a basis, in that isolation.

The sentiment of goodness to which we appeal or which we would excite, has two forms, as an axis has two poles. We distinguish as two correlates, sympathy and antipathy, love and hatred; for to every love a hatred corresponds; to the love of a thing the hatred of its contrary; to the love of goodness, the hatred of evil.

We have here two sources or two characteristics of eloquence. Although we cannot absolutely suppose one of these sentiments without the other, any more than the positive pole without the negative, one of them may have the predominance with one man, or on one occasion, the other with another man, or on another occasion. The bitter eloquence and chagrin of Rousseau answers to one of these sentiments, the happy and triumphal eloquence of Bossuet, rather answers to the other. Indignation is an ingredient of eloquence with which the pulpit cannot dispense. To be good to the wicked is to be wicked. "Lord, do I not hate them that hate thee." (Psalm cxxxiv. 21.) Still, it would be sad to have no love for goodness except hatred of evil. Indignation then must not be permitted to occupy the whole heart; how readily would it turn into wrath! Now, neither in the pulpit, nor elsewhere, does "the wrath of man work the righteousness of God." (James, i. 20.)

I mentioned first *goodness* or duty; afterwards I mentioned *happiness.*

This last motive may be presented by the preacher.

1. To some souls access is easy only on this side, and it is the side on which access to all is the easiest.

2. It is essential to human nature, it is a constituent part of it; it is not in itself evil; if it is the starting point of selfishness, it is also the condition of devotion and of sacrifice; it occupies a place amongst our most disinterested and most generous sentiments.

3. It abounds in that revelation in behalf of which we speak. "I have set before you life and death, blessing and cursing, therefore choose life, that both thou and thy seed may live." (Deuteronomy, xxx. 19.) "For why will ye die, O house of Israel." (Ezekiel, xviii. 31.) The first word in the public preaching of Jesus Christ, is the word *Blessed.* (Matthew, v. 3.) We may say that it is the first word of religion, which is a doctrine of happiness or salvation, as well as of perfection, and of which it is the peculiarity, that it identifies happiness with perfection. In this respect, the two motives which we have distinguished are but one.

Happiness then, in general, may be presented as a motive.

But on this point there are rules not to be disregarded by a Christian preacher.

1. He should give the preference in his addresses to our higher interests,* and have a subsidiary regard to the others. I call those high which are invisible, which are eternal. "If we were called," said a preacher, "to occupy ourselves with your temporal interests,† we would show you the beneficent character of the institution of Sunday.‡"

2. When he presents motives of a less elevated order, of temporal interest, he should do this from the most elevated point of view, less as motives than as indications of the good or evil of an action.§

3. The Christian should employ the motive of interest, only according to its nature. Interest is a motive, not an argument; it bears upon action, not upon belief. We shall here cite Pascal: "I blame them for having made not this choice, but any choice. It is equally wrong to take cross or pile; the true way is not to wager. Nay, but you must wager; you are committed, and not to wager that God is, is wagering that he is not. Which do you choose? Let us see that in which you are least interested, etc.;" and farther on, "What harm will befall you if you take this side? You will become faithful, honest, humble, thankful, kind, sincere, true. You will not, it is true, be given up to impure pleasure, to

* See MASSILLON, *Petit Carême,* Sermon *sur l'Humanite des grands envers le peuple.*

† We are no more called to do this, than was Jesus Christ to interfere as a judge in the disputes of his countrymen. (Luke, xii. 14.)

‡ See MASSILLON, *Petit Carême* Sermon *sur le Respect dû à la religion.* "Mais sire, quand ces motifs, etc."

§ See the sermon of BOURDALOUE on *Impurity,* tome i., p. 287, col. 1, édition Lefèvre: "En effet s'il cesse, etc." All the first part of this discourse realizes our idea by presenting impurity, not yet as a principle of reprobation, (that is the subject of the second part,) but as a sign of reprobation.

ambition, to luxury. But will you have nothing in their place? I affirm that you will be a gainer even in this life, and that every step you shall take in this road, you will see so much of the certainty of gain, and so much of the nothingness of what you lose, that you will confess, at last, that you have wagered for what is certain and infinite, and that to obtain it you have given nothing."*

Let us also hear La Bruyère: "Religion is true, or it is false; if it is only a vain fiction, then, if you please, the good man, the Carthusian friar or solitary, has lost sixty years; he runs no other risk. But if it is founded in truth itself, then to the bad man how dreadful the misery! The idea of the miseries he prepares for himself, overwhelms my imagination; thought is too weak to conceive, words too empty to express them. Even supposing that the world were less assured than it is, as to the truth of religion, there would be no better part for man than virtue,"† or rather, "than to live as if religion were true." Pascal alone is complete.

4. Combine hope and fear; do not appeal to one at the expense of the other. These are the two poles of interest, as love and hatred are the two poles of moral affection. We may not dispense with the influence of fear, (let us think of the terrible condition of a man who fears no longer;) but we must not let it be exclusive; even as we must not dispense with the influence of hatred, though not to the expense of love. Whatever practical advantage fear may have over hope, (fear acts more immediately and universally,) hope is still its superior; it is a principle of action and development; it dilates the soul, which fear rather contracts. The gospel has not said "Now abideth these three, faith, *fear*, and charity,"

* PASCAL, *Pensées*, partie ii., art. iii., § 5.

† LA BRUYÈRE *Caractères*, chap. xvi., *Des esprits forts.* See, also, MASSILLON, sermon *sur la Verité d'un avenir*, tome i., p. 171, édition Lefèvre.

(see 1 Corinthians, xiii. 13.) Fear is not a virtue, since it is the office of perfect love to cast it out, (1 John, iv. 18.) We may say that all our courage is fear, but this is not true of Christian courage; that is a hope.

When we employ fear, we must give it as moral and as generous a character as we can. But we are much mistaken in regard to human nature, when we employ terror under the name of fear. There is nothing moral, nothing noble in terror, it is a sentiment wholly selfish. It is not the same with fear. The evils which we fear may be of such a nature, that the impression we feel at the thought of them is rather adapted to ennoble than debase the soul. The fear which the preacher should excite is that of hell or the second death. But under the name of hell, may we not represent a different thing from those material sufferings, those terrible, but yet vulgar sufferings—the presentiment of eternal separation from God? We frighten our hearers with this mysterious future; but may we not bring the perspective nearer, and make them see and taste hell in the present? This hell, we carry it in us, and find it there. With the judgments of God, we must denounce on ourselves our own judgments. God may pardon us; we believe this, on the faith of the gospel: otherwise we could not believe it, for our conscience is more implacable than God; it cannot pardon us. Yes, although the eyes of God are pure, and our own impure, yet the pardon which it is most difficult to obtain, is our own, and this to many is a source of unbelief. Great orators have shown us how elevation may belong to the element of fear;—the fear of being separated from God. But so long as condemnation proclaimed from without does not resound within, so long as conscience does not sanction it, we are not in the condition which the gospel makes necessary to the reception of grace. We must combine fear with sentiments which expand and melt the soul. See how Bossuet could awaken in the heart at the same time terror and tenderness, in his sermon on *final impenitence.*

"Ah! God is just and equitable, unmerciful man of wealth, you yourself shall come to days of want and distress. Think not that I threaten you with a change of your fortune; events are uncertain, but what I wish to say is not a matter of doubt. It will come at the appointed day, that last sickness, in which, among a great multitude of friends, of physicians, of servants, you will remain without succor, more deserted, more abandoned, than the poor man who is dying on the straw, and who has not a burial garment; for in that fatal sickness what will these friends avail you but to afflict you by their presence; these physicians, but to torment you; these servants, but to run about your mansion in a fruitless hurry. You have need of other friends, other servants; the poor persons whom you have despised are the only ones who can succor you. Why have you not thought in good season of making friends to yourselves, who would now stretch out their arms to you to receive you into everlasting habitations. Ah! if you had assuaged their sorrows, if you had pitied them in their despair, if you had but hearkened to their complaints, your compassions would be your intercessors with God; the blessings they would have given you when you comforted them in their affliction would now shed on you a refreshing dew; the covering you would have given them, as the holy prophet says, (Job, xxxi. 20,) their refreshed bowels, their satisfied hunger, would bless you, their holy angels, as devoted friends, would keep watch around your bed, and night and day these spiritual physicians would hold consultation to find remedies for you. But you have turned away their heart from you, and the prophet Jeremiah presents them to me as themselves condemning you without mercy.

"Here, Sirs, is a great sight. Come see the holy angels in the death-chamber of a wicked rich man. While the physicians consult together on the state of his malady, and his trembling household await the result of the conference, these invisible physicians are consulting about a far worse evil: '*We would have healed Babylon, but she is not healed,*' (Jeremiah, li. 9.) We have even bestowed diligent attention on this cruel rich man; what mollifying ointments, what softening fomentations have we applied to this heart, but it is not softened, its hardness has not been subdued, all has gone contrary to our thoughts, and our remedies have only made the sick man worse. '*Let us leave him, they say, and let us go every one into his own country.*' (Jeremiah, li. 9.) See ye not on his forehead the seal of reprobation? The hardness of his heart has hardened against him the heart of God; the poor have laid their charge against him before the divine tribunal; proofs against him have been instituted in heaven, and though he should give away at his death, all the wealth he can no longer keep, heaven is iron to his prayers, and there is mercy for him no longer. '*For his judgment reacheth unto heaven, and is lifted up even to the skies.*' (Jeremiah, li. 9.) Christians, think whether you would like to die thus forsaken, and if you are horrified by the prospect, hear the cries of mercy that you may not hear the cries of reproach, which the poor will raise against you." *

These are the only springs of motion which the pulpit may touch, and the use of the second we have endeavored to restrict. We do not, with the ancient rhetoricians, give free course to all the passions: We do not say with Quintilian, *Haec pars* (πάθος) *circa iram, odium, metum, invidiam, miserationem, fere tota versatur;* † but in connexion with the generous motives of which we have authorized the use, we

* Bossuet, 2e *Sermon pour le jeudi de la,* 2e *semaine du Carême.*

† Quintilian, lib. vi., ch. ii. "This part, the pathetic, is almost wholly taken up with the passions of anger, hatred, fear, envy, pity." —Tr

indicate certain moral elements which enter into one or the other of the two grand motives above mentioned, or perhaps into both at the same time. We name them apart, because, each of them has something special, *sui generis*, and because it is not easy to say, at least with respect to some of them, to which of these principles they relate.

Self-love. We cannot determine ourselves to truth or duty, by self-love or vanity; but it is impossible not to see that truth is conformed and that error is contrary to the dignity of human nature. Here, in opposition to what we have said above as to the preference to be given to the positive over the negative, it is the negative that we prefer; we prefer exciting ourselves to goodness by the disgrace of being destitute of it rather than by the honor of practising it. When a preacher (and the most of christians may do this) shows how disgraceful is such an action, such conduct, such an opinion, what else does he but rely on the necessity of our esteeming or at least of our not despising ourselves.* It is true that the apostles scarcely appeal to the sentiment of human or personal dignity even under this form. It is not so much ourselves that they urge us to respect as God in us: "Your body is the temple of the Holy spirit," says St. Paul. (1 Corinthians, vi. 19.)

Ridicule. The difficulty is not to excite but to avoid exciting it, for wherever we find the unreasonable, there invariably ridicule may have place. "In truth," says Pascal, "it is honorable to religion to have such unreasonable men for its enemies."† "We must admit," says Boileau, "that God has insensate enemies." But we must not excite ridicule; for it is an impression which shuts the soul to religious emotions.

* See Massillon, sermon *sur la vérité d'un avenir*, tome i., p. 170, édition Lefèvre, and tome ii., p. 239, édition Mèquignon. "Mais je vais encore plus loin, etc."

† Pascal, *Pensées*, partie ii., art. ii.

We must beware of erecting the fear of ridicule into a motive; for men, under the power of it, will no longer avoid evil as evil, but as ridicule; they will no more repent of sin although sin is still a stupidity. We must guard against it, for ridicule attaches itself almost as easily to good as to evil. It is respect for man, nothing else, that ridicule invokes!

Moreover, though ridicule may make us avoid an action, it does not amend the soul. This shows that the pretence of correcting morals (*castigare mores*) by comedy is vain. If the use of ridicule may be admitted in familiar conversation or in a book, it is out of place in an assembly, when grave subjects are treated. Assembled men are susceptible of very diverse impressions, which are not felt in the same degree by a single man. We must beware of proceeding too far, when we use the *reductio ad absurdum.*

Sense of the Beautiful. What is the beautiful in such matters as preaching has to do with? Is it different from the good? Can we at least distinguish it from the good? The good is its ground, and under certain conditions the good becomes the beautiful. Analysis may discover these conditions, which are harmony, unity, grandeur. By making these characters prominent, we may give to the good the form of the beautiful. The preacher may do this; we see not why we should deprive truth and goodness of any one of their advantages; but he must not present the beautiful as a motive, to itself alone, and in itself. The manifest relation of the good to the beautiful has led to great errors, to the idea of the æsthetic culture of the soul, the idea that the development of taste is the best preparation for virtue. So far from this is the truth, that a literary education badly directed, will result in perverting the soul, in misdirecting it, and giving it a factitious nurture. Literary talent is a great snare; in man the sinner, it easily becomes the unrighteous mammon. The preacher is not to regard the subjects which he has to treat, from an essentially æsthetic point of view; there cannot but be danger in doing so.

Sympathetic Affections. The sympathetic affections, which, apart from the reflex idea of duty and the intention of obedience, unite our existence to that of others, of individuals or the community, and, for a moment, dispossess us of ourselves, coincide with the spirit and design of the gospel, and bear testimony to it. God, who put these affections within us, cannot condemn them, they are a law of our nature. We may avail ourselves of them, appeal to them, excite the domestic affections, patriotism, friendship, admiration, gratitude; still, however, giving to them a subordinate position and importance. Whatever of good remains in us since our fall, we must gather up in order to present it in homage to God. Let us cast all into the treasury of God; let everything lose itself in the ocean of his love. By exercising love to creatures, we exercise love to Him.

Of Emotion. Admitting the use of all these motives or means of impression, another question presents itself, Is it proper to excite emotion? And I ask whether it is possible not to do this, especially supposing that we have been able to make use of all the appliances of which we have been speaking? Is the distinction which some would make between moving and exciting emotion, between movement and emotion, a real distinction?

What is an affection but a prolonged emotion, an emotion diffused through the whole life? What is an emotion but an affection excited for the instant? Though we may in a given case, resolve on an action without exciting a present sensible emotion, we can only get the control of a life by exciting an affection, which is to emotion what the whole is to its parts, a tree to its branches, any fact whatever to its various incidents. It is impossible that our affection should not have its distinct exercises, which are emotions.

Affection, without being dormant or languishing, reposes, until something external, a fact or a word, touches and excites it; but this fact, this word, in some sort, rouses it; a particular movement has place in the general movement; this particular movement is emotion.

There is, likewise, a distinction to be made between emotions; some, by their very nature, or by the nature of the affected part, are more vivid, others less so; but I say of both kinds, that the distinct moment in which we make an appeal to them, is a moment when an emotion takes place.

It will be said: show this affection the objects which correspond to it, but do nothing more; give fuel to this flame, but do not blow upon it. These distinctions, which seem real at the first glance, vanish at the second. What then is it that produces emotion, but the act of approximating to the affection the objects which correspond to it? And when you say, "It is one thing to feed the flame, it is another thing to blow upon it," you deceive yourself with the image which you use; or rather, it does not deceive you, this human breath is also fuel for the flame. This breath is something; there is more than a simple disturbance or displacement of the air; breath, in eloquence, is its facts, its reasons. You cannot, without something of the kind, render more vivid for the instant the sense of the present affection. Just as you cannot present to an affection the facts or ideas which correspond to it, without exciting more or less of emotion.

On certain subjects, if we do not move the feelings we are not complete. If we have not done this, we have not said everything. We may appear to be complete; in one sense we may have been so; reason may have been convinced and conscience enlightened, but if we have reached only the speculative powers, if we have not, as far as possible, brought the emotional parts of the soul into contact with their appropriate objects ; if, in a word, we have not moved the feelings, we have stopped in mid-course. Will the hearers do the rest of themselves ? Shall we adopt the false idea that the generality of the hearers will address discourse to themselves which we were unwilling to address to them ? Will our appearing not to be moved, be a means of moving them ? For after all what we are not willing to do, it is necessary they should do ; they must penetrate their own heart with arrows which we throw at a good mark, but not with sufficient force.

If we are not permitted to move the feelings, what shall we say of the example which the writers of the Bible have set us—the most pathethic of all writers,—who did not think that Jesus Christ was fully preached, unless he was "so vividly set forth, that he seemed to be a second time crucified before their eyes." (Galatians, iii. 1.)

Is not the Gospel in itself, independently of the language of its writers, adapted to move feeling, by presenting facts, realities to us, instead of abstract ideas, and by pressing them on our heart ?

We may then, we should address the feelings, but not without rule or measure. Our rhetoric differs from that of the ancients. They might say : "*Dolus, an virtus, quis in hoste requirat.*" *

It is a remarkable thing—the distinction which the Athenians made in this matter, between the bar and the senate. They permitted no appeals to feeling in addresses to the judges of the Areopagus ; in other words, no motive was ever to be presented to them, except the motive, equable always, of justice and of truth. I know not whether the Athenians did not forget that the mind also has its illusions, and that the heart is the dupe of the mind, as well as the mind of the heart.†

* VIRGIL, *Æneid*, ii. 390.

† Louis XVI. and M. Desère.

But be this as it may, the Athenians, out of the Areopagus, abundantly indemnified themselves for this restriction, which they would not have imposed on themselves in judicial affairs, if they had not felt how contrary it was to their nature generally. Passion overflowed in political eloquence, where, since law, as Bossuet says, was no longer acknowledged by the people as reason, but where the will of the people was itself law and reason, the eloquence which, by any means whatsoever, swayed the general will, was always right.

Notwithstanding this, the Greeks did not refrain from maintaining theoretically, that eloquence ought to be devoted to the service of truth, and indeed, that eloquence and truth were essentially united, though in practice they showed little scruple as to the choice of means. The Romans, in practice, were the same, and their theory accorded with their practice. Their rhetoricians plainly authorized everything which was suited to deceive the mind, and to prevail over it, *per fas et nefas*. Their rhetoric does not imperfectly resemble the politics of *the Prince.**

We who do not think it necessary or possible to interdict emotion, give different rules. We are not envious of a triumph obtained by surprise or by violence.

We maintain that emotion should neither replace nor precede proof. The road doubtless would be shorter, for with the people an image is more forcible than an idea. For deciding great questions, passion is more suitable than reasoning.

We must neither multiply nor prolong sudden onsets, especially if they are powerful. *Crebris commotionibus mens obrigescit et est contra naturam, ut quæ summa sunt, diutina sint.*†

* "Deceitful weapons."

Ingenium velox, audacia perdita, sermo
Promptus et Isæo torrentior. (JUVENAL, *Satire* iii.)

† ERASMUS, *Ecclesiastes*, lib. 3, cap. lix.

In the next place, while we are in favor of emotion and even of agitation, we are opposed to perturbation. It is necessary that thought should react, that its action be not suspended. We must reserve space for contemplation. Emotion should not interfere with clearness and precision of ideas. Emotion otherwise would not be legitimate, or would pay no regard to our liberty; it would be passion.

Nothing in the soul is lasting, which has not an idea for its internal support. Nothing of a nature purely passive is lasting. *Nil citius arescit lacryma.*

An idea nourishes, renews emotion, which, left to itself, is dissipated. This consideration has weight, especially in the eloquence of the pulpit, which is not in haste as to the settlement of accounts.

We are mistaken also, if we think that affection will respond to an appeal in proportion to its greater vividness and force. "God is not always in the whirlwind." (1 Kings, xix. 2, 12.)

> Si vis me flere, dolendum est
> Primum ipsi tibi.*

The poet does not say *flendum*, but *dolendum* est. Reserve has a great force. Figuratively and literally too, sometimes, the remark is true, "The more you cry the less will you be heard." It is of more avail in regard to the effect we desire to produce, to *have the appearance of feeling* more than we express, than *that of expressing* more than we feel; and the hearer partakes the more of our emotion, the more he perceives that we are suppressing it.

There is in reserve, moreover, something manly and dignified. The eloquence of the apostles and prophets, though entirely free, is not a violent and convulsive eloquence. We add that nothing approaches nearer to the ridiculous than an

* HORACE, *Art of Poetry*, verse 102.

attempt to be affecting, which is, at the same time, violent and unsuccessful. It may be said:

Segnius irritant animos demissa per aurem;

but we have nothing to do with *irritating* minds.

We may apply to the pathetic or to passion what has been said of ridicule:

Ridiculum acri
Fortius et melius magnas plerumque secat res;†

but we have to do now not with cutting (*secare*) the knot, but untying it. To reason otherwise is to imitate that bad modern art of poetry, condemned by Aristotle two thousand years ago, which would strike hard rather than justly, and confound the understanding rather than touch the soul, and which boasts of this rudeness and exclaims that the art is in good condition.

It will be said, perhaps, that zeal cannot observe these rules, that those whom the voice of the preacher converts, are brands plucked from the fire, that his word is a cry of alarm, and that it is as unreasonable to wish to drown the voice, as it would be to prescribe a certain accent and volume for a man's voice, who, in view of a house in flames, should raise the cry of fire. Very well; but that religion which God made as he pleased, is a religion of thought and a religion of persuasion; it cannot renounce these characteristics without changing its nature; for they are essential to it; one is not a Christian if his religion be not the subject of his thought and of his consent. Now both are incompatible with this violent and boisterous eloquence.

Preachers of the highest order‡ are cited, whose words over-

* Horace, *Art of Poetry*, verse 180.

† Horace, *Satire* x., verses 14, 15.

‡ Wesley, Whitefield.

powered thousands of hearers crowded about them under the vault of heaven, and filled a vast plain with their groans and sighs. I reply, that truth in certain times and with certain persons, has in itself overwhelming force. I reply, that it is not certain that the most numerous and trustworthy conquests of these preachers were among those who were so overwhelmed. I reply finally, that the preacher need not concern himself with symptoms, provided he is conscious to himself of having preached not to the nerves of his hearers, exercising a physical violence upon them, but to their reason, their conscience, and their heart. Moreover, rules are not absolute; we condemn nothing until we have examined it, and we do not undertake to pronounce sentence on exercises of emotion. We only say, let not the exercise of thought be interrupted, and let there be no violation of internal liberty.

As examples of what may be effected apart from the exercise of reason, by an image, a recollection, a gesture, any word or thing, which abruptly and suddenly agitates the imagination or the senses, we cite Mark Antony uncovering, counting the wounds of Cæsar, and the English soldier who was mutilated by the Spaniards, and whose words Mirabeau introduces in this manner: "It is always under the illusion of the passions that political assemblies have decreed war. You are all acquainted with the remark of the sailor which was the occasion of the declaration of the war of England with Spain in 1740: '*When the Spaniards after mutilating me offered me death I commended my soul to God, and the revenge of my wrong to my country.*' This sailor was truly an eloquent man, but the war which he kindled was neither just nor politic; neither the king of England nor his ministers desired it."*

Mirabeau, himself, employed a stroke of this kind in a speech on a proposition to decree that the Catholic religion

* MIRABEAU, *Discours sur le droit de la guerre.*

should never be the religion of the State: "I would observe to him who has spoken before me, that no one doubts that under a reign signalized by the revocation of the edict of Nantes, all kinds of intolerance were consecrated. I will say further, that the remembrance of what despots have done should not be a pattern as to what ought to be done by the representatives of a people who desire to be free. But as historical references are proper on the subject which engages us, let me make one only: Remember, sirs, that from this place, this very tribune in which I am speaking, I see the window of the palace, in which factious men combining temporal interests with the most sacred interests of religion, obtained from the hand of the king of the French, feeble man, the fatal *arquebus* which gave the signal of the massacre of St. Bartholomew."*

We will also recall the example of Gerbier, presenting to the audience the orphans for whom he was pleading.

Without condemning any of the great effects of eloquence, which would be absurd and barbarous, we think we may generally prefer to abrupt effects, an effect which abides, which is more deep than violent, an eloquence little indebted to accidental causes, but penetrating.

We add another rule: We must give preference to the exercise of the most elevated affections. We may draw tears with a blow of the fist. There are generous tears, and there are tears too ready to flow. It is doubtless superfluous to say that we must not speak of our own emotions.

I have spoken of the sentiments which a preacher should endeavor to excite in his auditory. The same are the sentiments with which he himself should be exercised. We have yet, however, to speak of the general and characteristic spirit of christian preaching. It is comprehended in *unction* and *authority*.

* Mirabeau, tome ii., p. 305.

§ 3. *Of Unction.* *

This word, taken in its etymology, and in its primitive acceptation, denotes no special quality of preaching, but rather the grace and the efficacy which are connected with it by the spirit of God ; a kind of seal and sanction which consists less in outward signs than in an impression received by the soul. But as, in ascending to the cause of this effect, we distinguish particularly certain characters, it is to the reunion of these characters that we have given the name of unction. Unction seems to me to be the total character of the Gospel; to be recognized, doubtless, in each of its parts, but especially apprehensible in their assemblage. It is the general savor of Christianity ; it is a gravity accompanied by tenderness, a severity tempered with sweetness, a majesty associated with intimacy ; the true contemperature of the Christian dispensation, in which, according to the Psalmist's expression, "Mercy and truth have met together, righteousness and peace have kissed each other."—Ps. lxxxv. 10. It is so proper a thing to Christianity and to Christian matters, that we scarcely can think of transferring the term to other spheres, and when we meet with it applied to other things than Christian discourse, or Christian actions, we are astonished, and can only regard it as an analogy or a metaphor.

From the fact that the whole modern world has been

* The remarks on unction, promised in the preceding paragraph, are not found in M. Vinet's manuscripts relating to Homiletics. To fill up this chasm, we reproduce here the chapter on Unction in the Pastoral Theology, (pages 212–215, of our translation.) We think ouselves the more authorized to do this, as a very short summary of some of the ideas in this chapter in one of the author's note-books, seems to indicate, that as he was called to occupy himself with the same subject twice, he used the same notes in both courses.—(EDITORS.)

wholly imbued with Christianity, many modern works, which are neither Christian nor even religious, cannot be otherwise marked than by the word *unction ;* while there is no work of antiquity that awakens this idea.

The idea that Maury* gives of unction is no other than that of Christian pathos. The definition of Blair is more distinctly identical with ours. "Gravity and warmth united," according to this author, "form that character of preaching which the French call unction ; the affecting, the penetrating, interesting manner, flowing from a strong sensibility of heart in the preacher to the importance of those truths which he delivers, and an earnest desire that they may make a full impression on the hearts of his hearers."†

M. Dutoit Membrini thinks that, in order to define unction, an intimate and mysterious quality, we must guard against formal definition and analysis. It is by the effects of unction and by analogies that he would explain it, or, to speak better, give us a taste of it:

"Unction is a mild warmth which causes itself to be felt in the powers of the soul. It produces in the spiritual sphere the same effects as the sun in the physical; it enlightens and it warms. It puts light in the soul ; it puts warmth in the heart. It causes us to know and to love ; it fills us with emotion."

I willingly admit that it is a light which warms and a warmth which enlightens; and I would recall on this subject the words of St. John: "The anointing which you have received from him abideth in you, and this anointing teaches you all things."—1 John, ii. 27.

M. Dutoit Membrini continues thus: "Its only source is a regenerate and gracious spirit. It is a gift which exhausts

* MAURY, *Essai sur l'Eloquence de la Chaire* (chap. lxxxiii.) *de l'Onction.*

† BLAIR (Lect. xxix.), *Eloquence of the Pulpit.*

itself and is lost if we do not renew this sacred fire, which we must always keep burning ; that which feeds it is the internal cross, self-denial, prayer and penitence. Unction, in religious subjects, is what in the poets is called *enthusiasm*. Thus unction is the heart and the power of the soul, nourished, kindled, by the sweet influence of grace. It is a soft, delicious, lively, inward, profound, mellifluous feeling.

"Unction, then, is that mild, soft, nourishing, and, at the same time, luminous heat, which illumines the spirit, penetrates the heart, moves it, transports it, and which he who has received it conveys to the souls and the hearts which are prepared to receive it also.

"Unction is felt, is experienced, it cannot be analysed. It makes its impression silently, and without the aid of reflection. It is conveyed in simplicity, and received in the same way by the heart into which the warmth of the preacher passes. Ordinarily, it produces its effect, while as yet the taste of it is not developed in us, without our being able to give a reason to ourselves of what has made the impression. We feel, we experience, we are touched, we can hardly say why.

"We may apply to him who has received it these words of the prophet Isaiah : 'Behold, I will make thee a new sharp threshing instrument having teeth.'—Isaiah, xli. 15. This man makes furrows in hearts."*

From all that has been said, we must not conclude that unction, which has much the same principle as piety, is exactly proportioned to piety. Unction may be very unequal in two preachers, equal in piety ; but it is too closely related to Christianity to be absolutely wanting to truly Christian preaching. Certain obstacles, some natural, others of error or of habit, may do injury to unction, and obstruct, so to

* Dutoit Membrini, *La Philosophie chrêtienne.* Lausanne, 1800, tome i., pages 92 *et seq.*

speak, the passage of this soft and holy oil, which should al ways flow, to lubricate all the articulations of thought, to render all the movements of discourse easy and just, to penetrate, to nourish speech. There is no artificial method of obtaining unction; the oil flows of itself from the olive; the most forcible pressure will not produce a drop from the earth, or from a flint; but there are means, if I may say so, by which we may keep, without unction, even a good basis of piety; or, of dissembling the unction which is in us, and of restraining it from flowing without. There are things incompatible with unction: Such are wit,* analysis too strict, a tone too dictatorial, logic too formal, irony, the use of too secular or too abstract language, a form too literary; finally, a style too compact and too close, for unction supposes abundance, overflow, fluidity, pliableness.

It is the absence, rather than the presence of unction, that gives us its idea. It is from its opposite that we obtain its distinct notion, not, however, that it is but a negative quality; on the contrary, is is the most positive; but positive in the sense of an odor, of a color, of a savor.

But let us not contract the idea of unction by reducing it to an effeminate mildness, a wordy abundance, a weeping pathos. We must not think that we cannot have unction except on the condition of interdicting strictness and consecutiveness in argument, and that boldness of accent, that holy vehemence which certain subjects demand, and without which, in treating them, we should be in fault.

Massillon has unction, as Maury thinks, in a piece which contains nothing but reproaches.† As an example, we cite Bossuet also, in the conclusion of a sermon on *final impenitence.*

* Nevertheless, St. Bernard and Augustin have wit and unction.

† MAURY, *Eloquence de la Chaire* (chap. lxxii.) *de l'Onction.* See MASSILLON, the conclusion of the first part of the sermon, *Sur l'Aumône.*

§ 4. *Of Authority.*

Authority is, in general, the right to be believed or obeyed, the right to require confidence or obedience. But the word *Authority*, denotes also, the consciousness and exercise of this right; and in this sense, we may make authority one of the conditions of preaching, and one of the qualities of a preacher. It is not easy to say how it reveals itself; it is felt however, its absence is felt yet more; but it cannot be decomposed into separate and comprehensive elements. We can scarcely define and commend the sentiment itself, which authority may give to our language and our accent, but if the sentiment exists, the discourse will not fail to be marked with authority, and to put into relief, so to speak, its minutest details.

We cannot say that authority is exclusively appropriate to pulpit discourse. We look for it, it gives us pleasure to perceive it in all public discourse. The orator's confidence in his own word, inspires the auditory with confidence. We like to see a man sensible of what the force of his conviction and the seriousness of his object demands from others. Truth has rights which pass to its representative, its organ. The most modest man should be able to sacrifice his modesty to the dignity of truth, and firmness becomes him when he is speaking in its behalf. But authority is especially essential in a Christian preacher, who speaks on the part of God himself, and who announces the oracles of God. We should offend sincere souls by not putting this seal on our discourse; we should even surprise those who do not believe our gospel. They are not at our point of view, but they well know what it ought to be; if they allow us to be in earnest, they allow us at the same time to speak with authority, and by addressing them in any other tone than that of authority, we succeed only in scandalizing and estranging them the more.

We speak of true authority, that which rests entirely on

conviction and zeal, and through which humility and charity shine, as through a pure and transparent medium. Every one readily distinguishes it from that magisterial stateliness, that studied importance, to which ministers who have the spirit of their order rather than the spirit of the gospel, are necessarily exposed, from their holding an officially protected position, and from their being accustomed to speak without contradiction or interruption. If the Prince de Vendôme had heard only ministers of this class, one might excuse him for replying to Louis XIV., who urged him to go to church: "Sire, I cannot go to hear a man who says whatever he pleases, and to whom no one has the liberty of replying." For the circumstance of speaking alone, and of speaking without fearing a reply, only gives offence when it is made offensive. In itself it is not unacceptable, but we must acknowledge that arrogance is doubly repulsive in a man who knows too well that he is not to be replied to.

The accent of true authority, on the contrary, is welcome to almost every one. We are prepossessed in favor of men who, in this world of uncertainty and perplexity, express themselves on a grave subject with confidence and command. It is, indeed, what first strikes us in an orator, and what conciliates attention to him, especially when it is seen that he draws all his authority from his message and not from himself, and that he is as modest as he is assured. What was it that astonished the Jewish people in the doctrine of Jesus Christ? Was it that doctrine itself? It was chiefly the authority with which Jesus Christ expressed it. "For he taught them," says Saint Matthew, (vii. 28, 29,) "as one having authority, and not as the Scribes."

Authority doubtless became Jesus Christ, but it also becomes the truth; authority is inherent in truth; and those who, in the name of Jesus Christ, declare to the world that truth which regenerates and saves, have the right, or rather, are under obligation to speak it in the same accent with himself. If the servants are not greater than their master, neither are they in a certain sense less than their master; the truth which they bring to the world, is not less truth in their mouth than in his. It does not become them to speak as the scribes, for they are not seeking by a thousand subtile windings, to introduce their own inventions into the minds of men; they have a sovereign message to deliver; they are to speak as ambassadors of a king, whom they represent. Their person is nothing, their message is the whole; and not for their person, but for their message, do they claim respect; but they would be as culpable not to demand this respect for the divine thought of which they are the depositaries, as they would be foolish and ridiculous to demand it for their own thoughts.

Saint Paul, accordingly, fears not to enjoin on Titus, and doubtless on all ministers of the gospel, "to exhort and reprove with all authority." (Titus, ii. 15.) An injunction which must seem remarkable, when we remember that it came from him who of all men, perhaps, had most respect for the liberty of the human conscience, who most rigidly refrained from controlling the faith of his disciples, who most carefully avoided identifying his counsel with commands, and who has most strenuously insisted that the obedience of the faithful should be a reasonable or rational obedience. He is not inconsistent with himself. It is the duty of some to examine before believing; it is the duty of others to assert boldly what they believe. This boldness, this dignity, this gravity, in a word this authority, does not in the slightest degree touch liberty; it only warns conscience and gives it the alarm. And preaching interferes with liberty only when it disturbs the soul and overwhelms it with delusions, and when it takes advantage from the noise and tumult it has excited, to force from us an assent which we never would have given it, in an attentive, tender, but sedate frame of mind.

We are obliged to admit that the accent of authority is somewhat defective in the preaching of our times, and that comparing preachers of the same age with one another, the Catholics appear to have the advantage in the respect which we are considering. Beginning with the Catholics we grant that authority, in a peculiar sense, being the mother-idea and the fundamental characteristic of the Catholic institution, it is not surprising that it reproduces itself everywhere, and that the minister having not only individual faith in the religion which he preaches, but belonging to a body which interprets, and to say the whole perpetuates revelation, addresses his auditory, in one sense, from a greater height, which the Protestant preacher cannot occupy. It is true that he preaches, and so reasons, discusses, examines as well as the Protestant minister; but all these acts which imply similarity of position, are interpenetrated by a sense of sovereignty in matters of faith, which belongs to no other system. The subjects themselves, the form, the tone of the discussion, announce the Catholic priest; and when the priest and the minister maintain the same cause, the one pleads it as a lawyer the other as an attorney-general.

Now, without leaving the reformed church, if we inquire as to the difference in regard to authority, between our times and times more ancient, we find the explanation not in a feebleness of conviction on the part of ministers, but in a circumstance of another nature; and perhaps by looking closely at the matter we shall find that authority appears to have diminished, only because it had been exaggerated; or that the cords, if we may so speak, appear relaxed at present only because they had been drawn too tight. With the authority of conviction and of internal vocation which is the whole, there was unconsciously mingled the authority of position or of external vocation; and perhaps the latter had too great a share in the assurance and loftiness of tone in preaching.

There was not then more of true faith and less of real unbelief than there is with us; but unbelief declared itself less, and even less knew itself; unbelief was not then driven by circumstances to the necessity of declaring or even of examining itself; among those who on this point understood themselves and would no longer be deceived, the greater part, whether from prudence or policy, were silent; those who divulged their infidelity were few in number, and were blamed by those who agreed with them in opinion.

In the fiction of law, or to speak more correctly, in the common prejudgment, every one was a believer. The flocks remained in appearance entire and compact, the church was very much incorporated with the political institution, faith was always and with good reason taken for granted, the clergy were the quiet possessors of a strong position, and of privileges, for the defence of which some, I think, had made few sacrifices, but against which, on the other hand, others had made few efforts. I seriously believe that the change which has supervened, and which many deplore, is a divine blessing; and that if unbelief which was formerly unknown is now acknowledged, if opposition which was concealed is now discovered and declared, there has been in this nothing but progress. At first there appears to be an increase of infidelity; a more attentive examination discovers, in what has taken place, only an increase of sincerity and frankness; those who by the aid of carefully-maintained vagueness, and carefully-avoided discussions, supposed themselves and were generally admitted to be believers, have been forced to take account of themselves, and to render account of themselves to others. And on the other hand, those who have continued to believe and profess faith, believe in good earnest and profess to some purpose. Say and do as we will, there is a sort of disbanding of that compact majority which was called the Church; all kinds of causes have concurred to produce this state of things which is every day becoming more manifest and more flagrant. Ministers long since might have seen that their work was becoming more and more like that of missionaries, and that though nominally at the head of a church, they have scarcely a nucleus left, and are really called to gather and constitute a church. This state of things is essentially the same with that under which they have long lived, without knowing the fact; their real task was formerly what it now appears to have become; the difference is a constantly-increasing light as to positions and relations. But what should hence result in respect to authority. If we speak of a genuine authority, nothing, or rather a real advantage. Conventional authority is gone; we must cast ourselves on the other, that which every interpreter of truth, under the force of truth, may display. It is true that we can rely no longer on the implicit and silent assent of a flock; that is to say, we have one illusion less to remove; but we may always rely on the force of truth and the promises of God. It is true that the sheep no longer come to us, but that we have to go and even to run after the sheep. But did the apostles, who acknowledged that it was the object of their ministry to beseech men to be reconciled to God, (2 Corinthians, v. 20,) exhort with less authority on that account? (Titus, ii. 15.) Is the pastor less a pastor when he runs after the sheep, than when he feeds them with his hand in the fold from which they do not think of departing? This pursuit of the wandering sheep, which should always be the essence of our ministry, is more evidently so than ever; and if in this pursuit, the direction, the deviation, the length of which seem to be determined by the sheep themselves, we appear to be dependent on them, if through hills and valleys, brambles and ravines, that is to say, through all the paths in which passion and prejudice, knowledge and ignorance, levity or sophistry, may lead a soul astray from the knowledge of the truth, we are obliged to pant after them and patiently accommodate our course to their disorderly course, if each epoch by renewing the forms of error, constrains us to renew the forms of truth, what is there in this charitable condescension to take away the character of that authority with which preaching should always be marked? What! will charity take away anything from authority? Does authority consist and appear in always pertinaciously speaking the same language and maintaining the same formulas? And have the infinite condescensions of the divine charity ever debased, have they not rather embellished and softened the holy majesty of God which the Bible has revealed to us?

We must, however, confess that preaching in becoming more definitely an entreaty or a contest, has lost, with some, a part of the character of calm and serene majesty, which, in the apostles and especially in their master, was so admirably united with the holy vehemence of charity. Perhaps, also, dogmatic theology and the too minute exactness of doctrinal distinctions, have interfered with simplicity and dignity — the traits in which authority loves to appear. We must avoid these impediments, and, without affectation, without studious effort, by the mere spirit of our calling, acquire a manner, at the same time commanding and encouraging, which all our hearers, without exception, require in our preaching.

In regard to authority, I think we generally remain below what is legitimate, possible, necessary. The boldness and freedom of the prophets are not enough apparent in our discourses. We fight with mock arms as in a tournament, we forget that a serious combat demands sharpened steel, and that the semblance of a battle gives only the semblance of victory. If we had a livelier compassion for our people, if we had a deeper sense of our responsibility, in short, if we had a higher and more solemn ideal of our calling, we should be above vain considerations, and certain compliances, which, to say the truth, do not become us. I admit that this, perhaps, is not the idea, which, in the present day, is formed of the ministry ; but should we conform ourselves to such an idea, or reform ourselves according to it ? If the maxims of the world on this subject are the measure of our liberty, there is no reason why we should not descend lower and lower in our complaisance ; if, on the contrary, we claim all the liberty which Christianity allows us to claim ; if instead of suffering our ministry to be encroached upon, we demand for it all the authority which belongs to it, there is every reason to think that the world, though surprised at first, will yield and accommodate itself to us. It loves courage and independence ; it is strong only against the feeble, it is our timidity that produces its boldness. Everywhere and always, provided we follow truth with charity, we may make our ministry what we desire it to be. But whether acceptable or not it must have its proper character.

In regard to authority, character and position may have some influence. One orator has naturally more authority than another. One church encourages the tone of authority more than another. But before everything this accent in preaching the Gospel, is essential.

There is a difference as to principle between apostolic authority and a certain natural boldness, which, however, is not inconsistent with the other, but may very properly be associated with it. We may speak with authority, and this authority may be deeply felt, in great humility, and even in great inward humiliation, in great sadness of heart. He who trembles in the presence of God, is not on that account the less bold in the presence of men ; and his very confusion gives honor to God. Whatever may be his natural character or his external position, whether he have little or much talent, little or much understanding, I believe that under certain conditions which I shall enumerate, a minister may preach with much authority. The conditions are these :

1. That he speak in the name of God, and as to the things of God, have no wish to know anything, except what he has learnt from God himself. Our authority, as to its principle, is in our submission, and our authority over others is proportional to the authority of the divine Word over ourselves; we press upon them, if I dare speak thus, with all the weight with which the truth presses upon us. Here appears, at the same time, the apparent disadvantage and the real advantage of the position of the preacher when compared with that of any other orator.

The profane orator is master of his own thought; he modifies it only by itself; that the contrast may appear more striking, let us put him on the same stage with the evangelical preacher—that of morality and religion. He draws his principles from his own fund, that is to say, from his reason and his moral sense; he connects with them, according to the laws of logic, their consequences and bearings; no foreign force has broken under his feet the first round of the ladder, or removed the last; his course is free over the entire ladder, master alike of his point of departure, and of his conclusions. Reason and conscience may, it is very true, pass for authorities, but they are authorities we like to recognize, which, born and developed with us, are a part of ourselves; to which we at once adhere, by which alone we take cognizance of our own existence, and which, from their very nature, are perfectly exempt from the more or less arbitrary character which is inherent in all other authority. The same, at least we suppose so, in all thinking individuals, they ought to conciliate or subject them to us; and as all the means drawn from this source have the appearance of being at the same time ours and every one's, we have, in case of victory, the satisfaction of feeling that we are conquerors, while they, whom we have persuaded, have on that account no impression of having been conquered. An agreeable position for both parties, but very different from that in which evangelical eloquence places respectively the preacher and his auditory. The Christian minister unquestionably has much to do with reason and conscience; aided by these, he closes all the outlets through which souls would escape from the circle he would have them enter; since, when once in this enclosure, reason and conscience will retain, will fix, will establish them in it, will, in short, make them say, "It is good for us to be here, let us make tabernacles." (Matthew, xvii. 4.) So that he does absolutely nothing without conscience and reason. But these faculties accept, they do not create the truth; the truth is given; given as a sovereign fact, given as a divine thought, not as a deduction of our understanding; given as a fact which our faculties should explore, should employ, but which they would never have discovered. In a word, reason and conscience are the touchstones of truth, and not as in other spheres the very source of truth.

Is it not an unpleasant thing to a preacher, when he is always obliged to recognize an external authority, an authority which is not in him, which is not his? Yes, very unpleasant; if he would chaffer with this authority, to bend it, it is inflexible; if to corrupt it, it is incorruptible! Very unpleasant, as long as he labors to make it speak what every one wishes to hear, to naturalize the supernatural, to translate the untranslatable. But from the moment that he submits to it, that he is prepared to think human reason fallible and the divine reason infallible, then, walking no longer with one foot on the sand and the other on the rock, placing both feet on the true foundation, that which appeared to be a disadvantage becomes an advantage and a force. Then, after the example of Jesus Christ, he teaches with authority and no longer as the scribes, (Matthew, vii. 29;) he no longer looks to himself but to God; he no longer opposes man to man, but the majesty of the divine wisdom to the countless vacillations of human wisdom; divested of all personal authority, he is clothed with an authority more elevated, and the more he is abased as a man, the more is he exalted as a minister. But, what is important to be observed, he speaks with faith. Ponder this well. The lawyer, the panegyrist, the statesman may speak with faith; a firm assurance, a vivid conviction, is not naturally beyond their reach; but in speaking of morality and religion, faith is scarcely possible in ordinary and natural circumstances; there are few things in this class of ideas which one can maintain with entire assurance, and teach with sufficient authority; the spirit of secular analysis has so pulverized opinions, has left so few beliefs standing! So small is the advantage to be drawn from reasoning, in re-establishing the moral world and natural religion! Happy, then, he who has received from the hand of God a solution which earth was unable to give; an arbitrary solution, but which must needs be arbitrary, since fact has proved that reason cannot find a natural one. Happy he who has found it! he has something to give to souls; and in his humble reliance on revealed truth, he is really more independent, is more in the ascendant, than the preacher who would trust only in himself, and who is constantly surprised that he does not trust in himself.

We cannot forbear adding that the privilege exclusively assured to the preacher of occupying the auditory by himself, of having to combat only silent adversaries, would be an exorbitant and absurd privilege, if the preacher be not regarded as speaking in the name of God, and as repeating the oracles of inspired wisdom, in his developments and applications.

2. The preacher may preach with much authority, if to

the authority of God's testimony he unites that which springs from experience, since, in the plan of christianity, external truth is designed to become internal truth, revelation an experience, and since, in a certain sense, every man who preaches the gospel may say with the apostles: "That which we have heard, which we have seen with our eyes, which we have looked upon, and our hands have handled of the word of life . . . that declare we unto you." (1 John, i. 1–3.)

3. A third thing necessary to preach with authority: When the external life of the preacher is sufficiently conformed to his preaching to hinder his words from being put to the blush by his actions, and to leave it in no one's power to oppose him to himself. His character now deposes in his favor.

4. Fourth condition. When the more sensible he is of the excellency of his mission, the more he feels his own vileness; when he is seen to be the first to bow his shoulder to the burden he puts upon others; when he conceals himself behind his mission, when he puts himself forward only because it has become necessary, when he shows himself only that he may distinctly unite with his hearers in self-humiliation; when he separates himself from them neither in his thoughts nor words, and when it resounds through all his discourse, that he regards himself as the chief of sinners; in a word, when the authority which he displays, is deprived of every personal characteristic, when it is wholly relative to the object of his mission, wholly imbued and stamped with the sentiment which led Saint Paul to say: "Woe is unto me, if I preach not the gospel!" (1 Corinthians, ix. 16.)

5. Fifth condition. When in the pulpit, God gives him grace to forget himself, and frees him from the wretched perturbations of vanity. For, when the servant of the Most High becomes, through vanity, the servant of men; when at the very moment he announces to them the counsels of God, he is preoccupied with the desire of their approbation; when

he seeks solidity, pathos, unction, authority itself, from the secret desire of appearing to preach with solidity, pathos, unction and authority, then descending from the tribunal to the prisoner's stool, and an entire stranger to that noble independence which Saint Paul expresses in the words: "It is a light thing with me to be judged of you," (1 Corinthians, iv. 3,) he will in vain affect the tone of authority, he will not find it. The man who is overawed by men, was not made to inspire them with awe; he who trembles before them will not make them tremble; and if Peter when pronouncing his first sermon, his trial sermon, if you please, had been pre-occupied with what concerned himself, and with the judgment of his auditors, he would not have heard the conscience-stricken multitude say at the end of his discourse, "Men and brethren what shall we do?" (Acts, ii. 37.)

6. Finally, to preach with authority, the preacher must give evidence that he loves those over whom his word has command.

Reprehension. Saint Paul would have Timothy not only exhort, but *rebuke* with all authority. We do not speak here of individual or private reprehension, but of that which is given in public preaching. In some respects it is more easy than the other, in other respects it is less. If pulpit reprehension is more easy, because being addressed to all collectively, and leaving each one to do his own part, it does not so much irritate individual sensitiveness, on the other hand, the publicity, the solemnity, the small space which is at his disposal in preaching, makes this part of the preacher's work delicate and perilous. He cannot, as in a private interview, avail himself of interlocution, by which he learns the nature and extent of the impressions he produces, and is led to modify, to explain, and to shade his thoughts as he may find necessary, in a word, to adjust his discourse, not only to the individual character of the person to whom he speaks, but to all the successive movements of his soul. Collective reprehension, as it must always confine itself to a certain medium, which would be false if it included the representation of any individual's personal state, is always in danger of being feeble or exaggerated, and is with great difficulty hindered from being vague and arbitrary. And, meanwhile, the preacher cannot be exempted, cannot be permitted to withdraw himself from this thorny undertaking by reproving the vices or faults which are common to his own and other parishes, and which are chargeable to humanity in general. A true pastor knows his flock, and cannot keep silence as to the particular evils of that flock. We do not see why a man authorized to ascend the pulpit in a certain locality called a parish, a man set to defend the morality of a people, may not do what a private person does with entire propriety, what writers and orators of all times have done, whose zeal held the place of a commission. Only let me say, that independently of the counsels and suggestions of prudence and discretion given by christianity, the solemnity of temples, the very authority with which the pastor is clothed, his official position, his privilege also of speaking without being liable to contradiction or interruption, imperatively require of him the most severe thoughtfulness as to his words. What is public preaching but the last alternative of individual preaching, which alone is thoroughly direct and penetrating? Of what use is public preaching if it may not, to a certain extent, individualize each one of those who hear it? And why, while attacking evils less general than those which present themselves to an observer of general humanity, should it not avail itself of all possible means of rendering itself direct?

Admitting, then, that a good christian discourse must be useful and applicable out of the parish for which it was made, since all preaching for substance, relates to the fundamental traits of human nature, I think it ought be required that each pastor's preaching should have the unquestionable stamp of the place and circumstances in which he exercises his ministry. It is true that this kind of individuality in preaching has its local distinctiveness not only in the part of our discourse which we give to reprehension, and that in all the parts of an attentive and thoughtful minister's preaching the parish is reflected; but if he fully understands and accepts his position, if his parish is in his view a family of which he is the spiritual father, if he knows what is called the divine prerogative of the ministry, he will, with a noble freedom, reprove this parish for the particular evil which it cherishes, or favors, or tolerates. We are not to inquire whether this freedom will be favorably regarded, whether it will surprise, whether it will appear excessive. Is it so? is the question. The public, perhaps, do not regard the ministry as having this prerogative; but the fault, perhaps, is ours, and let us be assured that what is just and according to the nature of things, is always approved in the end. Men seldom will refuse us what we do not refuse ourselves; to him who hath shall be given; and we most frequently do wrong in complaining that we are not free, since to be free, we have only to will to be free. The barriers we see about us are very often the effect of an optical illusion. Let us advance as if they were not there, and we shall find that they are not. The whole depends on the point of view from which we contemplate the ministry. The form is not prescribed; the spirit alone is immutable, and it is this spirit of which we must obtain a just and complete idea.

There is a singular fact which we must bring into more notice. The people, because it is their custom, think well of having their ways examined into particularly, and sin called by its proper name, as often at least as one day in the year.* On that day the ministers have their freedom of speech, and they make a good use of it; but, frankly, is not what is good to be spoken, good to be repeated? And if it is important to each individual to be brought truly to repentance, to know his particular sins or the individual form of his misery, is it unprofitable to a people that their sin should be declared to them, that they may know where their evil, their danger lies, and how to direct their measures of reform?

Notwithstanding the difficulties connected with direct reprehension, we cannot think that the preacher should be exempted from it; we believe that it is a part of his office; but we can sanction or recommend it only on the following conditions:

Let the preacher, before he exercises it, be well acquainted with his parish, and let them also be well acquainted with him.

Let him feel assured that he has the esteem, the affection, and the confidence of his parish.

Let the evil be evident, general, serious, and such as calls for immediate repression.

I add in general, though not absolutely, that this office will be more appropriately performed by a preacher who, to the authority given him by knowledge, conviction, an exemplary life, and his mission itself, unites the authority of age.

I give here some rules which I think the preacher should carefully observe in his censures. The first: To avoid every kind and every appearance of personality; I do not say, to avoid every intention of being personal; that need not be said; I do not even say, to avoid what might lead his hearers to make some personal and malignant application of his words; that would be labor lost; I mean, that he must so speak, that no one may, with any appearance of reason, accuse him of having had some one in view, whether in or out of the auditory. He must, of course, endeavor to be

* Alluding to the character of the preaching on the annual fast which is celebrated in the Swiss Churches.

incisive and penetrating, without having recourse to the convenient and frequent form of the portrait. This negative mode is not impracticable; but the rule it refers to is not so easy to be followed as we may think, even though one has the greatest innocence of intention. It is difficult, perhaps impossible, to avoid finding about us some living type of the vice which we wish to paint or censure. The most ideal creations of the painter have had some individual model either to start from or rest upon. It is singular, that in drawing from the individual, one is sure of rendering well the species or the genus. There is perhaps no preacher who, while occupied on some one of the moral miseries of humanity, has not had before him, in distant view, during the whole of his labor, some figure well known to him. Unconsciously to himself, some one is always the subject from whom he forms the autopsy of the species; some one whom he does not name, whom, perhaps, he does not suppose he was thinking of more than another, has been the scape-goat of the reprehension. When it has been thus, let us carefully efface all signs which may be too distinctive, let us conceal the vicious man, the sinner, and let only the vice, the sin, remain.

The censure of certain classes or certain orders of society, may be chargeable with personality. Our ministry, which should always tend to harmony and union, ought to guard against signalizing one class to the hatred and contempt of the other classes. There may have been times and circumstances in which this rule should not have been followed. Thus Saint James reproached certain christians with their worldly compliances, and their obsequiousness to the rich by whom they were oppressed. I admit, indeed, that as certain vices spring from certain positions, it is impossible to speak of the vices without speaking of the positions which produce them; it is impossible to speak of the injustice of some without speaking of the sufferings of others. But christian ministers, aided by the example and the spirit of their adorable master, who did not hesitate, explicitly and publicly to address classes, whom he excited, not some against others, but all against himself, have been able to succeed admirably in reconciling frankness with prudence. The christian spirit, in its stern frankness, has never propagated hatred nor kindled resentments. Simplicity very often does the office of prudence, but it does not also affect to despise prudence. I think it must be only at the last extremity and under the impulse of the most powerful motives that a christian minister would permit, or rather force himself to speak like Père Bridaine in this celebrated and often cited exordium :

"In view of an auditory so new to me, it seems, my brethren, that I ought not to open my mouth, except to ask your indulgence to a poor missionary, destitute of all the talents which you require of one who comes to speak to you of your salvation. I have to-day, however, a very different sentiment, and if I feel humbled, yet think not that I am subject to the miserable agitations of vanity, as if I were accustomed to preach myself. God forbid that a minister of Heaven should ever think that he needs to excuse himself to you. For whoever you may be, in the judgment of God you are all sinners like myself. It is then only before your God and mine that I am constrained at this moment to smite upon my breast. Until now I have proclaimed the judgments of the Most High in temples covered with thatch. I have preached the austerities of penitence to unfortunate persons for the most part destitute of bread. I have announced the terrors of my religion to the good inhabitants of the country. What have I done? Miserable man, I have made sad the poor, the best friends of my God. I have filled with fear and sorrow, simple and faithful souls whom I ought to have pitied and consoled! It is here, where I see before me the great, the rich, the oppressors of suffering humanity, or daring and hardened sinners; ah! it is here alone, amidst so many scandals, that the holy word should be sounded in all the force of its thunder, and that I should place with myself in this pulpit, on the one side death which threatens you, and on the other my great God who is to judge you all. Already, at this moment, I hold your sentence in my hand. Tremble then in my presence, ye proud and scornful men who hear me. The ungrateful abuse of all the forms of grace, the necessity of salvation, the certainty of death, the uncertainty of that hour to you so dreadful, final impenitence, the last judgment, the small number of the elect, hell, and above all eternity! eternity! these are the subjects on which I come to discourse, and which doubtless I should have reserved for you alone. Ah! what need have I of your commendation, who would perhaps condemn me without saving yourselves. God is about to move you, while his unworthy servant addresses you; for I have long had experience of his mercies. It is himself, it is he alone, who for a few moments is about to stir your conscience to its depths. Smitten with sudden alarm, filled with horror at your past iniquities, while shedding the tears of compunction and repentance, you will come to throw yourselves into the arms of my charity, and under the power of remorse, you will confess me sufficiently eloquent."

In the second place, I would have reprehension whether in the pulpit or in private, frank and direct, never in the form of an oblique allusion. An allusion is understood or it is not. If it is not, the object is not gained; if it is, both the intention of the preacher and his timidity are discovered, and the question arises, why did he fear to be explicit? If it is found that fear was not his reason, he is on that account less respected; if the censure thus veiled is of a grave nature, it appears yet more grave, and the motive of it is exaggerated, when it is seen with what care the preacher thought it necessary to blunt its point; he is thought to have had a bad design equally in what he said and in what he did not dare to say; the feeling I admit is more vivid, but the dart thrown by fear is drawn out and cast far away. Let me not however be here understood, as by any means disapproving the attentions of courtesy, or the cautions and artifices of charity. The dullest in the auditory can readily distinguish between delicacy and timidity.

Finally, let the preacher, when he thinks himself called to censure the conduct of his flock, remember that "The wrath of man worketh not the righteousness of God," (James, i. 20;) and "that the fruit of righteousness is sown in peace." (James, iii. 18.) This deserves the attention especially of the young preacher. The just portion of sin and its earthly inheritance, we know, is hatred and derision; and it is impossible to love good without hating evil; but it is very possible and too common, to hate evil without loving good. This hatred without love, most certainly, is not that "perfect hatred" which the royal prophet had vowed against the enemies of his God; it is mixed with impure elements; but nevertheless, we cannot say that it is not hatred of evil, for evil is hateful to such a degree, and in so many respects, and is so contrary to our nature, that the wicked themselves hate it. But to be worthy of christianity, worthy of the pulpit, hatred must be sanctified, and, so to speak, steeped in love. The impatience or vexation which we feel toward sin, we may easily mistake for zeal; the ill-natured pleasure we take in blaming and condemning, we may regard as a holy grief; and more than one preacher, if he had not been a preacher, would have been a satirical poet. There is great pleasure in censuring, and the profession which seems to make this pleasure our duty, offers temptation to it, to minds of a severe and saturnine character. Let the minister mistrust this temptation; let him fear the exaggerated and declamatory emphasis which orators are accustomed to bestow on subjects of this kind, lest while censuring with authority, he follow his own impressions more than the counsels and inspirations of the Word of God.—Above all, let him beware of irony. Irony in the pulpit, as well as in private conversation, most frequently produces fruitless mortification, and nothing is more contrary to unction. I would not absolutely forbid it; sometimes it is not to be avoided; it is a means of severe correction, and among other offices of preaching, correction has a place. When our Lord said to the Jews who were about to stone him, "I have done many good works among you, for which do you stone me?" (John, x. 32,) he spoke ironically, but how appropriately, how noble and worthy of Him! The famous irony of Boileau, in his imitation of the Tenth Provincial, was but the natural form of a *reductio ad absurdum*, which, on such a subject, and against such errors, was almost the only possible way of reasoning.

Au sujet d'un écrit qu'on nous venait de lire
Un d' entre eux m'insulte sur ce que j'osai dire
Qu'il faut, pour être absous d'un crime confessé,
Avoir pour Dieu du moins un amour commencé.
Ce dogme, me dit-il, est un pur Calvinisme,
O Ciel! me voilà, donc dans l'erreur, dans le schisme,
Et partant réprouvé! Mais, poursuivis-je, alors,
Quand Dieu viendra juger les vivants et les morts,
Et des humbles agneaux, objets de sa tendresse.
Séparera des boucs la troupe pécheresse,
A tous il nous dira, sévère ou gracieux,
Ce qui nous fit impurs ou justes à ses yeux.
Selon vous, donc, à moi réprouvé, bouc infame:
Va brûler, dira-t-il, en l'éternelle flamme,
Malheureux qui soutins que l'homme dut m'aimer;
Et qui, sur ce sujet, trop prompt à déclamer,
Prétendis qu'il fallait, pour fléchir ma justice
Que le pécheur, touché de l'horreur de son vice,
De quelque ardeur pour moi, sentit les mouvements,
Et gardât le premier de mes commandements!

Dieu, si je vous en crois, me tiendra ce langage;
Mais à vous, tendre agneau, son plus cher héritage,
Orthodoxe ennemi d'un dogme si blamé,
Venez, vous dira-t-il, venez, mon bien aimé;
Vous qui, dans le detours de vos raisons subtiles,
Embarassant les mots d'un des plus saint conciles,
Avez délivré l'homme, ô l'utile docteur!
De l'importune fardeau d'aimer son Créateur;
Entrez au ciel, venez, comblé de mes louanges,
Du besoin d'aimer Dieu dés abuser les anges.
A de tels mots, si Dieu pouvait les prononcer,
Pour moi je repondrais, je crois, sans l'offenser,
Oh! que pour vous, mon cœur, moins dur et moins farouche,
Seigneur, n'a-t-il, hélas! parlé comme ma bouche! *

---

* BOILEAU, Epitre xii., *sur l'amour de Dieu*, at the end.
"A piece had just been read; one of their number
Insulted me because I dared to say,
A crime confessed, in order to be pardoned,
By love to God, in its first stage, at least,
Should be preceded. Purest Calvinism
The doctrine was pronounced. Heavens! I exclaimed,
Then I'm a heretic; then into schism
I've fallen, and am, of course, convicted.
But, I subjoined: When God shall come to judge
The living and the dead, and separate
His humble lambs, the objects of his pity,
From the vile herd of goats, He will declare,
With justice or with grace, what in His sight,
Makes us impure or just. If you are right,
He will, on me, adjudged a guilty goat,
Pronounce this fearful sentence: Go, thou vile
Reprobate, burn in fire eternal; wretch
Who didst maintain that man Me ought to love,
And much too earnest on this point, to insist,
Did'st hold, that righteous vengeance to escape,
The sinner touched with horror of his guilt,
Some sentiment of love toward Me should feel,
And of my law, the first command should keep.

This passage, which would not misbecome the pulpit if it had to treat the question of the tenth Provincial, this passage and others which the pulpit itself, perhaps, might furnish, do not hinder us from thinking that irony in general, does not agree with the character of evangelical eloquence ; together with invective, it must, I think be left, I will not say to profane, but to pagan eloquence, since a Christian lawyer or publicist should follow here no other maxims than the preachers.

But, after all, let us say, that a holy vehemence has a place amongst the most approved forms of religious eloquence. Indignation, the wrath of conscience, is as worthy of the Christian as wrath is unworthy. The love of good, we have said, implies the hatred of evil ; and why, if love has its outpourings and its transports, should hatred be without its own ? Why should we excite them if we may not venture to express them ? Did not the prophets, the apostles, Jesus Christ himself, give a free range to the grief and pious wrath with which their souls was filled. It is with godly wrath as with lightning that flashes in a blue sky ; this wrath does not interrupt or disturb the serenity of the soul ; it is not op-

If you I must believe, this language God
To me will hold. But to you, tender lamb,
His dearest heritage, orthodox enemy
Of doctrine hateful, these will be His words:
Come, well-beloved, you who in the maze
Of subtile arguments, embarrassing decrees
Of Holiest Councils, man has delivered
From the great burden of loving his maker,
Come, enter heaven, with my praises loaded,
And teach the angels Me they need not love.
To words like these, if God pronounce them should,
I, for myself, might answer, so I think,
Without offending Him: Alas! O Lord,
Has not my heart, less hard, less merciless,
Spoken for Thee as truly as my mouth ?"—Tr.

posed to charity ; on the contrary, charity is defective if it does not feel and express it. "Faithful are the wounds of a friend," (Proverbs, xxvii. 6.) Let us remember that our reprobation of evil and of sin cannot be comprehended if we appear to be unmoved by them, and that hatred, tranquilly worded, is no more confided in, than love coldly expressed. We are not, we cannot be on terms of politeness with sin—Saint Paul, as it seems to me, did not so understand it. We might be charged with rashness and violence by certain persons if we should repeat some of his apostrophes. Without meriting the reproach let us not fear to incur it. The Lord, who will keep the door of our lips, will doubtless permit the truth to pass through it; and truth consists in feeling as well as in thought; love is truth; hatred of course, and if needs be, wrath itself, also. But, O Lord and Saviour, give us to love as thou lovest, to hate as thou hatest, and to reprove as thou reprovest.

RÉSUMÉ

OF THE FIRST PART.

HAVING finished the first part of this course, I would measure with you, gentlemen, the space we have gone over, take the sum of the ideas we have collected and the convictions we have obtained. We shall have occasion, hereafter, in the sequel of this course, to show that an exact and concise Résumé assists the mind just as the reaper is assisted in carrying his sheaf by the osier-band, which surrounds and compresses it. Let us apply, beforehand, what we are, by-and-bye, to teach. We have also, I hope, a sheaf to carry, let us bind it as well as we can.

The Christian religion has the form of a word. The Divine Being, who has established this religion on the earth and in our hearts, is the Word himself, and here this term Word signifies thought, reason, the truth conceived as well as the truth expressed. By the Word the visible world was made; the Word also created the spiritual world, with this difference, that the Word acts from without on the visible world, while it produces the spiritual world from within. In regard to the visible world, God speaks *from* himself; but he speaks *to* the spiritual world; nay more: the Word creates the visible world which does not speak; the Word creates the spiritual world by making it speak; speak, I mean, internally, that is to say, think, and think externally, that is to say, speak. Christianity is a religion which is spoken and which should be thought.

To think and not to dream; to think with the heart the conscience and the understanding; to think, that is to say, to know and to believe; to think, that is to say, to act and live, consequently to *speak*, and not to stammer, as all human religions have done, this is one of the characteristics of christianity, one of its titles of honor. The minister of this religion then is the communicator and interpreter of a thought; whatever may be the speciality and the form of his ministry, he is the minister of a word. This minister speaks, that is to say, he thinks. The minister is a man who thinks christianity, and who endeavors to have it thought; for, once more, christianity seeks to be thought. Hence, among other reasons, the religion of Jesus Christ, alone among all religions, has founded a church. The idea of the church and that of the word are correlative.

This word of which the origin is divine, and of which the materials are divine, is a human word. It is subject to the same laws as every other word. It receives laws, it is true, from its peculiar object; but in these even, it follows the general rules of eloquence. These particular rules no more separate it from the common sphere of eloquence than they do the bar or the senate on account of the special nature of their object. Homiletics is only rhetoric applied to sacred discourse.

In Homiletics as in rhetoric, we must begin with a just notion of eloquence. This notion appears to us to include two elements. One subjective, which is but the power of persuading; the other objective, which is moral truth or goodness. It is not, in fact, we who are eloquent, but the truth; to be eloquent, is not to add something to the truth, it is to render to it its own; it is to put it in possession of all its natural advantages; it is to remove the veils which cover it; it is to leave nothing between man and the truth. We may be eloquent in a bad cause, but never without giving to evil the appearance of good. Eloquence dies in an infected air.

But eloquence leaves pure speculation to philosophy, pure contemplation to poetry; it strengthens and embellishes itself, by profitable intercourse with them, but it tends to action. Action is its very essence. Eloquence does not imitate, it acts. The drama of the poets is but the representation of the thousand dramas of which life is formed; public discourse is a real drama which has its plot, its incidents, its catastrophe. This catastrophe is the determination or conversion of the will. Poetry even when it simulates action, moves in the region of ideas; eloquence has life for its matter and life for its object. It dies as we have said in a corrupted atmosphere, but it also dies in an air too rarified.

This character, however, and consequently the oratorical element, is less prominent in the pulpit, where teaching has place more than elsewhere. Teaching indeed is the first end of ecclesiastical discourse. The eloquence of the pulpit is called *preaching*, that is to say, *public teaching*. To require preaching to be oratorical in the same degree and manner as the tribune, would be to change and pervert the mission of the pastor. But this teaching, most certainly, may and should be eloquent.

Is this art itself, the art of teaching eloquently, a thing which may be taught? The idea is opposed by reasons drawn from religion. But since eloquence consists essentially in putting the truth into its full light, since art and artifice are not the same thing, since art has the same relation to nature as civilization, since in instinct, even, to which some would reduce us, there is the beginning of art, since art is but instinct itself matured and developed by reflection, finally, since it is as proper, or rather as obligatory to observe and regulate our words (which are actions) as to observe and regulate our actions, properly so-called, our design is fully justified, unless we would give to truth the strange advice to disarm, while error and sin remain equipt for war. Now we must leave the weapons we are to use, we must leave the mode of using them, we must familiarize them, to him by whom they are to be borne. This is the object of Homiletics. Let us take care that scruples of conscience do not become pretexts of indolence and an excuse for levity.

But though Homiletics are something, they certainly are not everything; they are a substitute neither for conviction, nor zeal, nor talent, nor knowledge, nor the study of models. To hear a course of Homiletics is nothing less than to practice Homiletics; to a certain extent each one must teach himself; we know well only what we have learnt of ourselves. A course given, is not necessarily a course received; learning is a fact of the will; learning is taking, it is even creating.

The whole of art, say the ancient rhetoricians, consists in inventing, disposing, expressing; this is the whole of art, repeat the moderns. We pretend to no improvement. These three operations comprise the whole of art, and they are indeed three operations. We cannot better express ourselves than in terms borrowed from the art of architecture: matter, structure, style.

Invention is the only object of this First Part.

The act of invention, which is common to all the operations of art, (for we invent our plan, we invent our style,) is, at bottom, a great mystery. Invention is talent itself. We do not teach talent; we give to him who hath, not to him who hath not. To the inventive mind (and what is mind wholly destitute of invention?) there are means of inventing more, and of inventing better. The first point is *to know.* If knowledge does not give originality, it increases and nourishes it. Know man then: know life, know the divine word, know yourself; know everything if you can; all truth tends to the Supreme truth; all truth may serve it in the way of proof or illustration. Next unite yourself to your subject by intense meditation; warm it with your own heat; warm yourselves with heat from your subject; let your subject be a reality to you, and the preparation of the discourse an epoch in your history; think not only but live; try on your soul the same ideas by which you would influence the souls of others. Do one thing more: analyze according to the laws of a sound logic, the matter which you have before you. Having put yourselves by meditation into contact with the things themselves, now put yourselves by analysis into contact with their idea; having applied the logic of the soul in this study, now apply that of the mind. Inventing is finding; the same faculty of reasoning which you are presently to employ in proving, employ at the outset in finding. Such are the instruments of invention; make frequent use of them; study, meditate, analyze much; sharpen, by repeated efforts, the edge of invention, which, rust without them, will soon render dull; be not in haste to recur to that bank, if we may call it so, of superficial minds, that stock of commonplaces which are not contemptible, which have rendered service to every one, but of which the injudicious use has led talent to neglect its own resources. Have method, rather than a method.

Directions relating to the choice of materials are essentially embraced in that rubrick of *invention* which we have given in the first part of our course. But here appear two characteristics of the eloquence of temples; the first is this: Although, taken as a whole, preaching is a business-matter, each sermon is not one. Preaching is not *actual* in the same sense in which the discourse of the bar or the senate is so; it does not spring from an accidental fact, it is entirely spontaneous; that is to say, gentlemen, it chooses its subjects. The other characteristic is this: Not only is preaching connected with a document, (as also is judicial eloquence when it appeals to the law, and political eloquence when it refers to the constitution of the country,) but it consists essentially in unfolding this document, it flows from it as from its source; the document is its object, whence results, not necessarily, but naturally, the usage of preaching from a text. Before touching then the matter itself or the substance of the discourse, Homiletics, treat of the choice of subjects and the choice of texts.

Must we choose exclusively between subjects and texts? Since the sermon is connected with a text is not the preacher restricted to the selection of the subject, contained in the text? And is he not excluded from *subjects*, properly so called? This question led us to the examination of the custom which has become a law, of retaining a sermon under the control of a biblical passage. While maintaining, for reasons which we have seriously examined, the usage or law in question, we have not thought that it should be adhered to, to the absolute exclusion of subjects as subjects. Hence, apart from the text, we have spoken of the subject, the choice of which we subjected to two rules; one relating to unity, the other to interest. After having determined the idea and shown the importance of unity, after remarking that every discourse should be reduced to the terms of a simple imperative proposition, we enumerated the different forms under which this unity produces itself, or is sometimes disguised. As to the interest of subjects, we determined that it should be at the same time human and christian, and we thought to give a sure direction to preaching by urging that the just effect of the Gospel, the effect which preaching reproduces and seeks to realize, is to engraft divine sentiments on a human nature. We saw that in this sphere, as in that of life itself, liberty is proportioned to submission, and that to the truly christian preacher, as well as to truly spiritual christians, it has been said: "All things are yours, and you are Christ's, and Christ is God's." (1 Corinthians, iii. 22.) But inexperience may misapprehend this liberty, the narrow way is best suited to youth; and, at no age should one ascend the pulpit to speak of everything in a christian manner; Christianity alone is what is to be spoken there.

The text was now considered. We said, first of all, let it be taken in the specific meaning of the divine Word; let it be taken in the sense in which that Word has taken it. We were long occupied with the application of this great rule. The laws of a true and judicious interpretation, successively engaged our attention. From the verbal or external sense which is but preparatory, we passed to the real or internal sense, which is definition; from the interpretation of texts of the spiritual order, to that of texts of the temporal order, and from this again to the texts of a mixed nature, in which the passing world and the world of eternity combine their elements. After illustrating these important distinctions, after considering the relations and differences of languages, of times, of the economies of which the divine work is composed, we entered into the common enclosure of all kinds of eloquence, in treating of the matter itself or the contents of the sermon. Let it be farther remembered that the question as to texts conducted us to that relating to the Homily or Analytical Sermon, and that we considered the means of reducing this excellent kind of preaching to the universal and inflexible law of unity.

To know in order to believe, to believe in order to know, consequently, to know and believe, and both in order to action—this is the whole of religion—it is also the whole of preaching. As to knowledge, it embraces *facts*, that is to say, what appears in space and time, and *ideas* which have a reality independently of space and time. Facts are described or narrated. Ideas are defined. It was necessary to define definition, to establish the necessity of it, to distinguish its diverse modes, to show by what involuntary inclination, or by what necessity it comes under the laws of space and time, while it returns to narration or description, so that ideas without date and without place, are narrated and described as facts.

Belief, which sustains to knowledge the two-fold relation of end and means, since alternately we must know in order to believe, and believe in order to know, belief, by which we mean the two-fold assent of the reason and the will, demanded in its turn the attention of Homiletics. We thus passed from explication to proof, which employs *reasons* when the object is to reach the understanding, and *motives*, when it has respect to the determination of the will.

Intellectual decision, as differing from practical decision, has a three-fold source; experience, authority, reasoning. Each of these means implies the use of the other two; but they are nevertheless distinct from each other. It was our first care to appreciate their respective importance, to show the insufficiency of each in its isolation. Considering next, the two first, (to wit, experience and authority,) as materials of reasoning, and reasoning itself as the principal substance of the discourse, we attempted to distinguish the different forms of argumentation in oratorical discourse, and especially in sacred eloquence, the exigencies, the predilections, the repugnancies of which, we carefully remarked. To reasons which produce assurance of mind, motives succeeded which decide the will. A well-founded distinction. Between conviction and action, the connection is dissolved when there is no affection; affection throws a bridge over this chasm which binds truth and the will together. To speak more correctly, the truth becomes itself an object of the will. All motives may be reduced to two: Goodness and happiness. In the first of these motives or objects of affection, we distinguished and then reunited, *goodness in itself* and *the author of goodness;* we distinguished again, the two correlative sentiments of love and hatred, and the two eloquences which correspond to them. The appeal which the gospel strongly makes to the love of happiness, made it unnecessary for us to justify the use of this motive, for it is by responding to this imperious necessity of all life, that God opens our hearts to the love of goodness. We committed without hesitation, this honorable and necessary weapon into the preacher's hands. The motive of happiness, the axis of human life, presented to us the two poles of fear and hope; fear which contracts the heart, and hope which dilates it; fear which is only a passion, hope which may become a virtue. Around these two great objects, goodness and happiness, are grouped as satellites certain secondary motives of which we indicated the use.

Since it is true that the will cannot be determined without an appeal to affection, it follows that eloquence cannot attain its end without emotion; for emotion is but affection itself in the state of *actuality* or temporary excitement. But there is an economy of emotion. We guarded the moral liberty of the hearer and eloquence itself against excesses. We also gave the lower parts of the soul a direction towards the higher. We claimed in behalf of eloquence all those moral or spiritual emotions which stir within us not the natural but the new man. Passing in the conclusion, from the dispositions which are common to the orator and his auditory, since the latter receives them from the former, to those which are appropriate exclusively to the orator as such, we signalized unction and authority as two forces which adjust themselves to their one result, as two elements of a complex and mysterious nature, without which preaching falls to the level of ordinary eloquence, and even below eloquence.

This first part of our course contains, if you will permit us this expression, the chemistry of oratorical discourse; for we have distinguished not masses or successive movements, but the substances or ingredients of which religious discourse is composed. The second part, which will treat of Disposition, will present in some sort the mechanism of eloquence;

but we shall easily see in what strict relation the two parts are to each other, and at how many points they are interfused.

I hope, Gentlemen, that this *table of contents*, (for it is scarcely more,) has presented with clearness a series of ideas, of which, as separated from one another by the intervals between lectures, and, perhaps, not inserted into one another with sufficient distinctness, the order and connection may not have been apparent even to attentive hearers.

PART II.

DISPOSITION.

CHAPTER I.

OF DISPOSITION IN GENERAL.

§ 1. *Idea and importance of Disposition.*

I REMIND you, in the beginning of this second part, that we did not in the first treat of invention, properly so called, that is to say, of the faculty or the art of inventing, but rather of the nature and the choice of the materials which enter into the composition of the sermon. Invention controls the art throughout, and is applied to all the most diverse stages of the orator's work. He is always inventing; invention is talent itself; or, if you please, all talent is invention. We shall admit, I am sure, that to arrange well and write well is also to invent. Though we have said something on the sources and means of invention, it was in passing, and in a general manner, without anticipating the more numerous and more particular details which we shall give in the fourth part of this course, of which the title, *Method of the Work*, intimates with sufficient plainness the special object. *

Hitherto, then, we have been properly and exclusively oc-

* This fourth part does not exist.—[EDITORS.]

cupied with rules to be observed in the choice of subjects, of the text and the materials. We have been giving, in some sort, the chemistry of oratorical discourse, since we have had to do with the elements or ingredients which interpenetrate one another; *Disposition*, which is now to engage us, resembles more the physics or mechanism of discourse, as it has for its object the stages which succeed or the parts which are in contact with one another. I do not, however, intend to say that it abstracts entirely the inherent nature of the materials; it cannot do that.

Yet more, we had in view, in the first part, synthetic discourse, or the Sermon properly so called; not as though that were, in our opinion, the only normal form of pulpit discourse; we made our reserves in favor of the Homily; but the Homily itself aspires to synthesis; analysis is but a road to reach it, a road whose length, whose windings are determined only by the nature or the form of the text; in a word, all homily tends to the sermon, all homily ends in being a sermon; in all cases synthesis is the purpose, the summit, the very essence of oratorical discourse. It was, therefore, useful, it was even necessary to start in our instruction with synthesis and not with its contrary. Now, to use other terms, it was doubtless better, in treating of the sermon, to tighten a knot which might afterwards, according to convenience, be gradually relaxed, than to relax it at first and recommend the tightening of it according to necessity. Obedience first, liberty afterwards, is the order. With this understanding, we treat of the sermon as if the sermon was the only form of evangelical eloquence.

Our present task relates to the disposition of the materials which we procure by the first operation; it relates, in other words, to the construction of the discourse. Whether you announce or do not announce your design beforehand, you have always a proposition to establish, a conviction to produce in the souls of your hearers. I admit that all the ideas, all the facts you have collected, incline or tend to this conclusion; I admit that the opinions (not to say convictions) which are formed by the world, result in respect to each one, from a certain number of observations, experiences, reflections, which do not present themselves to the mind in a certain order, and which no one, after the end is gained, applies himself in arranging. Such is, if I may so say, the tumultous and spontaneous rhetoric of life. But you do not ascend the pulpit to do nothing better than this. It is with the orator as with the dramatic poet. The latter does not find in life a drama such as those which he prepares for the theatre. To mention but one detail, the entrances and exits are not made to seem natural in life, as has to be done on the stage. The poet submits to this rule; he observes others also. The same as to the orator. He does not throw at random the materials of his proof, even when they seem to be thrown at random in life. Chance with him, moreover, would be but a bad imitation of the other chance. When a conviction is formed in an individual or many individuals at once, apart from the direct influence of eloquence, it is not certain that the order in which the elements of proof were presented, grouped, arranged, was of no importance as to the result which is obtained; in the case given the apparent disorder was probably order; to which, of course, the chance corresponded. But in the composition which we have supposed the chance corresponds to nothing; the disorder is a pure disorder. Besides the element of time, that of repetition at long intervals is to be taken into the account; there are advantages from this, which compensate the want of order: oratorical discourse which is confined within the limit of an hour or two, is entirely deprived of them. It must then redeem inconveniences which are inherent in it, by its own peculiar advantages; order alone enables it to do this. Order is the character of true discourse; there is no discourse without it. We know not how to name a composition without order. It is disposition, it is order which constitutes discourse.

The difference between a common orator and an eloquent man, is often nothing but a difference in respect to disposition. Disposition may be eloquent in itself, and on close examination we shall often see, that invention taken by itself, and viewed as far as it can be apart from disposition, is a comparatively feeble intellectual force. "Good thoughts," says Pascal, "are abundant."* The art of organizing them is not so common. It requires, sometimes, a greater capacity to find the relations and the appropriate places of these organic molecules. Is not a relation also an idea, and a very important idea? There is then invention in this, and La Bruyère who said "that the choice of thoughts is invention,"† might have said the same thing of the order of thought.

I will not go so far as to say that a discourse without order can produce no effect, for I cannot say that an undisciplined force is an absolute nullity. We have known discourses very defective in this respect, to produce very great effects. But we may affirm in general, that other things being equal, the power of discourse is proportional to the order which reigns in it, and that a discourse without order, (order, be it remembered, is of more than one kind,) is comparatively feeble. A discourse has all the power of which it is susceptible, only when the parts proceeding from the same design, are intimately united, exactly adjusted, when they mutually aid and sustain one another like the stones of an arch. *Tantum series juncturaque pollet.*‡ This is so true, so felt, that com-

* See the development of this idea in PASCAL: *Pensées*, partie i., art. iii., "Rien n'est plus common que les bonnes choses," etc.

† LA BRUYÈRE, *Les Caractères*, chap. i., *Des ouvrages de l'esprit.*

‡ HORACE, *Art of Poetry*, verse 242.

plete disorder is almost impossible, even to the most negligent mind. In proportion to the importance of the object we wish to attain, or the difficulty of attaining it, is our sense of the necessity of order. It is, I think, not more commonly supposed that a discourse absolutely without order, is equally well suited to persuade, and especially to instruct, than that a multitude is a people, that a crowd of men in mail is an army, or that the confused masses which Darius drew after him were able to compete with a Macedonian phalanx.

We should perhaps be within bounds in saying that disposition in a discourse is not of more secondary importance than the mode of aggregation of molecules in a physical substance; this mode, in great part, constitutes the nature of the body.

Oratorical discourse, and especially that of the pulpit, has a double purpose: to instruct and to persuade. In considering only the first of these objects, we see that order is all important. We are instructed only in so far as we comprehend and retain; but we comprehend and retain easily, surely, only in the proportion in which the matters on which our understanding is exercised are consecutive and connected. Teaching, in which order is wanting, hardly deserves the name of teaching; all that it can do, is to give more or less valuable information. And the inconvenience of disorder in this respect, is not merely negative; if it is unhappy not to understand, it is more so to have a wrong understanding. Now, to this danger does bad disposition expose our hearer; sometimes we teach him nothing; what is worse, we sometimes teach him error; for truth which is not regarded in its true light, in its proper place, is changed into error, and often in respect to the greater part of minds, to pernicious error.

Thus as to instruction, or influence on the understanding. It is impossible that it should be otherwise as to persuasion, or influence on the will. A discourse badly ordered is obscure, and that which is obscure is weak. Decision cannot be conveyed to the soul of any one, by that which bears the tremulous impress of indecision. Conceive of a discourse in which the chief laws of order are violated, in which an idea is abandoned before it has been thoroughly presented, unless it is reverted to afterwards, by cutting, perhaps, the thread of another idea; in which an accessory has as much place as a principal idea, perhaps more; in which the advance is not from the weaker to the stronger, but from the stronger to the weaker; in which nothing is grouped, nothing compacted; in which everything is scattered, wandering, incoherent; such a discourse is contrary to the nature of the human mind, to its just expectation, to its wants; in the soul of the hearer, as in the discourse which is addressed to him, everything begins, nothing is finished; the elements, which by combination would have formed a solid mass (I mean analogous thoughts, homogeneous sentiments), are kept separate and at a distance; instead of a bright and burning flame, we have a whirl of sparks; lively impressions perhaps are produced, but transient and soon effaced; and although none of the materials necessary to the composition of an excellent discourse may be wanting, no comparison can be made, as to the two-fold purpose of convincing and persuading, between the work of which we are speaking, and another in which perhaps there are fewer ideas, but in which order renders everything availing. In the first case we had, in intellectual order, the spectacle of a great fortune badly administered, of an unproductive consumption, of a dissipation.

We may appear to be engaged in too serious a work to be allowed to refer here to the idea of the beautiful; but it is not perhaps unimportant to observe that nowhere are the beautiful and the useful so closely united and so nearly interblended. The same thing is, at once, strength and beauty.

Ordinis hæc virtus erit et venus, aut ego fallor,
Ut jam nunc dicat, jam nunc debentia dici.*

Order is in itself beautiful, and everything beautiful in itself, is more beautiful in its place. Disorder on the contrary diminishes, discolors, degrades everything. Quintilian, then, when representing with poetic eloquence, the inconveniences of disorder in discourse, is just in connecting with order the two attributes of beauty and force. Let us hear this great master: "Disposition has not without good reason been reckoned the second of the five points I mentioned, the first being of no significancy without it. If you cast or fashion all the limbs of a statue, it will not be a statue, unless these limbs are properly put together; and if you change or transpose any part of the human body, or of other animals, though all other parts remain in their due proportion, it will notwithstanding be a monster. Dislocated limbs lose the use of their wonted exertions, and actions in confusion are an impediment to any just manœuvre. They are far I think from being mistaken, who have said, that the universe is maintained by the order and symmetry of its parts, and that all things would perish, if this order was disturbed. In like manner a speech wanting this quality, must run into extreme confusion, wandering about like a ship without a steersman, incoherent with itself, full of repetitions and omissions, losing its way, as by night, in unknown paths, and without proposing to itself any proper beginning or end, following rather the guidance of chance than reason."†

The work of disposition is of very great importance, since it completes and perfects, as we may well say, the work of invention. We make invention a part *sui generis*, and independent: it is not so. We cannot, indeed, know our materials, we cannot measure, cannot appreciate them, except as

* HORACE, *Art of Poetry*, verses 42, 43.

† QUINTILIAN, Lib. vii., *Preface*, Patsall's translation.

a consequence, and by means of this second labor, which is very often simultaneous with the first. It has, in effect, the three following results:

1. It determines and reduces to strict unity, the meaning of the proposition. For disposing is decomposing; these two words are almost synonymous; in order, at least, to dispose we must first decompose. If we follow in the process the laws of sound logic, it is impossible that we should not look more closely at what we are to treat, that we should not have a better discernment of what belongs to it, and what does not, that we should not reduce it more certainly within its just limits. How many orators and writers have been unable to understand well the nature of their subject until they have proceeded to the arrangement of its parts.

2. As the labor of arrangement rests on a methodical analysis, it not only excludes and casts aside what interferes with the unity of the subject, but aids us in discovering what the subject itself contains. We see many things in it now, which we did not see before; many lines are completed, many intervals filled up. It is with order in the administration of a subject, as with economy in that of a fortune—it enriches.

3. Finally, disposition gives or renders to each of the elements of which the subject is composed, its real importance. By separating ideas which at the first glance seemed to be confounded, by grouping things which appeared to be separate, by attending to contrasts, relations, subjects of comparison, reflexions of light from one idea to another, we give a new and unexpected force to each of these ideas.

The small effect of a discourse in which the great law of order has been neglected, is further explained, we think, in another way. The orator, we know, must experience in himself the effect which he would produce; this is what is called inspiration.* Now, without a plan, without a plan strongly conceived, whether slowly meditated, or found as soon as sought, one cannot write with a true inspiration. Conceive of yourselves in the situation I suppose. You proceed at hazard, and as groping in the dark, by turns advancing and receding; the thread you have hold of is broken at every instant, and requires incessantly to be re-tied. Instead of completing the presentation of an idea at the first, after having presented it imperfectly once, you present it a second time still imperfectly; you have many *almosts*, many fractions of which the sum remains to be taken. You have skirmished on all sides of the place, one after another;—made false attacks which terminate nothing. One idea does not presuppose another; one idea does not produce another; in what you have, you have no guarantee as to what is to come, the passages (badly named, surely!) follow one another, but are not connected; as idlers who live by the day, you write by the sentence, not more sure of the second after the first, than they as to provision for the morrow. Now you have accumulated in one paragraph the matter of a discourse; now the discovery that you have failed in a first effort, throws you back upon an idea with which you should have nothing further to do; and these repetitions, these returns, these ambiguities, these digressions, you endeavor to dissemble by logical artifices, by subtile distinctions, turns of expression, playing upon words. This uncertain, hesitating, out-of-breath procedure is most contrary to inspiration, to that continuous movement which should be as one single expiration of a powerful chest. The regret of having so badly played your part, of having exhibited so imperfectly the

* We find here, between parentheses, in the original manuscript, the words "define, distinguish," which seem to have been merely designed by M. Vinet, to suggest to himself some more particular explication, which he thought it might be useful to give.—[EDITORS.]

richness of your subject and your thought, puts your talent in chains, if that can be true talent to which the power of organization is wanting ; the discourse, breathless, bridled, betrays perplexity and fatigue from the beginning. The orator is, as it were, oppressed by the painful feeling that he has not more than half gained his purpose or expressed his thought, that he has made only half impressions, which he vainly endeavors to complete by other half impressions. This discourse which is thrown away, this combat which terminates in a defeat, oppresses his spirit beforehand ; he feels himself conquered before the close of the battle.

Buffon has described perfectly, the two opposite states of the man who works without a plan, and a man who has formed one.

" For want of plan, from not having sufficiently reflected on his subject, an intelligent man finds himself embarrassed, and unable to begin writing ; he perceives at once a great number of ideas, but as he has neither compared or arranged them, nothing determines him to prefer some to others ; he therefore remains in perplexity. But when he has formed a plan, when he has once collected and put in order all the thoughts which are essential to his subject, he perceives readily at once which should engage his pen, he is conscious of full preparation for intellectual effort, he is in haste to make it, he has only pleasure in writing, ideas follow each other readily, style is natural and easy ; warmth, springing from this pleasure, diffuses itself everywhere, and gives life to each expression ; all is more and more animated ; the tone rises, the objects assume color, and sentiment, combined with light, increases it, extends it, transfers it from that which is said to that which is to be said, and style becomes interesting and lucid." *

* BUFFON, *Discours sur le Style, in Chrestomathie Française*, tome iii., p. 142, troisième édition.

Cardinal Maury also teaches excellently on the same subject: "Why," says this writer, "do we discover nothing at certain seasons? Because we really know, neither whither we would go, nor what we are in search of. We have here a poetic experience, which we gain every day from the art and habit of writing. We think we are in a lethargy of barrenness; we are only in the midst of a wilderness and a cloud."*

To recapitulate, then, what we have been saying, we remark: that order is essential to the very idea of discourse; that it is necessary to instruction and conviction; that it is the condition of invention itself; finally, that it is the condition of inspiration.

What we have just considered prepares us to hear without surprise this expression of Herder: "I readily forgive all faults except those which relate to disposition." Herder, un questionably, does not put false ideas and bad doctrines in the number of faults which he forgives; but, excepting these, we can understand why all faults in oratory should have appeared venial to him when compared with those of disposition, since it is disposition that properly constitutes discourse, and that it is in this especially that the orator reveals himself.

But where is the principle of that order which we recommend? May it not be as much in passion as in reason? Nothing I know is as logical, after its own manner, as passion; and that we may depend upon it for the direction of a discourse of which it is the principal inspiration. The beginning we may be sure will be good, and the beginning will produce all the rest. It will be repetitious, it will retrace its steps, it will digress, but it will do everything with grace and felicity which always accompany it; and it would be less true and consequently less eloquent if it were more logical in the ordinary sense of the word. It naturally finds the order

* MAURY, *Essai sur l'Eloquence de la Chaire*, xxxvi.

which suits it, and it finds it precisely because it does not seek after it. The rapid propagation of ideas, their concatenation by means of thoroughly vital transitions, which themselves constitute the movement of the discourse, suffice for the eloquence of passion.* When in *Andromache*, Racine makes Hermione speak,† it is evident that the disorder of the discourse is a part of its truth, a real order, and that this perfect logic of passion is a marvel in an imitated discourse. If there was more logical order in it the discouse would be less perfect.

But passion does not suffice in instructive discourse, in which disorder would not be order *sui generis*, because it would not be true; in which not being true, it would not be in taste; in which it would be simple disorder and confusion.

When we take logic in distinction from passion, as the principle of order, we have to meet greater difficulties.

Logic, as it appears to us, has its propensity as well as passion. But in relation to the sequence and concatenation of ideas, it is far from forming an instinct as true and as infallible as passion. The logical sentiment, if we may use this expression, has not, by any means, the vivacity of sentiments properly so called. Ideas are objects, logic then is objective; thought cannot, like passion, make itself its own rule and measure. It has its rule in the laws of thought, which are constant, immutable and independent of the transient states of the soul; and although these laws, taken abstractly, are the necessary forms of the human mind, and so to speak the instincts of the understanding, they do not, in application, retain their character as instincts, and though their operations may be sure, they are never independent of reflection. Exercise and discipline contribute much to their

* See le *Paysan du Danube* de la Fontaine, la prière de *Philoctete* à Pyrrhus, dans Sophocle, Pauline à Polyeucte, dans Corneille.

† Acte v., scene v., "Je ne t'ai point aimé, cruel, etc."

successful use, and although all minds acknowledge the same primitive laws, and present the same forms, all minds are very far from being equally perfect in their structure, equally logical.

The preacher, undoubtedly, has a sincere interest in his subject; but he is not agitated with passion; he ought not to be; the affection he feels is profound and serious, but it leaves him calm; he does not speak under the excitement of immediately perilous circumstances; he is not personally compromised; in fine, he is called chiefly to instruct. He may then, he should, have command of his feeling; not to commence wherever that may commence, nor follow the course in which it would lead him if he were under its direction. In order to be moved by his subject, he doubtless does not wait until he has explained its nature, presented its proofs and developed its consequences to his hearers; he is moved by it before he begins this work; it is because he is moved by it that he does begin; but it is not inconsistent with sincerity to delay the expression of an emotion until it can be advantageously expressed and communicated to others, because the object to which it relates, is well known and appreciated.

What we have here said of instructive discourse has a more extended application than the expression may indicate. Whenever we would instruct or persuade, whether from the pulpit or the tribune, or in common conversation, we ought to study economy of discourse, have a plan and follow it, because we should endeavor to impart to the mind, not a general impression,* but a distinct determination, founded on motives equally distinct. In this respect certain discourses of Racine in his tragedies are as perfectly conformed to the

* M. Vinet adds here the German word *Gesammteindruck*, doubtless as giving his idea better than the French words with which he approximates it.—[EDITORS.]

rules of oratorical disposition, as those of the most accomplished orators.* Read also the discourse of Phenix to Achilles in the ninth book of the Iliad, and that of Pacuvius in Titus Livius, (Liber xxiii. chapter ix.) The study of eloquence in these models may be further useful to us, by preventing us from taking the species for the genus.

The discourse of the pulpit is *didactic* and *oratorical.* Disposition should have respect to both these characteristics. Hence the study we are prosecuting is divided into two parts. We are to treat of disposition, first in the logical and then in the oratorical point of view.

§ 2. *Of Disposition under the logical point of view.* (*Decomposition—grouping or co-ordination—Progress.*)

We are obliged to assume that in the preparation of a discourse, things always proceed in the same way. This supposition, which simplifies our work, does not endanger truth. In certain cases, that which may be anterior in the order of time, may well be posterior in the order of thought.

Although we spoke first of invention and then of disposition, we are aware that disposition is sometimes simultaneous with invention, and that the *proposition* † sometimes comes last of all.

Thus, after regarding the Gospel *as great in what it demands ;* I regard it *as great in what it gives ;* these two ideas, which occur to me *one after the other*, are united and concentrated in the general idea; *the Gospel is great*, which forms my theme. The same with these two ideas : *The Gospel has liberty for its end ; the Gospel has liberty as a means ;* which are combined in this proposition : *The Gos-*

* See *le discours d'Agrippine dans Britannicus*, and that of Pyrrhus *dans Andromaque.*

† In German, *Der Hauptsatz.*

pel is a law of liberty. We must, however, be sure that the word *liberty* has the same sense in both of the particular propositions.

But, ordinarily, and perhaps too ordinarily, this is not the process. A proposition, either suggested by a text, or supplied by our theological system, or pre-adopted by our mind, presents itself to us completely formed, before we have actually in thought, either all the ideas which it embraces, or all the proofs which establish it. It is, we suppose, always with us in our study. What follows?

The theme is found. The idea of it, we will suppose, is fixed and well-defined in the mind of the orator. Now, whether he is to unfold or to prove it, he must decompose it, take it to pieces so to speak as one does a piece of furniture or a machine somewhat too large for a door-way.

This is the moment of meditation. Meditation is a slow and assiduous incubation of the subject, which fertilized, in a sense, by the natural warmth of the orator, by the interest which identifies him with his object, at length hatches and brings to view a crowd of particular ideas—a sort of pell-mell or mob, particles which are whirled in the air, but which seek to form groups, masses, and do not rest until they are in place and in order.

For when division is the only object, the subject goes on dividing itself until it becomes impossible to be divided any farther. But this pulverizing of the subject is not true division. Supposing what I do not believe that simple meditation might find again all these particles, it could accomplish only one part of the orator's task. The aggregation of the ideas forms a concrete mass, not an organism. We must attain to all these ideas, but not by a road traced by chance. The road is a natural one, a physiological one, like that of the sap to the principal branches, these to the boughs, these to the leaves.

Thus, as we just now excluded certain cases, in which invention of the subject itself, of the proposition, comes later and perhaps last, so we here exclude this work of meditation, this fermentation of the mind. This is a deep which at present we are not concerned with; and while the orator often passes from the branches to the trunk, or from the top to the bottom, we, on the contrary, shall pass from the trunk to the branches, from the bottom to the top.

We must then pass from the trunk, which is the proposition, to the principal branches; we must distinguish and seize them, that is to say, make a general division of the subject. It will sometimes be found that the subject (the proposition) has a necessary division, and will bear no other. In this first decomposition there may be no mystery; the division of a proposition into the exposition of a precept and its motives, of a truth and its practical consequences, is as easy to an ordinary as to an ingenious man; and it is below this first distribution, if we may so speak, that the difficulty and work of talent, true decomposition, begins.

We exclude these almost unavoidable divisions, in which invention scarcely has place; and we think we may say, as we give our thought to others, that the power and effect of the discourse depends, in great measure, on this first decomposition of the subject.

There are plans energetic and rich, which, applying the lever as deeply as possible, raise the entire mass of the subject; there are others which escape the deepest divisions of the matter, and which raise, so to speak, only one layer of the subject.

Here it is, especially, here, in the conception of plans, that we distinguish those orators who are capable of the good, from those who are capable of the better—of that better, to say the truth, which is the decisive evidence of talent or of labor.

We may here apply the well-known verse:

> Savoir la marche est chose très unie;
> Savoir le jeu, c'est le fruit du génie;*

and these other verses which are less known:

> Le Mieux, dit-on, est l'ennemi du Bien:
> Jamais le goût n'admit ce faux proverbe;
> C'était le Mieux qu'osa tenter Malherbe;
> Maynard fit bien et Maynard ne fit rien.
> Gloire à ce Mieux, noble but du génie!
> Il enflammait l'auteur d'Iphigénie,
> Boileau, Poussin, Phidias, Raphaël.
> Le Bien, timide, est le Mieux vulgaire;
> A feu La Harpe il ne profite guère;
> Il en est mort: le Mieux est immortel.†

Every one should at least strive, as far as possible, for this better, and not be content with the first plan which may present itself to his thought, unless, after having fathomed it, he finds it sufficient for his purpose, suited to exhaust his subject, to draw forth its power, unless, in a word, he can see nothing beyond it.

Many plans may present themselves on the same subject. If I am to prove that the thought of death is profitable, I may demonstrate successively:

* "To know the move is a very simple thing;
To know the game, is the fruit of genius."—Tr.

† The Better, they say, is the enemy of the Good:
Taste never admits this false proverb,
It was the Better Malherbe ventured to attempt.
Maynard did well, and Maynard did nothing:
Glory to this Better, noble aim of genius,
It inflamed the author of Iphigenie,
Boileau, Poussin, Phidias, Raphael.
The Good, timid thing, is the Better of the vulgar,
It scarcely profited the defunct La Harpe,
It caused his death: The Better is immortal.—Tr.

That it controls the imagination, regulates the affections, keeps conscience awake.

That it restrains and that it excites.

That it is the best introduction to the knowledge of man and of God.

That it teaches us at the same time to contemn and to value life.

That it reproves our ambition, our sensuality, our resentments.

That it places us at the true point of vision in relation to life, ourselves, our fellows, and God.

That it makes us afraid of evil, makes us courageous in respect to everything else.

In fact, under different forms and names, we may find the same matter in sermons constructed on these different plans. But the question we have to settle is, which of these plans it is that presents the truth under the most striking aspect, with the greatest affluence of detail, and of detail the most advantageous? It is very probable that we shall prefer Bourdaloue's plan on this subject, before any other.

. . . . . "I advance three propositions which I wish you to understand well, for they form the division of this discourse. I say, the thought of death is the most sovereign remedy for quenching the fire of our passions; this is the first part. I say that the thought of death is the most infallible rule for bringing our deliberations to a just conclusion; this is the second part. Finally, I say that the thought of death is the most efficacious means for inspiring us with a holy fervor in our actions; this is the third part."*

It is important to remark that in choosing a plan we often find a subject in the subject itself. Among the different points of view which the proposition combines, we choose

* BOURDALOUE, *Premier Sermon du Carême*, tome i., p. 131, édition Lefèvre.

that to which we would call attention. In the example I just now gave, all the plans proposed relate to the same point of view; but in dividing this proposition into its proofs, it may be decomposed into its parts, its species, its relations. Take this passage: "Perfect love casteth out fear." (1 John, iv. 18.) As I apply myself to one word or another, I shall have three plans, which will be three subjects.

Love.—It casts out fear, because it is *full of devotion, of hope, of joy.*

Casts out. Love casts out fear; for we cannot fear when we love; we have nothing to fear when we love.

Fear. Love casts out the fear of God's wrath, of ill success, of the judgments of men, of ingratitude.

This proposition, likewise, "Righteousness exalteth a nation," (Proverbs, xiv. 34,) is susceptible of different divisions, accordingly as we would develop the idea by means of fact, by its parts, by a comparison, affirmatively or negatively:

1. In prosperity,—in adversity;
2. Internally,—externally;
3. Without danger to itself,—without prejudice to others,—without envy on their part;
4. More than arms,—wealth,—science.

Thus when Homiletics gives us rules or directions as to the conception of plans, it is more properly instructing us in regard to invention. But assuredly, when it proposes to us different principles for the distribution of the matter, it does not leave us to chance in respect to them, but requires us to decide between them according to the end we wish to attain. We have now indeed to choose our subject, or rather to complete the choice.

The following are principles of division indicated by Doctor Ammon.* We may, he says,

* Ammon, *Anleitung zur Kanzelberedsamkeit*, p. 251, édition de 1812.

I. Decompose the whole into its particular notions and propositions.

Example. *Of the pernicious influence of ambition on human happiness.*

1. What is ambition?
2. Its unhappy influence on temporal good.
   a. It makes us habitually discontented with ourselves.
   b. It excites others to resist us.
   c. It does not secure to us the esteem of other men; and,
   d. Still less their love.
3. Its unhappy influence on spiritual good.
   a. It hinders self-knowledge.
   b. It prevents us from being just to others.
   c. It prevents us from loving others.

II. We may decompose the genius into its species. Example: *The veracity of the divine promises.*

1. General promises: "Who will have all men to be saved and to come to the knowledge of the truth." Timothy, ii. 4.)
2. Particular promises which God has made.
   a. To certain peoples. (The Jews.)
   b. To certain families. (Abraham.)
   c. To certain men. (David, Jesus.)

III. We may contemplate the principal thought in its different relations. Example: *The advantages of genuine culture.* *

1. To man as a reasonable being.
2. To man as a member of society.
   a. As a citizen.
   b. As a husband and father.
   c. As a friend.
   d. As a master. (*Lehrer.*)

* In German, *Aufklœrung.*

IV. We may decompose a general precept of the moral law into several subordinate precepts. I substitute here another example in place of that proposed by the author : *Respect for the reputation of others.*

1. Not to attack it.

2. Not to lead others to think, by our conduct, that we have no regard to it.

3. To defend it when attacked.

4. To admonish one when his conduct may lead to an unfavorable judgment of it; to care for his reputation, when he has no care for it himself.

V. We may decompose a theme into its different motives or its different proofs. Example : *The divine truth of the doctrine of Jesus.* It proceeds :

1. From its agreement with the laws of our reason.

2. From its divine effects on our hearts.

3. From the wonderful events which accompanied its introduction and establishment.

VI. We may, finally, decompose the proposition into its subordinate parts in a gradual manner. Example (substituted for that of Doctor Ammon) : *Idleness.*

1. It renders us unprofitable to ourselves.

2. It renders us unprofitable to others.

3. It renders us injurious to others and ourselves.

But, whatever mode of distribution we may adopt, or however great or small may be our success in the invention of the plan or principal divisions, we are to observe the following rules : *

* In giving these rules, we sufficiently indicate the chief difficulty or danger to young orators and even to experienced ones, presented by disposition. The ideas of the mind are not individuals but parts of that continuous and endless line, which connects all objects together in our mind, as they are connected in the universe. No idea separates itself spontaneously from other ideas. This logical fact is

1. Not to co-ordinate that which is subordinate, not to subordinate that which is co-ordinate. I call that subordinate in regard to an idea, which is comprised in the sphere or province of that idea. I call that co-ordinate, which, with this idea, forms part of a more general idea. The fault which violates this rule, consists in presenting as distinct and separate, two ideas which enter into one another, or of which one forms a part of the other.*

Thus, of the two ideas of *charity* and *indulgence*, the second is subordinate to the first; and the two ideas of *obligingness* and indulgence are co-ordinate the one to the other.

2. Not to present as two distinct ideas or motives, two points of view of the same idea or motive; that is to say, the same motive or idea taken in a particular relation which does not essentially change it. These ideas are like vases which differ from one another only as to the handle. Words the most different, do not always convey essentially different ideas, as in this division: "It is characteristic of christian faith, that it *excites*, *guides*, *supports*." But to prove successively that a thing is contrary to good sense or contrary to our interests, is to condemn ourselves to be in presence of nothing after finishing the first part. I may say as much of this plan: "Intolerance is contrary to the spirit of the gospel, and shows great self-ignorance." We are not sure as to our plan, until we have penetrated rapidly perhaps, but particularly, the ideas of which it is composed; if we have not done this, we may undertake a confused and barren subject, from reliance on a delusive presentiment of abundance and clearness.

indispensable to order, exactitude and clearness. It is logic that individualizes ideas. It reduces each of them within certain well-defined limits, which are, in fact, artificial, but which are necessary to all exact reasoning. This caution or this art comprises the whole secret of disposition.

* See HUFFELL, *Uber das Wesen und den Beruf des evangelisch-christlichen Geistlichen*, troisième édition, (1835,) tome i., p. 277.

I will extend this rule farther; I will say, that we must not distinguish ideas which, from their near relation to each other, cannot but be confounded, and which, without being identical, implicate one another. It is most difficult to treat under distinct heads *gentle*, *easy to be intreated*, in James, iii. 17; or indeed *peace*, *serenity*. In some passages of the Bible there are enumerations which are but little systematic.

3. To avoid being led by contiguity or affinity of ideas to put into one part of the discourse what belongs to another part, either preceding, or following.

4. Not to treat an idea before that which is to be used in illustrating or proving it. This rule condemns not only the grosser instances of *petitio principii*, but all distribution, the effect of which would be to introduce too late, that which is required to make an idea intelligible. This fault would be committed (*e. g.*) by proving, in the first place, that a thing will conciliate for us the esteem of good men, and after this, proving that the thing is just.

These, which are all negative, are fundamental rules, to which the plan must conform, and without the observation of which a plan is decidedly vicious. It is less so, doubtless, yet still it is vicious, when the system of decomposition is conventional, arbitrary, and when symmetry is preferred to natural order. This is the case when division is made previous to thorough meditation of the subject. We doubtless may make, artificially, a plan which does not contravene the laws of logic, and which pleases the eye by its regularity; but this external regularity may, nevertheless, do violence to the essential nature of things; it separates and keeps at a distance what requires to be united; the divisions of the matter are trenches and not articulations; the discourse is really interrupted at every turn; the artifice of oratorical transitions is no substitute for the force of those natural and vivid transitions, or rather the perpetual engendering of one idea from another, which distinguishes genuine order; the discourse is not compact, is not liquid; memory, which symmetry claims to aid, is much more and much better aided by a natural order. The greatest pulpit talents I know have accepted these shackles, and their success has been the misfortune of the pulpit.

All that we have said of the general disposition or plan of the discourse, applies, undoubtedly, to each of the parts the union of which forms the general plan, and has only to be transferred to them. We, nevertheless, think it may be useful to give some directions as to the plan of the parts of the discourse. We prescribe three rules relating to the ideas of which each of these parts consists: unity of bearing or direction, generalization, subdivision.

1. If the manner of proceeding in decomposing the theme of each part was necessarily the same in all, if all descended from the general to the particular, we should have nothing to add to what we have said; but here, more than in the general conception of the discourse, the mind chooses to take the particular as the point of departure, and we cannot think this wrong. If the other method has great logical advantages, this has substantial ones, as it leads us straight onward to ideas, and not by the ladder of analysis. But we must admit that, in this last case, as the point of departure or general idea has not been determined beforehand, we run the risk of not attaching ourselves, in each particular idea, to the stand-points which correspond to that of the general idea. Fractions are gathered which have not perhaps the same denominator. The idea we should find and accommodate to the general design of the discourse is indeed found now for substance, but as tending towards an object different from that of the general object, or of the part of the discourse in which it has place. The same idea may be presented under

the aspect of a means, when it should have been under that of encouragement. Thus, as to the ideas of utility and purpose, of censure and exhortation, of customs and rules, of obstacles and means, of duty and taste, of means and ways, of source and condition, of object and purpose, of illusion and pretext, of characteristics and rules, of shades and degrees, of motives and consequences, of proofs and motives, of effects and symptoms.—We hence see the danger of writing passages beforehand, without a view of the subject as a whole. We cannot, without modifying them, incorporate them into the discourse, and we are led by regret at losing them, especially if they are beautiful, to violate the natural sequence of the discourse, and the laws of proportion, in order to find a place for them, and we employ for this purpose logical artifices which never succeed, since the false can never be a substitute for the true. *

2. The particular ideas must not only have a unity of design and bearing, but there must be particular groups in the principal groups, that those which are susceptible of combination under the same leading idea, may have a common centre, tending to generalization. We do not mean, that we are to limit ourselves to general ideas and suppress details, but that we must strengthen particular ideas by giving them a centre and forming them into masses. By restricting ourselves to general ideas, we should make each discourse a *resumè* of many discourses, a broth too strong for weak stomachs; we should deprive ourselves of that multitude of aspects and applications, which are the life of eloquence; we should give little instruction, we should excite little emotion. Those discourses which comprise in one paragraph

* "Those who fear to lose isolated thoughts, and who write detached passages at different times, never combine them without forced transitions."—[BUFFON.]

the substance of a whole discourse, remind us, in one respect, of this verse of Boileau :

> Souvent trop d' abondance appauvrit la matière.*

The rule we give then relates purely to disposition.

In truth, are not sermons consisting of general ideas, which absorb at once what should form the matter of a series of discourses, distinguished in general, rather by poverty than affluence, and if an orator has seen but one subject where others would have seen many, is it not because he has employed himself too little in meditation, in deep study ?

3. The restriction or explanation of the second rule leads us to a third. We must learn to divide again, or to sub-divide; that is to say, to decompose the principal ideas into as many parts or points of view as we can, without approaching tenuity or subtility, by which attention is wearied and interest destroyed. We would in oratorical discourse imitate Corneille in the tragedy *d'Horace*, the subject of which, as supplied by History, would not have sufficed for a tragedy, if the poet had not been able to space it. *Divide et impera.* It may seem useless and puerile to be decomposing certain ideas, but if it is sometimes well to leap over intermediate spaces, it is also well sometimes to note them one by one, and to arrive at the end only step by step. Let us consider that in this matter the road, the travelling is itself important, and that it is not with discourse as with a ladder on which we may ascend or descend three rounds at once. In this ladder of discourse, every round should be touched. As I am now speaking of disposition only in the logical point of view, that is to say, in relation to the understanding and judgment, I shall not stop to show that the impression we receive from the truth is proportional not only to our

* BOILEAU, *L'Art Poëtique*, chant iii. "Too much abundance often impoverishes the matter of the discourse."

consciousness as to the end we have reached, but also as to our acquaintance with the road by which we have reached it. It must be evident to every one, that there is a great difference between the delay hence arising which has such oratorical force, and that which results from turnings and deviations ; for here we do not relax our movement ; we take short steps, but they are firm and energetic. Restricting myself to the logical point of view, I will say, that though the mind sometimes delights in rapid movement and in bounding over larger spaces in each effort, like Bossuet in his *Funeral Orations*, sub-division has two advantages :—*a.* It increases the sense of evidence ; it increases, so to speak, the truth, (not the word, for we surely mean not to teach the art of elongation.)—*b.* It aids the understanding of weaker persons, by dividing the division, and retaining their attention at each time but for a short space.*

§ 3. *Of Disposition under the Oratorical point of view.*

We have distinguished logical or didactic disposition, which is concerned only with knowledge and judgment, from oratorical disposition which aims to produce an effect on the soul and through the soul upon the will.

But these things are not different in such a sense, that a disposition which is not logical may be oratorical. So far from this, logical disposition is the basis of oratorical, just as reason is the basis of eloquence. Even more ; a discourse logically arranged, is, thereby, to a certain degree, oratorical.

* Resuming the comparison which he has several times used in this chapter, M. Vinet adds: "The ladder whose steps are as much less distant from each other as they are more numerous." [EDITORS.] See BOURDALOUE, *sur la Pensée de la Mort*, deuxième partie, tome i., p. 135, édition Lefèvre: MASSILLON, *sur le Salut*, première partie, tome i., p. 473, édition Lefèvre; *et sur la Passion de Jesus Christ*, troisième partie, tome i., p. 531, même édition.

It is evident that a fault in logical disposition, by impairing proof, impairs impression in the same degree, seeing that the soul is struck or penetrated with a truth in the proportion in which it is made certain and manifest; and in the same way it is evident that all progress in proof is progress in persuasion, and even immediate progress, since from the nature of the subject matter of sacred discourse, it is scarcely possible that what is spoken to the understanding should not be also spoken to the heart. The effect of argumentation in discourse on religion or morality, is always a mixed effect.* For when we speak of oratorical disposition, we assume that the materials to be arranged are themselves oratorical, and disposition can only give evidence and force to their oratorical character.

But while there is something already oratorical in a logical disposition of such a discourse, there are means of rendering it oratorical, which, though founded on or conformed to logic, are not suggested by it, and apart from the use of which, the discourse would still be perfectly logical. They correspond to a logic which may be called the logic of the soul, and we may consequently name them *psychological.*

The peculiarity of the soul, its first necessity in the absence of action, or in expectation of action, is movement, and because eloquence is the language which the soul would hear, movement is the characteristic of eloquence or oratorical discourse. *Eloquentia nihil est nisi motus animæ continuus.*†

It is the part of the orator then, to give the soul the move-

* REINHARD, (cited by HUFFELL, *Uber das Wesen und den Beruf des geistlichen*, tome i., p. 266, at the bottom,) *Uber die Wichtigkeit des Sinnes für Hæuslicheit*, says: "1. Die Natur, *bereitet* ihn vor;—2. Die Klugheit *ræth* ihn an;—3. Die Pflicht *gebietet* ihn;—4. Die Religion *heiligt* ihn."

† "Quid aliud est eloquentia nisi motus animæ continuus? (CICERO.)

ment which it requires, a movement tending to a certain end. But in what consists this movement? It consists in the hearer's proceeding from indecision, from indifference, from torpor of will, to a full determination, which has place in the proportion in which the soul unites itself more closely to the truth which is presented to it.

The movement of which we speak, according to the expression of Cicero, which we have cited, is a perpetual or continued movement.

We may, by a word or an isolated act, give a movement to the soul, inclining it immediately to a certain object, to perform an act of will; but this movement is only a shock. By the same means we may repeat, multiply these shocks. They are fractions of eloquence, eloquent moments; these are not eloquence, they are neither the oratorical art nor the oratorical genius. Eloquence consists in maintaining movement by the development of a thought or a proof, in perpetuating it according to the expression of Cicero.

To perpetuate this movement, is not an artifice unworthy of the candor of truth, as if it restrained the hearer from taking breath, from pausing, from knowing where he is. The violation of the law of candor, if there be any, begins with the choice of the elements; if we may not dispose of them oratorically, we should not have chosen elements which are themselves oratorical. The first error was that we did not address ourselves exclusively to reason. We have examined this point, and shall not now return to it. If in proportion as we move the soul we enlighten reason, if light increases with heat, if at each spot, where the hearer pauses, he can satisfy himself as to the way he has taken, and justify to his reason, the emotion of his soul, how is the procedure of the orator to be blamed on the score of rectitude? Truth was made to move the soul, the soul was made to be moved by truth. May we say that the truth which is supremely amiable, has been received when it has not been loved? It is in its bosom that the contemplative faculty of the soul is harmonized and interfused with the affective or emotional faculty.

The first rule of oratorical movement is, we have seen, continuity. This rule is negative. It only requires that the movement be not interrupted; and why should it be interrupted?

It is necessary that the movement be continuous, because whatever interrupts it, not only does that, but reacts destructively on the effect already produced.

That it may be continuous, it is necessary, that what follows an argument or an idea, though entirely different from the preceding argument or idea, should be suited to sustain the impression which the hearer has received from what has preceded, and not to give his soul a wholly different direction. Thus the continuity is broken, when after having interested the soul the orator addresses reason, intending to return to the soul afterwards. It is also broken by every digression, every excursion from the subject, which induces forgetfulness of the orator's design. And in this case, the intervening interest so far from excusing the orator, makes his fault more manifest.

Even when these faults find no place in the discourse, the continuity of the movement may be broken by yet another means; namely, multiplied subdivisions. Here is the condemnation of those symmetrical plans which have so invaded the pulpit. I question whether the traditional form of sermons, stiff and cold *schematisme*, has as much tended to instruction, as it has injured eloquence. On this account we owe thanks to those who have done honor to the Homily, in which there is always a kind of continuity arising, according to the nature of the text from the connection of the ideas, or the sequence of facts. Fénelon, in his second

Dialogue on Eloquence,* opposes divisions altogether as presenting only an apparent order, as dessiccating and forcing the discourse, as dividing it into three or four discourses. The great orators of antiquity and the Fathers of the Church did not divide their discourses, in which, nevertheless, they distinguished what ought to be distinguished, and in which also the law of progression was observed.

Let us however explain. We must not confound two different things: division itself, and the announcements which disclose it. Manifestly, it is the first of these things we have to do with; division in itself. Now does division break the continuity of the movement? We cannot here take division for every kind of division; for then we should have to renounce movement, all discourse being necessarily divided into parts more or less distinct, and disposition implying a decomposition. To what is Fénelon opposed? It cannot be to division in this general sense; but, on the one hand, to formal division announced beforehand, and on the other, to a too artificial and too extended decomposition. I think he was opposed, particularly, to a subdivision founded on unimportant distinctions; to that perpetual cutting up of ideas which suspends at every moment the progress of the discourse, and demands at every moment unseasonable halts; a method to be distrusted from its being too convenient. It may be necessary to a certain extent, but if carried to excess, it becomes a pillow to idleness, a substitute for meditation. When truly one has a series of little discourses, instead of one compact discourse, it is not a beautifully-veined marble, but a rough mosaic. Fénelon spoke of this the more seasonably inasmuch as this method was strongly accredited. In the most beautiful sermons of Massillon, after removing

* *Dialogue* ii., toward the end, "N'en doutez pas. Puisque nous sommes en train."

the cuticle from the discourse, we see beneath little fresh invention; everything lies in that superficial net-work.

As we have said that disposition, as far as it is logical, is already oratorical, we likewise say, that as far as movement is continuous, it is already progressive. It resembles the fall of heavy bodies, with this difference, that we speak not of acceleration of the movement but of its intensity.* Uninterrupted movement is always becoming stronger. But progress in movement has also something peculiar and special, as might be said of a body which, independently of the first impulse, and of the tendency which maintains and, so to speak, renews it, receives incessantly an additional impulse.

As progress in physical movement will at length displace the greatest masses, overcome the greatest resistance, so in respect to the increase of intensity,—oratorical progress, it affects the soul more powerfully, penetrates it more deeply.

The law of oratorical discourse is in this respect the same with that of the drama. Let us keep the drama always in view, with its plan always thickening, its incidents and its catastrophe. *Omnia festinent ad eventum.* †

1. But let us pass from the general idea of oratorical progress to its different forms, and let us first remember that progress is made when we pass from that which affects essentially the understanding only, to that which acts upon the

* "All real movement has its quantity. It is neither extent nor velocity only, it is the degree itself of its reality, of which velocity and amplitude are only the result and the sign: it is intensity. Now, intensity, the degree of reality, has its direct measure only in the energy of the cause, in force. On the other hand, if force is its own measure, it is also proportioned; it is proportioned at least to its actual energy, to the resistance which it has to overcome. Movement is the resultant of the excess of power over resistance." RAVAISSON, *De l'Habitude*, pages 18, 19.

† "*Semper ad eventum festinat.*" HORACE, *Art of Poetry*, verse 148.

will. Not that each one of these faculties is not, in its own sphere, as perfect as the other; but, in life, it is not the understanding which complements the will, it is the will which complements the understanding; thought in general, if not each particular thought, would resolve itself into action; in all his faculties man tends to action. *Facultas* comes from *facere*, it is the power of doing.

There is then, in all discourse, strictly, a progress, a progress from theory to practice, from idea to action. We violate this rule when we give explanation of a duty, after having presented its motives. The difference is here to be seen, between logical and oratorical disposition. The two kinds, as before indicated, are equally logical. And even in life, the explanation of a duty, or directions as to the manner of performing it, come very naturally after enforcements of it. But this would be perilous in a public discourse. The optics of a public and solemn discourse are not the same with those of a conversation.

2. Again, in a series of ideas relating wholly to the understanding, there is a progress from the abstract to the concrete, from *à priori* to *à posteriori*, because realized ideas or facts, though not intrinsically better as proof, act more directly on man, and sentiment is nearer the will than intelligence.

3. Among arguments of the same nature, whether addressed to the understanding or the will, we must advance from the weaker to the stronger. But what are the weaker and what the stronger? If the question relates to proofs for the mind, the simplest and most evident are the strongest, and presumptions are less strong than proofs.* If the question

* A singular idea of Cicero: He advises us to throw into the middle of a discourse the arguments on which we place the least value, that in company with the others they may escape detection. *Ergo in oratione firmissimum quodque sit primum dum illud tamen*

relates to facts, progress is from the less to the more important. If it relates to motives, the question is difficult. What are the weakest, what are the strongest? Are the most elevated the strongest? If so, Bourdaloue was wrong, when in treating of impurity he considered it first as a sign, then as the principle of reprobation.

A question presents itself. When a motive or argument is incomparably stronger than all others, when it is supreme and decisive, why pass through many others to arrive at that? Is it thus that we do in occasional and accidental discourses?

Perhaps not ordinarily; but perhaps we should do thus if these discourses were somewhat prepared, and were not accidental; in the majority of cases, we are confident that this method would be justified by the result.

There are cases, doubtless, in which public discourse itself would be acceptable, if it mentioned secondary arguments only in the way of pretermission, or even did not mention them at all. But in general, and especially in pulpit discourse, the point of view is different from that of occasional or accidental discourse in common life. The situation of the orator and his hearers is a tranquil one; the subject is not of momentary interest, a question suddenly started, a measure to be taken immediately. Not more is it an excited passion in unison with which the orator is to put himself.

Without intending to maintain that oratorical discourse is a poetical representation of real discourse (any more than a letter is an imitation of a familiar allocution or conversation), we may yet say that it is somewhat ideal. It is indeed reality, but an extraordinary reality; a point of view not met with, but given. The auditory is not a known individual; it

teneatur, ut ea quæ excellant serventur etiam ad perorandum; si quæ erunt mediocria (nam vitiosis nusquam esse oportet locum), in mediam turbam atque in gregem conjiciantur. De Oratore, lib. ii., cap. lxxvii.

is a collection of individualities whose mean we must calculate, a new being, a being *sui generis*. It is not a chance meeting, but a solemn assemblage. Finally, it relates to an act, isolated and regarded as single, in which everything is to be said, and to which we are not to return.

It is said that, in general, there is but one reason which is decisive. It is true that when a man is to give an account of an action which he has done or is about to do, we may be sure that one of the reasons which he gives is the strongest, that which has determined him,—that which he has given to himself; the others are for those to whom he may wish to commend the resolution he has taken. Why does he not express this first? or rather, why does he not express only this; for it is very certain that if he begins with the strongest argument the others will be neither felt nor listened to?

But the orator must give all the reasons; first, because he does not know which is the decisive reason, and because the same reason is not decisive with every one, nor with each one always; next, because truth should employ all its means; and finally, because it is useful to the mind to discern light from every point of the horizon; for it is not with truth as it is with the sun. We have not, however, the mistaken idea that quantity, in this case, may serve instead of quality; we do not regard conviction as a kind of intellectual oppression in which the mind is overwhelmed by the mass of arguments and the multitude of words.

Finally, the more suited an argument is to move and startle the soul, the greater the necessity for preparing the way before it is presented. The soul taken at unawares is disconcerted by vehement and abrupt challenges; it is rather confounded than conquered; it cannot react except from an appropriate disposition imparted by what has gone before.

4. Where, in accordance with the rule of progress or ascending movement, are we to place the solution of doubts and

the answer to objections? Should they be introduced before or after positive arguments? We cannot meet this question by the same reply in all cases. Let us, however, rest assured beforehand, that what logic suggests, physiology will approve and reciprocate. I think a distinction should be made. We may place before the positive proof, the examination of the prejudices, presumptions, equivocal expressions, confessions, logomachies, by which the question is obscured. This, if we may so speak, is to clear the ground on which we are to build. The refutation of objections, properly so called, is a different matter. If it does not constitute the entire discourse, it must come after the proof. But it is necessary that it should be clear, quick, rapid; that it should be turned into proof; that it should be an application of the positive arguments which was first presented.

In discourses composed of parallel parts, there may be progress, provided the parts follow in the order of their importance; but this progress cannot be compared with that of a discourse in which, instead of two or three lateral parts, everything is successive; in which there are not two or three discourses, in some sort, but one only, one single train of ideas, the first of which produces the second, then the third, and so on even to the end, so that the last pages share the strength of all which precede them, and the weight of the whole discourse rests upon the last paragraph. The progress here is as the accelerated fall of heavy bodies, not an arithmetical but a geometrical progression.

CHAPTER II.

OF THE EXORDIUM.

Among experienced preachers we find few examples of exordiums altogether defective; we find few good ones among preachers at their beginning. We hence naturally infer, that there is in this part of the discourse something of special delicacy, but nothing which demands peculiar faculties. It is with exordiums as with nice and exact mechanical operations, in which the workman finally succeeds, but not without having broken more than one of the instruments which he uses. We shall be able to judge of it from what we have to say concerning the nature and purpose of the Exordium.

Is the exordium necessary, natural? Or is it but a factitious and conventional ornament?

I remark that nature itself teaches us the art of preparation and gradation. We approve of it in everything, and we connect with it the idea of beauty. The beauty of the skies would be diminished by the absence of twilight and dawn. "*Sic omnia quæ fiunt quæque aguntur acerrime, lenioribus principiis natura ipsa prætexuit.*" *

I remark in the second place, that even in accidental conversation, no one begins *ex abrupto*, if he is free to do otherwise. If we do begin *ex abrupto*, if we hurry into the midst of things, (*rapit in medias res*,) if we enter the apartment by the window, it is when some circumstance or some word pro-

* Cicero, *De Oratore*, lib. ii., cap. lxxviii. "There is no cause in the compass of nature which pours itself into effect all at once, and suddenly vanishes; in like manner, nature hath disguised under gentle beginnings, the progress of more violent commotions." (Translation: London, 1808.)

nounced by another, has placed the auditory at the point of view at which we would have it. This is itself an exordium, and the exception confirms the rule. But apart from such cases, in which the preparation has been given, every one, without thinking of it, feels that the auditory should be prepared. There is a case in which this necessity is distinctly recognized. This is when some explanation is necessary to the understanding of the subject; when, for example, the passage of the Bible on which we are to speak, is intelligible only from its connection with what precedes it. But there are other reasons independently and in the absence of this.

In the first place, there is a certain degree of weight in the mere fact of beginning a discourse with an exordium. We appear to have more regard for our subject, when we do not approach it immediately, abruptly.

It is useful to compose the hearer for a moment, lest he enter into the depth of the subject with a wandering mind; now we can do this only by means of ideas in near relation to the subject.

But ordinarily, something more is required. The orator should seek to put his hearer in a state of mind in relation to his subject, similar to his own. It is with the orator and the hearer as with instruments which are tuned before a concert.

"The reason for an exordium," says Quintilian, "can be no other than to dispose the auditory to be favorable to us, in the other parts of the discourse. This, as most authors agree, is accomplished by making them *benevolent, attentive* and *do cile;* not but that a due regard should be paid to these three particulars, during the whole of the action; but in the exordium they are of singular moment, as by it we so far gain an ascendant over the mind of the judge, as to be able to proceed farther."*

The exordium, then, is a discourse before the principal dis-

* QUINTILIAN lib. iv., cap. i., (Patsall's translation.)

course, the object of which, in all cases, is to render the hearers benevolent, attentive, teachable, by which I understand disposed to receive instruction, and, in certain cases, to prepare them to understand well what is afterwards to be spoken.

We remark that it is not the personal interest of the orator, but much rather that of the hearer, which is here to be considered. And hence the word *benevolent* is not the most appropriate.

But, in no case is the choice of the idea in the exordium arbitrary ; it is less so than a prelude or an overture in music, not more so than a preface to a book. What is to be desired under the name of an exordium, is not a delay or an interval more or less well occupied, but an introduction, a preparation, the excitement of an expectation as distinct and vivid as possible. In our judgment, the truest exordium is that which has conducted the orator himself to his subject, or which is as the height to which the orator ascends after treating his subject, in order to contemplate it as a whole. After what we have said, it is not difficult to discover the rules of the exordium. If we pause long on a part which fills so small a space, let it be remembered that no part is either more difficult or in more danger of mismanagement.

I. The first rule for the exordium is confounded with the definition itself, in proportion to its proximity to it.

When an exordium is not supplied, or replaced by an explication of the text or context, it should be drawn from an idea in immediate contact with the subject, without forming a part of it.

These two things are self-evident. If the idea forms a part of the subject, it is no more an introduction or an exordium. If the idea has no relation to the subject, it is no more an exordium, it is a ridiculous outwork.* But if the first part of

* *Un hors-d'œuvre ridicule.* Fr.

the rule cannot be explained, it is otherwise with the second. It does not relate to an idea in the neighborhood of that of the discourse, but to an idea in immediate contact with it, between which and that of the discourse there is no place for another idea, so that the first step we take out of that idea, transports us into our subject. If we are not bound to this condition, we may allow ourselves, under the name of an exordium, all manner of divergence, and take the liberty to start with a digression. We may be assured that an exordium is not a good one, if it does not appear necessary, if it does not appear incorporated with the discourse, if it gives the idea of a foreign discourse stitched more or less ingeniously to the principal discourse, if it leaves the hearer at liberty to think some other exordium preferable, or as good. The exordium is good only in so far as it has been suggested by the subject, as it is born of the subject, as it is united to it as intimately as the flower is united to the stem. *Penitus ex ea causa, quæ tum agatur, effloruisse.** Gaichiès says: "The exordium should be excluded from the work, if one might retrench it without doing the discourse an injury."†

In all its rigor, the rule would require the exordium to be incommutable, that is to say, that it should suit but one subject; for whenever it should not be incommutable, there would seem to be a place between the exordium and the discourse for an intermediate idea. We must at least observe the rule as constantly and closely as possible. But it certainly is not absolute, and if your exordium endures the test which I have indicated, if it appears necessary, if the idea of

* CICERO, *De Oratore*, lib. ii., cap. lxxviii.: "It should be borrowed in a manner from the main stress of our pleading, whereby it will appear that it is not only not common, and not applicable to other causes, but shoots, and, as it were, flourishes from the cause which is your immediate business. (Patsall's translation, or rather paraphrase.)

† GAICHIES' *Maximes sur le ministère*, deuxième partie iii. 6.

another exordium does not occur any more than that of another discourse in connection with this exordium, we should have no scruples, no fear of censure. Who would condemn Saurin's exordium to his sermon on the *Necessity of Universal Obedience?** But it is doubtless very well to admit such exordiums only as exceptions. Otherwise we shall become vague and trivial, and make introductions which introduce nothing.

The orators of antiquity, having special regard to personal interest in the exordium, which, consequently, was less closely united to the subject, and was less integrant with the discourse, cared little to avoid commutable exordiums. Cicero, Demosthenes himself, had transferable exordiums. In general, we prefer exordiums more closely united to our subject and our design.

Though the rule we have given should reduce the number of the subjects or motives proper for exordiums, it would not be less excellent; but so far from reducing, it multiplies the number. By neglecting it, we may think that we set ourselves at large; on the contrary, we confine ourselves in a strait. An introduction, perhaps, might be more easily formed, but there would be little variety in choice. It is by adhering closely to the subject, that subjects are multiplied.

We may conclude, from the following indication of some of the subjects of the exordium, that matter for exordiums is not wanting to an attentive mind.†

But we remark that in indicating here some of the chief sources of exordiums, we do not undertake to give a catalogue of commonplaces, from which one may choose at random. There is always one exordium which is better than

* Saurin, tome iii., p. 125, nouvelle édition.

† Huffell, *Der evangelische Geistliche*, tome i., p. 286. Ammon, *Anleitung zur Kanzelberedsamkeit*, p. 271.

any other, and it is that on which the true orator ordinarily falls first.

There is then,

a. The idea of the genus, of which the subject is a species. This, in some sort, puts the subject in its place, or marks the place of the subject. This is the most common kind. * The text often furnishes us with an exordium in which we proceed from the idea of the species to that of the genus.

b. The approximation of the subject treated to another, in order to indicate the resemblance or the difference. †

c. Opposition between the idea of the subject and some opinion or maxim prevalent in the world. ‡

d. Commendation of the subject, that is to say, showing its importance and excellence ; the reasons for choosing it, sometimes even apologizing for the subject : *Vestibula nimirum honesta, aditusque ad causam faciet illustres.* §

e. Calling to mind a fact by which the subject is individualized, or from which it springs. ‖ A favorite method of Saurin. ¶

* See Reinhard, Sermons for the year 1797, Sermon xvii., on the proposition, "Nothing is more easily corrupted in the hands of men than religion." See also the exordium of my sermon, *sur la sanctification.* (Meditations Evangeliques).

† See Saurin, *Sur la Cantique de Siméon*, tome iv., p. 29, nouvelle édition, tome iv. p. 29.

‡ See Massillon, first of his Sermons, *Sur le Bonheur des justes.* Bourdaloue, *Sur la resurrection de Jesus Christ*, tome ii., p. 315, édition Lefevre.

§ Cicero, *Orator*, cap. xv. "He will give the portal of his harangue a graceful appearance, and make the entrance to his cause as neat and splendid as the importance of it will permit." (Translation : London, 1808.) See Chrysostom, *Première homilie au Peuple d'Antioche.*

‖ See Theremin, *Sermon sur la predication, Das Kreuz Christi*, translated in the *Feuille religieuse du Canton de Vaud Année*, 1847, p. 193.

¶ See *le Sermon sur la Campagne de* 1706, tome viii., p. 93.

f. Relation of the subject to circumstances of time and place.

g. Relation to the circumstances of the orator himself. This is more delicate; it is an exception. In freedoms of this kind the execution is the solution of the knot.*

h. An exordium has sometimes the form of a prayer, but this is a form and not an argument or idea of the exordium. This prayer in its essential ideas, will enter into some one of the categories which we have indicated.

i. Finally, there is the text and the context; that is to say, the explication either of the words themselves of the text, or of the connection of these words with those which precede. Theremin thinks that the text presents matter for the exordium already at hand, and always suitable; we have only to draw the idea of the subject from the text, by attaching to it a short explanation of the circumstances in which the words of the text were spoken, and which give them a particular application.†

Without wishing to restrict the preacher to this single kind of exordium, we also think the text and the context (in other words the *nexus*) always offer us the matter of a good exordium, an exordium with which we should always be content. We only subjoin that we must not create the *nexus*, that we must not present a problematical *nexus*, or ascend too high or too laboriously, or by too short steps, the borders of that stream of discourse, of which our text, so to speak, forms one of the waves.

II. When we said that the exordium should be drawn from an idea not remote from the subject, we gave our second rule, which, of course, was comprised in the first. It must, in

* See CLAUS HARMS, (*Predigten über das heilige Abendmahl,*) *premier Sermon sur la Saint-Cène;* and SAURIN, *Sur les Dernieres discours de Jesus Christ,* tome iv., p. 55, nouvelle édition.

† THEREMIN, *Die Besredamkeit eine Tagend,* p. 77.

truth, be *one* idea, one single idea. There are two ways of violating this rule; one by descending from a more remote idea toward that which is in immediate contact with that of the subject; the other by making two, in some respects, parallel exordiums, that is to say, an exordium composed of two ideas, one of which is not derived from the other.

There was a time when the exordium was invariably double. "Formerly," says Gaichiès, "two exordiums were made, one to lead to the invocation, the other to prepare the way to the division." I add, that the first seems to have had scarcely any other purpose than of getting rid of the text.*

III. There may be unity in the exordium without simplicity. It is necessary that it be simple; that it do not reason or prove too much; that it restrict itself to the exhibition of one known truth; that it relate to what the hearer already knows, or admits. In the first steps by which we approach the subject, everything should be easy.†

IV. For the same reason it is necessary that the development of the idea of the exordium should be brief. By detaining the people long on the threshold of a house into which we have promised them entrance, we give them good reason to be impatient.

We present additional rules relating, not as did the others, to the contents or substance of the exordium, but to its character.

I. The exordium which is intended to prepare, to compose the hearers, suppose them not prepared, composed. In general then, we cannot appeal in the exordium to powers which

* See Bourdaloue.

† Exordium of the sermon of Bourdaloue, *Sur les Tentations*, (Carême,) tome i., p. 175, édition Lefèvre. We find here the plan of three or four sermons, and three of these, at least, after the author had already announced the object and division of his own.

have not yet been awakened. Vehemence, splendor of style, solemnity, are not in season yet, and we must not exhaust ourselves at the outset. This rule, however, is not absolute. 1. In some cases the hearers are already excited before the discourse begins, and the orator need not put himself below their level. Let him now venture. Fléchier is judiciously bold in the celebrated exordium of his funeral oration for Turenne; Blessig, in that for Marshal Saxe,* and Bridaine at Saint Sulpice. 2. It is one mode, also, of preparing the hearer to impress him with the solemnity, the grandeur of the subject. It may be important, in certain cases, to deprive of authority the trivial or worldly ideas which the subject may awaken.†

It is the privilege of talent and the fruit of study and experience, to know when to venture and when to abstain. It cannot be allowed to teaching, strictly so called, to set aside talent or anticipate the dictates of experience.

II. It is a rule which seems to be implied in the former, that exordiums be characterized by modesty. The ancient rhetoricians insisted on this; nay, even recommend timidity. There is a passage in Cicero which shows forcibly the humble position which the ancient orator took in the presence of his auditory.

"If you insist that I should speak my opinion of the matter without reserve, as all of you are my intimate friends, I will now for the first time declare what I have hitherto thought ought to be concealed. Even the best speakers, they who speak with the greatest ease and grace, are, in my opinion, guilty of too much assurance, though really modest, un-

* See *la correspondence de Grimm.*

† As I have endeavored to do, in my discourse *sur l'Egalité*, (*Meditations evangeliques.*) A remarkable example is the exordium of the sermon of Bossuet on the taking of the religious habit by Madame de la Valliere. (Comp. Maury, *Essai* x. *De l'Exorde.*)

less they appear timid, and betray some confusion, in the commencement of their speech; for the more a man excels in speaking, he is the more sensible of its difficulty, he is under the greater concern for the event, and to answer the expectation of the public. As for him who discovers no sense of shame, as is too commonly the case, such a man I think deserves not reproof only, but punishment; for I have often observed in you what I have experienced in myself: I grow pale at the beginning of a speech, and feel a tremor in every part of my frame. But when a young man, I was so intimidated, that (I speak it with the highest sense of gratitude) Q. Maximus adjourned the court, when he perceived me thus oppressed and disabled with concern."*

We prescribe the same rule but not as a rule of art. Surpassing Cicero, who doubtless would commend modesty in every discourse, (*Quæ enim precepta principiorum et narrationum esse voluerunt, ea in totis orationibus sunt conservanda,*)† we would not have the exordium but the orator modest; we even approve of his being timid; but with this distinction of Marmontel, that he be timid for himself and bold for his cause.‡ The first sort of timidity is becoming, the second disparages the orator, and destroys beforehand the effect of his arguments. Now, as we may be at the same time timid and bold, the boldness of the sincere christian must terminate in bearing him above the timidity of the man.

III. Finally, I require in the exordium clearness, justness, correctness, purity of language and style; in a word, I may say perfection. In respect to ideas and style, the exordium

* Cicero, *De Oratore*, lib. i., cap. xxvi. (Translation: London, 1808.)

† Cicero, *De Oratore*, lib. ii., cap. xix. "As to the maxims which they lay down with regard to exordiums and narratives, these, according to them, are to obtain alike in all speeches." (Tr. Lond. 1808.)

‡ Marmontel, *Elements de Litterature*, tome iii., p. 323.

in truth, cannot be too faultless. The orator's position is critical now, for the hearer, not being as yet warmly interested, can give his whole attention to details, and the orator, as yet, has been able to do nothing to obtain indulgence even to his slightest faults. "No part of the discourse," says Gaichiès, "needs as much exactness, or as much address, as the exordium, none being heard with more coolness and none more severely judged." He may be well assured that the attentive hearer will not forgive those faults in the exordium which he will pardon in the body of the discourse, after we have communicated to him our own warmth. All incorrectness, redundance, exaggeration, want of precision, obscurity, he will remark, and nothing will he forgive. Now, this first impression is often decisive and always important. "The success of a discourse," says Gaichiès again, "often depends on the beginning; from first impressions, whether good or bad, we do not easily recover." * It is more important that it be free from faults than adorned with beauty.

Boileau has said, "That one faultless sonnet is of itself worth as much as a long poem."† We are inclined to say as much of a faultless exordium. But yet we may not add that "this fortunate Phœnix remains to be found." There are exordiums which are at the same time beautiful and faultless.

Some persons have thought, on account of the importance and the difficulty of the exordium, that we should not em-

* See also CICERO, *De Oratore*, lib. ii., cap. lxxviii. "Principia autem dicendi semper cum accurata, et instructa sententiis, apta verbis, esse debeant. Prima est enim quasi cognitio et commendatio orationis in principio, quæ continuò eum, qui audit, permulcere atque allicere debet. "As to the introduction of a speech, it ought always to have accuracy, acuteness, sentiment and propriety of expression. For the first judgment, and as it were, prejudice in favor of a speech, arises from its setting out, which ought instantly to sooth and entice the hearer." (Translation, London, 1808.)—Tr.

* BOILEAU, *L'Art Poetique*, chant ii.

ploy our thoughts upon this part of the composition until all the rest has been written. This is not our opinion. This mode of proceeding is not natural. A good exordium prepares the orator as well as the hearer. It is not with this as with a preface; a preface is less essential to a book, which, indeed, may dispense with one. We would rather adopt the idea of Cicero: "Having weighed all these particulars, I proceed to consider what I am to say in the first place, and how I shall set out; for, whenever I wished to consider the introduction first, nothing occured to me but what was dry, trifling, trite, and common." Cicero afterwards tells us on what his mode of proceeding was founded. "Your preamble is not to be sought from abroad, nor elsewhere, but must be taken from the very essence of your cause. For this purpose, after you have felt and surveyed the whole of your cause, after you have found out and prepared all its topics, you are to consider which of them you are to employ in the preamble; it is thus easily found out."*

CHAPTER III.

DECLARATION OF THE DESIGN AND ANNOUNCEMENT OF THE PLAN.

If the utility of the exordium is founded in the necessity of preparing the mind and disposing it favorably toward the special subject before us, it is idle to prove that the subject ought to be announced. Let us only say, that it ought to be announced in a precise manner, so that the mind may direct itself immediately, and without hesitation, to a determinate

* Cicero, *De Oratore*, lib. ii., cap. lxxvii., and lxxviii. (Translation, London, 1808.)

point. In this announcement of the subject, our language cannot be too perspicuous, the terms we employ too appropriate. The discourse here admits of neither circumlocution nor figure. Moreover, we must restrict ourselves to a small number of words selected with the greatest care.

Must we also announce the plan of the discourse? Here there is a diversity of opinion. Some have thought that even the general division should not be announced. "An order is necessary," says Fénelon, "but not an order promised and discovered from the beginning of the discourse. Cicero tells us that the best method is generally to conceal the order we follow, till we lead the hearer to it without his being aware of it before. I remember, he says in express terms, that we ought to conceal even the number of our arguments, so that one shall not be able to count them though they be very distinct in themselves, and that we ought not plainly to point out the divisions of a discourse. But such is the undistinguishing taste of these latter ages, that an audience cannot perceive any order unless the speaker distinctly explain it at the beginning."* "The harangues of those great men," (Demosthenes and Cicero,) says the same author "are not divided as our sermons are. . . . The Fathers of the Church knew nothing of this method of dividing. And for a long time afterwards, sermons were not divided. It is a modern invention, which we owe, originally, to the scholastic divines." †

Gaichiès, though not so absolute, inclines to the same opinion. "May not the preacher," he asks, "sometimes free himself from the bondage of divisions? Must he always promise whatever he intends to give? The Fathers were not in subjection to them. They proposed their subjects, and

* Fénelon, *Dialogues sur l'Eloquence*, deuxième dialogue. (Former translation.)

† Fénelon, *Dialogue sur l'Eloquence*, deuxième dialogue. (Former translation.)

conducted their discourses to the end without distinguishing their parts."*

But the greater part of the masters, many of whom are models, and have experience on their side, incline to the opposite course, if they do not even formally pronounce in its favor. They admit only as the exception, what Fénélon would make the rule.

Hüffell starting from the fact, which, according to him, is very general and manifest, that half of the hearers, especially in the country, are mistaken as to the very subject of the discourse which they hear, and carry away from it only accidental and particular points of view, insists on a method, the effect of which is to retain them in a straight course from the outset, to enable them to anticipate what is to follow from one point to another, and to prevent them from taking cross paths instead of the main road.†

Theremin expresses himself thus: "At the end of the introduction the orator may announce the two or three parts which contain the development proper; for why should he not carefully employ this, as well as every other opportunity, to aid the hearer's attention, and to facilitate his comprehension of the whole? If the hearer is compelled to stretch his power of attention too much, he either slackens it altogether, or else the effect of the orator is exerted on the cognitive powers alone, and not on the will, which, for the orator's purposes, is tantamount to no effect at all. If we do not find this practice observed in the orations of the ancients, or any announcement of the plan and division, this may proceed from two reasons: First, the method to which they were obliged to accommodate themselves, was prescribed to them by the occasion on which they spoke, far more than is the

* Gaichiès, *Maximes sur le Ministère de la Chaire,* liv. ii., chap. 5.

† Huffell, *Uber das Wesen und den Beruf, des evangelisch-christlichen Geistlichen,* tome i., p. 294.

case with the sacred orator; and since this method, especially in the instance of the orator before a court, was almost always one and the same, it seemed unnecessary to announce it formally. Secondly, and this appears to me to be the chief reason—such a formal statement of the plan would have been evidence of study and previous preparation, the appearance of which they avoided as carefully as they sought to maintain that of extemporizing. For they had to deal with a suspicious public, who would have attributed such previous preparation only to the design to deceive. But the case is different with the sacred orator, who may allow the diligence he has bestowed with an honest intention, to continually appear in his oration, since he can excite thereby in the hearer nothing but the expectation of a mass of information all the more fundamental for this. If, however, the sacred orator would, for any reason, omit the formal mention of the grounds of his oration, of the plan which he has sketched for himself, he is free to do so; for though, indeed, it is absolutely necessary that he endeavor to arrange his thoughts in the clearest and best manner, it is not absolutely necessary that he specify beforehand how he has arranged them.*

Let us hear Ammon: "After the exordium comes the announcement of the proposition and the principal parts. It is called the *partition.* This rule is not always followed in analytical sermons. . . . . But in synthetic sermons it ought not to be disregarded; first, because the partition determines the point of view in which the orator proposes to consider the proposition; next, because it is the best manner of evincing the justness of his division; finally, because the partition gives the hearer a view of the whole which enables him to follow more easily the development of the ideas, and to find

* THEREMIN, *Die Beredsamkeit eme Tagend,* pp. 60. 61. (Prof. Shed's Translation.)

more quickly the thread of the discourse when in a moment of inattention he loses it. The orator who clearly and distinctly announces the theme of his discourse, who at the beginning of each part announces further the secondary propositions which he would draw from it; who then develops them with care and accentuates them justly, will be perfectly understood by his auditors without numbering, as some do, each section of his discourse."*

We will endeavor to present a *résumé* of the discussion, while we complete it by some considerations which have not been indicated in the fore-cited passages.

In favor of the partition it is alledged:

1. That the attention and interest of the hearer are more vividly excited by it than by the simple announcement of the subject, (the partition is its complement; the plan sometimes is the true subject;) 2. That he is less apt to mistake as to the subject, or to hesitate between the principal idea and accidental ideas, or those of simple development; 3. That it aids the hearer in following the march of the discourse and in finding his way again, if in a moment of inattention it has escaped from him. 4. That it assists his memory, and aids him in retaining the whole and the principal parts of the discourse.

On the other side it is maintained:

1. That the partition is a modern invention; that the ancients did not use it; that the Fathers themselves did not; that we have received it from the schools. This first consideration has more show than strength: *a.* First, the ancients sometimes practised and recommended it.† *b.* If they used

* AMMON, *Handbuch der Einleitung zur Kanzelberedsamkeit*, p. 278.

† "Recte habita in causa partitio illustrem et perspicuam totam efficit orationem. . . . . . Ex qua conficitur, ut certas animo res teneat auditor, quibus dictis intelligat fore peroratum." "In speaking, the partition, rightly presented, makes the whole discourse luminous and

it less than pulpit orators there were reasons for this, which Theremin indicates.

Let us then dismiss this first argument and attend to the others.

2. Other kinds of eloquence make no use of the partition.

This is not absolutely true, but if it were we might answer: *a.* That in general they have to do with hearers not so apt to be inattentive: *b.* That the plan is most frequent-

clear. Its effect is, to enable the hearer by keeping certain things in mind, to understand from what has been said, that which remains to be spoken." CICERO, *De Inventione*, lib. i., cap. xxii.

Quintilian suppresses the partition only in cases in which we would take the judge by surprise or unexpectedly. With him, then, this suppression is but a *ruse de guerre. Interim etiam fallendus est judex, ut aliud agi quam quod petimus, putet.* "The judge sometimes is to be led into pleasing deceptions, and amused by a variety of stratagems to keep him from discovering our designs." But this is only an exception:

"Opportune adhibita, partitio plurimum orationi lucis et gratiæ confert. Neque enim solum id efficit, ut clariora fiant quæ dicuntur, rebus velut ex turba extractis et in conspectu judicum positis; sed reficit quoque audientem certo singularum partium fine, non aliter quam facientibus iter, multum detrahunt fatigationis notata inscriptis lapidibus spatia. Nam et exhausti laboris nosse mensuram voluptati est, et hortatur ad reliqua fortius exsequenda, scire quantum supersit; nihil enim longum videri necesse est in quo, quid ultimum sit, certum est." "The partition, opportunely adopted, gives great light and beauty to a discourse. This it effects not only by adding more perspicuity to what is said, things by it being drawn out of their confusion, and placed conspicuous before the judges; but also by recreating the auditory by a view of each part circumscribed within its bounds; just so mile-stones ease in some measure the fatigue of travellers, it being a pleasure to know the extent of the labor they have undergone; and to know what remains encourages them to persevere, as nothing can seem necessarily long, when there is a certainty of coming to the end." (QUINTILIAN, lib. iv., cap. v.)—Patsall's translation.

ly required by the subject; *c*. That the didactic kind of discourse, which is that of the pulpit, may have its own rules.

We dwell no longer on this second reason, which is only a presumption.

3. The proofs should distinguish themselves. Nothing more is necessary than well-marked articulations.

4. The announcement of the proofs deprives them of their force in some measure, unless the announcement be so vague that it amounts to nothing. Of what use is it to announce that we are going to explain a duty, and state the motives to its performance, or expound a truth and express the infer ences from it?

5. In refreshing the memory we connive at mental indolence. Would it not be better to introduce the division at the end of the discourse, under the name of recapitulation?

6. In order to refresh the memory, we begin by burdening it.

7. In order to refresh it, we are led to make symmetrical, artificial divisions, and to prefer external to internal order. It is symmetry which is to fix the division in the memory. If, on the contrary, we omit the partition, we oblige ourselves to employ more pains in giving the discourse connexion and coherence. Is not the best refreshment for the memory precisely such a concatenated order and coherence, that if the first link of the chain is raised, the whole chain is raised?*

8. The argument itself of Hüffell, in favor of the partition, leads us to this conclusion. He speaks of a strange way of understanding sermons, especially by country people, but he forgets that the sermons so badly understood, are ser-

* We may retain the division very well, and not be much advanced by it. "It would be," says Fénélon, "what most frequently happens, if the people should retain the division better than the rest. Generally speaking, sensible and practical things are those which they retain best." *Dialogues sur l'Eloquence*, deuxième dialogue.

mons well and duly divided; for of the other kind none are made.

9. If we should limit ourselves to the announcement of the general division of the discourse,* this, according to Hüffell, would not suffice; each of the great parts must be divided. Ammon, indeed, requires this also.†

It appears to me, that giving these considerations their full weight, they do not require absolutely the suppression of the partition. The partition cannot fill the place of internal order and exact sequence of parts, but it may in some cases, contribute to the effect which is expected from well-constructed oratorical discourse. I think that the direct injury to the hearer, from the use of the partition, is less than the danger to the orator himself. In observing it, I would have him do what he can in the way of omission, and so construct his discourse that it will not seem necessary. As to the use of the partition, moreover, we should distinguish between different subjects and different auditories. And perhaps this form should not be laid aside entirely, until we have attained to years of maturity and strength. It is certainly remarkable that since the time of Fénelon, and notwithstanding his objections, almost all orators have retained it.‡

* See Huffell, tome i., p. 296.

† See the passage cited on page 311.

‡ There would, perhaps, have been no objection to the strictures of Fénelon on division, if they had been expressed with as much definiteness and precision as those of Robert Hall, in the following extract from his admirable sermon on the discouragements and supports of the Christian minister:

"May I be permitted to remark, though it seem a digression, that in the mode of conducting our public ministrations, we are, perhaps, too formal and mechanical; that in the distribution of the matter of our sermons, we indulge too little variety, and, exposing our plan in all its parts, abate the edge of curiosity by enabling the hearer to anticipate what we intend to advance? Why should that force which

When we use the partition, I think we should restrict ourselves to the announcement of the general plan, rejecting a more extended programme.

The partition, unquestionably, should be clear and simple in expression. It may be useful to present the particulars of the division under several successive forms, but it would be puerile truly, to multiply unnecessarily, these variations of the same idea.*

surprise gives to emotion derived from just and affecting sentiments, be banished from the pulpit, when it is found of such moment in every other kind of public address? I cannot but imagine the first preachers of the gospel appeared before their audience with a more free and unfettered air, than is consistent with the narrow trammels to which, in these later ages, discourses from the pulpit are confined. The sublime emotions with which they were fraught, would have rendered them impatient of such restrictions; nor could they suffer the impetuous stream of argument, expostulation, and pathos, to be weakened, by diverting it into the artificial reservoirs prepared in the heads and particulars of a modern sermon. . . . . Let the experiment be tried on some of the best specimens of ancient eloquence; let an oration of Cicero or Demosthenes be stretched upon a Procrustes' bed of this sort, and, if I am not greatly mistaken, the flame and enthusiasm which have excited admiration in all ages, will instantly evaporate; yet no one perceives the want of method in these immortal compositions, nor can anything be conceived more remote from incoherent rhapsody." Works, vol. 1, London Edition, 1832.

* See the partition of Bourdaloue's sermon, *sur la Fausse conscience*, criticised by Roques, in le *Pasteur évangélique*, p. 406.

CHAPTER IV.

TRANSITIONS.

As punctuation, in written discourse, serves at once to mark the intervals and relations of the thoughts to one another, so transitions have two opposite purposes—one to distinguish, the other to unite. They are a kind of punctuation on a large scale.

We may obtain the ideal of a well-constructed discourse from the human body, in which the articulations are only a flexion of the members, and occupy no place, except as a joint or a hinge. A discourse corresponds to its ideal, when its paragraphs spring out of one another by a true necessity, by a truly generative process, so that each paragraph contains the germ or reason of the following one. The conclusion of one paragraph is the exordium of the next; but there is nothing between the two, as there is nothing between the stones of a wall, so cut as to rest exactly on one another. "Well-cut stones," says Gaichiès, "are united without cement." This image is from Cicero.

But this is the ideal, and consequently, the exception. We are acquainted with almost no oratorical *chef-d'œuvre*, none at least in the pulpit, that realizes perfectly this ideal. Cement is often necessary. We must often, unless we would have the discourse without continuity, throw between two ideas an intermediate idea, common, I would say, to that which precedes and that which follows. These intermediate ideas are called *ideas of transition*, or simply *transition*.

It is certainly better to use them than to leave a void between two ideas, which it is almost certain the hearer will not fill up.

Transitions have the advantage of maintaining continuity of movement, and of suppressing those unfortunate moments in which the mind, not knowing what to do, is diverted and dissipated. When they are good they aid the memory in retaining the connection of the discourse. The striking manner in which two ideas are sometimes united, is itself an idea, which conveys and represents the two others.

These are the advantages of transitions. But the art of transition, an art almost imperceptible, is not an art without difficulty. *In tenui labor.* Boileau was well aware of this when he said that La Bruyère had avoided the greatest difficulty, in sparing himself transitions. It is this art of transition that connoisseurs admire in *l'Histoire des Variations.** Some idea of transition it is not difficult to find; but some transitions are no better than a void, than a rupture of continuity. A good transition combines several qualities.

It should be as simple and as short as possible, with nothing harsh or abrupt. It is a contour, it is not an angle or an elbow; but the contour ought not to be a deflection. It is not a discourse intercalated in a discourse. The subsidiary idea must not efface the principal ones.

It would efface them, however, brief as it might be, if the connecting idea were as marked as each of the ideas which it is to connect; if the thread of the discourse in that spot were as strong and as thick as in the preceding and following parts, it would be no longer a transition, it would be digression.

Transition, nevertheless, must be interesting, strong and free; interesting, presenting an idea or relation which in itself is worth attention; strong, connecting one passage with another, not by an accident of discourse, by a chance expression,

* Transitions of Delille, (*buts, howevers,*) are not much better than *ands,* that is to say, numbers. "There is in *la Pitié,*" says some one, "seventy-six transitions made by the word *but.*"

by a word; it may connect them indeed, by the extremity of the idea, but not by the extremity of the phrase; not by the narrow side of the antecedent idea, but by one of its largest faces—by face not by profile; consequently free, and not as in Bourdaloue and Massillon, the result of some premeditated chance. Demosthenes rather spares himself transition.*

When it can be done, the transition must be effected by an idea, which is a sentiment or movement of the soul.†

Transitions are as much more graceful as they appear more sincere; and they are more sincere in appearance the more they are so in reality. May we go further, and say that they should not only be sincere but natural, (*naïve*,) that is to say, involuntary and purely objective? We go not as far as this; we ask only that the connection between two ideas or arguments, be created without effort and without artifice, and that they spring from attentive consideration of the ideas which are to be united. The great masters, let us observe, have either made natural transitions or made none.

It is needless to add that the transition cannot in any case be said to give the appearance of order to disorder.‡

In indicating the sources or objects of transition, we do not forget that we are not speaking of ideas which engender one another—the transition *par excellence*, or that which dispenses with all transition. The object may be either to enhance the idea, or to to indicate a new degree of intensity, or to extend the idea, or to confirm the preceding idea by

* See the discourse *Pro Corona;* see also the manner in which he passes from a defence of his own conduct to a series of recriminations against Eschines.

† See Bossuet, in *l'Oraison funèbre de la Duchesse d'Orleans:* "*Le grandeur et la gloire!*"

‡ Maury, in his *Eloquence de la Chaire*, gives very good precepts and very bad examples, as to transitions.

that which follows it, or to distinguish, contrast, or subordinate two ideas, or introduce an objection, or finally, to confess the insufficiency of an argument in a given case.

CHAPTER V.

OF THE PERORATION.

THE peroration, whatever may be its form, is a discourse added to the end of a discourse, as the exordium is to the beginning, and drawn, like the exordium, from an idea near to the subject, so that the peroration has place after the subject has been completely treated, as the exordium has before it has been entered upon. We hence see that a part of what we have said of the exordium is applicable to the peroration; we see also that the peroration being, from the place which it occupies, the contrary, in some sort, to the exordium, we ought, in order to treat it well, to observe rules, in some respects, the reverse of those of the exordium. If, following the example of wise men, I were to express the whole theory of the peroration in a few words, I should cite these from Quintilian, which, he who shall comprehend, will know perfectly what is a peroration: *Quæ plerumque sunt prœmio similia, sed liberiora, plenioraque.* *

We do not, however, confine ourselves to this comparison, but shall consider the peroration in itself.

All the discourses of the pulpit may be comprised in two kinds: discourse of doctrine and of morality, of fact and of right.

They have all the common characteristics of exciting to some action.

* QUINTILIAN, lib. vi., cap. i. "The peroration, for the most part, is like the exordium, but is freer and fuller in its manner."—Tr.

Moral discourse impels us to it immediately. It is its direct end, and its end is apparent from the first. It proves or assumes the necessity of an action. It treats of this action itself and nothing else.

Doctrinal discourse urges to it likewise, but not immediately, or in a manner distinct enough to exempt the orator from pressing the consequences of the truths which he has expounded.

These two kinds of discourse, in fact, involve one another, and differ only in the proportion of the two elements; we must always rise from right to fact, or descend from fact to right; the discourse, otherwise, is not complete.

If, when you have accomplished your design, you feel no necessity of adding anything, let nothing be added; you have probably made a peroration without suspecting that you were doing so. Massillon has shown judgment and taste by completing, in a few lines, the peroration of his discourse on the *Death of the sinner and the death of the righteous.** In some cases, the peroration may not be distinct from the discourse. In a doctrinal discourse it is the last inference; in a moral discourse it is the last argument or last direction.

With Reinhard, the last number of the division ordinarily furnishes the peroration. We cite an example. The subject is curiosity; the discourse treats of the inconveniences of this disposition and the means of resisting it. One of these means is an activity inspired and regulated by duty; the second, constant effort for the best possible discharge of the duty which is binding on us; the third consists in daily cherishing in ourselves the thoughts, the resolutions, the expectations which become us as Christians. In approaching this last idea the orator exclaims: "No, our mind could not descend to the miserable pursuits of curiosity if it was nourished every day with the sublime contemplations to

* Tome i., p. 22, édition Lefèvre.

which Christianity invites us, if every day it sustained itself by them, and cherished the remembrance of God and Jesus Christ. Our heart could not be polluted by the low pleasures of curiosity, if we every day reflected on our calling as Christians ; how sublime, how sacred the duties we have to fulfil, and what we have to become here below, in order to be conformed to the image of God and of Jesus. Our mind would not be carried away by the perishable objects of worldly curiosity, if we remembered daily that we are on the road to eternity, and that we have much to do to prepare ourselves for our entrance into that awful eternity, which, perhaps, is nearer to us than we think, and may be, perhaps, just about to open itself to us. Oh ! that to this end God would make us feel, my dear brethren, the power of the Gospel of Jesus ; that by this gospel he would purify, strengthen and elevate your mind, and give you that seriousness, that wisdom and that dignity which ought to distinguish the disciples of his Son. To him, with his Son and the Holy Spirit, be glory forever. Amen." *

Thus, the last division of the sermon, that is to say, a passage which forms an integrant part of the discourse, may hold the place of the peroration. But this so far from excluding the peroration, involves the idea of it, supposes its necessity. When we say that something else may perform the office of the peroration, we thereby affirm that the peroration should not be wanting in an oratorical discourse, and do but vary the form of expression.

The custom then of terminating the discourse by a peroration has some grounds. Let us search for them. In the first place, the peroration like the exordium is required in order to avoid abruptness. As we should not begin abruptly, neither should we end in this manner. When we are about to enter upon any matter we feel the need of self-recol-

* See *Sermons pour l'Année* 1797 ; Sermon xviii., p. 372.

lection, and the same when we are to finish any matter. Now self-recollection in this case is pausing upon the total impression of the discourse, or upon an idea at least as general as that of the discourse, instead of pursuing still the particular idea with which the orator has concluded: an elevation is occupied from which the work as a whole may be viewed.

It is required, again, in order to bring together the instructions which have been given, to compress them within a small space, so that they may be regarded collectively.

Yet again it is required, that by all the thoughts of the discourse as by only one and the same thought, we may be elevated to that which is the first and last object of the discourse, and of all preaching,—either prayer or praise.

These different demands, even if they are not met by the last sentences which complete the exposition or discussion, are obscurely felt by the hearer, in proportion to the interest he has had in the discourse. But whether he has felt them or not, the orator should wish to leave him under the most favorable impression toward the cause he has been maintaining, and what he may add at the close will not be the less a part of his work, than the exordium.

Now, in indicating the different necessities which the hearer may have felt in the process of the discourse properly so called, we have already indicated the different forms of the peroration.

There is the *résumé*, which reduces to a small number of ideas or even to one only, the ideas of which the discourse is composed. This is as a burning focus in which all the rays are concentrated. All the ideas of the discourse may also be condensed into a sentiment. This may be an idea yet more general than that of the discourse, an idea which while it enlarges the horizon, not only leaves the object in view but constantly recalls it. It may also be a new argument which presents the evidence under a vivid, concise, and unexpected form.*

There is the recapitulation,† a kind of after-partition, the parts of which, being already known, are no longer presented under an abstract, vague, incorporeal form, as in the division properly so called. These elements have been incorporated in the discourse, and now when collected and compressed in the peroration, formed into a bundle, clothed as much as may be in new expressions, presented in the tranquil and firm attitude of established truths, which have only to show themselves, they furnish a peroration not only useful but much more oratorical than Maury supposes.‡

There is the application or practical conclusion. It may seem strange that this is made a form of a peroration, since discourse is no farther oratorical and christian than it tends to practice. But we know that even a discourse of this character may require to be followed by some additional discourse, in order to appropriate to the hearers in a more impressive and direct manner, the truths to which they have just been attending. This may be done by interrogating conscience, by censure or exhortation, by promises or threatenings. The application, I think, should do something more than merely reproduce the idea of the sermon; it should present this under a new form, a new aspect, so that this kind of peroration may be substantially the same with that of which I spoke first.

Moreover, if we examine closely, we shall see that every pe-

* See the peroration of the *Plaidoyer pour Louis XVI.*, par LALLY-TOLLENDAL, *Chefs-d'œuvres de l' eloquence française.* Barreau, p. 200.

† "It is often proper at the end to make a recapitulation which collects, in few words, all the orator's force, and brings into view the most persuasive things which he has said." (FÉNÉLON, *Dialogues sur l'Eloquence*, deuxième dialogue.

‡ MAURY, *Essai sur l'Eloquence de la Chaire*, lxxvi., *De la Peroraison.*

roration is an application, and that we cannot even conceive of a peroration which is not an application—that, I mean, by which a nearer approach is made to the hearer, in order to impress more forcibly on his heart the truths he has just been hearing.

The application from being general, may become special, that is to say, suited to actual circumstances, or distributed among the different classes of hearers, accommodating to each the truths or the principal truth of the discourse; the rich and the poor, the young and the old, the converted and unconverted. There are preachers with whom this last distinction is never wanting. It is, indeed, unavoidable, and impliedly, at least, it has place in all sermons. The edge of evangelical truth would of itself make this division, though we should not make it. The gospel separates man into two men, life into two lives, of which conversion is the separating line. The pulpit teaches to some, certain principles, and requires from others the fruit of principles which they have already adopted. It would fail of its purpose, it would not fulfil its commission, if this fundamental distinction should not be enforced by all its teaching, and if its aim seemed to be to collect something better than wild fruit from a tree which had not been grafted. For the purpose of the gospel, its distinctive characteristic, is to engraft divine sentiments upon a human nature. This fact of itself is of much efficacy; but it would in general be better to oblige the hearers to class themselves than to announce this classification. Moreover, although we must be either without or within, and it would be melancholy if man should be made to dream of I know not what chimerical intermedium, we should not forget that there are shades, degrees of difference, that among those who are without, some are more, some less disposed to religion, and among those who are within, some are more and others less faithful to the grace they have received. Let us not speak slightly as to what is essential to being without or within, or rather as to the signs by which one may know whether another man is within or without. But let not form conceal reality, or abuse condemn use. The application of the sermon may then be distributed or divided; but if it is thought necessary to introduce, ordinarily, the classification we have mentioned, into the application, I could wish that variety of form might render the return of it less monotonous, or even dissemble it.

Finally, there is prayer, which is not so much a kind as a form of peroration, or if we may so speak, the peroration of the peroration, the conclusion of the conclusion. We must, in every case, end with a prayer or by a devout wish.

A peroration may be such as to present at the same time all these characters: recapitulation, *résumé*, prayer, application, as in Massillon's sermon: *Consummatum est.**

In whatever way we terminate the discourse, it is difficult to do it well, and more rare, I think, than to begin it well. We are naturally more desirous and careful to make a good beginning. Whatever idea occurs to us as proper for the exordium, the text, the subject gives it. We are more embarrassed at the end, since, on one hand, it seems that we have said everything, and find ourselves, so to speak, in presence of nothing, while, on the other hand, we feel the necessity of saying something more. We are fatigued, exhausted; we dread a new effort, and we dispatch the peroration with some common-place exhortation or wish, with exclamations, with passages of Scripture negligently introduced. It is, however, an essential part of the art to terminate well; it is at least as important to be assured in respect to the last impressions as to the first, on which the hearer may return; he is the conqueror who remains master of the battle-field. I cannot here apply the proverb, "All is well that ends well;" for a fine peroration cannot make amends for a bad discourse; the

* Tome i., p. 532, édition Lefèvre.

damage is not to be repaired, and the peroration which draws its force and its beauty from its relation to the discourse, cannot be conceived of as beautiful or good independently of that relation; but supposing the discourse to be what it should be, it is important that the conclusion should agree with it, and confirm the effect which has already been produced. In order to this, we must, in the peroration—

1. Introduce no new subject. I say *subject;* but I do not call a subject new, the general idea in which tends to expansion and enlargement, the new idea in which tends to renovate the particular idea in the subject of the discourse.

2. Present a truly distinct idea, not vague effusions. Let the bed of the river be enlarged, but let the river arrive at the sea entire and distinguishable.

3. Adhere to the idea of the discourse quite to the end, even where we seem to be throwing ourselves upon one more general.* It is interesting to remark that lyrics, which do not pretend to didactic order, follow the same rule. (See J. B. Rousseau, *Ode au Comte de Luc.*)

I give no other rules. I will not say, fill the peroration with the loftiest ideas, the liveliest sentiments, the most striking images, the boldest movement. Though all this be authorized, countenanced by the very nature of the peroration, it may not be precisely the object of a rule. I admit, indeed, that if we feel as much under obligation to timidity after as before proof, we should seem to have gained little ground.† I admit that though it is never proper to sound a trumpet, a firmer tone and higher pretensions are legitimate now; the peroration is the mouth at which the discourse dis-

* Nevertheless, Bossuet connects the peroration of his sermon, *Sur l'Impenitence finale*, with this idea, that the world without assistance attains to the greatest misery.

† Compare the *Exordium pro Coronâ*, with the peroration of the same discourse.

charges itself as the exordium is its source, and a river at its mouth is larger, fuller, more powerful, than it is at its source. I grant again, that the hearer warmed in the course, readily yields to rich and moving language. But yet again, all this does not furnish matter for a rule. Rather will I say, let the peroration be what it may. It is not a separate and independent discourse, it is the result of the discourse. It is truly excellent only from its relation and proportion to this. If we may give the peroration the bold, striking, impressive character of which I have spoken, we must be authorized to do this by the tenor of the discourse, by the impression we see we have made on the hearer. If we have something more urgent to say, let us say it; but often nothing remains but to give the mind a calm and solemn view of the subject, or impart to it a devotional frame. Very properly the peroration will often be in a less elevated and less vehement tone than the preceding parts. Here again the rhetoric of the ancients cannot be taken absolutely as our guide and model. "We may recommend the observation of this short precept: Let the orator keep in view the whole stress of the cause, and on seeing what it contains either favorable, odious, deplorable or heinous, in reality or probably so, say those things which would make the greatest impression on himself." * Truly, after rhetoric like this, the judges would be on their guard, and would only have to remain so. The *Cumulus*, of which Quintilian tells us,† as if the peroration was intended to gather into a heap all the impressions produced by the discourse, is not necessarily the character of the peroration.‡ Above all, it is not the essential and constant character of the peroration or epilogue of the sermon ; the sermon may be very properly finished in a

* QUINTILIAN, lib. vi., cap. i. [Patsall's translation.]

† QUINTILIAN, lib. vi., cap. i.

‡ See the peroration of the discourse of CICERO, *Pro Ligario*.

manner very different. It may be remarked that the perorations of the great masters of the pulpit are generally moderate and gentle.* We may compare them to a river, the waves of which, sure to arrive at the sea, become slow at the mouth, and present to the eye only a sheet of water, the motion of which is almost insensible.†

As, however, in citing examples of exordiums and perorations, they must be detached from the discourse, the former may be presented with more advantage than the latter. To judge of an exordium we have only to know the subject, to judge of a peroration we must have seen the whole discourse, because the beauty of a peroration is especially a beauty of relation, and resides principally in the suitableness of this conclusion to the discourse. As especially applicable to the subject of the peroration, we may recall those excellent words of Cicero: "He is the man of genuine eloquence who can adapt his language to what is most suitable to each. By doing this, he will be sure to say everything as it ought to be said. He will neither speak drily upon copious subjects, nor without dignity and spirit upon things of importance, but his language will be always proportioned and equal to his subject."‡ "Discretion, therefore, is the basis of eloquence, as well as of every other accomplishment. For as in the conduct of life, so in the practice of speaking, nothing is more difficult than to maintain a propriety of character." §

* See in the *Oraisons funèbres* of BOSSUET, édition de M. Villemain, the end of the first, page 51, and the remark of the Abbe de Vauxcelles.

† In the *Oraison funèbre de Turenne*, by FLECHIER, the peroration after a discourse wholly pathetic, is truly what it should be. The same in a sermon of the opposite kind—that of the Abbe Poulle, *Sur l'Aumône.* But especially we must remark that of the funeral oration for Condé, by BOSSUET.

‡ CICERO, *Orator*, cap. xxxvi. [Translation: London, 1808.]

§ CICERO, *Orator*, cap. xxi. [Translation: London, 1808.]

CHAPTER VI.

GENERAL CONSIDERATIONS ON THE FORM OF PULPIT DISCOURSE.

SUPPOSING that a sermon had never been made, what form would the precepts we have given require it to possess? Would it be precisely some one of the existing forms? Previously to a comparison of our theory with these forms, we may boldly answer, no. For the pure theory, or if we please the abstract idea and essential nature of an object, do not determine the form to the exclusion of every other cause. Time, places, circumstances, concur to this end; there is history in the form of every work of art, by which I mean, not only a correspondence of this form with contemporary circumstances, but the influence of tradition and ancient examples; influence, however, more sensible and more lasting in those kinds of work in which passion and actuality have less place. Passion and actual, palpable interest, exclude, in some sort, the arbitrary and the stereotyped; passion and actuality cannot be stereotyped. The bar and the tribune may suffer the imposition of arbitrary forms, but they are not slow in relieving themselves of them. These preservatives may seem to have substitutes in the eloquence of the pulpit, the one by the immensity of the interest it has to do with, the other by its majestic immutability and its universality; but no, there is no compensation in these; and mind, fashion, or tradition, which, in things of this nature is a fashion, have, and always will have, in this kind of eloquence, more control than in the others; a desire to please will have more place there where it ought to have less, and the forms of preaching, we may be assured, will be more frivolous than those of the bar or the tribune. I mean by frivolity, pedantry, which is only a grave frivolity.

Our theory then presents conditions of an ideal discourse, the forms of which answer only to the purpose of eloquence, and of christian eloquence. It supposes no form more particular, it has respect to nothing conventional. It does not teach one to make a sermon in the historical sense of the word, but it teaches him to speak the truths of salvation to an assembly of christians, in the manner which experience and the study of human nature have shown to be the most suitable for enforcing every kind of truth. This theory does not delineate before our eyes a particular figure, a kind of portrait of pulpit-discourse; each subject, each necessity, each circumstance, will give it the form which it ought to have.

When we spoke of the exordium and the peroration, we did not take our idea from the ordinary practice of eloquence, but from its very nature, its necessities. The exordium and peroration doubtless are not less rational than the division of tragedy into five acts:

> "Neve minor, neu sit quinto productior actu
> Fabula."*

We have spoken as if there were no sermons. We cannot, however, pretend that we have forgotten them, that we have no regard to them; and that we make a form to ourseves, absolutely according to theory. We think it impossible that there should not be, at each epoch, a certain predominant form. This form had, perhaps, its reasons and its truth; gradually these reasons are lost sight of, the form ceases to impart knowledge; the exterior alone remains.

The reverse may happen; that is to say, time may correct a form which is but little natural. Such, for example, as that of the schools and of the middle ages. This, to Bourda-

* HORACE, *Art of Poetry*, verses 189, 190.

loue and Massillon was what the system of the classical unities was to Corneille and Racine. Men of genius and of good methods do not meet at the same epochs; methods are wanting to men, and men to methods. May it not be the same as to institutions, which are also methods? The form of preaching has been gradually improved, though we can name no reforming genius of the times, by whom it has been displaced and renewed.* There remains, however, something of the old method. In greater or less variety which it has received from men of different individualities, there is still a general type in which the form of the seventeenth century, though softened, is reproduced, (not, however, that of the reformed preachers of the first half of that century.)

The principle of enumerations and distinctions was in vogue; the parallelism of parts was preferred to their succession and their production from one another, the logical method to the psychological; symmetry prevailed over internal order, and preaching bore the impress of the old scholasticism, and of a superannuated rhetoric.†

We must distinguish here between use and abuse. The use is not only legitimate but often necessary.

But when we make a genus of this form, what have we attained? Arbitrary divisions, such at least as are little philosophical, and as science never would have supplied, symmetrical plans, external order substituted for internal order.

Moreover, superior minds had protested against it. La

* It is mediocrity which *corrects*; it does the office of editor.

† See Bourdaloue, *sur la Passion.* But the ideal of this kind of preaching is realized in Massillon's sermon on *Consummatum est.* The three parts are parallel; then, in each part the sub-divisions are parallel to one another. Remark again this other parallelism of the recital, the application, and the exhortation. There is scarcely any gradation in this discourse, and, further, the gradation is not a logical succession, still less a logical genesis.

Bruyère had said: "It appears to me that a preacher should choose, in each discourse, a single leading truth, alarming or instructive; treat it thoroughly and exhaust it; abandoning all these divisions, so far-fetched, so trite, so hackneyed, and so nicely distinctive."*

These abuses also have occasioned the complaints of Fénelon.† In opposing them he should have avoided, we think, the word *division*, since, in one sense at least, every discourse is divided. His practice explains his theory. He was always faithful to it, if we may judge from the two principal sermons which we have from him. He wrote that *sur l'Epiphanie*, in his thirty-fourth year, and in his sixty-third, that *pour le Sacre de l'electeur de Cologne*.

To speak of the first only, nothing here is parallel, everything is successive; that is to say, speaking with exactness, the successive predominates, since without parallelism there would be only indications of ideas, no development. It is a river, which here and there widens and moves slowly, but which is always one and always flowing. See the partition:

"But I feel my heart stirred within me, and divided between joy and grief. The ministry of these apostolic men, (the missionaries,) and the conversion of this people, is the triumph of religion; it may be, also, the effect of a secret reprobation hanging over our heads. Shall it be on our ruin that this people is to be elevated, as the Gentiles were on that of the Jews at the birth of the Church? Here is a work which God has wrought to the honor of his Gospel, but is it not also in order to its removal from us? We should not love the Lord Jesus if we did not love his work, but we

* LA BRUYÈRE, *Les Caracteres,* chap. xv.

† FÉNELON, *Dialogue sur l'Eloquence.* Deuxième dialogue toward the end, in the section in which he opposes the use of *divisions.* See the citation from Fénélon, page 309.

should forget ourselves if it did not fill us with trembling. Let us rejoice then in the Lord, my brethren, in the Lord who gives glory to his name, but let us rejoice with trembling. These are the two thoughts which will occupy this discourse."*

There are discourses on this model in Bossuet, such especially are *his orations*. He proceeds thus when he can do so. He delights, like Fénelon, in this dichotomy; and in my judgment, divisions into two parts are ordinarily the most tasteful.

What we would say, is not: Choose such or such a form. This is not to be done independently of the work itself, and purpose of preaching; the form of the sermon should proceed from its purpose. "It is the mind that creates the body."† Yet it is a false point of view which suggests the questions, What can I find to say on this subject? What does the subject give me to say? How shall I fill this void? How shall I divide and subdivide, so as to fill up my framework? It is a false point of view, although truly the art of dividing and subdividing appropriately, is the art itself of oratorical development, and the means of instruction. But we must say to ourselves: How shall I serve my subject, and not how shall I serve myself of my subject? How shall I establish, how recommend the truth? We must oppose the constant tendency of a form to take the lead, by care to occupy ourselves exclusively with our subject and our purpose. It is only a lively sensibility to the real, the actual, that can secure us against formality. The golden rule is to regard the sermon as a means, and not as an end. Our point of view is false, frivolous, sterile, when we consider it as an end.

* FÉNELON, *Sermon sur l'Epiphanie.* An analysis of the second part of the discourse should here have place, but this analysis is not to be found, and appears not to have been written.—[EDITORS.]

† "Der Geit ist's der den Kœrper Schafft."

Doubtless nothing can be more false, more unworthy the seriousness of the pulpit, than to seek innovation for innovation's sake, or independence for the sake of independence.

But is it hence necessary to postpone the consideration of our subject and our purpose to that of some consecrated form, and permit ourselves to be pre-occupied with this? Abused as the word individuality may have been, I feel myself constrained to advise the orator to be individual. This does not imply that he is to withdraw himself from general laws, to forget which would be to separate himself from the community of mankind; it requires him to acquit himself of his mission, by being intelligent and trustworthy, and by having proper regard to the impression which the truth has made. Is it not necessary that the liquid take the form of the vessel into which it is poured, and does this form change the liquid? Without individuality, there is not truth. In art as in religion, objectivity, objective verity has *naïvete* as its condition, and naïvete has no place without individuality. When we renounce ourselves in favor of another, that is to say of a conventional model or type, what has the truth gained? We must then place ourselves before our subject, put ourselves under its power, receive from it our law, owe to it our form, and while profiting by models, accept no other form than that which the laws of good sense and the knowledge of human nature may impart to our work. It is evident, in fact, that our individuality should be employed in the structure of the discourse, as well as in all the rest.

Theremin attaches the highest importance to this privilege, which, in some sense, he regards as a duty.

"A deeper penetration into the nature of that life of faith, which is to be exhibited in the sermon, will give us the following results in respect to the form of the discourse:

"The life of faith, in every one who really lives it, and is not content with the imitation of a foreign type, is wholly and peculiarly his own; it may be like that of another, but can never entirely coincide with it. This individual stamp belonging to it, may and must be impressed upon all which proceeds from it, upon the ordinary discourse, the bearing and the actions, and hence upon the sermon also. If this be duly weighed, it must certainly seem strange that our sermons appear to be restricted to a single form, only slightly varied. One who is just beginning to be a pulpit orator, will do well to appropriate among the existing forms that which best suits himself; but it is to be expected, if his inner life is unfolded with something of energy, that it will soon break through this first form; and for every new stage it attains, that it will also create for itself a new form of discourse. No one in this matter should let himself be held back by traditional rules, which are often only limited and limiting prejudices, for there is no norm to be set up beforehand, to which every sermon must be conformed; but every sermon carries with it its own standard of judgment. It is, therefore, an auspicious sign of recent times, that distinguished pulpit orators make to themselves paths of their own, and that approved men, as Tholuck and Harms, in the works we have cited, impart directions which, taken generally, seem to contain the demand that one's own individuality should have a freer course in the sermon. Thus, what is new in the form of the discourse, ought to be willingly accepted, so far, that is, as it actually springs from the real life of faith, and does not gush out from an unregulated imagination, and is not a capricious device to excite attention. But such approval should always be prefaced by saying that the earlier form is not in the comparison considered as antiquated, and that it can remain, as one into which devout minds have shaped their thoughts, and which may still perform the same service for kindred spirits, and in like stages of growth.

"According to these principles, a just judgment, in my

view, may be passed upon that form of the sermon most current with us. It is the one in which we divide the theme derived from the text, into two, three and sometimes four parts, and unfold these in succession. It seems to me undeniable, that this method of constructing the sermon has its great advantages. It not only favors, but imperatively demands, a thorough and comprehensive elaboration of the subject, a luminous arrangement of the thoughts, and it gives to the mind of the hearer, often wandering and weary in a long discourse, a thread by which it can set itself to rights.

But this form has also, indeed, its disadvantages. In carrying an idea through thesis, divisions and subdivisions, it may easily lose something of the force and freshness, with which it at first came up to the mind. And in order to shape the two or three divisions with symmetry, something of importance must, occasionally, be left out of one, and something unimportant added to another. Several times, too, that is, in each of the divisions, we begin from a new beginning; for we must commence each part with a general statement, and close with an application to life; and this is a uniformity which may weary the speaker and the hearers. This form of discourse is found, indeed, among the French pulpit orators of the most brilliant epoch; for example, in Massillon and Bourdaloue; and that, too, even more severely than with us, since they also divide the divisions, and formally announce these subdivisions. Fénélon, even then, declared against this method, and expresses the wish that this form might be supplanted by another, which he proposes.* Sickel has also recently, and not without reason, urged many things against it.† But I cannot, in accordance with my general

* Dialogues on Eloquence, (pages 96–101.)

† Grundriss der Christlichen Halientik, s. 71 sq.

views, reject it; since I believe that it has rendered, and will still render, good service to many writers for the most impressive development of their thoughts. I would, therefore, advise all young ministers to try themselves in it, to carry it out with the greatest strictness; but also, I must add, to give it up as soon as they find that there is an irreconcilable contradiction between this method of exhibiting a subject and the natural course of their ideas and feelings. For such a case, among other conceivable forms, the following may be prescribed and recommended: Abandoning any formal division, let the writer avow only, in a general way, the intention of impressing upon the heart of the hearer the doctrine derived from the text. This doctrine may then be at once fully presented, without cutting it up into several parts, yet as concisely as possible, so that it do not form a main division of the discourse. When the leading idea has thus been brought into distinct view, it is then to be carried out in its relations to life, and brought into connection with the phenomena which are opposed to it, or which are conformed to it, and issue from it. Here the whole sermon is treated as we are wont to treat each part of it; it is, so to speak, only one part, it is wholly *of one piece*, for here there is not that breaking off from and returning to diverse general statements, which must be the case in beginning each of the formal divisions of the other method. Since the leading idea is not forced into any such definite bounds, we can have a greater freedom in the transitions of the discourse, and are not prevented, by regard to symmetry, from carrying out most fully the thoughts which are most important, and putting each one in its strongest place. It is, however, to be well remarked, that the method of procedure, though apparently lawless, must, for this very reason, be only the more according to law; and that the chief thoughts are not to be held fast less strongly, nor the illustrations selected with less care, than on the other method.*

We close with a citation from Herder:

"I have been careful, my friend, to remark, that we do not find in the Bible any model for the outward form of our sermons; for, what can we designate as such a model? The patriarchs blessed their sons, enjoined upon them to walk in the way of the Lord; but they did not preach in our manner. The fifth book of Moses is an address to the people, having for its theme and purpose that people's life, a most heart-felt, strong and importunate address, ending with the most solemn words of cursing and of blessing, followed by his eternal song and his humble benediction; but it is not the model of our usual discourses. Thus is it with the appeals of the prophets; they stand there as the mountains of God; who may say, mountain, come to me! From Christ we have sayings, parables, in part with their interpretations; there are also cordial addresses to his disciples and the people; but the *form* of our sermon is wanting. The *epistles* of the apostles are—epistles; in some cases with a theoretical and a practical division; they have become *texts* for sermons, upon which we preach, but how different is an epistle from a sermon! There then remains for us nothing but Luke's relation of the discourses of the apostles; but this is only a report of them, an historical epitome; it has not the form of an address written down as it was delivered. So far as I know, too, all these discourses are also different from each other, and which of them is properly like our sermon?

"You see, then, my friend, the *form* is not the essential thing, the form must be determined by the matter, it is only time which has given shape to it. That which is essential, which all the discourses of the Bible have in common, and

* Theremin, *Die Beredsamkeit eine Tugend.* Preface, pp. xxii.–xxvii.

which our sermons should also have in common with them, is, that they *proclaim the will of God*, that they set forth to the human heart and conscience the *word and counsel of God in respect to our true blessedness.* Patriarchs and prophets, Christ and the apostles, each in his way, did this ; this ought we to do in our way, *out of and according to the Scriptures ;* this is preaching."*

CHAPTER VII.

SELF-CULTURE WITH REFERENCE TO DISPOSITION.

RHETORIC directs us as to the mode of disposition as it also does as to the mode of invention, or rather it regulates our invention ; but it cannot be hence said to teach us disposition ; a too common error. In all things we scarcely learn more from rhetoric, than how to use the resources which it supposes us to possess, and which we find elsewhere.

It offers its counsels, and can give useful ones only to a man of upright mind, of open heart, who has disciplined his reason by the study of logic, and enriched it by that of philosophy.†

* HERDER, *Briefe das Studium der Theologic betreffend.* Letter xl.

† Cicero recommends philosophy less for that which it contains, and that which it imparts, than as gymnastics for the mind. *Positum sit in primis, sine philosophia non posse effici, quam quærimus, eloquentem ; non ut in ea tamen omnia sint, sed ut sic adjuvet ut palæstra histrionem.*

" *We may therefore consider it as a capital maxim, that the eloquent speaker we are inquiring after, cannot be formed without the assistance of philosophy. I do not mean that this alone is sufficient, but only that*

Eloquence penetrates into science and life by a multitude of roots.

Considering the disposition of the greater part of the sermons which we hear, a disposition ordinarily exact and according to rule, we may be inclined to think that disposition is not a great mystery, and that good sense and a little use would here be sufficient.

But all do not so easily succeed, and it is remarkable that the aptitude for disposition seems to be wanting in those who have at once too many and too few ideas;* success in disposition is best attained, with a mind sufficiently just, in the higher and lower spheres of thought. With very few or with many ideas, we have clear dispositions. But this clearness is profound with some, superficial with others; this order with some is more external, more internal with others; it has force, it has power with the first, it has not with the second; it is eloquent or it is not, for oratorical genius shows itself in disposition.

Now, the object is not to do *well* only, but to do *better*; and we really do *well* only when we endeavor to do *better*. Disposition may be more or less philosophical, more or less oratorical; discourse, more or less compact, formed of pieces fitted to each other or melted into bronze, creaking in the joints or playing with grace and ease; broken by that which should join it, or joined by that which seems to separate it, continuous or a mere patchwork.

To attain to the best possible, more and better practice and experience are necessary. Practice should be accompanied

it will contribute to improve him in the same manner as the palæstra does an actor. (*Orator*, cap. iv. Translation: London, 1808.) It does more.

* We often meet with such persons: they know almost everything, and yet they have very little true knowledge, for want of an aptitude for generalization.—Tr.

by, and should provoke meditation ; we should give thought to our modes of procedure, remark our faults, turn them to our advantage, interrogate our intellectual conscience.

I will say to those who have time : Be not vain of a foolish rapidity ; do again what you have done ; regard a first effort only as a trial of your strength, a rough draft of what you have in hand. Later, when you shall be in the bustle and hurry of active life, in vain will it be said to you :

> "Travaillez à loisir, quelque ordre qui vous presse," *

for the order which will press you will not comport with leisure, and you will have to substitute intensity for length in your work. But in the time of study and preparation, and as long as you can do so, work as an artist, the practical man will have his turn. By one trial after another see how you may better arrange, better fuse together the different elements of your work. Be not deceived, if a first attempt has succeeded, and succeeded so well that you do not return to it ; it was from a strong internal labor which had preceded it ; the force of this internal labor has supplied everything, and perhaps in the secret of meditation, many plans had given place to one another.

Finally, study models ; analyze their method ; endeavor to rival them ; on the same subjects, compare models with models. But be sure that the subjects are the same ; and not different subjects under the same names ; thus in Bourdaloue and in Saurin, the phrase, *The Word of God*, does not express the same subject.

* BOILEAU, *L'Art Poetique*, chant i. "Work leisurely whatever order presses you."

PART III.

ELOCUTION.

CHAPTER I.

OF ELOCUTION IN GENERAL.

You have chosen the arguments or principal ideas of your discourse; you have, by the same effort or by a subsequent operation, classified, arranged these materials in your mind; it remains for you to give a form and a body to the results of these first two operations, that your thoughts on the subject may become the thoughts of others. It remains to you, in a word, to write your discourse. This work is now to receive our attention.

This idea of *writing*, is less simple than it may seem at first. Is writing simply expressing in words the ideas and relations of which the two preceding operations have put us in possession? No one thinks so. A discourse reduced to this, strictly, is an analysis, and no more a discourse. But if writing is something more than expressing in language the ideas which have been furnished to us by the twofold labor of invention and disposition, is writing still thinking, still inventing, still arranging? Writing is in truth all these.

The work of style, properly understood, is but a prolongation of the two former works, of which one is called *invention*, the other *disposition.* Writing is still and always inventing and disposing. Does not an image include an idea? Is not a name a judgment? Is not the law of order and of gradation followed even in details? Is not a paragraph, not to say a phrase, a real discourse?

As invention and disposition re-appear on a small scale, in phrases and even in incidents, so elocution has place in the first rudiments of discourse, and even, so to speak, in the table of contents. It displays, however, all the characters of which it is susceptible, only in the development and the ramifications of the thought. Elocution is thought still, but on its surface or at its extremities. Here appears the whole importance of elocution. The simple announcement of the chief heads of the discourse, does little to enlighten and move the generality of the hearers. It is by the particular ideas that they are immediately impressed. It is with general ideas as with sapid and nutritious substances—they must be decomposed and mixed together in the mouth, in order to give us the sensation of taste; they must pass into the stomach and there be decomposed in another manner, in order to nourish the body. Thus, in general, we acquire the taste of truth, and it becomes nourishment to us only through its parts. To use another expression, would the larger blood-vessels of the body fulfil their purpose, if they were not ramified and attenuated indefinitely, in order to moisten and saturate the flesh? Elocution, then, has the two-fold function of clothing the thought with words, and of decomposing the truth so as to bring it into more immediate and sensible contact with us. But, at any rate, the work of style is a work of thought, and the direct complement of what, in the preparation of a discourse, is especially considered as appertaining to thought.

But it will be said: Is there not always this difference, that we invent and arrange without words, while elocution consists precisely in the use of words? But in the first place, it is not certain that we invent and arrange without the use of words. If, as I have said, every name is a judgment, every judgment is also a name. And then, what if elocution does make a more distinct use of these signs, without which it is nothing, provided the choice and arrangement of these signs is a labor of the mind? What would style be if it were not this? We ask what would a word be if it did not express an idea? The choice of words, the choice of forms, is from the thought or it is nothing. There is no essential difference between this part of the art and the two others. The signs appear more distinctly, and this is the whole.

"To write well," says Buffon, "is at once to think well, to feel well and to render well; it is to have at the same time, mind soul and taste; style requires the combination and exercise of all the intellectual faculties; ideas alone form the ground-work of style; the harmony of words is but its accessory."*

Though the principal ideas of the discourse are as to its purpose, the most important, it must be admitted that the ideas which we employ in the labor of elocution, the ideas which constitute the style, are of an elevated, delicate character, and in certain subjects, superior to the ideas which it is the object of the discourse to unfold. "A fine style," says Buffon, again, "is such only by the infinite number of the truths which it presents. The intellectual excellences which it contains, all the relations of which it consists, are so many truths not less useful, and perhaps of more value to the human mind, than those which may form the foundation of the subject."† We are far from giving other truths precedence, or equal rank to those of the gospel; but Buffon speaks only of the human mind, and within this limit, what he says is equally true and profound.

* Buffon, *Discours sur le Style.* † Ibid.

This, however, is not a point of view of immediate importance to us, in the question we are engaged in, and we confine ourselves to what has been before indicated. If it is true that the relation of elocution to discourse is analogous to that of the countenance or the hands to the human body, we see what is its importance and what also is its difficulty. It would be otherwise, if we had regard simply to *diction*, but what we have to do with is *style;* diction is not the whole man, while the whole man is in the style, or as Buffon says, "the style is the man himself."* Perhaps style is not merely, as this author maintains, the order and movement which a writer gives to his thoughts, but this order and movement form part of the style. Style, then, is a great matter, and even those who do not apprehend fully the reason of Cicero's thought, are not surprised that he expresses himself in this manner: "It is a great matter to know what to say and in what order to say it; but to know *how* to say it is a greater matter still."† If style is from thought, it would seem, that what makes a good mind will make a good writer, and that neither would a bad mind be found to write well; nor, especially, a good mind to write badly. It is certain that the great attributes of style are foreign to a feeble or badly-constructed mind; simple elegance, an elegance wholly external, is within its reach; but how many men are there who know how to think that do not know how to write? These two branches proceed from the same stem with an unequal force. In order to write well we must think well, but something more is necessary. Why should we be surprised? Is it surprising that a man who can walk very well does not know how to dance; that a man who speaks agreeably is not able to sing? There may be either a defect of some ulterior quality, or of two arts, which are related to each other, only the first has been studied. By cultivating

* BUFFON, *Discours sur le Style.* † CICERO, *Orator*, cap. xvi.

the art of inventing and of distributing a matter, we are prepared to write well, but we are *prepared* only; and elocution or style is the object of a separate study. Language, however, or the matter of style, is wholly independent of the writer. It is with language as with a violin; we must learn to play it. One does not come into the world with skill to handle the bow.

It certainly seems strange that a man who thinks well naturally, should hardly have reached a certain limit, before he all at once ceases to think well, and that he who has power for the greater, should have none for the less—this, if you please, is strange, but so it is. The same mind has not its thought equally at ease in all departments, even as the same man's chest is not equally at ease in all atmospheres. Although writing be thinking, still one may think well and write badly.

We would more readily accept this idea if we considered style in its inferior parts or its last details, confounding it with diction; for there is as to these things a *sense*, which may not have been given to all good minds. But it must be admitted that it is also true of the higher parts of elocution, of style, properly so called, in which we are much nearer to invention and disposition, much nearer to thought, properly so called. Style, even in this view, is a separate excellence, a separate quality.

But, though I admit that we may, in a certain sense, think well, and write badly, may I as readily admit that one may think badly, and yet write well? Yes, I may also admit this, if I reduce *writing well*, to its most external parts, and to the minutest details of elocution. But good style, taking this word in its full signification, style in the sense in which we may say it is the man himself, belongs only to the man who thinks well and powerfully.

"Scribendi recte *sapere* est et principium et fons,"*

says Horace ; and Cicero has said : "Sed est eloquentiæ, sicut reliquarum rerum, fundamentum SAPIENTIA."† Many works are well thought which are badly written; but all works truly remarkable in respect of style, are more or less so in respect of thought.

We may infer from all this, that the preacher, unless he may neglect and despise art on principle, should bestow a good portion of his attention on style. For style is a good portion of his total work, yet a work distinct, which demands separate aptitude and separate efforts.

Some are scrupulous as to this application. They question whether it becomes the most serious of writers, the preacher, to make elocution or the art of writing, a special study? If the question were not repeated every day, we would not raise it. Why should this study be unworthy of a serious man, if style is thought still, if the pains bestowed upon expression are but the necessary complement of the labor of thought, if that serious thought which is our whole concern, can reach the mind of our hearers completely and with all its advantages, only when it is well expressed?

For this is our point of view; and our doctrine, though in one sense very elevated, is entirely utilitarian. Even in the province of pure literature, we eschew the doctrine of *art for the sake of art;* how much more in the province of eloquence, and especially of christian eloquence. If poetry itself repels with alarm this sterile doctrine, eloquence, the purpose of which is practical, repels it much more. All arts, I admit, demand a noble disinterestedness of thought, aspire to pure idea; but this does not imply that art, in order to be pure, should be absorbed in occupation with form. "How

* HORACE, *Art of Poetry,* verse 309.

† CICERO, *Orator,* cap. xxi.

can it gain anything by being false to its origin? Does it not exist as a means before it is offered as an end? Do we seek first, ideas for expressions, or expression for an idea? To the view of human consciousness what then is art separated from its object, or when its object is made a mere occasion? Placed on this foundation, it is certain that art as art, perishes, and that the exclusive study of form destroys form itself. Literary teaching when obliged to treat of form separately, to concentrate attention for years on words and phrases; the greatest reputation of literary success; the highest charm of works in which the pursuit of form necessarily has much place; all this, directed seemingly in favor of art, has too often no other effect than to attenuate and relax it. Vigorous thinking, solid sense, are the first conditions of art; and, as has been very well said, it is only compact substances that are susceptible of a fine polish."

But how much more true is all this of eloquence, and particularly of the eloquence of the pulpit. The pursuit of an actual and practical purpose, which injures other arts, is the strength of this; it is its very principle; and every art, like every institution, is corrupted by separating it from its principle. The orator who supremely seeks to please, will not please; even as virtue which proposes happiness as its end, does not find happiness. Without insisting too much, as I have reason not to do, on this consideration, I affirm that the desire of speaking well, the literary point of view, just in proportion as it has ascendency over a minister, degrades his ministry. I affirm that the preacher is not, in the highest view, a man of literature. I affirm that there is a seductive intoxication in the use of speech, which should be feared. I affirm that we should fear being insensibly carried away from action into the imitation of action, from reality into poetry. This deviation is but too easy; such is the mysterious conjunction between moral beauty and literary beauty. Paul has said, "If I seek to please men, I shall not be the servant of Christ." (Galatians, i. 10.) We will say, "If I seek to please myself." To avoid this evil, a sure way is to hold art in contempt; but God has not made our way so easy. Jesus Christ says, "I pray not that thou should'st take them out of the world, (withdraw them from the conditions of human life,) but keep them from the evil." (John, xvii. 15.) It is between the idolatry of art and the contempt of art, that God has required us to walk.

Neither an anathema on art, nor art for art's sake, but art for God's sake, is what we insist upon. It results, as it seems to us, from what we have said, that good style is necessary, and that good style does not come of itself. If it is not necessary, no more is the rest; if it comes of itself the rest will also come of itself, and we shall have signed at once the condemnation of art altogether. For style is not added to all the rest, style is an integrant part of art; it is not its supplement but its complement. The limit which some would trace between invention and disposition, on one hand, and elocution on the other, is purely arbitrary. As there are invention and disposition in style, so there is style already in these first two parts. There is continuity, there is identity here, and the circumstance, very remarkable unquestionably, that there are persons who know how to invent and to arrange, who do not know how to write, is not inconsistent with what we have just said. Though a road becomes narrower in its asscent, and though certain travellers pause at this stage in it, panting and discouraged, it is still the same road. If the route henceforth becomes more difficult for some than for others, it by no means follows from this that it is permitted to them to pause, since the object, the prize of the course, is only at the end of the road, at the extremity of the race.

Some persons suppose there is an artifice in the application which is given to elocution. There is as much, we may say, in the first two operations of all eloquence, all art. We must not confound artifice and art. What characterizes artifice is the pursuit of an evil end, or the use of evil means, or both. Art is only the knowledge and use of means indicated by nature and experience, in order to attain a certain end. You do not deny that the end is good. It is even the only end, which is absolutely good; there is little probability that a good end will suggest bad means; if you should try such means, your end would array itself against your means. But in what do the means we propose consist? We pretend not to add to the truth, or to lead to the truth through falsehood, or to disturb the imagination in order to enlighten the conscience. No, we only would render to the truth that which belongs to it. Do we pretend to do violence to human liberty? No; for not to speak of our end, which is precisely to set souls at liberty, our means are conformed to our end, since we would only produce a more immediate contact between the truth and the soul of our hearers. There is then no artifice. Does art oppose itself, then, as contrary no longer to Christian rectitude, but to nature? We have elsewhere examined the supposed conflict between art and nature,* so like to that which has been imagined between nature and civilization, which is also an art and the first of arts; we have maintained that art is natural, that art is still nature, that the oak with an hundred boughs, is not less natural than the acorn. There is scarcely opposition here except between good and bad nature. If there are persons to whom it is natural not to care for their style, there are others who find it very natural to care for theirs. I know not by what right the first may impose their deformity upon those who have the instinct of the beautiful and the sentiment of art. They themselves may, if they wish, find from experience, that art may become a second

* See the *Introduction*.

nature. Is it maintained that it is more natural to write badly than to write well, since to write well requires more labor? But is not labor the universal law? Does it not add itself to all our gifts? Does the most gratuitous and the largest gift of all, exclude labor?* Eden, in all its beauty, was given to be cultivated. And finally negligence, is this fair nature? You do not accuse yourself of cunning and artifice. May we not with better reason accuse you of indolence?

You appeal to facts, and say that style has made dupes! Logic has done the same. Will you also proscribe logic? Because error is armed, would you have truth disarmed? And does not the same weapon from being criminal become virtuous, in passing from hand to hand? This weapon is only returned to the one who has a right to carry it. Say not that in a well-written discourse, truth is clothed with the armor of falsehood; it is falsehood which has stolen that of truth. It has it only in appearance; this armor does not fit it. On the contrary, we feel that when truth clothes itself in the form of the beautiful, it only enters into possession of its rights.

We have already answered those to which the labor of style seems unworthy of a manly and serious mind. Of what labor do they mean to speak? If the eloquence of style consists in speaking appropriately, *apte dicere*,† why should this style, necessarily manly and serious, be unworthy of the application of a manly and serious mind? What have we proposed except a labor of thought? "When I see," says Montaigne, "these noble specimens of speaking, I do not say they are well written, I say they are well thought." Style, like all the rest, comes from within, but it does not come by itself. It is a labor of the mind and of the soul which is only to be carried to its term.

* "*Work out your own salvation with fear and trembling.*" (Philippians, ii. 12.)

† Cicero.

Pascal has been cited, who has said: "True eloquence is the contempt of eloquence."* Yes, of false, of artificial, factitious eloquence, of that frivolous eloquence which is the study and delight of frivolous men; of artifice when candor would have sufficed; of conventional rules to which it is necessary to recur when nature fails. This pretended eloquence is truly wanting as to seriousness; but closely regarded, it wants art also; it is in the other, it is in serious eloquence that art, genuine art, triumphs.

But it will perhaps be said, since to write well is to think well, elocution, excepting that which is arbitrary, and is addressed only to the ear, does not constitute a particular art, and is not the object of a special study. Admitting this to be so, the importance of style is not denied, and we only ask that this importance be recognized. If a man is able to write well without the necessity of a labor *ad hoc*, of a new study, he need not fear being questioned as to the way in which he has made the attainment; it is the end, not the means, to which importance is attached, and no one thinks of recommending the labor for its own sake. If you attain, by a single impulse, the end we propose, the better for you, and we have nothing to object. We are well persuaded that things do end thus, and that there are writers to whom it is as difficult to write badly, as it is hard to others to write well. But if it were important to discuss the question, and we had not already replied to it, we would say that the experience of all times, and the testimony of all teachers, present to us as inseparable, these two propositions: 1. That we must not flatter ourselves that we shall have a good style, without an interesting fund of ideas. 2. That even with an interesting and substantial supply of ideas, we must not flatter ourselves that style will come of itself. D'Alembert separates these: "Eloquence," he says, "properly consists only

† PASCAL, *Pensées*, partie i., art. x., § xxxiv.

in vivid and rapid traits, its effect is lively emotion, and all emotion is enfeebled by being prolonged. Eloquence, then, in a discourse of any length, can reign only at intervals; the lightning darts and the cloud closes. But though shades are necessary in a picture, they should not be too deep; the hearer doubtless must have places of repose; in these places, the hearer should take breath, not sleep, and he should be kept in this tranquil and agreeable state by the quiet charms of elocution. Thus, (what is no less true than apparently paradoxical,) the rules of elocution, properly speaking, have place and are truly necessary only in the passages which are not properly eloquent, which the orator composes when he is cool, and in which nature has need of art. A man of genius should fear falling into a loose, low, grovelling style, only when he is not sustained by his subject; then it is that elocution should have his attention. At other times, his elocution will be as it should be, without his thinking of it. The ancients, if I mistake not, were apprized of this rule, and hence in their works on oratory, they have treated principally of elocution."*

In all this there is a delicate mixture of error with truth. Eloquence does not consist only "in vivid and rapid traits;" it has these traits, but eloquence pervades the whole, and continuity is one of its elements, one of its conditions. Elocution is truly something special, as the author thinks, but it is not detached from eloquence. The following passage from Cicero, appears to me to present the true principles of the subject before us: "As every speech is made up of things and words, words can have no place if you take away things, nor can things be explained without the help of words. We are assailed by contrary opinions, not only from the vulgar, but even from the smatterers in learning, who find it easier to handle those points, after they are torn,

* D'Alembert, *Melanges*, tome ii., p. 329, *Reflexions sur l'Elocution Oratorie.*

and as it were separated from one another, which they are unable to comprehend in a general view, and who sever words from sentiments, which is, as it were, separating the body from the soul, and producing immediate death. I will intimate, in a few words, that the ornaments of expression can no more be attained without inventing and arranging sentiments, than a sentiment can be intelligible without the lustre of expression."*

It is said, that in the work of style we must use imagination, and that imagination is a deceiver. But, in the first place, is everything in the labor of style, an affair of the imagination? In the next place, is the imagination itself only a fabricator of error? The imagination, essentially, is the faculty not of believing in what has no existence, but of representing to oneself that which one does not see, not of imagining what is *not*, but of *imagining*.† Whither will you go to escape from it? Not even to science, not even to faith. The most austere are susceptible of it. See only the *reflections on eloquence*, by the celebrated Doctor Arnauld. Imagination may henceforth say with Boileau:

Arnauld, le grand Arnauld, fit mon apologie.‡

Respectable men are cited, who in writing and speaking on these subjects, have disdained the study of their style. The apostles, including Saint Paul himself, are among this number. I begin by declaring that I am not scandalized by defects

* CICERO, *De Oratore*, lib. iii., cap. v. and vi. [Trans.: London, 1808.]

† "Non de *s'imaginer*, mais *d'imaginer*." Fr. Perhaps the former word might be rendered by *fancying*.

‡ BOILEAU, *Epitre* x.:

"Arnauld, the great Arnauld, has made my apology."

See on the attention to be given to Elocution, SAINT AUGUSTINE, *Christian Doctrine*, lib. iv.; and ROLLIN, *Traité des Etudes*, livre v., chap. ii., art. i., on the fault of neglecting too much the ornaments of discourse.

which may be shown me in the style of Saint Paul. He may have defects, and not be less St. Paul. You, in fact, do not wish to write in every respect like him. Why not allow yourself in his digressions? If attention to expression is blamable, attention to arrangement may well be also. Saint Paul had a spiritual power which might put him above the rules of art; have this as he had, and we allow you in those digressions and that obscurity which Saint Augustine has remarked, and which he counsels us to avoid, as being referable to some secret design of God. But, after all, write as St. Paul does; we ask nothing more, provided you write altogether as he does. Saint Paul has style. I know not how he acquired it; but have it equally; here is the whole question. If you can have it without labor, we ask nothing better. We are not hindered by St. Paul's irregularities from seeing the writer in him. There is no form of style which may be pronounced absolutely good or absolutely bad, independently of the particular circumstances or character of the writer; and if St. Paul was an ordinary writer, an artist, we might be reminded by his irregularities of these verses of Despréaux:

> Quelquesfois dans sa course un esprit vigoureux,
> Trop resserré par l'art sort des régles prescrites,
> Et de l'art même apprend à franchir leurs limites.*

"Men may convert, edify, console others, without aid from style." Do it then; do without style what we would have you do with the aid of style; we shall speak no more to you concerning style. Men also have converted others without the word. Do that, and we shall hold you quit of the word But, as a general truth, men are converted and edi-

* Boileau, *L'Art Poetique*, chant iv.
"A powerful mind, in its course, sometimes,
Confined too much by art, set-rules forsakes,
And learns from art itself to pass their bounds."—Tr.

fied by the word, and style is nothing else but the word rendering more or less justly the thought or inward life of the speaker. He acts through the word only as the word expresses truly all his thought; in this sense, there is neither paradox nor levity in saying that men are converted by means of style. The truth is so powerful, and, in some cases, the hearer is so well disposed, that all speaking, all style is good. Say, then, that you have succeeded in spite of the imperfections of language, but go no farther. If you imagine that this success authorizes you to speak without application and without rule, why not also say that it is the means of speaking better? And you will come to this. It is the doctrine of quietism applied to the use of speech. You will be the mystics of eloquence.—Moreover, we have not forgotten, in speaking of style, that every one has his vocation and style. If you have the overwhelming vehemence of a Whitefield, of a street preacher, go into the streets, and speak there what language you will; you will have the style suited to your position and your purpose; nothing more will be required of you, but this is required, it still is style. If, with the missionary of the Romish Church, your hands have been burnt off in an incipient martyrdom, stretch forth to the multitude your mutilated arms, and they will speak. When the word itself is superfluous, of what importance is the form of the word? But if the word is used, if it is through the word that we act, the form is important. The form and the substance are inseparable, and in truth they are one.

Nothing, assuredly, is more serious, nothing greater than the mission of Moses. Nothing is more eloquent than his life, except the miracles which he performed by his voice. He might, it would seem, have been exempted from speaking or speaking well. Eloquence is considered among the Arabs as the greatest of natural gifts, because it has more influence with them than with any other nation. Moses being conscious that this talent did not belong to him, could not entrust himself to his mission; he shrunk from it no longer, however, as soon as the Lord united with him Aaron, his brother, saying: "*Scio quod eloquens sit.*"†

This is an answer to those who say, that the application given to style is appreciated only by a small number. I presume we are not to understand by this, that to be appreciated, admired, may be the end and the recompense of the preacher; but only that it may be the sign and proof that his true purpose has been reached. Now it is certain, I admit, that a good style is justly appreciated only by a small number, but if no one has remarked that your style is good, does it follow that you have lost your labor? If a good style has produced its effect, it is of small importance whether the hearer knows distinctly by what this effect has been produced. An assiduous and attentive hearer, after awhile, will make proper acknowledgment of certain merits. If a christian preacher may think himself called to form the taste of the public, it is ours certainly to form the taste of our auditory.

"Still the form may withdraw attention from the substance." It is too true. As the thinker, when the time for writing has come, may pause, may yield, before a more delicate, perhaps more complicated labor, and leave expression to become what it may, another, in his turn, may prefer attaching himself to the labor of style by its most external parts, by those which have the least connexion with the interior of the subject and the substance of things. It seems, in truth, that if you form a just idea of style, the form cannot so easily divert you from the substance; for true style comes from thought, as the complexion comes from the blood, as the flower springs from the vigor of the sap. Style is not

* Leon De Laborde, *Commentaire sur l'Exode, etc.*, Paris, 1841, in fol., p. 14.

the mask but the physiognomy of thought. Still the difficulty remains, and I wish neither to deny nor enfeeble it ; I will endeavor to avoid doing so. I say more ; I know of but one remedy for it, the spirit of mortification and the spirit of prayer. For to say : Let words come as they will ; let us not use all our advantages ; let us refuse our thought its form, that is to say, in some sort, the life and the faculty of communication ; this is what we should not do. Eloquence is a whole, a unit, which we cannot divide. We have not imposed on it any form, we have not recommended any style in particular, we have only required that the word of the sacred orator should render his life and his thought as perfectly as possible. This thought he owes, in its fulness, to his hearers ; he ought to convey it to them, with all its elements, all its characteristics ; now, if he cannot do this without a particular application, without a labor *ad hoc*, this labor, this application, is matter of obligation like all the rest.*

* We think we ought to reproduce the more extended developments which M. Vinet gave to his thought in a former digest of this part of his course :

"The labor of style thus conceived, that is to say, as little subordinated to things as possible, and even subjecting these to itself, making thought its instrument, instead of its being the instrument of thought, may certainly be a snare, and form may withdraw attention from the substance. Such is it in the case of the man with whom writing is the first thing, to whom principles, ideas, facts, are of little value in themselves, and are only the substratum, and, so to speak, the *gangue* of style. His business is to make the most vulgar articles valuable by the chasing, and, in fact, he is to the true writer what the chaser is to the sculptor. The agreeableness of his style consists in ideas, like the excellence of the most solid style, for with these he cannot dispense, but it is in ideas of tinsel, ideas without roots and without power, or if some thought is mixed with it, it is external to the subject, sustaining nothing, and unsustained. One can scarcely say that the form has withdrawn attention from the substance, of which, to say the truth, this man has scarcely

A man of letters, to whom, when he was sick, a priest endeavored to represent the joys of paradise, interrupted him by saying, "Speak no more of them, my father, your bad style disgusts me with them." This profane pleasantry is intellectual epicurism to the last degree. But, frankly, we have no right to speak of divine things in a bad style. In vain will it be said, that the things should speak; for what is a bad style, but something which hinders them from speaking,

dreamed. We must not indeed distinguish here between writers, we must distinguish between subjects. The subjects here are such that the form is every thing, the form is the thought itself, the form is the whole work. I refer to those common thoughts, those common places, (using the phrase in the best sense,) in which everything being given once for all, nothing remains but to express well, and in which one author can differ from another only in expression. Now, as Buffon says, the art of saying little things may become more difficult than the art of saying great things. In every case, the form does not take attention from the substance, because all is form.

I do not mean to deny that, apart from these subjects, form may draw attention from substance, though to the great damage, when it does, of form itself; for, in great subjects, the style, that is to say the truth and character of the expression, can come only from great thoughts. Thus then, in these subjects, the labor of style may indeed be a separate labor, a thing *sui generis;* so that we may have thoughts without style, substance without form, but we cannot have form without substance. If the labor of style does not proceed from within, if it is not intimately united to the labor of the thinker, and the internal activity of the man, if it is applied from without, if it does not spring like the flower, from the force of the sap, it is neither a true style nor a style true, for style is not the mask, it is the physiognomy of thought.

If then we say that the form will draw us from the substance, it is not of true form, it is not of true style that we speak, since it is consubstantial with thought. We must charge the fault not to the form but to the man; he has not thought of the true form of the object, because he has not thought of the object. But if we are pre-occupied with the true form, we are not withdrawn from the substance

an infidel style, a style which is not true (and in this respect it may be at the same time elegant and bad); what, on the other hand, is a good style, but a style which is true in every respect? For it is with the truth that it has to do, and we do not give as a motto to eloquence, these well-known verses:

Les sucs reparateurs dont la coupe est remplie,
A l'enfant qui se meurt sont en vain presentés,

---

of things; for it is in view of the substance that we seek a form and the form returns into the substance.

This is all I have to say to the preacher, on whom I must acknowledge, the external labor of style, the attraction of fine words, the pomp, the harmony, the decorum of language, may exert their seductive influence, as well as on another; and in proportion to his youth, especially if he be a man of taste, he will scarcely be able to resist it, and to recognize a style in the naked simplicity of a Demosthenes and a Pascal. He will long perhaps be under the charm of words and images, and in works of art, will take show for beauty. It is important that without repressing too much a fine and tasteful imagination, he should study eloquence in the models which I have named; not that theirs is the only manner of being eloquent and true, (that of Bossuet is not less so, since he faithfully renders the internal life and character of his thoughts;) but because in this school he is less exposed to mistakes, because in this simplicity we rather recognize what it is that forms the essence of a good style, and that liberty is no longer dangerous after continuing for a season so severe a discipline.

When one says to you, that form withdraws us from the substance, reply, that you must, after all, seek the form of your thought; but seek this form in the thought itself; and condemn yourself beforehand, yourself alone and not art, if you have sacrificed substance to a form, which, from that very circumstance, was not its own; for a thought cannot perish in an expression which is conformed and adequate to it.

All this discussion is founded on a misunderstanding; it would not have had place if it had been agreed beforehand that the essential merit of style and the foundation of its beauty, is in being true; true relatively to the subject, true relatively to the writer.—[Editors.]

Mais que d'un peu de miel les bords soient humectés
L'enfant saissit la coupe, et, trompé boit la vie.*

We would neither deceive nor seduce; falsehood and error often kill, but never give life.

Finally, it is said: How much time does this labor of style take away from us? We should satisfy ourselves that this time is lost—that what we obtain is not worth the sacrifice we make for it, and that we gain as much in respect to the final purpose of discourse by writing rapidly and indifferently, as by writing slowly and well. Moreover, I am not sure that we save much time by neglecting style. I think we learn from this exercise, both to write rapidly and to write well; and that in this matter, as in many others, in order to gain time, we must know how to lose it; for good style becomes an instinct, and in the end is as a flowing fountain. But I hasten to take the objection in its full force.

"Time presses," it is said; "each instant which escapes from us, becomes our accuser; preaching should be abundant, and preachers be multiplied; discourses, were it possible, should follow each other without an interval, and each discourse declare the whole counsel of God."

Should preaching, then, be but a cry of alarm? Why, if it should be, has religion been presented to us in so long a series of facts, so long a chain of deductions, so vast a system of ideas? It is thus presented according to the will of God, and it probably does not belong to us to wish it were otherwise; and in view of his patience, it ill becomes us to be impatient. Whether preaching be for *appeal*, as it is said, or for *confirmation*, it is something besides a cry; it is a word,

* Tasso, *Jerusalem delivered*, chant i.

"In vain the dying child is urged to take
The cup with juice invigorating filled.
But let the edge with honey be but touched,
The child deceived, receives the cup and lives."—Tr.

an instruction, a discourse. Some are gently called, and others gently confirmed; perturbation has its value, and may have its hour; but taking the work as a whole, we may say, in every sense, "The fruit of righteousness is sown in peace." (James, iii. 18.) And we should not fear to apply to pastors what has been said to poets:

Travaillez à loisir, quelque ordre qui vous presse.

Putting each instant to profit, and working in haste, are two very different things; the second is not implied in the first, and it is precisely that we may do nothing in haste, that we should be avaricious of time.

Situations, certainly, are not always the same; there are missionaries as well as pastors, and pastors, in our day, are half missionaries. Would we make the pastor do less in order to his doing better? God forbid! But, if when he had leisure for it, he had studied art, had practised it, he would speak well naturally; he would not be long in seeking the best terms, the best forms of expression; they would come to him of themselves. He would slowly have acquired the secret of meditating quickly, he would, by labor, have rendered himself able to find with ease, just and new plans, happy combinations, interesting points of view. It may be thought, from its naturalness, that he owes everything to talent, to emotion; he himself may think so; but if he carefully examines his consciousness, he will soon understand the matter, and will be surprised to discover that he never defers so much to art as at the moment when he thinks he is obeying instinct. Art, with him, has in fact become instinct.

For what, moreover, do we contend? What? For a certain measure of perfection. Who may determine it? We have maintained but one thing, that each one should do as well as he can. We have not so much required the practice of art as esteem for it and the acknowledgment of its rights.

In gaining this we think we gain everything. It is a principle on which we are insisting; and circumstances being parallel, difficulties equal, there will be an entire difference in practice between him who confesses the principle and him who denies it. It is impossible to acknowledge art and wholly to neglect it; for it is always possible to practice it in some measure. An artist is always an artist. Always, as far as he can, he meets the exigencies of art; and when he wants leisure for preparation, he improvises his preparation, so to speak, and meditates in execution. There have been, we doubt not, true artists among popular orators and street preachers, and their theory, the secret of which they would confide to us if they themselves had possession of it, is a wise theory.

Must we repeat again, that we regard art as a means and not as an end, and that it is only the result we are in quest of? Produce us, without preparation, without meditation, by the mere powers of instinct, a logical, connected, solid discourse, pure as to language, natural as to expression, and happy to find that you have arrived at the end of your journey, we will make no inquiry as to the way in which you have come. What does it concern us? Moreover, to tell the truth, we know it. Say what you will, you are an artist, and your instinct is not a blind one. But as to those, and their number is very great, who write negligently and badly, nothing forbids us from saying to them, that they write badly because they write negligently, and that in order to write better, they must have either more of instinct (which they cannot give themselves) or more of art, (which they may acquire.) As there are so many ministers to whom one cannot listen, as slovenly discourses are so frequent in the pulpit, as the feeblest lawyers can hardly descend to the level of the feeblest preachers, we conclude that art, yet more necessary in the pulpit than at the bar, is disowned by idleness or repelled by prejudice. The opposite doctrine would certainly elevate the level of ecclesiastical eloquence. Let the younger among the more ardent make trial of it; they will not be long in disabusing themselves of the idea that art is something essentially voluminous, which demands for its display, a great space; that is to say, much time; they will soon understand, and afterwards know by experience that much art may be contained within an hour; intensity of labor is as available as length. When this discovery has been made, there is already much advancement. What in many minds has disparaged art, is not art in itself, nor even its abuse, but much rather its absence.

A discourse of which the progress is measured, the plan rigidly symmetrical, the style pompous or brilliant, the sentences always rounded and sonorous, distresses or wearies us by its cold elegance. We condemn strongly a kind of writing so false. We even venture to blame, in works much more simple and grave, a certain stiffness of form and a certain starchness of language, the last and too persistent vestiges of an epoch in which eloquence was a pageant. We would banish if we could, the rhetoric of rhetoricians to make place for that of the philosophers. We insist on the rights of individuality, which is to art, what liberty is to law. But we do not arraign, we do not banish art, which has nothing to do with the whims which offend us. Art is necessary, art is immortal; the reformations we recommend depend upon it, and will be its work; and when we shall have accomplished them we may say with equal justice, with equal truth, Nature at last has regained its prerogatives; art at last has triumphed. Art in fact consists essentially in following and perhaps in retrieving nature. There is only one real opposition; it is not an opposition between nature and art, but between false art and true. If we adhere to this formula it is because this formula is a principle.

Let us be understood. We only require for the pulpit, the style of thought, but this we do require. We require it for the village as well as the city pulpit. A popular style is not a degree but a kind of style. No more do we maintain that preachers, as a whole, should surpass in this respect writers as a whole; but that a bad style, a trivial, dull, loose, dragging style, does not seem to be an appendage of the pulpit; that there is no exception to be made here as to good language; that the preacher, called as he is to reason and to speak is not to be a worse reasoner or speaker than any other writer or orator.

It would be strange and unfortunate if, at an epoch in which every one is more exacting or more severe, the pulpit should be more indulgent to itself than at an epoch in which less was required.* It would, in truth, be an odd way of showing, that weak things confound the mighty; this means, in our opinion, is not to be relied upon.

CHAPTER II.

FUNDAMENTAL QUALITIES OF STYLE.

We are to consider the different conditions of elocution in sacred discourse. Now, of these there is not one that is peculiar to sacred discourse. And if we must restrict ourselves to what is peculiar to it, we should have to be content with the few loose notes which, in a treatise on oratorical elocution according to the general principles of rhetoric, might be thrown at the bottom of the page, assuming at the

* There are not more, perhaps there are fewer men of genius than formerly; but good speaking has become common, and many more persons are capable of judging.

same time, that our hearers are already acquainted with rhetoric in its general principles or without application to a particular kind of eloquence. But it would neither be possible nor useful to proceed in this manner. We shall, therefore, with special regard in each instance to the eloquence of the pulpit, pass in review the principal points of a treatise on oratorical elocution, or indeed of elocution in general.

We are then to give an enumeration of the different qualities of style, as if we were treating generally of the art of writing, but still with a special reference in everything to the object of sacred discourse. We begin with qualities which are indispensable to style in every kind and instance of writing, and without which, or at least some measure of which, style is decidedly bad.

Those essential qualities which make a writer irreproachable, as obedience to the laws makes an honest, though not a virtuous man, are the following : *perspicuity*, *purity*, *correctness*, *propriety*, *precision*, *order*, *naturalness*, *suitableness*.

After qualities comes virtues, or style, properly so called, which is the character impressed on language by the subject, or by the individuality of the writer; after truth, beauty, as far, at least, as these two things may be separated, the beautiful being " the splendor of the true."

D'Alembert distinguishes between diction and style : " Elocution," he says, "has two parts, which it is necessary to distinguish although they are often confounded; diction and style; diction, properly, has respect only to the grammatical qualities of discourse, correctness and perspicuity; style, on the contrary, includes qualities of elocution, which are more particular, more difficult and more rare, and which mark the genius or the talent of him who writes or speaks; such as propriety of terms, nobleness, harmony, facility."

We would for ourselves remark, that some of the qualities of style which we are now to consider, are not purely negative, that is to say, do not consist in the absence of faults; propriety, precision, even perspicuity, may become virtues of style, when carried to a certain point.

§ 1. *Perspicuity.*

If we consider the first or proximate end of discourse, we cannot, I think, hesitate to give the first place to perspicuity. *Nobis prima sit virtus perspicuitas*, says Quintilian.*

The importance of perspicuity ought not to be questioned; still there is a predilection for obscurity. Man rejoices in perspicuity, but yet he is imposed on by obscurity. As that which is profound is sometimes obscure, he mistakes obscurity for depth. We do not maintain that perspicuity answers every purpose. In some subjects we distrust it. "In eloquence, perspicuity is often of itself a great force, a great means of persuasion; may we not add it is also a snare? It is not always decisive as to justness of reasoning; especially is it not, as to justness of views; it may, as may also elegance, accompany and recommend error. We may doubtless be at the same time superficial and obscure; but some who may be clear if they are content to be superficial, would, by a loftier aspiration, be lost and left in the clouds. We must always distrust obscurity; but we must not yield to perspicuity an absolute confidence. Self-love and indolence conspire to prejudice us in favor of what is clear; but in order to judge of an author, it is not enough that from his own point of view, we can easily comprehend him; we must first of all examine his point of view itself. On the top of a hill the horizon appears distinct to us because it is limited; on the top of a mountain we take in a horizon which, as to its limits, may be obscure, but then it is immense."† We freely

* QUINTILIAN, lib. viii., cap. ii. "Let us regard perspicuity as the first excellence."

† *Chrestomathie française*, tome iii., p. 207, troisième édition. Re-

say with La Bruyère : " We do not write merely to be understood; but in writing we must at least be interesting as well as intelligible. It is abusing purity and perspicuity in discourse to employ them upon arid, unprolific topics, which have no poignancy, no utility, no novelty. Of what advantage is it to readers that they understand easily and without effort, things which are frivolous and puerile, perhaps insipid and vulgar; and that they are less uncertain as to an author's thought than tired of his work."* This, I think, is readily enough conceded; but after all, obscurity is not a good, but an evil. Everywhere is it an evil, where there is a necessity for perspicuity. We speak in order to be understood, and if we do not wish or expect to be understood, it were well to be silent. It is scarcely worth while to say that which cannot be said clearly. It is true that everything is not naturally clear, in matters upon which we may profitably discourse to men, but then we must either overcome the obscurity or confess that it is invincible, and show clearly the obscurity of the subject.

Let us endeavor, ourselves, to be perspicuous on this point, and to have it well understood, that it is perspicuity of style, and not perspicuity of subjects, to which we have reference. It would be unjust to charge an author with obscurity, who is obscure to us only because the subject he treats is above the reach of our minds. He may have erred in bringing such a subject before such an auditory, and in this matter shown want of judgment; but his discourse may be very perspicuous.

Perspicuity is to be determined by its result, facility of being well understood. A man who has not understood you, may have no right to say to you : " You have not been clear."

marks of M. Vinet occasioned by thediscourse of Barnave, *sur l'exercise du droit de la paix et de la guerre.*

* La Bruyère, *Les Caracteres*, chap. 1er, *Des ouvrages de l'esprit.*

You ought to be perspicuous, in exact proportion, first to the perspicuity of your subject, then to the understanding of the hearer, and finally to the attention he gives you.

On subjects as to which our design is not only to instruct but to persuade and determine the will, we have no power if we are not perspicuous; we are powerful sometimes merely by being perspicuous. There hence results a particular necessity for perspicuity in the pulpit; but this necessity results also from the nature of public discourse, and from the character of the auditories to which preaching is addressed. The labor of understanding what is spoken prevents the soul from yielding itself to its power. The precept of Quintilian may here be applied: *Oratio debet negligenter quoque audientibus esse aperta.**

It may be added, that, in this respect, the French mind is exacting. The French language, it would seem, is eminently perspicuous from the influence of causes which might be thought to make it obscure. Other languages, in which the meaning is always made obvious by turns of expression, are negligent in respect to perspicuity. In the French language, which does not offer this facility, the difficulty is avoided in a different manner. There is a demand for perspicuity in French auditories, which is perhaps peculiar to themselves. The preacher should satisfy this demand. The mere possibility that a phrase may have two meanings, may suffice to divert and alienate the attention of some hearers. He must accommodate himself to this peculiarity, so much the more since it has saved the language which has escaped only by an exigence which could not bear the obscurity from which, with so much difficulty, it has emerged.

But perspicuity should not be carried so far as to render discourse insipid. Time has enfeebled the notion of the word

* QUINTILIAN, lib. viii., cap. ii. "An orator should be clear and intelligible even to hearers who give imperfect attention."

perspicuity as well as that of many others. It formerly signified *effulgence*, *brightness*, and Racine, in his day, might speak of Jerusalem as "brilliant with perspicuity." Giving perspicuity its full force, it will not be merely negative, it will be brilliant. Explaining everything, filling out every detail, satiating the mind with evidence, is failing of the end by getting beyond it. Style produces its effects not only by what it says and shows, but by what it does not say; perspicuity does not exclude reticence ellipsis, half-lights which are truly occasions of activity to the mind. When the hearer is able to work his own way, he does not wish to be carried. The orator should doubtless offer aid to indolent hearers, but not so far, assuredly, as to impair the sprightliness of active minds. He must leave neither too much nor too little to be supplied by his hearers.

There are very many beauties in style which, in truth, are improprieties of language, exaggeration, obscurities of diction. There are rhetorical figures which are nothing else. In hyperbole, something is given to the hearer to retrench; in litotes, something to be added; in irony, the true to be put parallel to the false, etc. But all this does not trench upon the rule which we have given.—Let us now inquire for the means of perspicuity of style. They are of two kinds. Some apart from the labor of elocution or preliminary to it; others which have their application in this labor itself. We first note those of the former kind.

1. Sincerity. We do not say *truth*, because truth is sometimes less perspicuous than error,* and we are speaking only of subjects which are perspicuous in themselves. There may hence be an advantage to the defender of error; but in error

* "Certain errors have the appearance of perspicuity," says Bernardin de Saint Pierre, when speaking of Condillac. Eclecticism also has this appearance, and it is by a great appearance of perspicuity that certain erroneous systems, certain heresies, have succeeded.

as well as in truth, sincerity is a means of perspicuity. The position of him who defends truth without being convinced of it, is worse on this account, than the position of one who defends error, believing it to be truth. The latter perhaps cuts the knot which he thinks to untie; but his position is true; he is in a state of liberty and of ease; he is not troubled to adjust his thought and the truth to each other, to insert a crooked blade into a straight scabbard. He, on the contrary, whose thought is out of harmony with itself, undertaking to reconcile two adversaries that never can be in agreement, error which he defends and truth which he cannot avoid recognizing, is to be pitied both in defending the one and in recognizing the other. Obliged to be partially true, in his use of language, he experiences perpetual embarrassment, which he endeavors to disguise by the elaboration of words, by industrious dexterity in giving turns to expression, by stealthy subtility in connecting things together. In all this there is nothing favorable to perspicuity which has its life in freedom, in decision, and in unity. Now, a discourse can no more be eloquent with obscurity than a figure be striking in the dark. A sophist may be eloquent, but only when he is sincere.

2. Distinct conception of ideas, or understanding ourselves well. Boileau has said:

> Selon que notre idée est plus ou moins obscure,*
> L'expression la suit ou moins nette, ou plus pure,
> Ce que l'on conçoit bien s'enonce clairement,
> Et les mots pour le dire arrivent aisèment.†

The last two lines are true only with restriction. Words

* He does not say, Accordingly as our idea is more or less *true*,—but more or less obscure.

† BOILEAU, *L'Art Poetique*, chant i. "As our idea is more or less obscure, the expression which follows it is less distinct or more pure. What one conceives well he announces clearly, and words for expressing it come readily."

do not always occur readily to him who has clear conceptions. It may indeed be sometimes said that one conceives clearly only when he has found words. For we think in words, and speech evidently is the analysis of thought. But still it is not less true, that we may not flatter ourselves that we make that clear to others which is not so to ourselves. Perhaps our thought is obscure to us because we have not yet found its expression; perhaps we have not found this expression, because our thought is obscure to us; it matters not; we must not pretend to give what we have not. If, on the contrary, by any means whatever, with words or without them, we have succeeded in taking account of the object of our thought, if our thought, like a logical mechanism, plays without effort and without embarrassment, and if there is no interruption of continuity between the parts of our thought, we have at least a very great chance of being understood, and if this be not an infallible means of perspicuity, it is an indispensable condition of it.

3. Care to put ourself in the hearer's place. Without this care, we may be obscure. Signs which may serve as an adequate expression, and recognition of our thought to ourselves, may not always suffice to express it to others. We know what we would say, they do not. We may, then, in speaking only to ourselves, be indulged in what cannot be allowed to us in speaking to others. Let us remember how often a reader detects an equivocal expression in an author, who, after reading it himself the tenth time, did not discover it.

"We will venture to apply to human speech in general, and to style in writing, what a sacred author has said of prophecy: 'Nothing should be of private interpretation,' (2 Peter, i. 20,) that is to say, thought should be clothed in a form at the same time individual and general, which, in order to be understood and accepted, does not assume entire conformity of the reader's mind to that of the writer. It may be that our expression is subjectively true; that it conveys, with perfect fidelity, the aspect in which the object presented itself to us, and the impression we received from it; we may fall in with some one who finds in our manner of conceiving of the idea, an anticipation of the difficulty which it has occasioned in his own mind; we may perchance have spoken admirably for this mind congenial in this respect with our own; but we may have spoken well only for this mind, or at least for some few others besides; we have thought too solitarily; we have thought, or rather felt, instead of speaking, if it be true that in speaking we seek the mind of others on ground which is familiar to them; their adhesion, their lively assent, their rapid association with us, all, things which are necessary to meet one of the first instincts of eloquence, have been too little felt to be necessary on our part, and it is to be feared that their understandings will not come to seek us in this proud solitude, in which, far from them, we have secluded ourselves. A book is not a monologue. It is a very long *aside*, which lasts through a volume. We must write in the view and presence of others; in a manner, borrow of the reader the discourse we would hold with him; listen to him as much as speak to him; make each of our sentences an answer to his silent questions; permit him to suggest to us our own words. Still these words must be our own. And that they may be affecting to the reader, they must strike him as foreign, while suitable to him as his own. It is this happy combination which has always made skilful writers, true orators, and in proportion as one or the other of these two elements has been wanting, whether the first or the second is of no importance, eloquence has been defective; for eloquence is maintained at once by individuality and by sympathy; to live much in yourself, to live much in others, this is the two-fold requisite to powerful speaking.

The majority of writers ought to be re-translated; few of

them are translated when born—that is to say, clothed with a form suitable for communication. What one writes at first, for his own sake, should be written a second time for the sake of others."*

Pascal, on re-perusing his thoughts, would not perhaps have understood them all, and might have hesitated between one sense and another. If Rousseau, who had so much difficulty in finding words, could write his *Emile* nine times, in pursuit of different ones, we may well write our sermons at least twice.

La Bruyère has said: "In order to write clearly, every writer should put himself in the place of his readers; should examine his own work as something which is new to him, which he reads for the first time, in which he has no peculiar interest; and which the author has submitted to his criticism; and should expect to be understood not because he understands himself, but because he is in truth intelligible."† We should even do this, if we wrote for ourselves. "We do well to give account of our thought to others in order to give account of it to ourselves. We are not sure of understanding ourselves perfectly, unless we have done what we can to be intelligible apart from ourselves. Our thought indeed is ours only when we have communicated it and have gained it acceptance. Till we have done this, we are in much danger of resting in vagueness, and in being almost correct. It is useful to have to do with those who are not content with this, and in this class let us be sure that the public is to be reckoned."‡

We must know our hearers in order to put ourselves in

* M. Vinet here cites himself. See *Le Semeur*, tome vii., (année, 1838,) pp. 307, 309.

† La Bruyère, *Les Caractères*, chap. i., *Des ouvrages de l'esprit.*

‡ M. Vinet here cites himself. See *Le Semeur*, tome vii., (année, 1838,) p. 309.

their place; after sermon, let us inquire if we have been understood, and in what manner.

To these general means of obtaining perspicuity, we subjoin particular ones.

1. We must avoid expressions too little known or too abstract. Style on account of these will not be absolutely less perspicuous, but we speak of a perspicuity relative to the ordinary auditory of the preacher. The pulpit should give great attention to this. We ought in speaking to an auditory, on matters of the highest concern to them, to be intelligible to them. It is a singular thing that sacrifices made for the sake of perspicuity sometimes interfere with precision; but perspicuity is before everything.

2. We must avoid too much ellipsis.

3. We must exclude ambiguity, even though it may not lead to error. It is always disagreeable, and divides attention.

4. We must shun labored and embarrassed turns of expression. An unpractised mind will find much trouble in discriminating the principal point in a phrase but a little overloaded. This, however, does not exclude the periodic style.

5. We must allow no want of unity of phrase. We cannot determine anything as to the length of a period, but it must be as to thought, grammar, the ear, a unit. Unity of thought exists when all the ideas are integrant parts of the principal idea. The period should have the effect of concentric circles drawn around the same centre.

6. We must not admit into the same sentence too many accessory or too many subtile ideas.

7. We must have no want of order in our plans, narrations, etc., by which the parts would be hindered from throwing suitable light on one another.

§ 2. *Purity, correctness, propriety, precision.*

These different qualities, and the latter two more evidently than the former, are aids to perspicuity. Purity and correctness are important chiefly from their relation to perspicuity of style.

Correctness is but a branch of purity. They both have strict regard to the conventionalities of language, one in respect of words, the other of construction. "Language is a conventionality, which, like that of society, of which it is the instrument and the basis, binds at once every person, willing or unwilling. Language is as sacred as society. It is not, it cannot be immutable, but it suffers no arbitrary or capricious change, no gratuitous violence, no purely individual modification." * It is a conventionality not less regarded than it would be if the law had said, "such a word shall signify such a thing, or such a thing shall be designated by such a word." Indeed, the acts of the tribunals themselves are based on this convention, which is nowhere written. Words are the representative signs of ihtellectual values. Writers, without purity or correctness, are as false coiners who introduce disturbances in intellectual transactions, and diminish the credit of speech. Respect for language is almost a matter of morality. It would doubtless be extravagant and unjust to charge a man with immorality for speaking badly; but we may say, at least, that the general corruption of language is a mark of the declension of morals. We add, that with those who are capable of judging, a preacher is discredited by bad language.

Some of the defects now referred to, those especially which indicate affectation or too much intercourse with the world of fashion, are contrary to the gravity of the pulpit.†

* Le Semeur. M. Vinet here cites himself.

† In certain countries, in certain times, language has to be reduced to the level of the multitude, and to be corrupted, in order to be intelligible. This is not the case with us. We have nothing between

Propriety or *justness* consists in using terms which suit exclusively each of the ideas we would express.

Perfect synonyms we cannot have, for every language, when compared with the ideas to be expressed, is poor. Two forms cannot be applied to the same idea; they would give us two ideas. For each idea there can be but one word; any other would not express the same idea. When language is enriched, it gains nothing superfluous ; expression, taken in a superfluous sense, is improper. No language in the world can contain any superfluity. A word to be found with difficulty goes to fill an empty nitch, and to name a solitary idea which has been waiting for a visible existence, or which could have such an existence only by means of circumlocution. Not but that we may, in certain cases, substitute one word for another, especially when we have in view a general idea. For example, though in defining indigence (the want of what is necessary) and poverty, (the want of everything superfluous,) we must mark well the difference, yet if we should speak in a sermon of the general idea of well-doing, it would be indifferent whether we urged the giving of aid to indigence or the giving of it to poverty.

La Bruyère says on this subject: " Among all the different expressions which may render one and the same thought, only one is good; we do not always fall in with it in speaking or in writing. It nevertheless exists, and every other

French and patois, we have indeed patois no longer. For example, we are not obliged to say *vite* for *tôt ; se rappeler de quelque chose*, for *se rappeler quelque chose ; nous avons convenu*, for *nous sommes convenus ; aimer lire*, for *aimer à lire ; distraisent*, for *distraient ; observer à*, for *faire observer à ; il craignait que je ne l'eus perdu, ses alentours*, for *ses entours; la maison que j'ai faite batir, un mesentendu*, for *un malentendu, je me suis en allé, l'endroit où la forêt est la plus épaisse ; recouvert*, for *recouvrê ; empecher â malgré que, etc.*

It is from us that the majority of the public learn French. We are at once the guardians of good manners and good language.

except that is feeble, and a man of mind who wishes to be understood, can be satisfied only with that."*

La Bruyère here indicates two disadvantages of impropriety, obscurity and weakness; and two advantages of propriety, perspicuity and force.

Improper expressions render the style not wholly obscure, but confused, of diminished perspicuity. The style may, however, become decidedly obscure, through impropriety. As to force, it is always proportional to perspicuity; we may add force to perspicuity; but never, without perspicuity, can we be strong; force is only a higher degree of truth.

The law of propriety condenses, not only expressions which are not just, (the first degree of impropriety,) but expressions which are not applied closely enough to the idea, or between which and the idea an interval is left. There is, accordingly, an impropriety in the last of these verses of Boileau on Juvenal:

Soit que sur un écrit arrivè de Caprée,
Il brise de Sejan la statue adorée
Soit qu'il fasse au conseil, courir les Sènateurs,
D'un tyran soupçonneux pâles adulateurs,
* * * * * *
Ses ècrits pleins de feu partout *brillent aux yeux.*†

Propriety may be extended so far as to be no longer purely negative, but positive, striking; it may become a *virtue* of style.‡ D'Alembert we know has said: "Among ordinary

* La Bruyère, *Les Caractères*, chap. i., *Des ouvrages de l'esprit.*

† Boileau, *L'Art Poetique*, chant ii.

"Whether on the arrival of a writing from Caprea,
He breaks in pieces the image of Sejanus,
Or hurries together in council, the Senators,
Pale flatterers of a suspicious tyrant,
* * * * * *
His writings full of fire, *sparkle in our eyes.*"

‡ Buffon here is specially remarkable. See among others his *description de l'Arabic.*

authors expression, so to speak, is always by the side of the idea; reading them gives the same kind of pain to good minds that a singer, whose voice is between false and true, gives to delicate ears. Great writers, on the contrary, are distinguished by propriety; their style, by this means, is always on a level with their subject; it is this quality which reveals the true talent for writing, as distinguished from the futile art of disguising common ideas by a vain coloring."*

That the want of propriety may be felt, it is not necessary that you should be overtaken by the reader in a flagrant instance of impropriety; the negative effect is sufficient; that is to say, it suffices that the exact correspondence of the term to the idea is not felt. And how is this felt? After a more or less frequent use, the greater part of the readers or hearers have received a just sense of the import of a word; conformably to the purpose of its formation it must have been, used in its true sense often enough to make a just impression of itself, even on the minds of persons who cannot define it; so that if they do not distinctly notice that the term we employ is improper, they at least do not receive from it the impression, the stroke, so to speak, which they should receive; the hammer has struck by the side of the nail or struck the nail on the side.

There may, moreover, be an affectation of propriety, as there is an affectation of purity. The painful toil of distinguishing and analyzing, is not necessary to it.

Attention given to propriety of expression, may contribute not only to the perspicuity and force of the discourse, but to the richness and beauty of the language. Whence the poverty of our vocabulary? Is it from unacquaintance with our tongue? No, but we are not accustomed to distinguish between words

* D'Alembert, *Mélanges*, tome ii., p. 345. *Reflexions sur l'elocution oratoire.*

of a similar signification, that is to say, words which express the same general idea in a particular shade of meaning. From not noting carefully the shades of meaning, we use for each of them, either the generic term which embraces them all, or a special term taken at hazard. This word, rather than the others, almost always recurs, the others remain unused; our vocabulary is contracted, our language is poor. There are fortunate minds, favored too by education, to whom language yields up at every moment all its affluence of expression and form. They are, it is said, well acquainted with it, but what is this that is said? Are others to whom none of the terms it consists of are strange or new, less acquainted with it? The first in this sense know it better, that having received from each of the words a more distinct and vivid impression, by observing better, and feeling its power more perfectly, and being in more intimate relation to it, it is more at the command of their thought. We may, to a certain extent, appropriate this advantage by study, the thoughtful study, I mean, of good authors; it would also be a useful labor to inform ourselves in a case of uncertainty as to the import of a word, or the choice which should be made between two words, that is to say, to recur to the most valuable works on synonyms. We may also recommend, in this connection, the exercise of translation.

Propriety in the expression of moral ideas is difficult and uncommon; yet propriety is not naturally foreign to these ideas. For, although there is scarcely a perfectly simple moral state or fact, *in concreto*, we have succeeded in distinguishing clearly the elements which are combined in each state or fact of this class, of which I desire no other proof than the names we have found for them.

Precision.—These two qualities, propriety and precision, are, assuredly, not without a relation to each other; the necessity for one supposes the necessity for the other, and we can hardly find a writer who has cultivated one and neglected the other. Still, they are distinct, and ought to be studied separately.

The word *precision* appears to designate a language which expresses neither more nor less than one means to say, and it is often used in this sense; but the Rhetoricians and the Academy define precision: "Exactness in discourse, by which one so confines himself to the subject of which he speaks, that he says nothing superfluous." The Academy adds: "by which, also, he expresses himself with justness, regularity."

We will say, for ourselves, that while propriety is concerned with the justness of signs, precision has respect to their number, which it reduces to what is simply necessary. But if it is opposed to saying too much, it is not content without saying everything. "Precision," says M. Lémontey, "consists in banishing from discourse everything superfluous, and omitting nothing which is necessary. It must be distinguished from one of its branches which is called conciseness, and which pertains to the husbandry of words and to the compactness of the sentence, rather than to the strict adjustment of the expression to the thought. Conciseness may be applied indifferently to falsehood and to truth, while precision cannot be conceived of apart from justness and perspicuity; conciseness, also, may be but an affectation of the mind, while precision consists especially in the combined vigor of judgment and character. In man it is the attribute of force and reason; in social order, the language of the law which prescribes, and of the authority which commands; in science, the end and perfection of method and nomenclature."

Precision, nevertheless, tends to conciseness, since, as its name indicates, it retrenches, it cuts around. Conciseness is distinguished by an economy of words greater than the object of precision requires; for precision only suppresses what is decidedly superfluous, and would spare the mind a fatigue, that which springs from the necessity which an author puts upon us, of condensing the thought, or reducing it to a few elements. Conciseness, stopping somewhat short of what is necessary to complete expression, is not designed, doubtless, to fatigue the mind, but it gives it labor, and thus it enters into the category of those procedures or figures of which we have before spoken. It is an ellipsis, not of words but of thoughts. Taking it as figure, or at least as a particular force of style, it can scarcely constitute the form of an entire composition, especially that of the sermon. It is too apt to produce obscurity;* it approaches to affectation and the epigrammatic style. It is often but the false semblance of precision; and nothing is easier than to have at the same time much conciseness and very little precision. For it is possible to be at the same time parsimonious and prodigal, and with all this affectation of strictness, to leave only vague ideas in the mind of the reader.

Precision is opposed to repetitions, unmeaning epithets, pleonasms, expletives.† Proceeding farther, it becomes a real virtue of style, and furnishes us with the most apt and neat forms of expression, and urges us to concentrate many words in one, which one word, in truth, contains the substance of many. It aims to spare the reader the pains of taking the sum of the ideas, by enabling him to comprehend them at a glance. Still, redundance and a certain accumulation of circumstances and of words, may not be inappropriate.‡

* See Rollin, *Traitè des etudes*, lib. v., ch. ii., art. 1.

† See Boileau, criticised by Condillac, *Art d'ecrire*, p. 115, édition de Genève, 1808, and P. Corneille, tome i., pp. 129, 132, édition Didot, 1800.

‡ See Pelisson, *Discours au Roi*, pour M. Fouquet. (*Chrestomathie Française*, tome ii., 254, 258, troisième édition.) See, also, 1 Corinthians, xv. 53, 54.

Precision is not equally necessary in every kind of composition. Prolixity is always repulsive; but a certain abundance is necessary, when instead of writing we have to speak, and especially to speak to a promiscuous auditory;* and some diffuseness is suited to the fulness of the heart. A heart which is moved wants to multiply the thought which agitates it, and to express it at large, by multiplying words and images. It is difficult to move others by very condensed language, unless we follow and enforce it by thoughts more fully developed.

In the same discourse, different degrees of precision may have place. But we seldom advance from more precision to more abundance. The wave appears to compress itself in order to break with greater force. "Oratory," says Lémontey, "is prodigal of rich developments, only that it may conclude its harangues with more cogent recapitulations, and finish often like Demosthenes, that which it began like Isocrates."†

* Precision, which is a stranger to the protestations of love, to the confidential expressions of friendship, to the freedom of the epistolary style, and to the obscurities of diplomacy, finds its own obstacles in eloquence, in poetry, and in the dramatic art. Whenever we address several men simultaneously, we must adapt ourselves to the attention of the most frivolous, the capacity of the most simple, the indolence of the most sluggish. Whenever we undertake to convince various minds, what a variety of tone and imagery, what repeated attacks are necessary in order to oppose the different degrees of malevolence, and prejudices of many roots! Thus the sacred pulpit, the political tribune, try different methods, and employ alternately vehemence, authority, unction, imagination, and argument.—LÉMONTEY.

† *Satius est aliquid (oriatoni) superesse quam deesse*, Quintilian, lib. iv., cap. ii. "That which ordinarily causes obscurity in discourse, is the desire of always explaining with brevity. It is better to offend by too much than by too little breadth; a style always spirited and concise, such, for example, as that of Sallust or Tertullian, may suit works which, not being intended to be spoken, allow the

Precision is not to be restricted to isolated sentences. As there may be too many words in a sentence, there may also be too many sentences in a paragraph; and the general tissue of the style may be loose as well as that of a period. A rule which we have given for discourse as a whole, may here be applied. Everything must hasten to the conclusion. We must not have two sentences where one will suffice. We must not delay the reader when he would advance. Our motion must not be less rapid than that of his mind.* He doubtless might suffer himself to be amused on the way, by brilliant displays of thought and flights of imagination; but the pleasure he would hence find, would be no apology to the orator, whose business is not to amuse his hearer, but to lead him on to a determinate end. Everything, even the ornaments of style, ought to tend to that result; oratorical discourse admits of no useless charms. What, then, shall we say of those deviations and diversions which have not even the merit of amusing, of those unmeaning sentences which do nothing but retard the movement, of a loose tissue, whose frettings are not even disguised by the embroidery? Let us adopt this general rule: That there be nothing intervening between ideas which complete one another, and between which the mind does not require a pause. If there be anything between two ideas, it should be an idea which is suited to smooth

reader leisure and liberty to review; but not a sermon, which by its rapidity, may escape from the most attentive hearer. We must not suppose, indeed, that it is always thus; such, at least, should be the perspicuity of the discourse, that it will convey light even to the most listless minds, as the sun strikes our eyes when we are not thinking of it, and almost in spite of us. The highest effect of this quality is reached not when one may understand what we say, but when he cannot but understand it." (ROLLIN, *Traité des études*, livre v., chap. ii., art i., *De la maniere dont un prédicateur doit parler.*)

* See D'ALEMBERT, *Reflexions sur l'elocution oratoire*, in his *Mélanges*, tome ii., p. 345.

the passage from one to the other, like sluices which prevent a boat from making too sudden and too forcible a descent. I admit that without such intermediate ideas, the texture of the style might, by its compactness, become hard and rigid. But if they be superfluous, the style is loose and dragging. The orator is a traveller; the hearer travels with him.

De leur robe trainante ils relevent les plis.*

We must never—and with this remark I conclude—allow precision to render our style abstract and dry.

We may doubtless fall upon lively expressions, we may attain to elegance which is closely allied to precision, we may become ingenious by the habitual study of forms in which thought is compressed and condensed, but the whole is wanting in richness and in color.†

Precision, applied to the general texture of the diction, becomes *rapidity*. This is not only a form but a quality of style; style to the general composition is what man is to the world, a *microscosm*. Man is a world in miniature, and style is discourse in miniature, with all its laws and all its characteristics. Rapidity is not precipitance, but the economy of time and space. There are two forms of style; one which concentrates the elements of each idea, the other which amplifies them. Bossuet's sentences are Massillon's paragraphs, and neither of them is to be censured. Bossuet, sometimes, is too rapid, and Massillon too long; but the first also is often brief and the other long, with propriety. The movement of Bossuet is more majestic, more imposing; the phraseology of Massillon, flowery as it is, is sometimes dragging. The *Petit Carême*, which is regarded as his most highly-finished work, is not the most eloquent. It often de-

* "They raise the folds of their training garments."

† The substantive instead of the verb. The reply of children to the question, "What is a thing?—It is when we . . . ."

velops, and it develops exceedingly well; but it also amplifies, expressing the same idea under two or three different forms. There is a difference between them, for the words are different, but it amounts to almost nothing, and is not worth the trouble which it costs. This form, which is reproduced in every part of the volume, is somewhat tedious. Bossuet doubtless is often too rapid. We must, in short, amplify when it is proper, but we must also know how to retrench.*

This leads us to speak of *proportion*, which consists in giving each idea the place and the degree of development, which belong to it, in the plan of the discourse. In regard to proportion Bossuet often fails in his sermons, and hence, though he has more genius than Massillon and Bourdaloue, we place him below them as a preacher. While every one reads Massillon and many read Bourdaloue, Bossuet is read by few, although exceedingly brilliant, because he is wanting in proportion. This same fault injures passages otherwise excellent.†

§ 3. *Order.*

Precision led us to speak of the texture of style. We condemned everything which retards or interrupts the succession of thought. Herein we applied to style what we have said of the general composition of discourse. Within reduced proportions, we have been but insisting on that continuous progression which Theremin recommends. We now touch on another quality of style: order.

* We contrast Bossuet and Massillon in a passage taken from each of them. See BOSSUET, *Oraison funèbre de Michel le Tellièr*, (*dans le choix d'oraisons funèbres*, édition Villemain, 1827, p. 273,) and MASSILLON, tome vii., p. 128, édition Méquignon, "*Nous n'avons de grand.*" The paragraphs of Massillon are so many couplets. They are wanting in freedom and variety.

† See, on this point, the sermon of MASSILLON, *sur l'Oubli des injures*, and that of P. de la Rue, *sur le Pechcur mourant*, p. 569

All the other qualities of which we have spoken are, as it were lost, without order, which puts in its place each paragraph in the discourse, each sentence in the paragraph, each word in the sentence. And as to perspicuity, of which we first spoke, it cannot dispense with order; order is chiefly essential to it. As there is no force without perspicuity, so there is no perspicuity without order. Apart from perspicuity, moreover, it is with style in which order reigns, as with a wall, the stones of which are well united; it is much more compact and strong. Now, it is the effect of order in style to connect the ideas closely, whence also results strength.

The law of order not only proscribes gross faults, manifest transpositions; it is opposed to everything in the arrangement of the ideas, which is not as well ordered as possible. It requires the texture of the style to be as compact as possible. It does this, by the very formula which it uses, since, according to this formula, for which no other can be substituted, it is necessary that each idea should be followed by that which among all the author expresses is nearest to it. I do not say, absolutely the nearest possible, since this would forbid the suppression of those intermediate ideas which constitutes the rapidity of the style and contributes to its beauty. If the idea which is logically nearest to another idea is separated from it in the discourse, by some other, there is already disorder in it, which, though not visible perhaps, is not on that account without influence. And if this fault, small as it may be, is often afterwards reproduced, if this negligence is habitual, an effect results from it, not appreciable, perhaps, because it is negative, but nevertheless considerable. It produces weariness and doubt in the mind of the hearer, which prevent him from receiving a complete and well-sustained impression.

Every mind instinctively requires order. Every mind

delights in order and is pained by its opposite. It suffers for the want of it, without knowing why, and perhaps without being apprized that it does suffer; we have an uneasiness like that which one feels in a tainted atmosphere, or, not to leave the intellectual sphere, like suffering which we experience from sophistry, when the fault in the reasoning is not detected. If it is man's destiny to err, still his natural element, his essence so to speak, is truth. However unjust a mind may be, and whatever errors it may allow in itself, it does not allow errors in others. The same mind which does not lead others aright would itself be so led, and every deviation from the true route which perhaps it is itself unable to indicate, disconcerts and wearies it. The mere interposition of a thought which the progress of the ideas does not yet call for, or calls for no longer, destroys rising interest. A mind hesitating, uncertain, no longer lends itself to the orator's intention, if we may say indeed the orator has an intention; for we see him assailed by several ideas at once, without knowing to which he is to attend, and in the perplexity, breaking his thought at every stroke, retracing his steps, mistaking gradations and confounding relations. The fact may be inexplicable; it is nevertheless real, and the certainty is, that where there is less of order, there is, equally, less of power.*

If order, or the connection of ideas, is always necessary, it is especially so in the eloquence of the pulpit, in which we should spare the hearer every useless and unwelcome trouble. We should even leave something to be supplied by a hearer

* M. Vinet proposed to introduce here two passages on *Singularity*, which he wrote for the purpose of exhibiting in the way of comparison, the importance and necessity of order. Only a fragment of the first of these passages has been found, and as it is on this account impossible to make the comparison designated by the author, we have thought it better to suppress the unfinished paragraph.—[EDITORS.]

as well as a reader; but it is by no means allowed to us, to require him to do a work which properly belongs to us.

There is the same difference between logical and oratorical order in style, that there is in the composition as a whole. Applying then to style, the rules of oratory, we say:

Let that which is more general precede that which is more particular;

Let that which is less striking precede that which is more so;

Let the form in which an idea is concentrated, follow one in which it is expressed more at large.

This order is violated by precipitance, by the attraction of accidental or *terminal* ideas, which create connections which are true, but not the true connections.

No great writer, no writer who is classed with models, is defective in this point, any more than in the preceding ones; or rather no writer who has not strictly and exactly observed this law, has ever been placed among models, however distinguished for invention, for strength, or for brilliance. It is well indeed to observe, that if the combination of all the qualities which we have enumerated does not form a great writer, others, though they may seem to be of a superior nature, will not suffice for this, independently of the former.

Let these verses from Racine, in *Athalie*, be examined after this statement:

> L'enterprise, sans doute, est grande et périlleuse,
> J'attaque sur son trône une reine orgueilleuse,
> Qui voit sous ses drapeaux marcher un camp nombreux,
> De hardis etrangers, d'infidèles Hébreux;
> Mais ma force est au Dieu dont l'inérêt me guide,
> *Songez qu'en cet enfant tout Israel réside,*
> Déjà ce Dieu vengeur commence à la troubler;
> Déjà, trompant ses soins, j'ai su vous rassembler. * etc.

---

* Racine, *Athalie*, acte iv., scene iii.

"Th' attempt doubtless is great and perilous;
I attack a haughty monarch on her throne,

And these verses of André Chénier in *le Mendiant:*

Il ouvre un œil avide, et long temps euvisage
L'etranger. Puis enfin sa voix trouve un passage;
Est-ce toi Cléotas? toi qu'ainsi je revoi!
Tout ici t'appartient. O mon perè! est-ce toi?
Je rougis que mes yeux aient pu te méconnaître,
O Cleotas! mon perè! O toi, qui fus mon maître,
Viens, je n'ai fait ici que garder ton trésor,
Et ton ancien Lycus veut te servir encor.†

Compare the same group of ideas differently arranged in the two following passages. The subject is the foolishness of Christianity:

1. "Those who accuse Christianity of foolishness should at least admit that it foresaw and braved this reproach. It was in haste to charge itself with it. It has avowed the bold design of saving men by foolishness. It was not under an illusion; it knew that its doctrine would be regarded as madness; it knew this before experience, before any one had said it, and with this foolishness in its mouth, with this foolish-

---

Who sees advancing under her banners,
A numerous band of intrepid strangers,
And unbelieving Hebrews. But my strength
Is in that God whose cause directs me;
Conceive all Israel bound up in this child.
Already does God avenge himself on her,
Already eluding her wrathful vigilance,
You I have been able to muster, etc."—Tr.

*"With eager gaze, he long the stranger eyes.
His tongue at length finds utterance. Is't thou
Cleotas! thou, whom thus again I see?
All here is thine. My father, is it thou?
I blush that thee my eyes should have mistaken.
O my father Cleotas! O thou who
My master wast, come, here nought have I done
But thy treasure keep. Thy ancient Lycus
Still longs to be thy servant."—Tr.

ness as its standard, it went forth to the conquest of the world. Christianity then has not left to infidelity the satisfaction of taxing it with foolishness, and if it is mad, it is in good earnest and willing to be so."

2. "Christianity has not left to infidelity the satisfaction of being the first to tax it with foolishness. It has been in haste to bring this accusation against itself. It has avowed the bold design of saving men by foolishness. It has not been under an illusion; it has known that its doctrine would be regarded as madness; it knew this before experience; it knew it before any one had said it, and with this foolishness in its mouth, with this foolishness as its standard, it went forth to the conquest of the world. If then it is mad, it is in good earnest, and is willing to be so; and those who reproach it with foolishness, are at least contrained to confess that it has foreseen their reproach, and braved it."*

§ 4. *Naturalness.*

This is one of those things which can be defined only by their effects or their symptoms, inasmuch as any different definition would itself have to be defined. We will say then that the natural style is that in which art is not perceptible; whether because there is no mixture of art in it, or from the force of art. For the triumph of art is to cause itself to be overlooked or to be undiscoverable except on reflection.

Art is not the mere imitation of nature, as it has long since been said to be; we reject this definition, and maintain that art aspires to give to its creations the character of natural productions. It is successful, when it is able to combine the

* VINET, *on the foolishness of truth*, in the *Nouveax discours sur quelques sujets religieux.* Study, with the same object, a paragraph from Massillon, *Sur l'Oubli du dernier Jour:* "Sur quoi vous rassurez, vous encore? etc.," and the passages from Fénélon and Bossuet, examined by Condillac, *Art d'Ecrire,* liv. iii., cap. ii. Massillon winds up an idea admirably.

true and the extraordinary. Neither the true which is not extraordinary, nor the extraordinary which is not true, is an object of art.

That which in one age or country seems natural, does not seem so in another. From our point of view, the panoply of St. Paul (Ephesians, vi. 13–17) is not natural. The oriental style does not appear more so. Epochs of half-civilization, epochs, also, the exquisite performances of which appear to be of a species of naïvete, and those of extreme civilization, are little favorable to the natural in style; to restore us to this, is the object of mental culture.

It is as the proof or sign of sincerity that the natural pleases. The absence of it induces a suspicion of that of sincerity, although one may be very cordial without being natural; in that case, however, we must indeed be cordial. Who are more cordial, more moved and more moving, than Saint Augustine and Saint Bernard? and yet they are not natural.

In works of art, in writing, the natural pleases on two accounts; as more unexpected and as more uncommon. It is partly from the rarity of entire naturalness, that we experience such pleasure in meeting with it. "When," says Pascal, "we meet with the natural style, we are surprised and delighted; for we expected to find an author and we have found a man. Whilst men of good taste who look into a book, in the hope of finding a man, are altogether surprised to find an author."*

Boileau, in his *Eloge du Vrai*, has not forgotten to praise the natural style:

> Cessons de nous flatter. Il n'est esprit si droit
> Que ne soit imposteur et faux par quelque endroit,
> Sans cesse on prend le masque, et, quittant la nature,
> On craint ce se montrer sous sa propre figure,

* PASCAL, *Pensées*, part i., art. x., § xxviii.

Par là le plus sincère assez souvent déplaît.
Rarement un esprit ose être ce qu'il est.
* * * * *
Chacun pris dans son air est agréable en soi;
Ce n'est que l'air d'autrui qui peut déplaier en moi.*

The natural may rise to naïvete, and this naïvete is admirable in men and subjects of a grave character. In a child the natural proceeds from naïvete; that a man should become a child without losing his gravity and maturity, is most uncommon and most interesting. The difference between the natural and naïvete is this: The natural possesses and recognizes itself; naïvete does neither; it allows itself to be surprised by its own impressions; when all is over, it will be itself surprised at its own utterances. Bossuet has impressive exemplifications of the natural.

Apart from situations in actual life, it is very difficult to be perfectly natural, that is to say, perfectly true. Either we must avoid wholly the influence of art, or give ourselves wholly up to it. Even sincerity gives no security for the natural. It is so rare, that when we meet with an orator who is perfectly natural, we are tempted to ask of him:

Est ce vous qui parlez, ou si c'est votre rôle?†

If there is pleasure in finding a *man*, we should have it when we hear discourses from the pulpit; and here it would

* Boileau, *Epître* ix.

"Cease thyself to flatter. No mind so pure,
But has some taint of error and of falsehood;
We take the mask, and, nature disowning,
Fear to be seen in our proper figure.
The truest, thus, oft most displeasure gives.
How seldom dares the mind be what it is!
* * * * *
Each, in his own shape taken, pleases us:
The shape of others only me disgusts."—Tr.

† "Is it you who speak, or are you playing a part."

seem there should be less place for the pleasure of surprise. May we venture to say that there is in fact greater? That which may be natural in poetry may not be so in eloquence, and that of the pulpit, the chair of truth, from which we speak of God and the most weighty interests, is behind other kinds of eloquence in regard to this quality.

According to Theremin, the cause, in part, is the physical condition of the preacher who is removed from his auditory and elevated above it. All the fervor of Christian charity is needed to transform the discourse into a business matter. D'Alembert, complaining of the academic style, says: "It were better called the style of the pulpit."* Fénélon has earnestly endeavored to restore nature to the pulpit, in respect both of style and of conceiving and planning,† which are all closely connected.

I forbear to indicate the different ways in which we fail of the natural. Why should they all be enumerated? On this subject, of what use were negative rules? We should not be rendered natural by being put on our guard against violations of nature. The source of the natural is more positive and more vital. Darkness should be absorbed by light. In avoiding one fault, we shall fall into another, unless we strongly adhere to principle; and to do this, an orator must determine to be true, and to make his discourse not a work, but an action. It is to this that Brougham ascribes the superiority of the style of Demosthenes. What, in fact, is it that a man calls natural, in a discourse which he hears? It is a mode of expression which he feels he himself would have involuntarily used, if he had been in the position and frame of mind which are professed by the orator. A mode of expression which leads him to say: How could one have spoken otherwise? And is it not the first form of expression which must needs have come to the mind?

* D'Alembert, *Mélanges*, tome ii., p. 348.

† See *his dialogues on Eloquence.*

Not then to speak of affectation, of exaggeration, of witticisms, of prolonged metaphors, of antitheses, etc., we only remark, that there is danger of not being natural in transferring to the pulpit traits or forms which are natural in secular oratory, or in imitating the particular form of the master-pieces in our own kind of oratory. Not without caution, not without reserve, should we study the orators.

Be that which you would appear to be.

§ 5. *Congruity.*

In a very general sense, all the qualities above recommended are *congruities* of different kinds. We now speak of congruity in a special sense, namely, the correspondence of the expression to the character of the ideas which it should invest, to the kind of the composition, the subject it treats of, the end it proposes. The style may be perspicuous, correct, precise, natural, without being congruous. Congruity proceeds from a just sense of the subject, and consists in not offending or obscuring this sense in others.

We restrict ourselves of course to the particular kind of discourse we are treating of, to preaching; for what have we to say of congruity in general, which the name alone has not already expressed?

A preliminary question occurs. We speak of a language of the pulpit; is there a language of the pulpit? Doubtless there is, if we take the question as referring to the assemblage of congruities required in a discourse which is connected with worship and pronounced in a sacred place. But if we go beyond this, if the question relates not to *congruity*, but *conventionality*, if a certain dialect be intended, if it be asked whether a sacred orator is to use a language subject to different rules from those which result from the nature of his mission, and which a just sense of his position suggests to him, we answer, no. In this sense, there is not a language of the pulpit.* Let us for a moment hear M. Theremin :

"To this question, What language is suited to the pulpit orator ? some answer, the language of the Bible ; others, that of books ; others, again, that of ordinary life ; some, a language simple and natural ; others, a language elaborately artistic, a poetical language, rich with imagery. The language of some celebrated preachers, is also sometimes given as a model. For my part, if I am asked what language ought the preacher to use in the pulpit, I can only answer, his own. He has an inward experience of the christian life, and is constantly nourished by the word of God, with many expressions and images of which he has become familiar. Now this christian life does not form a separate current in his life, but unites and mixes itself with his whole internal life, consisting of his imagination, his sensibility, his character, all the faculties of his mind, of the experiences of his life, of his scientific and literary culture. From all these combined elements results an inward speech, the language in which he speaks the truths of salvation to himself and to God. This is the fundamental tone of the speech which he should use in the pulpit. Let every one then assume his own individuality, without exaggeration, without expressing more or less than is in him, always endeavoring not to exhibit whatever he may have that is rough and severe, but rather to allay it by imitating Jesus Christ, the most perfect of models."†

These ideas, well digested, lead us into all the truth on the style of the pulpit. Let us, however, consider more in detail, the congruities of this style.

The first is *simplicity*, which must not be confounded with *naturalness.* The natural which should reign everywhere

* *Kanzel*-sprache, *Kanzleis*-sprache. "*Pulpit*-language, *Chancery*-language."

† Theremin, *Die Beredsamkeit eine Tugend*, pp. xxvii., xxix.

cannot distinguish the style of the pulpit. But simplicity, which does not strictly belong to every kind of discourse, is one of the congruities of sacred eloquence. Besides, simplicity may be subjected to rule; it may be regulated, not so the natural.

Naturalness and simplicity are sometimes confounded. They are, it is true, related to each other. One can scarcely be simple without being natural; but we may be natural without being simple. The natural consists in being oneself, a thing assuredly very rare; the perfectly natural, also, is little common; naïvete still less so; but art furnishes no means of becoming natural; it can only show to those who explore it that nothing is gained by separation from nature, and that the beautiful and the natural are inseparable. The natural, moreover, is not an object of art; it is the first prerequisite of art; it is, in some sort, a security against the abuses of art; it is the ground of art. Literary advancements have been essentially but a return to the natural; the natural cannot be imitated; the worst of affectations is the affectation of the natural.

But as we may be wanting in simplicity without being wanting precisely in naturalness; as the natural is equally necessary in all kinds of discourse, while some require more, others less of simplicity; there is something to be said concerning simplicity, in a course on Rhetoric or Homiletics.

Etymologically speaking, *simplicity* is the contrary of *multiplicity;* simplicity, the absence of all *folding* or *doubling*, excludes the expression of a second idea when a first suffices. This, at first view, gives it the appearance of conciseness; but conciseness spares words, simplicity is the economy of means. It is this form of style that least disturbs the labor of thought, and advances it to the end by the most direct road. It is, however, in some degree relative. What is not simple enough for one class of readers is sufficiently so for another,

We shall here call that simple which will appear to be such to all the individuals, or at least to all the classes of which the preacher's auditory is ordinarily composed, and with this understanding we add, that simplicity excludes, on the one hand, useless circumlocution and complexity, profusion of figures, ambitious ornaments; and on the other, tenuous thoughts, subtility, abstractness. It excludes, however, neither shades nor affluence of expression. One may be at the same time magnificent and simple, simple and delicate.

Simplicity in a pulpit orator is especially important. It is the ornament of great thoughts, as perspicuity is of profound ones; and all the thoughts which the preacher is charged to transmit are great.

Simplicity is inseparable from seriousness. Nothing has less the appearance of seriousness, nothing more induces the suspicion of insincerity than nicety and refining.

Finally, simplicity is included in the consideration and respect which are due from the preacher to an auditory consisting of persons of different degrees of intelligence.

In oratorical discourse, the true name of simplicity is that of *popularity*. Popularity, which should also characterize strongly the thoughts and arguments, consists, as regards the style, in language composed of expressions which are familiar to the majority. Popular language is that which all classes of society alike understand, the common ground on which they meet and communicate with each other; it is a language in their habitual use of which, some add, others retrench something, but which is not on that account less the language of every one, the only language of every one, although it may not be, such as it is, the language of any one.

The word *popularity*, awakens at this day the idea of a peculiar manner in art and style, and one which is more or less disreputable. Popular writing is writing of its own sort, which is scarcely allowed a place in literature. It has not been always thus distinguished. Not to speak of epochs of barbarism, in which all classes are alike rude, there have been highly-civilized ages which have had but one language. Grecian literature has no writings which are specially popular; popularity is the character of all. Even at our point of view, the great productions of ancient art may be regarded as popular. And among the highest modern achievements in art, the most distinguished are, on the whole, the most popular; and we ought not to be surprised at this; what interests man in all classes, is superior to what can be understood and relished only by men of a certain class. One may be popular without being great, but not great without being popular. To be pathetic, to be sublime, we must, by proceeding with the mean degree of culture and development, strike the keys which are the same in all men.

Before a promiscuous auditory, we incur a risk in not being popular; we always gain when we are so. What we do with a view to being popular, that is to say, to reach at once the greatest number of good minds, is not lost upon those of the highest cultivation; they enjoy it the more from their superior cultivation; and in this view, the orator's success, in this way obtained, is of the highest kind, while that which is done for the special purpose of pleasing a certain class, is lost on others, without, in fact, succeeding better with the class whose applause was desired, or whose assent was sought.

The true region, the natural medium of eloquence, embraces the thoughts of all, and consequently, as far as possible, the language of all. Eloquence is the contact of man with man, by their human, not by their accidental or individual sides. The language, then, which is adapted to eloquence, is a general, common, customary language; nothing rare or exceptional is here in place. I do not say that one cannot be *eloquent* on very special themes, or in their behalf; but one cannot be *oratorical* on such themes, except before a very select auditory, to whom such themes present no difficulties, and who can readily resolve special ideas into general ones, the only ones which are oratorical. Cicero doubtless rested no less on experience than theory, when he said: "*In dicendo vitium vel maximum est a vulgari genere orationis atque a consuetudine communis sensus abhorrere;*"* a passage, of which this, from D'Alembert, seems to be a translation: "An orator should never forget that it is to the multitude that he speaks; that it is them which he is to move, to melt, to draw. Eloquence which is not for the majority is not eloquence."†

If this maxim is just in application to eloquence in general, it is especially so as to the eloquence of the pulpit. Nothing is more popular than the themes of preaching; for nothing is more general, more common to all. Nothing more completely effaces the distinctions of rank and education among men. Nothing is more purely human. It is then, if we may so speak, a purely human language that the themes of the pulpit require. Here, if we would rise, we must descend; and if we descend, we shall rise. As the body is more than raiment, substance more than accident, the genus more than the species, so man is more than any of the particular conditions or forms of humanity; to reach man through the subdivisions and shades of humanity we must rise; and the majesty of the pulpit displays itself chiefly in separating man from whatever is accessory to him or added by events, in order to seize him in that lofty generality in which he corresponds to God and touches the infinite. The

* CICERO, *De Oratore*, lib. i., cap. iii. "In eloquence, the greatest error that can be incurred, is to deviate into abstruse expressions, and out of the beaten track of *common sense*." [Tran. Lond. 1808.

† *Reflexions sur l'elocution oratoire, dans les Mélanges, de* D'ALEMBERT.

eloquence of the pulpit, then, is great in proportion to its popularity, or popular in proportion as it is great. Its language, of course, avoiding what is particular to some, must, in the selection of its elements, have respect to what is common to all. The preacher is not permitted to use abstract terms, scholastic formulas, learned allusions, subtile and nice distinctions, ingenious but complicated terms of expression, a certain kind and even a certain degree of elegance, certain delicacies of art highly appreciated by professional men, but lost upon the people.

Still *popularity* is not the true name of the simplicity of the pulpit ; this word rather indicates the elevation on which we place our auditory, than the relations in which we place ourselves, or suppose ourselves to sustain toward it. Now, the preacher's auditory is more than a people, it is a family ; and the simplicity of evangelical discourse is not only *popularity*, it is *familiarity*. Familiarity which was long confined to the order of relations from which it has borrowed its name, ought not be restricted to a circle so narrow ; it should exist among men who are not united by the ties of blood, who do not live under the same roof. It is needless to advert here to the causes which have compressed it within its actual limits, which have rendered ceremony and *decorum* so indispensable among those who have sprung from the same dust, are subject to the same necessities, and alike exposed to death. Among generous and congenial souls, intimacy soon induces familiarity ; that is to say, the decent and noble freedom which becomes brothers. So great are the advantages of familiarity, that when it does not spontaneously arise, we should be able to establish it. "There is not," says Vauvenargues, "a better or more necessary school than familiarity. A man whose whole life is pent up in a state of reserve, commits the greatest faults when occasion obliges him to leave it, and business occupies nim. The only cure of presumption, of timidity, of foolish pride, is familiarity; it is only by free and open intercourse that man can be known, that one can test himself, that one can analyze himself, can compare himself with others; here it is that naked humanity is seen in all its weakness and in all its strength. They who want courage to seek truth in these rough experiences, are profoundly below all true greatness."

Between those whose relative position prevents their meeting on a true footing of familiarity, if anything intermediate can create this relation, it is assuredly God, or the thought of God, a thought before which all differences and all inequalities disappear. Now, he whose function it is to speak to his fellows of God and of God only, can recognize among them only men and brethren; he approaches them only in this character, he assembles them around him only under this title, expressly indeed under this relation; not only does familiarity become his discourse, but a different character misbecomes it. The ceremony of polite intercourse carried into the pulpit takes from the discourse of the preacher all communicative virtue; there remains, I know not what, between the speaker and the hearers. There is, in the intercourse of friends, one of those symbols so abundant in our social life and conversation, which long survive the remembrance of the ideas which they express. When two friends meet they give one another the hand; if it is covered they first make it bare; man must touch man; the contact and pressure of two naked hands make each one sensible to the life of the other. A preacher who is not familiar, and who carries into the pulpit the formalities of worldly politeness, who holds himself in reserve, who is not free, is a friend who extends a hand to his friend, but a hand in a glove, through which no warmth or life can be felt. What then of him who, before he gives his hand, is careful to cover it,—of the preacher, I mean, who allows himself less freedom, less flow of heart in the pulpit than he does in the ordinary greetings and the superficial intercourse of social life? If we understand well the preacher's position, who, for a few moments at least, is invested with the liberty of a father and a brother, his language should be familiar, inasmuch as it ought to be open, and to consist entirely of terms, of movements and forms of expression taken from the relations of the family and of friendship. This language will indicate, in a lively manner, the relation which should consciously exist between his auditory and himself; it will make the impression that it is not a mere idea, but a common, present, urgent interest that is at stake between him and his hearers; it will bring them nearer to him. It is unnecessary to distinguish the familiarity we have in view, from another familiarity which is indecent and irreverent; it is in and before everything animated by christian sentiment; this sentiment at the same time creates and limits it; as it is christian familiarity, it is accompanied, necessarily, with those holy restraints which are not wanting even in the freest intercourse of two christians with one another.

Familiarity, I think, is not wanting in any of the masters of the sacred pulpit; it characterizes the most eminent among them, more strongly and completely than any others. It is almost unknown among the orators of the senate or bar; they may be popular but hardly familiar. How can they be so? Is their auditory to them a family? Nay, these citizens, these judges, are they in respect to the orator, even for one instant, men, nothing besides men? Are they not always citizens and judges? I do not then hesitate to make familiarity, in an exclusive sense, characteristic of pulpit eloquence.

In the daily relations of life, and of individuals with one another, familiarity leads us to call things by their names; it prefers individual to generic designations, direct affirmation to reticence and insinuation, precise to vague indications. In some measure, it may, it should do the same in the pulpit; it thus imparts to the objects here treated a vivid impress of reality.

On one trait of familiarity we ought for a few moments to dwell. It may seem to us, that a sense of familiarity towards his hearers, must make it difficult to a preacher to avoid speaking of himself. A minister of the word of God is justly blamed for being occupied with himself; he ought to wish to forget himself; but while forgetting himself completely, charity may still induce him to speak of himself. Oratorical discourse is not a book, it is a direct, proximate, personal, urgent action. The orator's personality is to be here regarded as something. He, a man, comes as a representative of God, but he comes spontaneously, prompted by love, to discourse to a certain number of his fellows and his brethren, on their interests and his own. In every case, but especially if he addresses his parish, he is in the position of a father of a family and not of a stranger. He is an ambassador or a deputy in a sense different from that in which a man is one who has been sent by men. He may, he ought to speak as from himself, although the doctrine which he teaches is not his own. Observe these two points in which personality bears on what he does. He is a father and he is a brother. As a father, he exhorts, he entreats, he urges; he delights in sympathy, he is grieved by indifference, he fears on account of his own weakness, he depends on the power of God, he invokes his aid, he calls upon him for it. As a brother of his hearers, what he says to them he says to himself; he wants to make common cause with them and to testify this to them, not to appear as having no part in the interests in which he seeks to engage them. Doubtless he never seeks to turn upon himself an attention which ought to have a different direction ; he would censure this as a disloyalty ; but he does not claim it for his own sake, in testifying his sympathy with the truths he announces and the hearers he addresses ; and how can he testify his sympathy without speaking of himself? Is not every sympathetic movement, at the very moment, and by the very fact of its union with the personality of others, an external exhibition of our personality? Thus then, charity, humility, will control, but not interdict the manifestations of personality.

I do not speak here of that form of oratory, in which the preacher personifies his whole auditory in himself, and expresses in his own name the sentiments with which he supposes them to be penetrated. This is a figure of style, very proper at certain times, in which the *I* and the *me* do not designate the orator personally,* but the flock considered as an individual. No one can mistake here, no one does mistake. "There are occasions," says Maury, "on which a christian orator may modestly take himself as the subject of a moral development in which the multitude are interested : but he does not call the attention of the auditory to himself, by putting himself forward ; on the contrary, he concentrates on himself alone the weaknesses, the mistakes, the errors, the inconsistences of the human mind or heart ; and in such a manner that the more he speaks of himself, the less is he personal. Massillon excels in this humble method of thus putting himself in the place of sinners, while deploring his own contradictions, errors, distress and remorse. He excites the most touching interest, he melts his hearers into tears when depicting them with the most striking truth, he unveils the depth of his conscience, and condemns himself before God as *ungrateful*, as *miserable*, as *insensate*."†

* See Romans, vii., 7–25.

† MAURY, *Essai sur l'eloquence de la chaire*, lvi. *De l'egoisme dans les orateurs.* See two ways in which MASSILLON speaks of himself

There is no preacher, among those who are regarded as models, who does not often speak of himself in his discourses, though this is always done in the design and spirit which we have ascribed to oratorical familiarity. Their *me* has not the same meaning with the strictly personal *me* so veritably egotistic of a Demosthenes and a Cicero. It is the communicative *me* of sympathy and humility.

While the style of the pulpit should be simple, popular, familiar, it should still be *noble*. There is nothing more noble than christian truth. Its nobleness is the first characteristic of it that strikes us. Style should correspond to it; it ought to be noble. But in what does nobleness of style consist? In style as in society, nobility imparts the idea of distinction and even of exclusiveness. There is a class of images and words which is regarded as noble, as there is in aristocratic constitutions a class of men separated from the community of citizens by a visible and distinct barrier. Language also has its ignoble element, confounded in dictionaries, though not in discourse, with the aristocratic element. A low term is one which brings one's thought into too close contact with an object which it disdains, that is, judges unworthy of being occupied with, except from absolute necessity. Man does not willingly submit or wish to have the appearance of submitting willingly, to what too distinctly reminds him of what is humiliating in his nature or condition. Nobility in manners, actions or language, springs from a sense of human dignity, and every one feels that this dignity resides in thought or in the faculty in us which thinks.* Hence we are, in the first place, led to exclude

in his sermon, *Sur le jeune*, at the end of the exordium and at the end of the discourse.

* "All our dignity consists in thought, not in space which we cannot fill; nor in duration, which is nothing."—PASCAL *Pensées.*—TR.

certain ideas, or if we cannot wholly avoid them, then to exclude the words which recall them too directly, and to give preference to terms which present them obliquely and by a retreating side to the mind which recoils from them. It here concerns us to consider whether, from any cause, such or such a word impeaches our conscious respect for ourselves, or for such or such an object which we cannot despise without despising ourselves.

This impression we should avoid making on our hearers, first by the choice of thoughts, next by the choice of words. But, understand us well. We have respect to legitimate invincible disgusts, not to those which proceed from effeminacy of manners and culture; these last, if we would be noble, we must sometimes be able to bear, for nothing is less noble than the reciprocal conventionalities of fastidious politeness. We give them their place, and do not distrust them in it; but neither let them undertake to impose their yoke on the generous freedom of apostolic language. Religion, which embraces true nature, the truly natural in itself, constantly tends to restore civilization to its just conditions, and it approximates it to nobility in the proportion in which it removes it from effeminacy; for if coarseness is ignoble, effeminacy is scarcely less so. This spirit of Christianity should be that of the pulpit. In the choice of his terms the preacher should have respect to the state of the society from the bosom of which his flock has been drawn; but in this policy there should be no unmanly complaisance; he ought boldly to attempt to raise above itself, above its vain ideas of delicacy, this society to which Christianity only can impart natural beauty.

According to Buffon, nobility of style depends on "care to name things only by the most general terms."* And true it is, that whatever extends the horizon of thought, whatever

* BUFFON, *Discours sur le style.*

detaches it from its dependencies, raises it to its source and gives it space, is agreeable to the nature of man, suits its dignity. In passing from the notion of the individual to that of the species, from the idea of the species to that of the genus, we feel ourselves to be ascending. We become sensible of our liberty, our spirituality in this upward movement. But if general expressions are the most noble, they are not the most vivid or the most touching, and eloquence has want of breath in this ethereal region. General ideas, certainly, must cover particular ones; we must see in the particular ones the presence of the general; but this does not authorize in eloquence the exclusive use of the most general terms. Nobleness of style is not to be so gained. The greatness of eastern monarchs consists in their making themselves invisible; there is something of this kind of greatness in a style which, as far as possible, is rendered invisible by substituting a series of formulas for the presence of objects, and by making language, which is the painting of thought, a species of algebra.

Let us not be misunderstood. The laws of the sermon are not those of a poem. Preaching would seem to be for our amusement, not our edification, if it should be as precise and particular as poetry delights and has a right to be. Preaching, doubtless as well as poetry, should endeavor to make its objects present to us; but its objects are different. Some facts it details, others it expresses in a general manner. When it would represent the urgency of our projects and the ardor of our enterprises, under the very natural image of a car or a horseman borne along the course, of what use were it to attach the reins nicely to the foaming mouth of Bucephalus, or to imbrue in blood the rowels of Alexanders spurs? In scrutinizing our honesty in matters of interest, of what use were it to keep up the technical terms of which the peculiar language of the Exchange or the Counting-room is composed? In such cases it is seldom that a general designation does not suffice. But still we should be able to make use of these terms, when we have the hope that by employing them we shall be better and more promptly understood.

Periphrasis, though not requisite to nobleness of style, is a proper method of avoiding the direct mention of things, the true names of which give the impression of shame or disgust. Periphrasis is often indeed the definition, the true name of the object. It is sometimes a means of diminishing the too interesting quality of an object. Again, it sometimes enables us to avoid the use of a word.

It appears to be almost superfluous to speak of the *gravity* of the pulpit style, because what we have said of nobleness in this style implies or supposes gravity. In ascending to the principle of the one we ascend to the principle of the other, and what stamps our discourse with the first of these characters, engraves on it necessarily the second. Still, nobleness and gravity are distinct. We have said what the first shuns and repels; gravity, which, according to the etymology of its name, bears the weight of a great thought or a great interest, suffers not itself, suffers not the mind of the hearer to be withdrawn from that thought, by thoughts of less importance or of no importance, relatively to the object of preaching; it would interest us indeed, amuse us never, still less permit anything to arise in our mind resembling a hurtful or profane gayety. The most innocent smile, one which might be admissible in the most religious conversation, would not be innocent in the temple. I mean we should not be innocent in provoking it. In the most serious conversation there is not what there is here, a consecrated place, a solemn assembly, a worship of which the discourse is a part, and of which it wears the character; the emotions are all contagious, they spread electrically through the assembly, they become stronger and greater as they multiply; what then will an emotion of gayety become, and what is a temple, what an hour of worship in which we remember to have laughed? I do not suppose the preacher to intend to produce either laughter or a smile. I only admonish him to be on his guard lest he use terms which, in spite of him, may have this effect. We have said that it is not permitted to the preacher to use the weapon of ridicule.

In short, gravity requires that the mind be not even transiently occupied with any idea with which it should not be occupied in a sacred place, and in the exercise of worship.

It remains to me to speak of one more congruity in the style of the pulpit, a particular congruity which is, however, the substance and test of all the others. I mean the *scriptural tone of the language*. I would guard myself here, against all prejudice. A discourse, doubtless, may be christian, eminently christian, and not have the quality I speak of. The converse, also, may have place, that is to say, a sermon strongly tinctured with biblical expressions or allusions may not be christian. It is not, indeed, proper to express thoughts and feelings only in biblical formulas, to make sacred discourse wholly out of selections from scripture. We recall here the maxim of Theremin: "Each preacher should use his own language; Christian thought should individualize itself in him; the Word of God should become his word; the truth becomes his own, only when he is able to give it a form which is from himself; in short, a sermon composed only of quotations, even the finest quotations, would not be a *discourse*, it would want oratorical unity and force, because there would not be perceived in it the continuous presence and progressive action of a soul in which all the truths contained in the discourse are, in a sense, personified." But, admitting all this, let us still remember:

1. That we have a written religion, and that we are not

to forget this nor suffer it to be forgotten, and that when God himself has condescended to give a form to the truths of salvation,* it would be strange and disloyal not to cite, and cite abundantly, expressions which, though they came from human lips, have a character of authority which belongs to no other words. Their presence in preaching imparts majesty to it, and reminds believers, as we ourselves should be reminded in citing them, that we are only messengers, ambassadors, that we do but accommodate to a certain time and place, a word which is not our own, so that he who despises our word, despises not man, but God himself.

Moreover, the question relates not only to language and coloring, but to facts and persons also.

All the facts of the Bible ought to be present with us, for everything is either proof or symbol; and this history is the national history of the Christian church; here are its beginnings, here are its vouchers. The history of the kingdom of God on earth, doubtless offers for citation other facts also, and we are to refuse nothing in this department; but the facts of which the Bible is the sacred memorial, have doubtless the highest claim, and are of the greatest authority. After all, facts, persons, form the chief substance of the Bible and of our religion; may we cite nothing besides doctrines and precepts? It is of great importance that religion should retain its historical and providential character. We should be constantly reproducing this character, either directly, by using its facts as starting-points or confirmations to our reasonings, or indirectly, by multiplied references and allusions. Abundant opportunities for doing both will present themselves to a preacher who is nourished by the holy word, and possesses some imagination. Saurin, for the purpose of showing the influence of the trials of this life, in leading us to long for a

* Maury has in a singular manner reconciled the Bible and mythology. (*Essai*, lxix. *De l'emploi de l'Ecriture sainte.*)

better, says that "when the dove found, out of the ark, furious winds, overflowing waters, the open flood-gates of heaven, the whole world buried beneath the waves, she sought a refuge in the ark, but when she found valleys and fields, she stayed in them. See, my soul, an image of thyself." Elsewhere, when insisting on the necessity of uniting prayer with labor in the work of our salvation, he says: "We ought to follow the example of Moses when in the battle with the Amalekites, he divides with Joshua the work of conquest. Moses ascended the mountain, Joshua goes down upon the plains; Joshua fights, Moses prays. Moses stretches out his hands in supplication to heaven, Joshua raises the arm of a warrior; Moses opposes his zeal to the wrath of heaven, Joshua opposes his weapons and his courage to the enemy of the Jewish people, and by this wise union of prayer and action, of trust and vigilance, Israel triumphs, Amalek is discomfitted."*

Having Him for our master who is the Word full of grace and truth, to whom the Spirit was given without measure, who alone having the truth in himself as he has the life in himself, teaches with *authority*, how is it possible that we should not joyfully and fervently repeat his words, not as common citations but with reverence, with marked intention?

2. The Bible contains thoughts, "which never would have entered into the heart of man," sublime paradoxes on our nature, our condition, our future state, the purposes of God with respect to us, and, to use an expression scarcely to be dispensed with, on the CHARACTER of God. None of these extraordinary, unheard-of thoughts, could have received a more complete and pure form than that which they have received from the Spirit who conceived them. This form is sacred, fundamental; the thought which it invests can never be perfectly separated from it; we may express it, develop

* SAURIN, tome i., p. 56, nouvelle édition.

it, in our own language; but we can never be justified in omitting the very terms in which it has been expressed by those who first revealed it to us. We must rely upon extraordinary authority when we utter extraordinary things. It seems to me that we cannot suitably treat of what is most ineffable in our religion, unfold the unsearchable mercy of God, repeat his terrible threatenings, without at least starting with the very words of scripture. Are we not happy to have forms already prepared for truths which man would hardly have dared to pronounce, so greatly do they transcend and overwhelm him? *

"The imaginations of the thoughts of their hearts are only evil continually."—(Genesis, vi. 5.)

"The heart is deceitful above all things and desperately wicked."—(Jeremiah, xvii. 9.)

"Man is without all glory in the sight of God."—(Romans, iii. 22.)

"As he (the wicked man) clothed himself with cursing like as with his garment, so let it come into his bowels like water, and like oil into his bones."—(Psalm cix. 18.)

"For after that in the wisdom of God, the world by wisdom knew not God, it pleased God by the foolishness of preaching to save them that believe.—(1 Corinthians, i. 21.)

"Can a woman forget her sucking child, that she should not have compassion on the son of her womb? Yea they may forget, yet will I not forget thee."—(Isaiah, xlix. 15.)

"And the Lord spake to Moses face to face, as a man speaketh unto his friend."—(Exodus, xxxiii. 11.)

"In all their afflictions he was afflicted."—(Isaiah, lxii. 9.)

3. After Rollin, and especially after Fénelon, after Maury, I will not attempt to speak of the eloquence and the poetry of the Bible. I will only remark, that what distinguishes it

* "These passages (of the Bible) are as a rich vein of gold which winds its way through other metals of a gross kind."—RICHARDSON.

and sets it above all literary performances, is, that its beauties are not literary, that the thought always gives the form, so that the union of the thought and form was never so intimate. The beauty then of biblical language has everywhere something substantial, which connects the mind immediately with the essence of things, without permitting it to take pleasure in the exterior covering. We are impressed before we have had time to be delighted or scarcely to admire. It is remarkable too, that oriental language, at first view so strange to western imaginations, should be at the same time so human, and on this account so universal, that it assimilates itself to all people, all forms of civilization, all languages, much more readily, than the languages and literature of any age or people, though much less remote from us, would do. Whatever, in the holy book, relates to man, whatever portrays man, has a depth and simplicity to which there is no parallel; the Bible here speaks a universal language, displays a universal poetry; the Bible in this respect as in all others, was intended as a book for the human race. Setting aside authoritative claims we can draw from no other source, images, descriptions, more suitable to the subjects we have to treat in the pulpit, or adorn religious discourse with beauty more becoming or more grave.

All the forms of beauty which are proper in religious discourse abound in holy scripture, and our position in relation to it gives us the privilege, imposes on us the duty of appropriating them all. We alone can do this; what everywhere else would be plagiarism or affectation, is one of the highest congruities, is truth, in the kind of discourse we have to do with. In discourse of other kinds who would venture, however he might desire to do so, to intersperse his composition with so many vivid allusions, to color it with so many reflected rays? But the Bible is more than a source or a document; the Bible we may almost say is our subject; we have to speak from it, our voice is as its echo; it is as a forest which we subdue, as a field which we reap; the labor is less an addition to our task, than our task itself; boldly and freely then may we draw from this treasury. And what a treasury! This book has in everything reached the sublime. The most perfect models of the grand and the pathetic, of the human and the religious, of the strong and the tender, are here as in their depository. Among all the books which have expressed ideas of the same class, if we were free to choose, if the authority was equal, we should always recur to this. It has given names to all divine and human things which are definitive and irrevocable. Its manner of expressing things could not without loss of strength be exchanged for any other manner. Whole nations have appropriated this lauguage and interfused it with their own; the Bible has given to human speech a multitude of expressions as it has also given to human thoughts some of the most sacred of its forms. We remind men of their family traditions when we repeat to them the words of the Bible.

Have you a different image from this to give to creative power; God said, "Let there be light and there was light"? (Genesis, i. 3.)

To describe the Creator's authority over the two worlds of physical and moral being, is there anything to be preferred to this word: "Who stilleth the noise of the seas, the noise of the waves, and the tumult of the people"? (Psalm lxv. 7.

Can we better attain to the sublime of grief, than has been done in these words: "In Rama was there a voice heard, lamentation and weeping and great mourning, Rachel weeping for her children and would not be comforted because they are not"? (Jeremiah, xxxi. 15. Matthew, ii. 18.)

Can the desolation produced by sin, ever be expressed with so alarming a power as has been exhibited by Isaiah, when he says, "There shall be darkness in the ruins tnereof"? (Isaiah, v. 30, *French* translation.)

To present the divine harmony of all the perfections of Jehovah, and the ineffable unity of his purposes towards us, can you find anything which approaches the mildness and grandeur of this expression: "Righteousness and peace have kissed each other"? (Psalm lxxxv. 10.)

But we might transcribe the whole Bible. We make a concluding remark. It is this, that we should be deprived of a large number of the most original and striking beauties that the Bible supplies, if we are not to draw from the Old Testament as well as the New. The Old Testament, we must maintain, is a continued parable, or a rudiment of the New; and the application of the Old Testament to the ideas of the New, from the very consideration that it is less direct than an application of evangelical language, has a peculiar, inexhaustible charm, which must not be neglected. Without allowing place for groundless allegory, without permitting anything to be forced, by natural accommodation, the entire Old Testament may be used in the service of christian ideas—may present them under a surprising and touching aspect. After all the happy and natural resemblances which have been discovered and applied, an attentive study of the Old Testament will draw forth a multitude more.*

Let us remark, however, that all these beauties are discolored or lost in a discourse without individuality, in a discourse which has no depth, no intrinsic power, as flowers whose stem is not rooted in the soil, hang their head, grow pale and die.

4. After passing in review all the congruities which I think should be found in the style of preaching, simplicity, popu-

* We may cite here the exordium of SAURIN's sermon, *sur le Cantique de Simeon*, and the peroration of that of BOSSUET, *sur l'Impenitence finale.* See this latter passage, p. 211.

larity, familiarity, nobleness, I think I see them all united in the scriptural style, and that this, as I said a moment since, is its compendium and its measure. The Bible I regard as the true *diapason* of the preacher, who assuredly should take from it the general tone of his discourse; his imagination should be steeped in the Bible; he should come forth in the spirit of this book, if he would have true power, dignified simplicity, noble and grave familiarity. It is the Bible, let me say with emphasis, that imparts and preserves to pulpit discourse the just measure of popularity, which from the existing state of civilization we are constantly liable either to fall short of or to exceed.

What I have named *popularity*, I am willing to call *humanity*. It is what reminds men of the community of their origin and condition. It is the living impress of what equalizes or resembles men to one another. In great refinement of manners, in too intellectual habits, this equality, this resemblance, is too much forgotten. Even in an intermediate condition, life is so artificial, nature so transformed, that we can no longer discern its original purity; and as to the poor, the miserable, it is as a corrupt text which repels and offends us. It rejoices me, I confess, to see all classes promiscuously brought back under a divine authority, to a world in which nature and common life pass for something, in which kings and shepherds speak the same language, in which the most distinguished teachers are as watermen or tent-makers, in which the language of the poor becomes the language of all, the poor feel themselves to be divinely exalted, and the rich truly humbled. The Bible adapts itself to the middle point, the centre of human life, to its sincerest forms; it here unites the two extremes of society, those who are below and those who think themselves above this region; it makes man sensible of his simple humanity, and by this means of his true greatness which dire necessity conceals, and effeminate conventionality curtails.

We have said that this is the aspect in which humanity appears greatest, inasmuch as it is the most comprehensive aspect. Now, a simple and naïve form best becomes that which is truly great. While the Bible imparts its greatness to our discourses, it gives them its own simplicity. It places us with itself on an elevation, from which we may say everything. By intermixing it with our own speech, we embolden our style, which is at once ambitious and timid; it becomes throughout and in just proportion, serious and free. The Bible gives now a passport, now inspiration to ideas and traits, which, apart from it, perhaps we should not have hazarded; on its behalf and in its terms, we say what in our own name we should not have ventured to say. What other image could better express the principle of destruction which infidelity involves, than this of the prophet: "This iniquity shall be to you as a breach ready to fall, swelling out in a high wall, whose breaking cometh suddenly at an instant. And he shall break it as the breaking of the potter's vessel that is broken in pieces; he shall not spare, so that there shall not be found in the bursting of it a shred to take fire from the hearth, or to take water withal out of the pit"? (Isaiah, xxx. 13, 14.) This is an image of which we should not have thought, or which, if we had found, we should scarcely have dared to present; but as it is taken from the Bible, we freely use it, and it is well received. One, in order to represent the insufficiency of human wisdom to solve all the doubts and satisfy all the wants of men, would hardly have employed on his own responsibility if the Bible had not used it before him, the following image: "The bed is shorter than that a man can stretch himself on it, and the covering narrower than that he can wrap himself in it." (Isaiah, xxviii. 20.)

The God whom the gospel reveals, appears to approach us

with this word: "*Homo sum, humani nihil a me alienum puto.*"* But it belongs to him to speak thus; to him who is pleased to borrow from the language of men, all sorts of terms by which he may express the inexpressible condescension of his love. Let it be then himself who says in our sermons: "As a beast goeth down into the valley, the Spirit of the Lord caused him to rest." (Isaiah, lxiii. 14.) "Ye shall be borne upon her sides and be dandled upon her knees." (Isaiah, lxvi. 12.) But the more we cite scripture, the more shall we dare to speak as it does. We shall end also, by saying: *Homo sum* . . . . We shall, in truth, become so. Nothing is so human as christianity. No one is so much a man as a christian. The eloquence of the pulpit, when inspired by scripture, readily attains that mingled greatness and familiarity, that familiarity so full of greatness, which should be and always has been the inimitable signet of preaching.

We cannot give particular rules as to the manner of introducing Biblical language into pulpit discourse. The only one I would give, one which is altogether general, is this: Feed upon the Bible, live in the Bible, unite yourself to it; let it abound in your memory and heart; let a frequent personal study of it reveal to you the force, give you the secret of a multitude of passages, which without such study, would remain to you as mere commonplaces, and take no root in your memory; mix the recollection of them with your most tender affections, with your prayers, your gravest occupations; let the words of scripture gradually become the natural and involuntary form of your most inward thoughts;—then meditate on a subject for the pulpit; write; preach; your word will come filled with the richness, inter-blended with the colors of the word of inspiration. The prophetic

* *Terence, Heauton,* act. i., scene 1. "I am a man, and nothing human is foreign from me."

word will be interfused in yours; it will not be distinguishable from it; it will not appear to be applied to it from without; it will not impair the individuality of your expression; you will never fall into imitation, and thus will it come to pass, as the nature of the evangelical ministry demands, that a *man* will be heard by *men*.

CHAPTER III.

SUPERIOR QUALITIES OR VIRTUES OF STYLE.

§ 1. *Of Strength and Beauty of Style in general.*

Although several of the qualities we have considered, may, by a certain measure of elevation, advance from simple qualities to virtues, still we have prescribed negative rules rather than positive precepts or means; we have removed the barriers, marked out the field of eloquence. All these qualities, I admit, are comprised in the idea of truth; it is the truth, under different points of view, that we have been all the while recommending. Admitting that truth is not all, what more is there besides it? There is, if you please, the *extraordinary*, "the superfluous, a thing very necessary;" the union, the reconciliation of the true with the extraordinary, is the problem to be solved. In the kind of composition we are concerned with, the proper name of *extraordinary* is eloquence, an eloquent style; but this word teaches us nothing which we do not already know. In what does this *extraordinary* consist; of what elements is this *eloquence of style* composed?

We may say with propriety, of *strength* and *beauty*, and this is indeed to say something. There is here some instruction. The truth, doubtless, is not a purely negative thing; strength and beauty are not perhaps only truth at its highest stage; the word truth, however, may be and often is taken in a restricted sense, and in this sense truth is distinguished from beauty and strength, and remains this side of them. Style, in a word, cannot be eloquent without being true; but it may be true without being eloquent.

Thus we may say, that in collecting in the preceding chapter, the elements of which the truth of style is composed, we raised the barriers, within the interior of which we leave eloquence to move. *Leave* is the word, because there are not rules and a method for being eloquent; we cannot give to him who has not. We may, however, give to him who has; an exposition of the resources, the means, and the procedures of eloquence may be of advantage to him who has the talent of eloquence. It may not be impossible to him to reflect on the causes of the effects produced by the genius of oratory; this study leads to the exercise of unconscious faculties, and while we preach morality to the regenerate man, we may preach art to the man of talent, that he may know how to use all his strength, and also that he may learn to regulate it.

Strength and beauty, which are essential attributes of religious and moral truth, should exist in the form in which it is clothed. Now, *strength* in works of art, is whatever exalts in us the sense of life; *beauty* is what, in the manifestation of life, gives us the sense of harmony and proportion. It is with strength and beauty as with other couples of things that aid while they resist one another, and complete while seeming to restrain each other. It is with them as with righteousness and peace, which though distinct and often apparently opposed, "meet together and kiss each other." (Psalm lxxxv. 11.)

Strength and beauty have not, distinctively and exclusively of each other, affinities for certain kinds of composition.

But there are kinds in which we aim especially at strength, and others in which the study of beauty is most important. There are times, also, which appreciate highly one of these excellencies, and are indifferent to the other; a more decided inclination towards strength or towards beauty distinguishes some nations and some epochs from others. These differences of taste arise from profounder differences. The lowest depth of moral existence is discovered in the diversity of these tendencies.

In respect to what remains to be said, we gave no indication of our plan by calling that which is beyond the simple truth of style, *strength* and *beauty;* we only comprised under two leading ideas, what, in eloquence, is the complement of the truth of style.

We may be inclined to distinguish poetry from eloquence, according to the exclusive predominance or presence of these two elements, strength and beauty. They should not however be so distinguished; for neither does poetry dispense with strength nor eloquence exclude beauty. We must look elsewhere for the principle of discrimination between these two kinds of composition. It is that one, eloquence, has facts for its objects, the other has ideas; eloquence, I mean as far as it is eloquence, and poetry as far as it is poetry; for these two arts sometimes touch and intermingle more or less. Eloquence seeks to produce changes in the world of reality, poetry would produce them only in the ideal sphere. Eloquence does not ignore ideas, poetry does not take away facts, but the former goes from ideas to facts, the latter from facts to ideas, that is to say, eloquence transforms ideas into facts, and poetry transforms facts into ideas. Eloquence, indeed, must rest upon ideas, (ideas of justice, honesty, fitness,) but it uses them as a lever, to act upon facts; poetry also must rest upon facts, upon reality, upon experiences, but only that by means of them it may rise to ideas or to an ideal.

Let us remark, however, that the word *ideas* does not, in both cases, mean the same thing; in the former it means laws, the laws of nature, reason, conscience; in the latter, ideas are only types of existences—types, however, more pure and complete, than any real or concrete existence, separately taken, or all such existences collectively, can present. Eloquence, then, leads us to action, poetry to contemplation. Eloquence is a combat, poetry a representation or a vision. Eloquence speaks of what is, poetry creates that which ought to be. Eloquence flows in the same channel with life, poetry digs a channel for itself by the side of life. Eloquence, so to speak, raises itself with the wave of life which it enlarges and bears along; poetry suspends it. Let it be understood, that I do not here speak of inward or contemplative life, but of external or practical life. They are two rivers which are not always separated; they may unite and flow together from and to a great distance; poetry may become eloquent, eloquence may become poetical; but eloquence and poetry are not less distinct in their principle than in their end and consequently in their means; and so true is this, that if eloquence, which is an action, passes from action to contemplation, it ceases to be eloquence; and that if poetry omits contemplation in order to act, it ceases to be poetry.*

The rule for each is not to deny but to remain faithful to its principle, and constantly maintain it, and to avail itself of the aid of the other, without allowing itself to be absorbed by it. We are not here giving advice to poets; our business is with orators. What shall we say to them?

Everything with you should be subordinate to action, everything, even to the minutest details of style; all with you should be activity, what is not is lost; all your words should be winged

* See reflections on the difference between poetry and eloquence in the earlier *Mléanges de philosophie et de littèrature d'*ANCILLON, tome i. p. 269.

and armed. And if you do not yet comprehend us, if you say that in poetry also everything tends to an end, everything advances toward a goal, and that on this account, poetry is also an action, we complete our explanation by adding, that poetry is an internal action, a contemplative ideal action, while eloquence is a real action of man on man, of will on will, and through will on the world. This is the action which the orator proposes to himself, it is this as his end which makes him an orator, and of which he is not to lose sight for a moment.

Must we hence infer that poetry is to remain foreign to the style of the orator? We must infer only that poetry with him is a means not an end; for, how otherwise will he dispense with it? How distinguish from poetry, the talent or art which gives the objects of discourse presence, presence both to himself and his auditory, which gives ideas a body, which transforms definitions into pictures, which invents, which creates, which paints? Imagination and poetry are the same thing; and if in the economy and combination of our faculties, reason and sentiment do not dispense with imagination, how shall eloquence dispense with it, which is at one and the same time reason and imagination? But a river need not retard its course, in order to reflect the rays of the sun or to receive tints from the color of its shores, and eloquence need not be suspended or annulled in order to discover the poetry with which it is penetrated, and which flows with it. In short, we must admit the claim of beauty as well as strength, the claim of poetry as an oratorical element. Style must be left to appropriate whatever is suitable to it; only one character should everywhere prevail, should accentuate everything, should form the general tone. That character is activity, the active style.

This principle of activity which we have already laid down in the chapter on oratorical disposition, we are constrained to lay down anew in speaking of the superior qualities or virtues of the oratorical style. We need not remind you that we were treating of qualities which do not endanger this principle; neither purity nor correctness, neither perspicuity nor precision, neither naturalness nor congruity, even distantly opposes the principle of activity; none of these qualities interfere with action; not one of them requires its suppression or suspension. It is not the same with ulterior or superior qualities, as we may call them; for though they have nothing to lose but much to gain from the observance of this principle of activity, they are liable to isolate themselves and to arrogate to themselves an independent existence; style may seek strength and beauty, apart from this principle; and we ourselves, when we undertake to indicate the elements of which strength and beauty of style are composed, would be implicated in this same error, if we did not first take care to lay down certain general principles which should direct and control the writer in this part of his labor.

The first of these principles, is that nothing, in eloquence, can be given to the mere desire of pleasing; that eloquence admits of only useful beauties, and that nothing in it is mere ornament. And we use the term *useful* here with no vagueness of meaning. Utility with the orator lies in proving, convincing, determining. Eloquence, in this view, has its type in nature, where everything beautiful is useful or springs from what is useful. Nature so admirably combines the useful and the beautiful, that according to the aspect in which we regard it, it appears alternately to have intended only the beautiful, and to have had no thought except of the useful. Nature hastens to its result, but when we consider the beauties it develops in its course towards its end, can we say that it ever declines being at leisure? Under another view nature is like a harp with a thousand vibrating cords, or an immense mirror of ideas; but all is activity, all is life, all is production in the sounds of this harp, and in the images of this mirror; nature is not only a poet, (under this title even, we are permitted to recognize in its works an end, a severe unity,) nature is an orator; it acts, it produces, it argues; whatever it does is beautiful, but whatever it does is useful, that is to say, suited to prudence, apart from itself, the sense of happiness.

We borrow from Cicero this comparison between the works of eloquence and those of nature: "In speaking, the same thing happens which may be discovered in most of the other surprising operations of nature, that the subjects which are of the greatest utility contain the greatest dignity and often the greatest beauty. We see that the economy of the universe and of nature is accommodated to the general safety and happiness. The concavity of the heavens, the centrical position of the self-balanced earth, the rotation of the sun through all the gradations and revolutions of the seasons, the access and recess of the moon, by which the radiance she derives from the sun is regulated; and the unequal revolutions of the five other planets, are all so many convincing proofs of this truth. So unvarying are the proportions which effect all these causes, that the least alteration would dissolve the whole system, and so beautiful is their economy, that fancy can form nothing so fair.—Let us now reflect upon the form and figure of man, and even of the other animals; there you find that every member has its proper use, and that the finishing of the whole speaks not a blind chance but a providential wisdom.—How wonderful is the vegetable creation, where there is not a stalk, a bough nor even a leaf which does not operate in preserving and propagating its own nature, yet all is beauty.—Let us pass from nature to the arts. The same observation holds good with regard to eloquence; for there wit and humor almost attends utility, and I may say necessity.*

* CICERO, *De Oratore*, lib. iii., cap. xlv xlvi. (Translation: London, 1808.)

Cicero gives *number* as an illustration, which is intended to spare the speaker fatigue.

Now, eloquence, like all the arts, is a product, a development of nature. It ought to present the same phenomena as nature. Cultivated according to nature, it is impossible that it should not produce the beautiful when it produces the useful; but as in morality, the useful is produced from the honest, and not the honest from the useful, so that we cannot reach the useful except through the honest; so in art, the beautiful, the truly beautiful, can spring only from the useful. The useful here holds the first place; but the useful in this sphere is conviction, is precisely the determination of the will, and the useful, according to the laws of morality, is confounded with the true, the just and the good. It is then from the essence of our subject that we are to draw our ornaments, here are the only true ornaments, and consequently, the only truly beautiful ones; nothing is absolutely beautiful in itself, but only in the place which it occupies; it would be then an unhappy calculation which should lead us to look for ornaments apart from our subject, that is to say, apart from our end. Our subject is to supply them to us; no necessity is to lead us away after others.

"The choicest expressions," says Quintilian, "are for the most part, (I would say always,) adherent to things, and are seen in their own light; but we search after them as if always hiding and stealing themselves away from us. Thus we never think that what ought to be said is, as it were, at hand; we fetch it from afar, and force our invention. Eloquence requires a more manly temper, and if its whole body be sound and vigorous, it is quite regardless of the nicety of paring the nails and adjusting the hair."*

To this first rule we add a second, or rather deduce a second from it, which is that the whole is never to be sacrificed to

* QUINTILIAN, lib. viii., proem. [Patsall's Translation.]

detail. This is less a new rule than another form of the preceding one. Subordinating the beautiful to the useful, is subordinating detail to the whole, since the useful in oratorical discourse, is not renewed from space to space, being one and the same throughout the discourse. There may be agreeableness of diction without this subordination, but not true beauty of style; I would rather say no style in reality. As a useless beauty is no beauty, since the beautiful in all discourse is inseparable from the useful, a beauty of detail which is not related or subordinated to the whole, is not a beauty; the idea of the useful and of the whole being equally inseparable from oratorical discourse. Periods, sentences, can be constructed apart and for themselves, but the ingenuity bestowed on them is the effect of a mistaken diligence, since it injures continuity, proportion and the total effect. If the orator is not constantly occupied with his end, if at every moment, so to speak, his whole subject is not present to him, if each passage is not really a *passage*,* a *step* towards the end, his discourses will be composed of inlaid work, that is to say, of pieces which are not related; and the detail will suffer no less than the whole, since the idea of the beautiful cannot be separated from that of congruity and relation. In this respect, writers may be divided into three classes: some write well a discourse, others a paragraph, others a sentence. The first are not the most numerous.

"Many are seen," says Quintilian, "to stick at single words, even whilst they invent, and reflect on and measure what they invent. If this were done designedly, to use always the best, yet would this unhappy temper be detestable, as it must check the course of speaking, and extinguish the heat of thought by delay and diffidence. For the orator is wretched, and I may say poor, who cannot patiently lose a

* *Act of passing*, the first sense given to the word by the Academy.—[Editors.]

word. But he will lose none, who first has studied a good manner of speaking, and by reading well the best authors, has furnished himself with a copious supply of words, and made himself expert in the art of placing them. Much practice will afterwards so improve him, that he will always have them at hand and present to him, things naturally occurring, with the proper way of expressing them.*

Quintilian has shown us the danger: it is the desire to lose nothing; it is a mistaken avidity which loses all from a wish to gain all; it is the love of effect, a love which has always distinguished writers of no genius, or epochs of decline, but often, likewise, at all epochs, true talents in the age of inexperience. Did it never happen to a young man, to undertake a discourse that he might have occasion for setting forth a picture or a happy movement; did it never happen to him to make out of a vast subject, the case or frame of a word? Mortifying error; but one which should be pondered if we would be aware of all the danger and insignificance of such a way of writing; *miser et pauper*, says Quintilian. "It is," says Buffon, "from the fear of losing isolated, fugitive thoughts; it is from the desire of introducing everywhere striking traits, that there are so many compositions formed of inlaid work, and so few that are founded at a single cast. Nothing is more opposed to warmth of style."†

I would not exclude striking traits; they are useful;‡ but to a man of talent they come of themselves in the natural series of the ideas of a well-ordered discourse. Never, per-

* QUINTILIAN, lib. viii., proem. [Patsall's Translation.]

† BUFFON, *Discours sur le style.*

‡ "Leave not everything to your heirs; know how to be yourselves heirs."—(BOSSUET.) "The fool in his presence shut his impious lips, and retaining, under a forced silence, his vain and sacrilegious thoughts, was content to say in his heart—'There is no God.'" —(FLECHIER.

haps, are they so striking, so happy, as when they have not been sought, and when a kind of logical necessity has led to them. By whom are they so abundantly obtained as by writers who never sacrificed the whole to one of the impulses of composition? "For my part, I look upon the luminaries of an oration, as so many eyes planted in eloquence. But I would not have eyes disseminated all over the body, lest they might obstruct other members in performing their respective functions."*

We think that the qualities of an eloquent style may be reduced to two general ones—*color* and *movement.* The first element in the eloquence of style is that by which objects, of whatever kind they may be, are represented so as to take the place of the immediate view of them, or, perhaps, give us a more vivid intuition of them than we should obtain from the objects themselves. For want of another word† I call it *color;* but the talent subdivides itself, and its effect is not fully expressed by the word *color.* One writer partakes more of the painter, another, of the sculptor; the style of one is as a warmly-colored picture, that of the other, as a deeply-cut bas-relief. Both by speech have happily presented the objects they would make known, but one attempts to give the very idea of the object prominence, the other to indicate it by its effects or circumstances. Examples:

"He who is most like the dead, dies with most regret."

"Death plunders all without shame."

"The people ought to be the favorite of a king."

"He who hath pity on the poor lendeth to the Lord."‡

"True eloquence is the contempt of eloquence."§

* QUINTILIAN, lib. viii., chap. v. [Patsall's Translation.]

† The German has the word *Anschaulichkeit.*

‡ Proverbs, xix., 17.

§ PASCAL, *Pensées,* part i., art. x. § xxxiv.

"Without envy, without disguise, without ostentation, always great in action, and in repose, he appeared at Chantilly as at the head of his troops. Whether he adorned that magnificent and delightful palace, or supplied a camp in the midst of an enemy's country, and fortified a place; whether he marched with an army amidst perils, or conducted his friends through these superb walks, amid the murmurs of fountains which were silent neither day nor night, he was always the same man; everywhere his glory followed him."*

La Bruyère, an admirable sculptor of thoughts, gives us examples of a different kind:

"False greatness is severe and unsociable; conscious of weakness, it conceals itself, or at least does not show itself openly, and displays itself so far as is necessary in order to be imposing."†

"A great soul is superior to injury, injustice, sorrow, and reproach, and if it did not suffer through compassion, would be invulnerable."‡

"Every one says of a fop that he is a fop, no one dares to tell him that he is one; he dies without knowing it, and without any one being *avenged*."§

A second law requires the proper arrangement of the ideas among themselves, such a regulation of the movement of the discourse as will give the hearer a sense of activity, of progress. of a series of distinct phases in the drama in which he has part, as will not leave him long in the same situation, and will transport him into another in a spirited manner, as will give him, in a word, a deep and continued consciousness of his life, here is a second law, in truth, the general and highest law of oratorical discourse, but as it is in the style that it is realized,

* Bossuet, *Oraison funèbre du prince de Condè.*

† La Bruyère, *Les Caractéres*, chap. ii.

‡ La Bruyère, *Les Caractéres*, chap. xi.

§ Ibid.

it is here that it should be studied. These two laws, though distinct, never admit of being fulfilled, the one by the other; images may aid movement; movement in its turn may become a painting; the orator may, should indeed, endeavor to obtain one of these effects by means of the other; but the two effects are not on that account the less distinct from one another, and require to be contemplated separately.

Let us first inquire for the chief means of painting thought, of giving character and relief to objects, and color to style.

§ 2. *Of Color.*

All discourse, that of books, of conversation, aims to substitute for immediate experience, something which takes the place and reproduces the impression of it. Speech ought to be something more than the formula of things. We must have an image in order to have knowledge; an image is sometimes as impressive as reality. Nothing short of this will suffice in the pulpit; thought must be painted. I mean, that the expression should produce an image, that is to say, should not only impart to us an idea, but, in some sort, a view—a vivid intuition, of the physical or moral things which are spoken of; should clothe ideas in a form in which they will be vividly and distinctly presented to our imagination. In this process, we may contemplate the act itself, the nature of the idea on which it is exerted, its immediate object or its mode, and the means which it uses. Let us take:

I. The act itself. Each of the objects comprised in the subject of the discourse must have its character and its value. What is painting the thought, but adding to perspicuity a vivacity which ordinarily it has not, a force which it knows not? It is not, of course, painting for its own sake; it is a means and not an end. This draws the limit, excludes extension and minuteness. The object in general is to paint and not to write ; to insinuate everything, not to show everything. All is to be subordinated to instruction and emotion. Splendid imagery in pulpit discourse, is scarcely more unacceptable, to me, than gold on the priests garments, or luxurious display in the sanctuary. Still we must give vivacity to objects. Figures slightly bold are not adequate ; style slightly colored, is seldom proper for the temple. I would have no one force his nature ; for here also, " Whatsoever is not of faith is sin." (Romans, xiv. 23.)

II. The nature of the objects to be represented. These are now material, now immaterial objects : now persons, now situations or scenes ; sometimes individual, sometimes collective facts.

III. The immediate object or mode of representation. This is sometimes the character, the idea of the object, sometimes its external symptoms which the image makes prominent. One of these procedures more resembles sculpture, the other painting. In their perfection, they are equally valuable. Bossuet excels in both.* Often a word gives a character. " The lightning cleaves the clouds, the night returns," but we have seen, that is enough. The idea may then be seized, whether from some particular characteristic circumstance, or from a variety of details. Painting doubtless, ought to be oftener employed, because it is more generally appreciated. But the other method, which consists in bringing the object itself to view, has great force when properly employed. It is common with La Bruyère.

IV. The means which are used. They are direct when they are taken from the object itself which is to be presented ; indirect, when we have recourse to comparisons.

A. Direct means consist in announcing the characteristics

* "Fountains which cease not their murmurs day or night." BOSSUET, *Oraison funèbre du prince de Condé.*

of the object. This procedure in its most ample form is *description*, that is to say, such an indication of circumstances as renders an idea present to the imagination, or as visible, as present as possible in the absence of the object.* I have said *indication*, not *enumeration*, because though a complete enumeration may sometimes be useful, perhaps in certain cases even redundance, or at least accumulation, a well-chosen circumstance may often answer our purpose. Not the number but the choice of details, is chiefly to be regarded. There are frequent circumstances which are of as much avail as a complete and methodical analysis of a character or situation. The point is to be sought in which the rays converge and light becomes flame.†

Great writers require but little space for a complete picture. They are able to condense the elements of a thought or an image, to suppress intervening ideas, to substitute combination for juxtaposition of parts; thus Bossuet: "This word of confidence bore her holy soul to the abodes of the just."‡ And elsewhere: "He expired while writing these words, and prolonged the sacred song with the angels."§

In the most concise recitals of the Bible, the characteristic, comprehensive word is never wanting.‖

* Antique genius, from which ours differs too much. Contingent circumstances added to the principal fact; always descending from the genus to the species.

† "Pontum adspectabant flentes." VIRGIL, *Æneid*, v. 616.

> Son coursiêr bondissant, qui sent flotter la rêne,
> Lance un regard oblique a son maître expirant
> Revient, penche la tete, et le flaire en pleurant.

> His bounding courser feels the reins relaxed,
> Darts a glance side-ways at his dying master,
> Returns, inclines his head, and weeping scents him.

‡ BOSSUET, *Oraison funèbre de la princesse palatine.*

§ BOSSUET, *Oraison funèbre de Le Tellier.*

‖ See the exposition of the Cantique sur Pharaon, by M. Hersan,

Massillon excels in the art of fusing images in the texture of the style, though his images are sometimes bold, as in this example: "Your actions put your titles to the blush." Yet his images appear only as far as is necessary, their way having been prepared, and being legitimated by what preceded them.

Often, moreover, the best painting is done not by happy combinations and words, but by a simple and naïve expression, which aims not at painting but only at a mere designation of the idea. Thus we read in the Bible: "Let there be light and there was light,"—(Genesis, i. 3;) and elsewhere: "Rachel weeping for her children refused to be comforted because they were not."—(Mathew, ii. 18.) But often also more pains are necessary.

Epithet is often a powerful and formidable means, and to this an image is frequently reduced. An epithet is a word added to the name of the object or action, to distinguish a characteristic of that action or object. Every epithet is an adjective or an adverb; every adjective is not an epithet. An adjective or adverb without which the noun would remain incomplete or be suspended, is not an epithet; but it is an unmeaning epithet which does not give a more complete or more vivid sense of the object.

In all languages the middling class of writers make a great abuse of epithets; it is the resort of indolent minds, the inadequate supplement of imperfect meditation, and the cause of that effeminacy of style which we remark in many writers. An epithet is unmeaning if it does not condense a judgment, if it does not abridge a picture. It ought not to be the rule, but the exception. An epithet is always an injury if it be not an excellence, and useful epithets are of less advantage

in *le Traitè des etudes de* ROLLIN, lib. v., ch. iii., § ix: "*Interficiet eos manus mea,*" for "*Interficiam eos.*" See, also, Genesis, xliii., 26–31.

than hurtful ones are hurtful. See the imitation of Psalm xix., by J. B. Rousseau:

Quel plus sublime cantique, etc.

Who does not feel wearied in the first strophe with epithets which are not needed because they are comprised in the substantive? We may here recur again to the principle of activity; the mind must be left to do something of itself; nor will it thank you for what it might have found or what it really has found without your aid.

We must distinguish the cases in which the substantive carries with it the entire train of accessory ideas, or in which every accessory idea will be importunate, and in which the substantive will itself answer for an adjective; for in truth, is not every substantive by implication an adjective?

A very vivid sentiment now suppresses, now multiplies epithets. In a compact cogent argument, speech, intent on its purpose, rejects qualifying words, which are not absolutely necessary. It may have a style, in that case, made up of substantives.

But if adjectives conceal themselves, and retreat, so to speak, into the bosom of substantives, when thought is concentrated, when it girds up its loins to move more quickly, there are moments of flowing emotion, when epithets will re-appear and abound; there are not enough of means for characterizing objects. The adjective now is as necessary as the substantive; it makes part of it. In this case, redundance itself is pleasing.

Votre crime est énorme, exécrable, odieux.*

Description delights in multiplying epithets when they

* Ducis, Hamlet, act v., scene iv. See, also, the exordium of Cicero's third oration against Cataline.

form an image, or when they characterize the object, or put it in relation or contrast with its situation.* But the more freely we use these, the less are we permitted to use trivial ones; they must express something. Not that we should aim to be extraordinary; the simplest epithet, that which every one would think of, is often the best,† best suits true style. But in general they ought to be striking, to present a picture, or to contain a judgment. Some epithets paint, others characterize; the first are images, the others are thoughts. We present an example of the use of both:

Et dans les flancs affreux de leurs roches sanglantes,
Emportent, a grand cris, leurs depoilles vivantes. ‡

Poursuivant des proscrits, les troupes égarées,
Du sang de ses sujets souillait ses mains sacrèes,§

Combined epithets often have great force:

La mort pale et sanglante etait à ses côtés.
. . . . De l'enfer il ne sort
Que l'éternelle soif d'une inpossible mort.‖

* Virgil here is admirable; see *Georgics*, lib. iii., verses 494–500, and 515–524. *Æneid*, lib. ii., verses 204–211.

† Naïvete of antique epithets. The most common are again becoming piquant. We are beginning to say *perfumed rose, fresh dawn, rapid river, green meadow.* We say with propriety, *blue lake.* I cannot condemn epithets such as those in *Esther*, act i., scene ii.

Sacrès monts, *fertiles* valleés,
Du *doux* pays de nos aieux
Serons-nous toujours exilées?

‡ VOLTAIRE, *La Henriade*, chant ii.
"Their living spoil, with shouts, they bear away,
Into the dread sides of their blood-stained rocks."

§ "Pursuing outlaws, wandering hordes, the blood
Of his own subjects stained his sacred hands."—Tr.

‖ "Death, pale and bloody, was at his side.
. . . . . From hell,
Nought proceeds save the eternal thirst
For a death impossible."—Tr.

"When all parties were prostrated, he seemed still to sustain himself alone, and alone to threaten the victorious favorite by his sorrowful and intrepid looks."*

The same may be said of contrasted epithets.

"More powerful death removed her from us while in these royal hands."†

> Le temps, cette image mobile
> De l'immobile eternite.‡
>
> Pour reparer des ans l'irréparable outrage.§

New epithets, adjectives turned aside somewhat from their ordinary signification, may, if practicable, be employed, provided no violence be done to the language, as in these association of words: "Disciple lumineux, un homme irreparable; une âme douleureuse."‖

But I cannot commend the use of extraordinary epithets in the pulpit; it should avoid exciting surprise.

And, in general, use epithets soberly. A style made somewhat substantial by the addition of an adjective to a substantive, becomes feeble, you may be assured, by the abundant use of epithets. Observe how economical of them are the masters. Massillon has more than Bossuet, but although he has the art of multiplying them appropriately, he is very far from using them profusely.

B. Indirect means of painting relieve the object by giving boldness to some features of it, by heightning the color through the approximation of some other object. We approach here the figurative style.

* Bossuet, *Oraison funèbre de Michel Letellier.*

† Bossuet, *Oraison funèbre de Henriette d'Angleterre.*

‡ J. B. Rousseau, *Odes,* livre iii. ode ii. "Time, that changeable image of unchangeable eternity."—Tr.

§ Racine, *Athalie,* acte ii., scene v. "To repair the irreparable wrongs of years."—Tr.

‖ "Luminous disciple, an irreparable man; a painful soul."—Tr.

Antithesis is at the same time one of the most powerful and most perilous means of giving prominence to objects. It is an opposition of ideas marked by words; so that there is no antithesis when the things alone, or when the words alone are contrasted. But, in the first case, we have no figure; and in the second case, we have a puerile figure, a play of words a falsehood in expression. "Those who make antitheses," says Pascal, "by forcing words, are like men who make false windows for the sake of symmetry."* The taste for antithesis belongs especially to epochs and minds defective in simplicity; it is a spice for giving edge to a blunted palate. Good authors seldom use it; Demosthenes never; Bossuet rarely; Fléchier more frequently, who in his funeral oration for Turenne ventures to say: "After so many actions worthy of immortality, had he nothing more to do with mortality?" Wit is but a poor supplement of eloquence, it is much more common; and the orator should not suffer himself to be ensnared by it. Far-fetched antithesis is always bad; it is admissible, if ever, only when it escapes involuntarily, and proceeds from the soul. When there is an opposition in things, we must not fear to mark it in words; but opposition in ideas sometimes gains by not marking it in words.

Christianity favored the use of antithesis, and was itself, we may say, full of it. In order to reconcile certain opposites, it was absolutely necessary at first to make them prominent. Christian writers, also, of all times, have more or less abounded in the use of it. Modern languages, and we may say to a certain extent, manners and thoughts also, are christian in one complete aspect. It is this that explains the difference which may be remarked between modern and ancient authors, in respect to the use of antithesis. Paganism suppressed it, that it might, so to speak, give a certain unity

* PASCAL, *Pensées*, partie i., art. x. § xxii.

to life, a factitious unity, unquestionably, which arose from the negation or ignorance of one of the terms of those great contrasts which human life presents to us. Christianity, by boldly exhibiting the contrasts it would reconcile, has brought into view the antitheses of our existence. It is not therefore surprising that many of the great achievements of the christian pulpit result from the use of antithesis. But we repeat what we have said, that we ought in this matter to rely on the substance of things, to guard against witticisms and a pliant and cold rhetoric which characterizes periods of decay, and indicates a want of inspiration.

One of the most effectual means of giving character and color to expression, is *metaphor*, a name under which we may comprehend all the forms of the figurative style. It transfers to one class of objects qualities which belong to another. The reason for the substitution is that the mind is more struck with an idea when it is appropriated to an object in which we do not expect to meet with it. Metaphor has two forms which have their ground in the complex nature of man. Man unites in himself two natures, which influence one another, which continually have need of one another, and he always endeavors to interblend them. Hence it comes that we give a body to metaphysical and moral objects, and a moral life to physical objects. These two forms of metaphor or transference are as ancient as man; but the primitive metaphors have ceased to be figures; on the ground of language, they have no longer any prominence.

The most common form of the metaphor is that which consists in giving a body, a form, a color to things which are destitute of them; compelling language to assume a material element. The other, which designates the physical by the spiritual, is of a higher order; it refers us to our spiritual nature as the former does to our physical. Metaphors of this class, show that mind prevails over everything; for though we are obliged to give things of the moral order names which are taken from the physical, we are not obliged to name physical things from moral ones. These intellectual metaphors are of great beauty; they abound in holy scripture: "For my sword shall be bathed in heaven; behold it shall come down upon Idumea, and upon the people of my curse, to judgment, " (Isaiah, xxxiv, 5;) but they are found in the texture of all languages. The pantheistic tendency which poisons so many modern writings, has contributed to their revival; but they are confined to no system, no times. See Bossuet: "How different this voyage from that which she had made over the same sea, when going to take possession of the throne of Great Britain, she saw, so to speak, the waters bending beneath her, and subjecting all their waves to the mistress of the seas."*

Metaphor is very powerful; it is like a mirror in which we see what is behind us, and what cannot be seen without it. It has often all the force of a syllogism. It, moreover, gives an additional idea, a wider and fuller view of an object. Thus La Bruyère has said of true greatness: "that it graciously condescends to its inferiors, and returns without effort into its native element."†

We cannot but desire that the style of the pulpit were less insubstantial, less abstract, more figurative, than that which it commonly employs. Our style, as Bossuet said of Calvin's, is somewhat *triste.* We have to do with the people, for religion reduces its hearers to the quality of men, it approximates them to nature, it makes people and children all one.

"When," says Marmontel, "we give ourselves up to natural impressions, we all become children together." I will reverse this proposition, and with him I will add: "Our

* Bossuet, *Oraison funèbre de la reine Henriette.*

† La Bruyère *Les Caractères,* chap. ii. *Du mérite personnel.*

natural condition is that of the people." We must then, in a certain sense, speak like the people; and popular language is metaphorical. We must not, however, force our talent. In literature as well as in morality, what is not of faith is sin. The free use of metaphor implies a fruitfulness of imagination which does not belong to all. But to those who by the cast of their mind are inclined to be imaginative, we must say in the way of caution:

1. That the habit of expressing everything figuratively may become a mental indolence, and make us forgetful of the true names of things.

2. That it is what may happen, and it is a great fault, to be satisfied with imagery; to be content with weakness of ideas, if intrinsic vacuity, may, though but a little, be disguised by an agreeable or captivating form.

Vauvenargues, on this point, has well said, that "when a thought is too weak to bear a simple expression, it shows that it ought to be rejected."*

3. That preaching by an abuse of metaphor may introduce false ideas. In this way metaphor, which gives life to inanimate things and personifies abstractions, may be dangerous. It has sometimes misguided and retarded the progress of moral and social philosophy; as when it has represented society as an individual being.

4. Finally, that the affluence of imagery is unsuitable to the pulpit. If the style of the preacher ought not to be sombre, still less should it be frivolous; and profuse imagery, even if perfectly proper, regarded in itself, destroys its gravity. For the same reason we must exclude metaphors which show too much ingenuity, and which incline to wit. In general, wit and eloquence are hostile to each other, especially wit and pulpit eloquence, with which every appearance of frivolity is especially incongruous.

* VAUVENARGUES, *Reflexions et Maximes.*

Voltaire thinks that passion should always supply metaphor; a too absolute, yet a valuable judgment. It implies that beauty and strength of style should be one and the same thing, and that whatever interests the imagination must, as far as may be, touch the heart. An image in which the writer's soul is revealed, is more excellent than every other which simply displays intelligence.

In this respect Bossuet is admirable. For example, he says: "Thus we proceed, always drawing after us the long, dragging chain of our hopes." Ornaments should be closely united with ideas, and be, as it were, interfused into the very texture of the composition.

Allegory, which is very little used in preaching, though it has for its authority divine eloquence itself, is a form which might be introduced anew, by one who has a talent for it. It is ancient, but it may be modernized, and though it would at first produce surprise, it would become acceptable, for it is eminently popular. Still, if metaphor has the dangers which we thought we ought to indicate, allegory, which is a metaphor prolonged, should be used with great caution, for it may easily assume the appearance of intellectual amusement. The parables of the gospel which resemble allegory, have so pre-eminently serious a character that they allow the mind no liberty to withdraw itself from religious influence and lose itself in amusement. We must not now venture on such an allegory as that on old age, (Ecclesiastes, xii. 2–9;) it is strictly an enigma; but an allegory like that of the vine (Isaiah, v.) might be admitted into a modern discourse. We must have respect, too, to the auditors we address.

Comparison is an explicit metaphor, as metaphor is an implied comparison. Comparison is more artless, and, as an ornament, it is more ancient than metaphor; it abounds in Homer, who spreads out all its folds, while with moderns its form is more rapid and concentrated. It is somewhat sluggish in its nature; it walks instead of marching or running; it seems to imply that we should to be at leisure, that we may delay; it suits poetry better than oratory. We should not think of excluding it from the pulpit, but it is not specially proper to it. Excepting Bossuet, great preachers make but little use of it. Even he uses it more freely in panegyric and in funeral orations, than in sermons.*

Rapid comparisons thrown into the midst of recitation and reasoning, as the discourse advances, are to be preferred:

> Henri, plein de l'ardeur
> Que le combat encore enflammait dans son cœur,
> Semblable à l'océan qui s'apaise et qui gronde.†
>
> Par levibus ventis, volucri que simillima somno.‡

And Bossuet: "Greatness, far from impairing goodness, does but contribute to its enlargement, as a public fountain is elevated that it may send forth its streams farther."§ And again: "This formidable infantry of the Spanish army, whose great battalions in close array, like so many towers—towers which are able to repair their breaches, remained immovable."‖ We do not, however, condemn altogether extended comparisons even in the sermon.

They may be familiar; they ought to be so in one sense, that is to say, they should be taken from objects which are

* See *le Panesgrique de saint Paul et l'oraison funèbre du grand Condé.*

† VOLTAIRE, *La Henriade*, chap. vi.:

> "Filled with the zeal with which the battle still
> Inflamed his heart, Henry, like ocean seemed,
> When calm yet murmuring."—Tr.

‡ VIRGIL, *Æneid*, lib. ii., vs. 794:

§ BOSSUET, *Oraison funèbre du prince de Condé.*

‖ Ibid.

well known ;* still they should be noble. This of Bossuet is not so: "The soul is not less eager, its desires not less excited, when it is in want, than when it has abundance. It is with the soul as with the hairs of one's head; we feel the same pain, whether they are plucked from a bald head, or from a head covered with hair."†

Saurin is more happy in the passage already cited:

"If God had given us a life full of attractions, we should have had no desire for another. It is natural to love an abode in which we find delight; whatever attracts us to earth abates the ardor we may have for heaven; the inward man is renewed when the outward man decays, and our faith is built up on the ruins of our fortune. When the dove found, out of the ark, the unchained winds, the overflow of waters, the flood-gates of the heavens open, the whole world buried under the waves, she sought refuge in the ark. But when she found valleys and fields, she remained in them. My soul see the image of thyself."‡

* Demosthenes has said: "Like moulders of clay you fabricate taxiarchs and tribunes for exhibition, not for war." And again: "As in an edifice or a ship, the lower parts should be the most solid, so we make justice and truth the foundation of government."—"While a ship, great or small, is not yet lost, sailors, pilot, passengers, ought to unite earnestly to prevent perfidy or rashness from destroying it; but all effort becomes useless when it is buried in the waves. Thus, Athenians, so long as our republic is still erect, sustained by great forces, by numberless resources and the most brilliant renown, what shall we do?" In regard to the comparisons which he employs, the great Greek orator may serve as a model. They are remarkable for their rapidity and their practical character.

† See the artless comparison with which Segneri commences his first sermon *du Christiano instruito nella sua legge.*

‡ SAURIN, *Sermon sur le jeune celebrè à l'ouverture de la campagne de* 1706.

§ 3. *Movement.*

This is the second character or element of an eloquent style. Physical movement is passing from one place to another; internal movement should be the same; the movement of style will then consist in transferring the hearer from one moral place or situation into another. This movement is not life, but it is the effect and evidence of life. We cannot conceive of life without movement, and after a time immobility appears to us to be death. These two ideas of movement and life unite so naturally in our minds, that wherever we see movement, we assume or imagiue there is life.* The beauty of a quiet lake charms us in vain by the purity with which it reflects its shores; we would see it agitated and the image of its shores trembling in its waters. Thus as to style; we are not satisfied that it purely reflects objects, we require movement in it; but between the two mirrors there are two differences; in the second we would always have movement, without the trembling of the objects, that is to say, the movement of the style, without any interference with perspicuity of representation.

What an orator desires, if he is truly an orator, is not only to give clear or even bright reprnsentations, nor to connect his ideas with each other so exactly that there shall be no interruption of logical continuity from the beginning to the end; nor even that this chain should be so complete that the proof should not be one moment suspended, but the discourse be, so to speak, as a single breath;—oratorical discourse is an action; this action, which proceeds from the soul, supposes *emotion;* it would, of course, represent but a part of what ought to be represented, if it were only logical, clear, bright, and even profound, and the hearer would

* See Marmontel, *Elêments de littérature*, tome iv., pages 441, 454, article, *Du Mouvement.*

receive only a part of the impressions which he should receive from it. If the orator is not wholly united to his subject, if the discourse be not an action of man upon man, if it be not, as we have said it should be, a drama with its plot, its incidents and its catastrophe, it wants that communicative life, and, we may even say that truth, without which the end of oratorical discourse is wanting in respect to the majority of hearers, who require to feel the truth as identified with him who exhibits and endeavors to unfold it.

The orator, moved by his subject, moved by his auditory, cannot but transfer to his style the emotion which he feels; now, emotion is a movement, that is, to speak exactly, passing from one moral place to another; a momentary emotion is a change of place, a continuous emotion is a succession of changes which arise one after another. Movement must be distinguished from movements. There are abrupt movements which are very fine, but still oratorical movement is not necessarily abrupt. It is different with different orators, with some it is gentle and soft. In vain might we smite the sides, multiply blows, strike with the foot, the soul of the hearer yields only to a true movement. To adopt any other, as Cicero has somewhere said, "is to leap, not to walk."

Movement is the royal beauty of style, the characteristic of great writers and great epochs. In the models, images interblending with movement are furnished by movement itself. Color and life come together. Thus the pale countenance of Atalanta acquires color from the swiftness of her course. Images are not contrary to movement; they may even contribute to it, since they may be impassioned; but in themselves, they produce it no more than would a mirror, since they are but the mirror of things. Movement corresponds to the soul; eloquence may dispense with everything except truth and movement; the most naked, the most austere, the least colored style, may be eloquent. The first beauties are beauties *en blanc*, or *between lines.*

We are taught by experience that one may have been very much interested in his subject, and yet not have movement in his style; force of thought, seriousness of language, may, to a certain extent, take the place of it. It is no less certain that a discourse of a grave, calm, and so to speak, immovable style, may, in certain circumstances, make a sufficiently deep impression. But in general, the emotion of the hearer is in direct proportion to that of the orator, if the subject is deserving of it. And as a christian orator has a two-fold object of interest, his subject and his hearers, we may with the more reason expect to see him moved.

Pulpit eloquence, however, is in this matter restricted within narrower limits than eloquence of other kinds.* It can scarcely be vehement, that is to say, impassioned. The preacher is as much an instructor as an orator; movement in his discourse, therefore, will be more quiet than in that of political and judicial eloquence. The love of a minister of God's word, for divine things, ought to be immeasurable; still we dare not call that love by the name of passion. Reverence demands discretion, and christianity would win us to goodness only by good means.

Movement has very different forms, many of which it is difficult to seize and name. We can indicate only those which are least delicate. We must, in the first place, distinguish those which have place in the expository style, and those which consist in passing beyond the limits of this style.

The expository style is a style *in repose.* But here I distinguish between movement of style and that logical movement of which we spoke when treating of *disposition.*

It is indeed true, that movement may show itself in the expository style, by rapidity in the succession of ideas and by

* Read the third Philippic of Demosthenes.

vivacity in turns of expression. But movement of style is especially apparent, when we forsake the expository style. Strictly speaking, the expository style regards only the idea, excluding the personality of him who expresses and those who hear it. Whatever recognizes these elements removes us from it; we leave it always in *direct address.* This is not a momentary characteristic, an accidental form; it is the normal permanent characteristic of the true oratorical style, and this single characteristic draws after it all the rest in a greater or less degree, all the movements, I mean to say, by which style may be enlivened.

It is characteristic of the direct, or as it may perhaps be also called the *frank* style, that it never seeks the end by oblique or circuitous means, but confronts the idea directly, openly, and uses expressions adapted most immediately to awaken it in the hearer's mind. We speak here, however, not of a moral quality. A style destitute of the characteristic at which we have just glanced, may breathe frankness and candor. We intend what in business matters is expressed by the phrase, going straight to the fact. There is an indirect or oblique course which in certain compositions is appropriate and agreeable. No style is more indirect than La Bruyère's; none is better, if we take into view the author's design: "I suppose men immortal here on earth; I then set myself to thinking in order to acquaint myself with what they would do, in that case, beyond what they are doing as things now are, to make more of their condition."* What shall we say of the *Provincial Letters*, which are written in the same spirit? No other than the direct style is proper in a work intended to be of the popular character, to affect immediately the masses. The less the interval between the thought and the expression, the less the reader is obliged to transform the expression in order to receive the direct im

* La Bruyère, *Les Caractères* chap. xi. *De l'Homme.*

pression of the idea; in a word, the more your language is the vehicle rather than the equipage of thought the greater your success in oratory. You may be elsewhere tenuous, circuitous, cunning, sinuous; elsewhere you may allow yourself in implied meanings, in reticence, in allusions, in reflex ideas, in glimmerings, in indifference and affectation of doubt, in simulation, in giving the principal thing as an accessory, and *vice versâ*, in whatever renders style ingenious; elsewhere it may suffice to make what you wish to say intelligible; here you must say it.

The means of retaining the direct style, is the use of the allocutive form, that of direct address to the hearers. Without this a discourse is not a discourse, but a book. The use of this form compels us constantly to recur to the direct style, which is the truly powerful, truly oratorical style. For two reasons, I recommend this form; first, because the constant use of it will make you almost sure of attaining the direct style, which is so rare and so difficult; next, because, in discourse properly so called, it is the true, the only true form, and whatever is false is feeble. But this same form, how is it to be maintained, how, at least, when the discourse is written, as our reasoning and teaching have hitherto supposed it to be?

That it may be maintained, facts, the examples of the great masters, demonstrate. In writing a discourse, we may truly speak it, address it directly not to a public, but to an audience, imagine ourselves in the orator's position; in short, write oratorically. Whoever would write thus, should assemble his flock about him; the habit is easily formed.

The orator's style then is never purely expository. But a preacher is also a doctor; he teaches, and, therefore, simple exposition in his discourse may be in place. We first distinguish the figures or movements which are included within the limits of the expository style.

1. The simplest, most short, natural, and also one of the strongest and sometimes boldest, is *repetition*. We must not here be imprudently venturous, for from the very simplicity of this form, we fall very low if we have not complete success. It is with it as with the refrain in poetry, which has great power when it is well managed. But repetition must, in some sort, spring out of the subject, must come without being sought, and as it were spontaneously. Repetition is an artless figure. It supposes the orator to be profoundly excited, and absorbed by his subject. Bossuet is artless, and among the great masters of the pulpit, he alone is distinguished by this characteristic. The Bible is artless, and it supplies us with remarkable examples of repetition: "And I also have given you cleanness of teeth in all your cities, and want of bread in all your places. Yet have ye not returned unto me saith the Lord. And also I have withholden the rain from you, when there were yet three months to the harvest; and I caused it to rain upon one city, and caused it not to rain upon another city; one piece was rained upon, and the piece whereupon it rained not, withered. So two or three cities wandered into one city to drink water; but they were not satisfied; yet have ye not returned unto me, saith the Lord. I have smitten you with blasting and with mildew; when your gardens and your vineyards and your fig trees and your olive trees increased, the palmer worm devoured them; yet have ye not returned unto me, saith the Lord. I have sent among you the pestilence after the manner of Egypt; your young men have I slain with the sword, and I have taken away your horses; and I have made the stink of your camps to come up into your nostrils; yet have ye not returned unto me, saith the Lord. I have overthrown some of you as God overthrew Sodom and Gomorrah, and ye were as a firebrand plucked out of the burning; yet have ye not returned unto me, saith the Lord. Therefore thus

will I do unto thee, O Israel; and because I will do this unto thee, prepare to meet thy God, O Israel."*

2. *Gradation*, which is an important form of movement and an essential quality of style, rises, sometimes, to the rank of a figure, by the approximation of parts, their number, and the rapidity of their succession. Thus at the close of the fourteenth *Provincial*, the summing up of the doctrine of the jesuits on homicide, and the last words in particular: "Remember that the first crime of fallen humanity was a homicide committed upon the person of the first righteous man; that its greatest crime was a homicide perpetrated on him who was chief among all the righteous, and that homicide is the only crime which destroys at once the State, the Church, nature, and piety." And in the *Satyre Ménippée*: "Thou hast barely sustained thy king, so meek, so gentle, so affable, who became as a townsman and a burgher of his city. What do I say? Barely sustained? Much worse; thou hast banished him from his city, from his house, from his bed. What, banished? Thou hast pursued him. How pursued? Hast assassinated him, canonized the assassin, and made bonfires at his death."†

3. *Accumulation*, which is often combined with gradation, may also produce a very great effect. The sermon of Massillon on the *Passion of Jesus Christ*, contains many examples of it. We cite only one: "I conjure thee," he said to him, "in the name of the living God to tell us if thou be Christ the Son of God. But if there is a sincere desire to know the truth, why interrogate Himself on the holiness of his ministry? Ask John the Baptist, whom ye have regarded as a prophet, and who confessed that he was the Christ; ask his works, which none before him had done, and which

* AMOS, iv. 6, 12. See also SENECA, *Natural quaest.* lib. vi., cap. xxiii., and the *Life of Bridaine*, p. 170.

† *Harangue de M. d'Aubray, pour le tiers état.*

testified that it is the Father who sent him ; ask the witnesses of his life and you will see if imposture was ever accompanied by such marks of innocence and holiness; ask the Scriptures, ye who have the key of knowledge, and see if Moses and the prophets have not borne testimony to him ; ask the blind whose eyes he opened, the dead whom he raised, the lepers whom he healed, the people whom he fed, the sheep of Israel whom he restored ; and they will tell you that never has God given such power to man ; ask the heavens which were so often opened over his head, to make known to you that this was the well beloved Son ; and if these testimonies are not sufficient ask hell itself, and learn from the demons who, in obedience to him, went out of bodies, that he is the Holy one of God. But there is here no serious inquiry after truth, but a snare laid for innocence; and, as often happens, especially to the great, pre-occupied by their passions, they consult and do not wish to be undeceived ; they seem to desire instruction, and would be grieved to be enlightened."

4. *Reticence* should be little used in the pulpit. The preacher speaks with open mouth, he has nothing to conceal. The orator, however, from various motives, may pause before he develops an idea, especially when he would not present to the imagination too vivid pictures of what is gross or disagreeable. The orator of the senate or bar, unquestionably has more frequent occasion than the preacher, for reticence. The preacher, however, should not be altogether deprived of a movement of so much efficacy. But reticence is never proper, unless the hearer knows with certainty what is not expressed. In a discourse of my own, on the *Principle of Human Equality*, I do not follow this rule in an instance of reticence, the effect of which is lost. "How soon in fact, does inequality insinuate itself among brethren according to the flesh, whom fortune favors unequally ? How often does

a brother find a haughty patron in a more influential brother, and the latter a servile and low dependent in a brother less fortunate? How often indeed, ... But let us not go too far; let us not wantonly profane the idea of the sweetest of earthly relationships."*

5. *Correction* is an excellent figure when it is not a figure, when the orator perceives that his emotion has involuntarily overpowered him, and recovers himself without calculating how he is to correct, restrain, or complete what he has said. It may be very beautiful or very vulgar. Such expressions as, *What do* I say, though common in oratorical discourse, are very far from being always happy. But Bossuet is admirable in this passage from *the funeral oration of Henrietta of England:*

"No, after what we have just said, health is but a name, life but a dream, glory but an appearance, grace and pleasure but a dangerous amusement; all that pertains to us is vain, except the sincere confession of our vanity to God, and the settled judgment which leads us to despise whatever we are.

"But do I say the truth? Is man whom God has made in his own image only a shadow? Is that a mere nothing which Jesus Christ came from heaven to earth to seek, which he supposed he might redeem by his own blood without dishonor to himself? We acknowledge our mistake. This gloomy view of human vanity has doubtless deceived us. The sudden frustration of public hope by the death of this princess, has carried us too far. Man must not be permitted to despise himself altogether, lest while thinking with the impious that life is a jest or the reign of chance, he walk at the impulse of his blind desires, without rule and without guidance."†

* *Nouveaux Discours sur quelques sujets religieux*, edition of 1841, p. 284. See an example of reticence in Cicero, *Pro Ligario*, cap. x.

† Compare the *Correction* of Flechier, in *l'oraison funèbre de Turenne:* "But what do I say? We must not, etc."

6. *Pretermission* seems to imply a desire to pass in silence what is too well known or too manifest to need mention, while expressing it with an emphasis proportioned to the orator's appearance of being opposed to dwelling upon it. Cicero often uses it happily.* Pretermission is used to classify two orders of ideas or arguments; and while it seems to put one class aside, which yet it takes pains to represent as far from having no value, it gives in advance to those which are to follow, a great appearance of strength. But ideas which are thus introduced, must satisfy the expectation which is excited.† A too frequent use of this procedure is not perhaps in perfect accordance with the candor and frankness of the discourse of the pulpit. Massillon seems prodigal of it, for he often presents an entire argument under the form of pretermission.

7. *Irony*, which was much employed by ancient orators,‡ cannot be excluded from the pulpit, for the Bible makes frequent use of it; but it should be introduced with caution, on account of the dangers which accompany it. It should never be otherwise than serious, and never offend charity. We may cite here the beginning of the application of Saurin's first sermon on the *Delay of Conversion:*

* *Pro Milone*, cap. xi. In *Pisonem*, cap. xxxvii.

† See FLECHIER, *Oraison funèbre de Turenne:* "I can show you, sirs, as many trophies on the shores of the Rhine, as on those of the Escaut and the Sambre, etc."

‡ See DEMOSTHENES, *Second Philippic.* "Then you who attend are better qualified than Philip, either to plead the justice of your cause, or to apprehend it when enforced by others; but as to any effectual opposition, in this you are entirely inactive. You see then the consequence, the necessary, the natural consequence; each of you excels in that which hath engaged your time and application; he in acting, you in speaking." (Leland's Translation.) Cicero pushes irony even to sarcasm. See *Pro. Milone*, cap. vii., and in *Catilinam*, i., cap. x.

"To be truly converted, it is not sufficient to perform some act from love to God, this love must be the ruling disposition of our heart. There are visionary persons who are offended when we urge these great truths of religion, and incessantly proclaim in our ear these maxims: 'Take heed to yourselves, christians; they shake the foundations of your faith; there is poison in this doctrine.'"

"My brethren, if this were a subject less grave and serious, we could not forbear turning such scruples into ridicule. Take heed to yourselves, indeed, there is poison. We would urge you to love God with all your heart; we would urge you to consecrate your life to him; we would urge you not to defer your conversion, to prepare yourselves for a holy death by the constant exercise of piety and repentance. Is it not obvious that we should have great care in admitting such a doctrine, and that the church would be in a deplorable condition, if all its members should assume these dispositions. But, as we have said already, this is a subject too grave and too serious to admit of raillery."

8. We may mention *hyperbole*, which is very ancient, and which abounds in the Bible. But we can scarcely give positive rules for its use; here everything depends on the posture and movement which the discourse has given to the minds of the hearers.

9. *Paradox* approaches hyperbole. It gives a striking and often an affecting form to a thought, and fixes it in the mind. Saint Paul frequently recurs to this means of compelling, in a manner, and fixing attention. But it must be used with care when it is introduced in the pulpit. The preacher speaks to men who cannot always take his meaning at once, and he ought to be on his guard, lest he give errors instead of truths, to the simple.

10. Finally, we mention *vision*, or *oratorical hypothesis*, a supposition by which, in order to impart a vivid impression

to the soul, we give presence to certain objects. It is one of the boldest of figures. Bourdaloue sometimes employs it; but pulpit eloquence, unquestionably, very seldom rises to the height of this passage from Massillon's sermon, on the small number of the elect.

"I confine myself, my brethren, to you who are here assembled; I speak no longer of others; I regard you as if you were the only persons on earth, and here is the thought which possesses me and fills me with dread. I imagine that this is your last hour and the end of the world; that the heavens are about to be opened over your heads, and Jesus Christ to appear in his glory in the midst of this temple, and that you are here assembled only to await his coming, and as trembling criminals on whom he is to pronounce either a pardon or a sentence to eternal death; for, in vain have you flattered yourselves; you will die such as you are now; all those desires of a change which have deluded you, will delude you even to the bed of death; this is the experience of all times; all you will then find new in yourselves, will perhaps be an account somewhat larger than that which you would to-day have to render; and from what you would be, if you were to be judged this moment, you might almost determine what will happen to you at your departure from life.

"Now I demand of you, and I do this impressed with dread, identifying in this matter my lot with yours, and assuming the position into which I wish you to enter; I demand of you then: If Jesus Christ should appear in this temple, in the midst of this assembly, the most august in the world, to judge us, to make the momentous separation between the goats and the sheep, think ye that the greater number of those who are present would be placed on his right hand? Think ye, at least, that the numbers would be equal? Think ye that he would find here ten righteous, a number the Lord at another time could not find in five entire cities? I demand it of you, you know it not, I know it not myself; thou alone, O my God, knowest those who are thine. But if we know not who are his, we know at least that sinners are not of this number. Now of those here assembled, who are believers? Titles and honors are to pass now for nothing; in the presence of Jesus Christ they will be taken away from you. Who are believers? Many sinners have no wish to be converted; still more would be, but delay their conversion; many others would be converted only to relapse; lastly, a great number think they have no need of conversion. Remove these four classes of sinners from this holy assembly; for removed they will be at the great day; now ye righteous come forth; where are ye? remnant of Israel pass to the right; wheat of Jesus Christ, separate yourselves from this chaff which is destined to the fire. O God! where are thine elect? and what remains for thy portion?"

We come now to figures which pass the limits of this purely expository style.

1. *Interrogation*, which is often used, and sometimes extravagantly, is a form of affirmation; it is affirmation enforced by a sort of defiance, and so distinct from ordinary interrogation, that it is pronounced with a different tone. It may be employed in reasoning, to which it gives a more cogent character; but we must be careful in doing this, for this form is very apt to become monotonous.*

* In a celebrated example of this form in the beginning of Cicero's first oration against Catiline: "Quousque tandem, etc."

On the abuse of interrogation we cite the following very forcible passage from Robert Hall's review of Gisborne's sermons:

"Another blemish which strikes us in this work, is the frequent use of interrogations, introduced, not only in the warm and impassioned parts, where they are graceful, but in the midst of argumentative discussion. We have been struck with the prevalence of this practice in the more recent works of clergymen, beyond those of any other order of men. With Demosthenes, we know interrogation

2. *Exclamation*, a very simple figure, is very apt to become commonplace. It is the ready resource of frigid minds. Buffon charges J. J. Rousseau with using it too freely. But this common figure is enhanced by genius, and still more by a true emotion. It is always beautiful when it is well employed; that is to say, when it is artless and flows from the heart, like that which the remembrance of a recent affliction drew from the soul of Bossuet: "O disastrous night, O dreadful night, in which, like a peal of thunder, suddenly resounded this surprising news: Madame is dying, Madame is dead!"*

Exclamation is enforced by *apostrophe* and *prosopopœia*, figures of great boldness and power. Apostrophe is a loud call addressed to an absent person. We give a fine example of it from Massillon: "An angel must descend from heaven to comfort him, to strengthen him, to assist him to bear this invisible cross, as Simon the Cyrenian the cross of calvary. Angels of heaven! this heretofore has not been your ministry; you have heretofore approached Him to serve and to worship; now He is debased below you."†

was a very frequent figure; but we recollect, at the same time, it was chiefly confined to the more vehement parts of his speeches, in which, like the eruptions of a furnace, he broke out upon, and consumed his opponents. In him it was the natural expression of triumphant indignation; after he had subdued and laid them prostrate by the force of his arguments, by his abrupt and terrible interrogations, he trampled them in the mire. In calm and dispassionate discussion, the frequent use of questions appears to us unnatural; it discomposes the attention by a sort of starting and irregular motion, and is a violation of dignity, by affecting to be lively where it is sufficient praise to be cogent and convincing. In a word, when, instead of being used to give additional vehemence to a discourse, they are interspersed in a series of arguments, as an expedient for enlivening the attention and varying the style, they have an air of undignified flippancy."—(Works, vol. iv. London, 1831, pp. 141,142.)—Tr.

* Bossuet, *Oraison funèbre d'Henriette d'Angletere.*

† Massillon, *Sermon sur la Passion de notre Seigneur.* We recall, also, Saurin's celebrated Apostrophe to Louis XIV.

Prosopopœia approaches apostrophe, from which it is distinguished by this only, that the calls are addressed to inanimate or deceased persons. The use of such energetic means can be justified only by the orator's emotion and the state into which his discourse has put his hearers. It is indispensable that in the use of it he be sincere; he will be cold and repulsive if he feign or affect to be moved. It is of the genius of eloquence to sympathize with the hearers, to unite itself with their impressions while it takes the measure of them, and to say what they are able to bear. Saurin uses this figure quite often without, however, being prodigal of it: "Give place, give place to our calamities, ye catastrophes of former ages, ye mothers whose tragical stories astonish posterity, who, forced by the horrors of famine had to eat the flesh of your sons, and to preserve your own life by taking that of those who had received life from you. However dreadful your condition, you took from them only a transient life, and by a single stroke you saved them and yourselves from the rigors of famine. Here all follow one another into the same abyss, and by an unheard of prodigy, the mother, the mother feeds, if we must so speak, on the very soul of her son, and the son in turn devours the very soul of his mother."

Bossuet abounds in prosopopœia: "Why will you have prodigies so expensive to God? One prodigy only do I now announce to the world: O heavens, O earth, be astonished at this new prodigy! It is that among so many testimonials of the divine love, so many remain unbelieving and insensible." And elswhere: "We give thee thanks, O death! for the light thou hast cast on our ignorance. Thou alone hast taught us our baseness, thou alone hast made us acquainted with our dignity. If man is high in his own esteem, thou art able to abase him; if a man is too self-abasing thou canst give him courage; and to moderate all his thoughts, th-

teachest him these two truths which open his eyes to the true knowledge of himself; that he is infinitely mean as he comes to an end in time, and infinitely great as he passes into eternity."*

We cite one example more from Massillon: "In this degraded condition, Jesus Christ came forth from the pretorium. He said to them, behold the man, *Ecce homo.* Holy kings sprung from the loins of David! inspired prophets who announce him to the world; is this the personage whom you so longed to see? behold ye then the man? *Ecce homo;* behold ye then at length the Deliverer promised to your fathers so many ages ago? Behold ye the Great Prophet whom Judea was to give to the earth? Behold ye the desire of all nations, the expectation of the whole world, the substance of your types, the fulfilment of your worship, the hope of all your just men, the consolation of the synagogue, the glory of Israel, the light and salvation of all nations? *Ecce homo*, behold the man! Recognize ye him under these marks of shame?"†

3. *Dramatisme,*‡ of style, which consists in presenting in action what may be presented in another form,—didactic or narrative. Oratorical discourse is always a drama; each word of the preacher is a question to which the hearer responds in himself, and his response becomes as a new question, to which the orator replies. There is then a close conference in every oratorical performance. But this general character may become more marked in certain places, as a lofty region may be strewed with eminences. These places are as so many, more or less, intense accents. Dramatism in discourse has place whenever a distinction of persons appears, which is not required by the nature of the idea, whenever

* Bossuet, *Sermon sur la mort et l'immortalité de l'âme.*

† Massillon, *Sermon sur la passion de notre Seigneur.*

‡ We retain the French term. There is no word in English by which we can render it.—Tr.

respect is had to a relation of persons different from that which exists naturally between the orator and the hearer. This figure is not peculiar to eloquence; it is one of the beauties of poetry, of history, of all animated discourse. Actions show men; but words exhibit actions. "Speak that I may see thee." We do not condemn the discourses which the ancient historians put into the mouths of persons to express externally that which is within. The Bible makes the prodigal son to speak, although his actions speak already of themselves. Dramatism, we add, should not only be introduced in large portions but should be insinuated into the smallest details of the discourse. "Have you an important secret," says Bossuet, "pour it out without fear into this noble heart; your affair becomes his by confidence."*

A very bold form of dramatism consists in putting into the mouth of God the instruction which the orator wishes to give. It may be used, but not without the greatest reverence, moderation and caution. The prophets often make God the speaker, and pulpit orators have followed this example. "What hinders you from fulfilling the law?" says Bourdaloue; "what makes you despair of ever fulfilling it is, you say, the vicious inclination of your heart, that flesh which is conceived in sin, and which wars incessantly against the spirit. But suppose, my brethren, Saint Chrysostom replies, that God should address you in these terms: O man, I would to-day take away this heart and give you another; you have only the power of a man, I would give you that of a God. It is not you alone who are to act, who are to combat, who are to resist; I myself will fight within you, I myself will overcome this inclination and this corrupt flesh. If God should thus address you, if he should make you this offer, would you still dare to complain? Now, in how many places of scripture has he not made you this promise? Does he not speak to

* Bossuet, *Oraison funèbre du prince de Condé.*

you by the prophet Ezekiel: *I will take from you this hard heart, and give you a new heart, a heart teachable and submis sive to my law?* What then do ye fear? That God will not keep his word? That were to distrust his faithfulness. That notwithstanding God's word, you would find it impossible to observe his law. But that were to distrust his power."*

The personification of the whole auditory by the preacher, is another form of dramatism. We have an example of it in the following passage from Saurin, which has been already cited in part: "When the dove, out of the ark, found the winds unchained, the overflowing waters, the flood-gates of heaven open, the world buried beneath the waves, she sought refuge in the ark. But when she found plains and fields, she stayed in them. My soul, see the image of thyself. When the world presents to thee prosperity, honor, wealth, thou hearest the voice of the enchanter, and sufferest thyself to be taken in its charms. But when thou findest in the world only poverty, contempt, misery, thou turnest thine eyes upward to seek happiness in thy centre. Now, notwithstanding the disappointments with which our life is accompanied, it is exceedingly painful to us to tear ourselves away from it. What would it be, then, if everything prospered here according to our wishes."†

The most complete form of dramatism is *dialogue*. Demosthenes often employs it; but one of the most beautiful examples of it that can be produced, is this passage from Saurin: "But regarding this whole text as applicable to you, my brethren, you are permitted to-day to pour out your complaints freely, and to declare before the face of heaven and of earth, the evils God has done you. *My people, what have I done?* Ah, Lord, what things hast thou done to us. Ways of Zion covered with mourning, desolate gates of Jerusalem,

* BOURDALOUE, *Sermon sur la sagesse et la douceur de la loi chretienne.*

† SAURIN, *Sermon sur le jeune célébré a l'ouverture de la campagne de* 1706.

lamenting priests, wailing virgins, prostrate sanctuaries, deserts peopled with fugitives, members of Christ wandering over the face of the world, children torn from their fathers, prisons filled with confessors, galleys crowded with martyrs, the blood of our countrymen poured out like water, dead bodies venerable as having witnessed for religion, but now cast out as refuse, and given for food to the beasts of the field and the fowls of heaven, ruins of our temples, dust, ashes, sad remains of houses consecrated to God, fires, wheels, gibbets, punishments till our day unheard of, answer and witness here against the Lord."*

We must finally mention *prayer*, as contributing to movement in discourse, although the preacher, certainly, should not allow himself to use it simply as an instrument of oratory. But it is very impressive when used appropriately. In certain solemn moments, crises of discourse, recomposing the heart in God has great power and produces great effect. We should never forget, however, with what seriousness and sincerity this means should be employed.

It remains for us to speak of certain qualities of style which relate alike to imagery and movement. We mention first, *variety:*

> Sans cesse en ecrivant variez vos discours.
> Un style trop égal et toujours uniforme
> En vain brille à nos yeux, il faut qu'il nous endorme.
> On lit peu ces auteurs, nés pour nous ennuyer,
> Qui toujours sur un ton semblent psalmodier.*

---

* SAURIN, *Sermon sur le jeune célébré a l'ouverture de la campagne de* 1706. Tome viii., p. 112, nouvelle édition.

† BOILEAU, *L'Art Poetique*, chant i.

> "In writing strive to vary your discourse.
> A style too equal and always the same,
> Dazzles in vain. We can but fall asleep
> Few read those authors, born to tire us,
> Who always seem to sound the self-same note."—Tr.

I would not regard the subject in this view only. Variety has a close connection with truth, with propriety, with precision. A style possessing these three qualities, will thereby be made various; as no one thing is absolutely like any other, if we express a thing just as it is, we shall vary our words and phrases; variety arises from the essence of the things when the things themselves are different.

The constant recurrence of the same forms and phrases is owing ordinarily to a crude or at least imperfect analysis of thought. If we would be, not nice or subtile, but simply true, we must have distinguished well, analyzed well, inwardly at least. Too many authors are accustomed to do what is done in printing, when words and even whole sentences, which it is foreseen there will be occasion to use, are kept standing in type. A number of clauses or oft-cited passages are in circulation which each applies to his present thought, even though it does not correspond to it perfectly. Writers of strongly marked individuality are distinguished by this, that while they are different from themselves in different places, they are to be recognized in almost every line. Bossuet for example. He has no standing phrases, no frequent returns of the same forms of expression, no mannerism, no refrains.

Thorough analysis of thought then is the first, it is not the only condition of variety. Not only the object itself, but the instrument, that is language, must have been studied. And it is to be remembered, that the study of the instrument or the forces of language, favors the study of the object, since in seeking the sign for an idea we seek the idea itself. We generally study language too little; we know it only in gross; we do not explore its resources; we do not endeavor to make it productive; we leave those who have the instinct, the living and inward sense of language, to enjoy their advantage; we have no care to gain by study, what with less of natural talent, we may acquire by that means. Those who give so little attention to language, have but a poor vocabulary, are capable of but few constructions; it is to others that language unfolds its affluence.

Finally, with all our diligence, we must keep up a constant watch, for every one has his favorite expressions and forms into which he too readily falls. It is only writers of the second order that commit this fault. We do not meet with it in the masters.

Variety of expression, of construction, and of movement, is of special importance in didactic works, and above all in pulpit discourse.

Elegance.—Variety of which we have just spoken, is one of the elements, or, at least, one of the conditions of elegance; still we thought it ought to be considered separately, as it is an excellence which may exist in a greater or less degree, apart from elegance, and be the object of distinct attention.

The meaning of the word *elegance*, in the language of the seventeenth century, appears from Boileau's use of it, in two well-known passages of the *Art of Poetry:*

> . . . . . Une élégante idylle.*
> . . . . De Marot l'élégante badinage.†

It is the avoidance of what is common and flat, the most natural danger in pastoral and playful composition. Everywhere as well as in idylls, it chooses forms which are remote at once from the trivial and the subtile, without betraying the slightest effort. It is in style what refinement is in manners.

But its avoidance of the vulgar and the trivial is not confined to what offends moral or social propriety, it also ex-

* Chant. ii. "An elegant idyll."—Tr.

† Chant. i. "The elegant pleasantry of Marot."—Tr.

tends to whatever violates the proprieties of wit, for that also has its proprieties. Wit is opposed to whatever is coarse, clumsy, awkward, too full or too empty of meaning.* It rejects repetitions, uniformity, embarrassed or heavy forms of expression, nice discrimination and too formal logic. It delights in freedom and agility, in a simple and easy conciseness; in delicately appropriate expressions; in ingenious turns which seem only fortunate hits; a style which in these respects gratifies wit, is an elegant style.

The elements of elegance often escape us, and it has been said to be wholly negative; but it has positive ingredients. Elegance implies an aptitude in multiplying the relation of ideas, in combining, in condensing; it not only polishes, it cuts the diamond. It does not limit itself to relations of the greatest importance or necessity; it seizes subordinate relations, bearings of things which are little observed; of course it possesses imagination, or at least wit; in an elegant style there is always wit, though there may be none in thought, for elegance consists of the same ideas which give us wit.† We may see this in a few examples:

"In each genus the first species bears away all our praises and the secondary species are left to the contempt which arises from comparison with them."‡

"The work obtained a success in all Europe, which malignity put to the disadvantage of Louis XIV."§

* There is a coarse wit, so called; but wit violates its law when it is not elegant. "The definition of wit," says Dryden, "is only this, that it is a propriety of thought and words; or, in other words, thoughts and terms elegantly adapted to the subject." Buffoonery is not wit; Locke somewhere suggests that buffoonery is to wit what pedantry is to learning.—Tr.

† Yet, Montesquieu has much wit and is not elegant.

‡ Buffon.

§ Villemain.

"The bishop of Antioch strove to unite to Christian society the hope of so fine a genius."*

Elegance appears not only in a separate sentence, but also in connected sentences, in the texture of the diction; simple sentences, from the manner of their succession and combination, may form an elegant whole. Here we have pleasure in citing Massillon: "It is a light thing, my brethren, that almost the only work of the great and powerful should be the corruption of our times; ages to come also will perhaps owe to you a part of their licentiousness and disorder. Those profane poems which, but for you, would not have seen the light, will also corrupt the hearts of men in the ages which are to succeed you; those pernicious authors whom you honor with your patronage will pass into the hands of your offspring, and with the fatal poison which they carry in them, and which they will communicate from age to age, your crimes will be multiplying; your very passions, immortalized by history, after scandalizing your own age, will do the same to ages following; others, by reading the story of your excesses, will be led to imitate you after your death; they will learn new lessons of crime from the recital of your adventures; and your irregularities will not die with you. . . Such is the consequence of the vices and passions of the great and the powerful. They live not for their own age only; they live for ages to come, and there is no limit to the duration of their scandal except that of their memory."†

Elegance is not beauty, but it takes the place in style which *tournure*, carriage, and dress have in the figure of a woman of fashion. Elegance is seen to advantage from the mechanism of verse, which makes it more apparent by the two-fold exactness of rhythm and thought, as in Racine.

Elegance is apt to be cold, because it is less the effect of

* Villemain.

† Massillon, *Petit Carême.*

imagination which paints and colors, than of wit which sketches and engraves, (otherwise would geometry itself ever have had its *elegant* demonstrations to boast of?) and because it is only to a certain extent that it accords with vivid emotion. For when the heart is moved, too much elegance is not the supplement but the contrary of beauty. Should we be pleased to see a person in a transport of grief, watching lest his gestures should derange his toilette, or his tears wash off his paint?

Neither does it accord with gravity beyond a certain point. Elegance is social, it is mundane. It springs from the refinement of society, and all its graces point to the leisure and luxuries of polished life.

There is, however, even in grave and pathetic subjects, a degree of elegance to which style should attain; a chaste elegance scarcely to be observed, scarcely to be distinguished from the natural, the just, the concise in style; these qualities appear and assert themselves, alone, it is not until afterwards that elegance is recognized. The preacher in order to be elegant, must have had recourse to practice, and another and much greater effort will be necessary not to appear so; elegance which announces itself, elegance which shows itself, is unskilful and unhappy; but chaste elegance is appropriate to the pulpit.

CHAPTER IV.

THE MATERIAL PART OF DISCOURSE, OR SOUND.

If it is not right for us to flatter the ear, we ought at least to accommodate it, and our instructions in this chapter have respect only to this object.

It would doubtless scarcely be proper to speak of harmony

or even of the other qualities of style, if the attention to the subject required of the preacher were too absorbing, or such as might withdraw him from more important labors; but art is not or ought not to continue to be a severe and minute labor; it should become a second nature. Habit makes that easy which was difficult at first; the movement on the keys of the organ becomes at length a real *play*, and in itself, perhaps, is less difficult than that of the eye over the note-book.

Art would not be art if it did not become nature. Inspiration is possible only when all the faculties contribute to it without interfering with one another, and it is to this equilibrium of the faculties that we must attain. All art unquestionably requires instruction, and this is as true of the art of writing as of other arts; but when once the habit is acquired, and art becomes nature, it will be as difficult to write ill, as it is to write well without it.

Harmony comprises three things, *euphony*, *number*, and *imitative harmony*. This last belongs to poetic language, and without desiring to exclude it from the pulpit, we should exclude at least the pursuit of it. But we must say something concerning euphony and number.

Euphony is the combination of agreeable, and the exclusion of discordant sounds. The latter point, the care to avoid cacophony, is doubtless essential.

> Fuyez des mauvais sons le concours odieux.*

I do not add:

> Le vers le mieux rempli, la plus noble pensée,
> Ne peut plaire à l'esprit quand oreille est blessé.†

---

* BOILEAU, *L'Art Poetique*, chant i.

"Shun the hateful concourse of bad sounds."—Tr.

† Ibid.

'The most finished verse, the most noble thought,
The mind cannot please if the ear be pained."—Tr.

I would not be so nice, but an offended ear turns away the mind.

Doubtless there is a harmony of words which becomes a kind of music, which intoxicates the hearer; and we must guard against exciting or cherishing frivolity, by effeminacy, a sort of epicurism of style; but let us also avoid falling into the contrary excess. Cacophony is less hurtful in intensely accentuated and agitating language, in which prosody makes amends for the want of euphony; but the French wants this advantage; it is dull, nasal, abounds in mute *e*'s, and should fear more than other languages, the *superbissimum aurium judicium* of which Cicero speaks. We should therefore do wrong to give no thought to euphony, for it would seem to be no less unhappy to disparage ideas by bad sounds than by agreeable ones.

Number is quite as important; a sentence which to the understanding is a unit, should be one to the ear; but unity is perceptible only through plurality. We perceive no longer a first, where we do not perceive a second. It is with a sentence as with verses, in which musical unity is perceived only from the divisions or pauses. There are spaces, pauses, numbers or number, in prose as well as in poetry. But the difference between them is, that in prose any number of syllables is proper, whether of an entire sentence or any one of its parts, while verse restricts itself from the outset to certain numbers and divisions, which render the musical intent more apparent, and these it verifies by means of rhyme. Poetry sings, prose does not exactly sing, it speaks; but the ear requires to be pleased; and this is done by pauses at the proper places, by phrases of the requisite length, and by agreeable cadences, now loud, now low, now strong, now feeble; cadences corresponding to rhyme in verse.*

* See the description of the *Swan*, by BUFFON, in *Chrestomathie Française*, tome i., p. 172, troisième édition.

The first object is not to amuse the ear; it is to spare the hearer the painful impression which he feels when he perceives that the orator is out of breath; for he involuntarily sympathizes with him, measures the compass of his voice, and knows when he needs rest. "A discourse," says Gaichiès, "is not pronounced with one breath; pauses enable us to take breath again, and aid the voice by grateful variety; thus the necessary introduces the agreeable." Cicero had said before: "The stops and divisions of periods were first introduced for recovering the breath and opening the lungs; and yet in their own nature they are so musical, that though one's lungs were inexhaustible, yet we should not wish for continuity of style without any stops. Such a sympathy exists between what is agreeable to our ears, and what is not only possible but easy for our lungs."*

Even the unpractised hearer perceives when propriety is violated, when proportion is wanting; the discerning almost distinguish the imperfect sound of a syllable.

By attending to this matter, we may afford assistance in understanding and retaining the discourse; number supports the voice and favors hearing in a temple. Let us not think that there is any artifice unworthy of the gravity of the pulpit, in giving this subject our attention. We ought, doubtless, to sacrifice number to thought;

Le *nombre* est un esclave et ne doit qu'obéir:†

But it may obey always; the resources of language are so numerous, that the sacrifice of thought is never necessary; and if good poets have used so much liberty and propriety

* CICERO, *De Oratore*, lib. iii., cap. xlvi. (London Translation, 1808.)

† BOILEAU says this of *Rhyme*, (Ed.:) "Number is a slave, and should only obey."—Tr.

under the constraint of rhyme, surely the orator may much more do this under the easier constraint of number. Number must seem to present itself spontaneously; after a period of practice the appearance becomes reality: *Ut numerus non quaesitus, sed ipse secutus esse videatur*, says Cicero.* We cannot, however, allow ourselves what was not only allowed but required in the Grecian and even Roman orators before an artistic people.

Number should not be confounded with the introduction of unusual phrases into a discourse, which form verses and have the same kind of measure. Paul Louis Courrier often has such phrases, and they are set off, by elegies with which we have no sympathy. It is a sort of dissonance, which gives to prose a somewhat equivocal and indeterminate character; something between singing and speaking; and besides, there is something of affectation and puerility in being occupied in such work.

Number is not peculiar to the periodic style; it should have place in any style in which one writes. It is, however, in the involutions of the oratorical period, that number appears to the most advantage; here it is that we look for the *numerous* style. We should carefully avoid the periodic style, if the style called *numerous*, would not suit our discourse. It is not the ear only that suggests the periodic style, neither does it, first of all, relate to the ear. It delights in assembling around one and the same thought, as around a trunk, a certain number of thoughts, which spontaneously bloom, and form above the principal idea, as it were, a tufted summit. This style imparts the idea of calmness, of power and dignity; the period is also suited to the style which inspires awe and solemnity. But it is not a style to be labored at, as a painter labors according to his particular talent, at a landscape or a portrait; it is a form which style should assume from the movement of thought,

* Cicero, *Orator*, cap. lxv.

and it should beware of embarrassing itself with long sentences; they are not suited to it.

I say the same of the laconic style. We should habituate ourselves to neither. The laconic style has precision and vivacity; sometimes it has authority, and is very proper in its place. Pomp and grandeur belong to the periodic style. It sounds well; but it may relax the vigor of thought, and is unfavorable to emotion. We should then intermingle these two styles, and use them alternately. Bossuet here, is to be preferred before Fléchier, and is an excellent model well worthy to be studied. Though we may recognize him in almost every line, he is always different from himself. But Massillon surpasses all others in the happy mixture of the laconic and the periodic style.

APPENDIX.

A DISCOURSE DELIVERED BY M. VINET, AT HIS INSTALLATION AS PROFESSOR OF PRACTICAL THEOLOGY IN THE ACADEMY OF LAUSANNE, NOVEMBER 1ST, 1837.

Honorable Counsellor of State, Vice-President and Members of the Council of Public Instruction, Rector and Members of the Academy, Regents and Instructors of the Academical College, Students of this Academy, Honored hearers of every order,—

SIRS,—

The discourses we have just heard* suffice to grace this solemnity and to allay the anxiety which it naturally causes in me; you have been gratified and my heart has been encouraged; and if this service had no other object it might now properly be brought to a close; but the law which imposes on me the difficult task of following two orators so worthy of commanding your attention, doubtless has its reason, and does not merely aim at meeting a conventional propriety. He who occupies the post of an instructor in our Academy, does not discharge his important functions before the public; yet he is responsible to the public, he in a man-

* Alluding to the address of M. Jaquet, President of the Council of State, who presided on the occasion, and to that of M. J. J. Porchat, Rector of the Academy.

ner belongs to it, he is its man, and as such it is fitting that once at least, on entering upon his charge, he should appear before it to do honor to his sureties, to those, I mean to say, who have appointed him, those first delegates of the public who have delegated him, and publicly installed him. It is fitting at least that at their risk and his own, he should make himself known. Especially is it fitting that when a serious mission is to be undertaken, every one should know in what spirit it is to be fulfilled. It is under this last impression that I regard the obligation which I am now to meet. Even without designing to do so I should meet this obligation, by what I am now to say. Desirous chiefly to show, at my entrance, what I think and what I am, though I should see it for my interest to do otherwise, though ignorant, as a new-comer, as to what it is expedient I should say, what disguise and what suppress, on whatever subject I might speak, I could not but show myself openly, with whatever there may be in me, good or bad. And as an affected reserve would betray me more than my words, I shall approach at once the questions relating immediately to the office which has been assigned to me. Only may I have grace from Him whose good Providence to-day has made frankness a demand of my position and of good sense, to add truth to frankness, that what I speak, I may speak according to the oracles of God, and that my discourse may communicate grace to my hearers.

Called to be henceforth occupied with the subject of preaching, that chief lever of the evangelical ministry, I have not been able to regard it in a purely abstract view; it has not presented itself to me simply as an art, of which I am to inquire into the principles and trace the theory, but as a matter of fact in the regulation of which I am to take part, as a christian work in which I am to be employed with others;

and I could not but regard it at the stand-point of a certain time, our own, and of a certain place, our country. And at the outset a two-fold question claimed from me an exact solution. How have the circumstances of time and place modified preaching; and what influence has preaching had in its turn on that state of things which has modified it?

I could satisfy myself as to this question before an examination of facts; for I could not be doubtful either as to their action or reaction; of their nature alone might I be ignorant. Every epoch has its characteristics, more or less prominent, and if the influence of these is felt in private society, in individual life, and even in the most hidden life, how could a public fact like that of preaching be unaffected by it, especially in a country in which religion is one of the interests, and, in some sort, a property of the State? It is true that as religion has its rise in no human fact, and claims, by its nature, ascendency over everything, its principle seems to withdraw it from that mysterious attraction which draws all the concerns of an epoch within the orbit of an idea or a passion; but in man, religion becomes human, he transports it into his own sphere, using, for the purpose of drawing it to himself, the chain which fastens him to it. Incorruptible in itself, its institutions and its characteristics become more or less changed in the atmosphere of human passions; the dust of this world adheres, in some measure, to its august feet; in a word, whatever springs from religion, whatever is connected with religion, and, above all, preaching, which is its most lively representation, receives, unavoidably, the impress of times and places.

Every epoch has its characteristics; but every one has not as its signet, its proper name, a mighty fact, which strikes the least attentive observer; a fact, which materializing itself in its effects, becomes, by means of its external manifestations, familiar to all, and receives from all a popular appellation; a fact, in short, about which there may indeed be different opinions, but which no one thinks of denying. Such an impress is not wanting to our epoch; and the fact, which, among others, characterizes it, is that which is conventionally termed *the religious movement.*

The very name of this fact would seem to exclude it from the number of those of which I have spoken. It is religious, and its influence on religion may seem to be a spontaneous evolution of religion itself. It is not so, however. A religious fact is not religion. Brought to pass by means of man, it is a human fact, a fact at least of a mixed nature, in which we perceive both the presence of the divine idea and the influence of humanity. But, be this as it may, the confusion, if there be any, has not reached the question which we have presented, and nothing in reason is more legitimate than to ask: What has been the bearing of the religious movement on preaching, and how, in turn, has preaching reacted on the religious movement?

It is incontrovertible that a movement has taken place in the sphere of religious things. The complaints of some, the congratulations of others, the interest of all, bear witness to this movement; and as we are among those who are thankful for it, the question we have brought forward resolves itself naturally into this: What has preaching received from the religious movement, and what in return can preaching give to it?

Ought we here to inquire for the date, to trace the history, to determine the extent, to appreciate the nature, to conjecture the future of a fact at once so serious, so vast and so delicate? This task perhaps does not belong to us, and in its full extent transcends the limits of our subject. Still our subject itself requires the examination of certain parts of it. The religious movement, in its most essential elements, has had influence on preaching. These elements ought to be ascertained and expressed.

What impartial and thoughtful observers have called a religious movement, has received from another class a name which embraces a complete judgment. This movement with them is an *awakening*. We enter fully into their meaning when in our turn we define it a reaching forth of christianity towards its source, towards a more comprehensive view of the evangelical system, towards a more exact and extensive application of christian principles to human life. But let it not be thought that we ascribe to this movement, regarded in its purpose an entirely novel character. We deny that it has this character, or rather to express our thought better, we exempt the movement from the imputation of it, for absolute novelty would lead us to distrust it. Jesus Christ has promised to be with his church till the end of the world; now Jesus Christ is not divided; the truth which is himself, and by which alone he remains with us, this truth is one and indivisible, not one of its essential elements can perish; every truth, without which truth would be incomplete, is permanent and perpetual; and we are sure of finding it virtually at least, wherever we meet with life. Formulas may have an end, names may disappear, and when they do, doubtless we may have reason to think that ideas are obscured; now, ideas can be obscured only when sentiment or faith has suffered; such is the order of facts in parallel cases. Nevertheless, wherever we recognize life, truth is not far off; wherever, again, a part of the truth is frankly acknowledged and cordially professed, other parts, though concealed it may be in silence and shade, and seemingly disregarded, have a secret residence in the soul by the side of other elements of truth, from which they are inseparable. If Jesus Christ may be divided in theory, that is to say, in formulas and words which are external to man, he cannot be divided in sentiment which is man himself. If life, then, has always flowed in the church either in large streams or in rills, there has been, in one sense, a continuity of truth as well as a continuity of life; an unbroken tradition connects through intervening darkness the most remote and the most different epochs: Those which are termed *awakenings*, are in this view the offspring of antecedent epochs; the strong have descended from the strong, life has sprung from life, and though unquestionably the sovereign Lord can at any time make even nothing prolific, history witnesses that he has always employed that which *was* for the advantage of that which *was* to be; that he has chosen that men should receive the truth at once from God and their fore-fathers; that each generation should be indebted to the preceding one, and that no one should be able absolutely to disown its sire.

Yet more than this: In proportion as an epoch has been more embarrassed with sophisms, more destitute of believers, those who then, cherishing the flame of life, thereby witnessed for the truth—these, I say, whether from forgetting in part the doctrines of salvation, or misunderstanding their mutual and essential relations with each other, or whether from their having in their haste protested against the dawn of that new day which they will bless forever—these witnesses, in keeping alive the smoking flax, continuing the holy tradition of the ages, preparing a starting-point for the next generation, had need of more courage and more energetic faith than will be necessary perhaps for their successors. If truth is inherited, equally certain is it that courage is borrowed or given; it is easy to be sincere and strong, when we are compassed about by a cloud of witnesses, sustained by a thousand sympathies; but it is not good for man to be alone; we cannot live a higher life of any kind alone; we cannot, in a certain sense, believe alone. If Jesus Christ experienced this solitude, if he left the world without having tasted the sweets of spiritual communion, if nothing, neither faith nor love failed in him, the cause was that he was in all respects the SOLITARY ONE. Something, however, there is, which feebly recalls this unparalleled example; it is the life of his servants in a degenerate and infidel age: woe to us if we have no regard to it; if certain speculative errors, though perhaps serious in their principles and results, shall withhold our homage from those valiant and humble continuators of the everlasting testimony.

More favored, sirs, than other nations have been, we have witnessed with us no rejection of the truth, either in its documents or its essential articles, or in its just representations. The monuments of our Fathers' faith have remained sacred among their children, and examples are not wanting in our theological history, of an explicit reception of this inheritance, in confessions substantially the same with those which, three centuries ago, raised the standard of the everlasting gospel. We may say that at least, in our church, Jesus Christ has never been wrapped in the grave-clothes of oblivion, or contemptuously arrayed in the mantle of Socrates; that his holy Name has never been blasphemed—has always been praised and adored amongst us; that in our youth, our ears were wont to hear and our lips to proclaim the praise of Jesus, and that we, his messengers especially, have been familiar with a venerable voice which commended to us the love of Christ, the Mediator, as the chief qualification, and the sole efficiency of the evangelical ministry. Our Réals,* our Curtats and others, themselves the heirs of more ancient witnesses, have bequeathed to us confessions and examples; and if they were not in their day the centre of a movement

* RÉAL was the author of an excellent Course on Religion, for the publication of which we are indebted to Professor Dufournet.

like that which it is our privilege to behold, it was because God has times and purposes which he reserves in his own knowledge.

Less to the honor of certain men than to the glory of God, it was needful, sirs, to allude to these examples. But in respect to the Divine glory, itself, we must acknowledge in these times a progress beyond that of former days—a movement of reform and renovation. This is neither the place nor the season for presenting the defects of this human work, or the humanity which is visible in it. Let us note to-day only the Hand of the Master; and let us hasten to say with thanksgiving: Languid faith has relighted her torch; convictions are more frankly declared, more exactly expressed; belief, which had fallen into the condition of a corporate, and so to speak social affair, has become a personal and thus a living thing again. Many souls having become serious, have seized the good part which cannot be taken away from them; a larger number, affected in a less direct, more superficial manner, have begun to respect at least what they do not yet love; and the multitude are so accustomed to hear certain truths announced, that they would be now as much disturbed by their absence as they would perhaps have lately been offended by their presence. We must acknowledge that many in whom formerly the natural man would take almost nothing from the man of religion, have been brought to feel the need of strict consistency of life; that christianity, zealous as to fruit, has given an external manifestation of its truths in works as vast as itself is great; that it has caused its presence and reality to be felt in all spheres, even in the highest conditions of human life; that it has compelled society to take it into calculation; and, in fine, that a multitude of questions all of which imply the vitality of religion and a sense of its importance, and which, a short time since, would have been regarded as frivolous and antiquated, have become serious and urgent questions. Such is the state of the facts which we are endeavoring to represent, not from memory, but ex perience, for they are present and manifest. If now we consider the ideas themselves whence they have derived their strength, the doctrines they are connected with, it is impossible not to see that they have drawn not from the sepulchre but the shade, certain parts of the evangelical system which had fallen into desuetude; that to truths which have been always maintained, they have found a necessary complement in other truths which prescription seemed to have attainted; that elevating a fallen side of that mysterious triangle whereby christianity is the exact image of God himself, it has reinstated the doctrine of the Holy Spirit, and thus imparted substance to the words *regeneration* and *conversion*, so long unmeaning and dead; that these words, now become powerful ideas, have vitalized and illumined many others; that, by this means, christianity has formed a chain in thought, a chain in life, and in regard to both, has shown itself ascendant and energetic. It is, sirs, by these characteristics that the religious movement of the nineteenth century has been distinguished in every country to which it has extended. Admirable constancy, impressive unity, since no force has been employed, since in every country its principle has been the reinstatement of the Divine Word, which, whenever it obtains from the heart the respect which is due to it, restores to the church the same convictions, the same Christ, the same God.

If it is by means of preaching that the religious movement has been communicated, still preaching is not its principle; we may then inquire how far and in what respects it has modified this movement. But let me repeat, nothing here is absolutely new, nothing which has not already exist-, at least as an exception, and what we have to show is precisely this,—the exception making itself the rule.

Preaching has become more thoroughly Biblical; not only in this sense that textual citations from the Bible have been multiplied in sermons, and that the language of our ministers is more deeply imbued with that of the apostles and prophets, (the modern pulpit here should indeed confess to some abuse;) but in this more important sense, that the Word of God, in substance, abounds in it, that divine authority everywhere stamps its seal upon it, that the preacher, eclipsed by his mission, leaves nothing to be seen but the ambassador of the Most High. If, as we cannot deny, individuality has suffered loss, the fault is ours, not that of the principle, which, so far from requiring such a sacrifice, does not accept it. Truth requires to be individualized in each man; the better to illustrate its unity, it seeks to multiply itself in each of the souls by whom it is received; it does not regard itself as enriched by our loss; it does not spread ruins around itself; a living thing, it has no fellowship with death; it converts James, Peter and John, into saint James, saint Peter, and saint John, but in adding sanctity it does not take away humanity. God, moreover, by instituting preaching designed to bring man into contact with man; he attached to this contact a mysterious and singular virtue; now, who knows not that there is no real man except the individual, and that it is by his personality that one man acts on another? Besides, when the preacher is animated by a true zeal, individuality will guide itself aright; it is always with his own soul that one loves, entreats, laments, and, through too much uniformity of language and method, perhaps, the personal being will appear even in spite of itself, and set its seal on a work to which its trembling humility would assert no claim.

This profound respect, this reverence for the inspired

Word, has made it literally to abound in our pulpits from which it had before descended only in drops. The sermon has more frequently been replaced by the homily, the paraphrase; explaining holy scripture, and, as much as possible, explaining it by itself, appears to be, as it was in the first days of the Church, the more immediate mission of the preacher; the gospel flows in full tide in our churches, enlivening at once the eloquence of the minister and the interest of his hearers; the most insensible are made to feel the charm of his perpetual novelty; prejudice itself often expires before the divine unction of the Word; its sternest asseverations give less offence than our most prudent discourses; and preaching, as penetrated with this fresh savor, appears to gain equally in tenderness and in authority.

The teaching of the pulpit, in becoming more Biblical, must needs become more conclusive, more connected, more complete. In a system which is truth itself, every truth challenges another truth as its complement or its support, until at length the entire chain is gone over and joins indissolubly the infinitude of our misery with the infinitude of the divine wisdom and goodness. The mind, of itself, in the absence of every motive, requires this consecutiveness, and it cannot be doubted that God has designed to give peace at the same time to our understanding and our heart; and such satisfaction pulpit discourse has actually imparted to us, since doctrine in all its completeness has been set forth in relief. Since we have seen each particular subject so exhibited as to conduct us irresistibly to the beginning and the end of Christianity, and to introduce, as of itself, the whole of religion within the circle of each sermon, we have understood what we obscurely experienced formally, at the conclusion of some of our best sermons; we have thought, after so long a time, how many a truth appeared as if it were suspended in the air, how such another truth supported nothing, how all of them together did not bear on life taken in its full extent and depth; and how, in a word, something incoherent and incomplete was perceptible even in the best performances of the most logical men.

It is true that a delight which should peculiarly fill the soul, is too often diverted to the understanding, and, from the intimate connection between the different parts of our being, we may be sometimes deceived as to the seat of this delight. Possibly, a religion perfectly consistent because perfectly true, may have had in the view of some minds, the charm of a perfect syllogism. Possibly the satisfaction of being able to reason out our religion, may have led us into a little excess of reasoning: possibly we may have been desirous of extracting our religion, body and soul, out of logical abstractions, and by deducing the effect from the cause, we may have produced conversions rather intellectual than moral; possibly, even, we may have attempted to perfect a divine logic, and in order to open a plainer and more direct path to christian reasoning, may have excluded by silence at least, some inspired passage, and consequently some truth which God has set as a snare for logical pride. Possibly, indeed, a little of that rationalism which orthodoxy attacks with so much spirit, may be one of the characteristics of the new orthodoxy. But this abuse, the seriousness of which we would not conceal, is far from counterbalancing the unquestionable merit of a more systematic instruction in preaching —a merit of which the practical results should teach us the great importance.

If logic may be defined a necessity of the internal man, every element of our being has its logic, since every one conceals the germ of a necessity. The heart, the conscience, has its logic, as well as the understanding ; for each of these parts of our internal man when once a principle is recognized or felt, immediately demands the conclusion as a sacred debt. Now, when these three necessities coincide in one point, when in their union they bear upon the will with the weight of the entire man, how can the will resist, or rather is it not already absorbed in what absorbs the entire man? See, sirs, what the christian preacher becomes armed with, this triple logic. See what vivacity then will be in his word, what urgency in his demands. See with what strength a doctrine must bind souls, all the knots of which are so closely tied. See what importance preaching must possess, in which each discourse, by a happy necessity, contains the whole counsel of God.

But if you would test completely the principle of this urgency and this vehemence of reason, (I may well so name it, for it lies in things not in discourse, and the most moderate eloquence leaves it its full range,) mark the characteristic doctrines of the awakening: that vivid coloring which has displaced all half-tints; that thought which, comprising the whole gospel in the most urgent and commanding dilemmas, divides mankind into the friends and enemies of the truth, and the whole of life into two thoroughly distinct eras, that of the natural and that of the new man, the reign of the flesh and the reign of the spirit. Mark the new meaning given to this word *conversion*, which no longer signifies a gradual and imperfect reformation of morals, but a resurrection of the whole man redeemed from the most radical error and restored to the most fundamental truth; mark the abolition of that at once charitable and fatal assumption, which regarding an external and most superficial profession as serious, considers all those as believers whom baptism has devoted to faith, and, making no other difference between them than that of different degrees of zeal and purity, obliges the preacher to preach sanctification only, that is to say, to insist upon the consequence before the principle has been obtained. Truly must we confess, that in preaching according to this idea of it, Jesus Christ, not designedly but by logical consequence, had become a veritable out-work;* except by his example and teaching, he was no longer the starting-point of morality; and even then it was necessary to separate carefully from his teaching whatever suspended the moral destiny and eternity of man, on anything beside man himself: the only means of reaching the roots of moral life, of transplanting it into a new soil, of changing the wild into the true olive-tree, of engrafting a divine life on the human nature, of removing man from himself and restoring him to God—this means, rationally, existed no longer; and the most solemn words of Christ, and even his blood, were lost, and his name was a pleonasm in our discourse: and against the gospel thus understood there arose the most formidable of presumptions—one most auspicious to the hopes of infidelity, namely, that God, who is always constant in adapting the end to the means; God, who in all his works observes the most rigid economy and an exactitude absolutely mathematical, had accomplished less than he had undertaken, and had moved heaven and earth in vain, that is to say, without wisdom; in a word, that God who always calculates with perfect precision, and is always sure of his end in action, had been disappointed!

A sounder knowledge of the gospel, then, has saved, to the eye of reason, the honor of the government of God; and has furnished the preacher, if we may so speak, with a longer lever, by which he may raise up the very roots of our life. The word of the preacher has become more energetic, more vital, more incisive; it can arm itself, on each occasion, with the whole gospel, charge with the weight of the entire

* *Hors d'œuvre.*

truth, each particular truth of detail or application. Hence, that lively surprise, that astonishment in our temples, as if a new gospel was preached; hence those emotions heretofore unknown, those salutary wounds, which are not healed until he who inflicted them comes to bind them up; hence that rumor in society, that trouble in lately tranquil relations, to say the whole, those divisions in families,—a result which sometimes arises, it must be admitted, from the alarms of a suddenly-awakened indifference, and from the rudeness of a too impatient zeal. In a word, preaching in these same temples, these same consecrated forms, under the same official costume, has returned, through the gospel, to forgotten times, whose boldness, whose vehemence, and whose rudeness, in some instances, it has reproduced. Under the robes of a minister of the nineteenth century, a reformer of the sixteenth is often discovered; the pastor in his parish appears as a missionary; he would seem to have come from farther off than the neighboring borough; and, in fact, it is from farther off that he comes; he suddenly appears like a stranger in the midst of his flock, and, in fact, he is a stranger; he is a stranger on the earth, how much more in his village, in his town; and it may be said of him, without exaggeration, and almost without a figure, that "his place knoweth him no more." (Psalm ciii. 16.)

A change so important in the substance of teaching must needs have affected the form of pulpit compositions. The zeal of the messenger excited by the very nature of his message leads him to multiply himself, to abound, so to speak, in places, persons and occasions. Discourses in which applications of doctrine replace the connection of ideas, and the regularity of the didactic process, discourses which employ familiar analogies, pointed allusions, those spirited apostrophes which seem to decompose the auditory in order to maintain a colloquy between each individual and the preacher, those pressing alternatives, which, forcing the hearer to declare for or against the truth during the session of the assembly, make the hours of worship really hours of trial and initiation, naturalize in the bosom of our churches the popular eloquence of the highways or the desert. From the multiplicity of oratorical exercises, in season and out of season, extemporizing proceeds, a practice which had been almost unknown amongst us. It even becomes necessary to those of our ministers who desire that religion amongst and around them should assume the character of a reality, and who cannot be content that a living word should exist only in a word recited. Even discourses which are written and committed to memory, sometimes become, through haste in the labor, another form of extemporizing. What is termed *meditation*, that is, all discourse in the least degree meditated, becomes abundant. Perhaps use here has a tendency to abuse. It seems to be forgotten that it is necessity alone that justifies exclusive extemporizing; that ordinarily the retrenchment of written composition, instead of excluding, requires a severe preparation, and that nothing indeed should be better premeditated than an extemporaneous discourse. We may, perhaps, at the present time, satisfied with having received to ourselves an aptitude in which we were wanting, think ourselves obliged, by the importance of the subjects of the pulpit, either to cultivate this aptitude with extreme care, or to reserve the use of it to circumstances which require it, allowing the habitual exercise of it only to those special and consummate abilities which cannot be made a precedent, since the very exhibition of their force teaches us, in spite of ourselves, the useful secret of our weakness.

In describing so far the influence of the religious movement on preaching, I have been unable to avoid noting an immediate reaction of preaching on this movement itself. But this latter reaction is wholly spontaneous; it springs without design from the very nature of things; there is another reaction which is voluntary, the result of reflection and free choice in which preaching, not content with allowing religion to re gain by a natural tendency the advantage which it has drawn from it, seeks to derive from other sources additional advan tage which study and reflection from time to time make manifest to it. It here appears purely as a means, as an instrument, and offers to christianity the tribute of certain resources which it has not directly borrowed from it. There is no profane temerity in speaking in this manner; there would be, certainly, if we sought to add to the intrinsic value of the gospel, or wished to make it more perfect, to improve it; to say that we wish to serve it, to say even that it has need of our services, is not to ascribe to it a decrepit and precarious existence; it is but entering into the very spirit of its author. In the moral world, the force of God which is not to be appreciated, consists of our forces, even as the work of his providence is very often the sum of our works; if you decompose the power displayed by christianity into visible elements, you will find in the last analysis only human forces. Whatever God works in this arrangement, he works through us, but it is he who evokes our will, who determines it; it is he who permeates and coördinates the elements offered to him by our nature; we give him only what he has given to us; we work only what he works in us; he is, in a word, the force of our forces, he consequently is all; our life is his life, and we are always himself.*

* Is there any one to whom these last lines require to be explained? I hope no one will see in them more than I have intended, namely, a persuasion that all good flows from God, and ought to be ascribed to him; that every moral agent, in doing good, fulfils the purpose and performs the work of God; that it is impossible to dis-

Now, assuming these principles, how may the pulpit subserve the religious movement? It may be replied, partly by purifying, partly by accrediting it. But this distinction is superfluous. The last of these effects is contained in the first. Whatever shall purify this movement, will also propagate it. Let us not misunderstand what the gospel affirms respecting the natural opposition of man to the doctrine of salvation. This opposition indeed is certain, but not less so is the adaptation of the gospel to the deepest necessities of our nature, or to embrace all in a word, the perfect humanity of the christian religion. When a heart is gained *to* the gospel, it is gained *by* the gospel, by something which is in the gospel; and lest you should impute the change to nothing more than some occult influence, or as Saurin says, to I know not what "fabulous enchantment," that heart will be careful to tell you what has gained it, and it will tell you this so perfectly that you will be astonished at only one thing, namely, why it is that all hearts appealed to by the same means are not also gained. Here is the mystery, but it is only here. The gospel is reason itself, hence it gains us; the gospel is reason itself, hence it repels us. Be this as it may, its force is in showing itself as it is; and whatever manifests it more fully, makes it more powerful, and the more it shows itself divine,

tinguish and separate from God's work, what he does not work directly and personally, that is to say, in few words, whatever is not, strictly speaking, a miracle; that it is even a contradiction to suppose that anything which is true, anything which really *is*, does not always and in every instance flow from him. This is my thought, not that there is any confusion of essence between God and man; not that our personality is absorbed in that of God, not especially that our personality is absorbed in his liberty. In my view, and so must every one think who examines his consciousness, man, in respect of good or of God, is a living channel, personal and free; God is the fountain which flows through this channel.

the more will it be human; it ceases to be human, that is to say, suited and adapted to humanity, only when man by robbing it of its crown of miracles and its veil of mystery, would bring it down to himself. If Jesus Christ should cease to be perfect God, he would cease to be perfect man.

To extend the religious movement, then, we must purify it. If it has been restricted within limits narrower than our hopes, it was, on one hand, I readily acknowledge, because it was christian; but it was also because it was not enough so. The day of repulsion draws to a close; let us hasten that in which the power of attraction is to prevail. How are we to do this? By imitating Jesus Christ.

In his actions as well as in his nature, Jesus Christ was perfect man. Let us consent to be so. Jesus Christ accommodated his word and his action to the circumstances in which he acted and spoke; his apostles followed his example. Let us follow their example and his. Let us ever keep before us humanity and the age. Let us descend (if indeed it be descending) from the pure region of ideas into the domain of the real and the actual. By so doing we always approach nearer to Christianity and the Gospel.

Thus preaching, faithful to its mission, walking in its own footsteps, will continue to publish those doctrines which abase all human pride before the counsel of God; it will announce this God on earth, this God on the cross, perpetual folly to the Greeks of all places, perpetual scandal to the Jews of all ages; it will proclaim as the sole condition of salvation, that new birth, the necessity of which abolishes all pride in the human soul—dangerous preaching, which provokes the meekest, and moves the contemptuous pity of the most ignorant of mankind! This way though sowed with thorns, is the good one; let preaching always walk therein! But, faithful, in every respect, to the Master's example, let it always combine the characteristics of humanity with the characteristics of the age.

Our imagination here does not labor without assistance; the existing pulpit, sirs, you are aware presents us fine models, fine in our sense of the term, of evangelical orators who are attentive to the signs of the times and the characteristics of humanity.

The few ideas which we have yet to propose to you, we shall not arrange distinctly under the two leading ones, which we have indicated, namely, humanity and the present age; they correspond to both at the same time, as with propriety they may; each age taken in its reality conceals the real man as a whole; and that which meets the legitimate demands of an epoch, meets the exigencies of human nature.

Thus the present epoch requires what humanity requires, when it demands that the rational side of christianity, its philosophy, be set in relief, and that it become, as it were, the instrument of an intellectual, as well as of a moral regeneration. This demand or this right, consequently this duty, is one of all times; there certainly has not been an epoch in which the gospel should not have been held as reasonable. We may even, in a sublime sense, call that *reason* which in all ages has determined mind to submit itself to the gospel.* But

* Fond as we are and justly fond of faith,
Reason we grant demands our first regard:
The mother honor'd as the daughter dear.
Reason the root, fair Faith is but the flower,
The fading flower shall die but Reason lives
Immortal, as her father in the skies. * * *
Wrong not the Christian; think not reason yours;
'Tis reason our great Master holds so dear;
'Tis reason's injured rights his wrath resents;
'Tis reason's voice obey'd, his glories crown:
To give lost reason life, he pour'd his own,

the equilibrium which is now demanded, has not been always so distinctly demanded. The conscience and heart, the processes of which are essentially summary and synthetic, have often left little place for the analyses of reason. We may even go further. The conscience and heart have often had to be reasonable, in place of reason, which has not been so; and everything has been clear and logical in the soul, when everything in the mind has been embarrassed and subtile. The epoch in which we live appears to have taken as a motto, the apostolical precept: "Let your obedience be reasonable." It has, perhaps, demanded not so much the exposition of the external proofs of religion, as the demonstration of its internal consistency, and its agreement as a whole with whatever belongs to the heart and to human affairs. It requires an explanation of christianity and its philosophy. Not, sirs, a philosophy which it would obtain in exchange for christianity, but a philosophy which it desires to receive from the hands of christianity.* Nor does it ask for an intellectual exhibition for the satisfaction of certain superior understandings; it asks for a satisfaction in which the popular reason is to have a share. What it requires as an end, it also requires as a means; it supposes that christianity so taught, would become to the people the most powerful incentive to reflection, the most effectual means of intellectual elevation, and the source of all the substantial and

---

Believe, and show the reason of a man;
Believe, and taste the pleasure of a god;
Believe, and look with triumph on the tomb,
Thro' reason's wounds alone the faith can die.

(YOUNG, *Night IV.*)

* "Allerdings ist Dogmatik eine Philosophie und muss als solche studirt werden; nur eine Philosophie *aus der Bibel* geschœpft, und diese muss immer ihre *Quelle* bleiben." (HERDER'S *Briefe das Studium der Theologie bettrefend.*)

sound ideas by which their life ought to be governed. I readily admit that preaching, so far as it is christian, has met these necessities and demands; but who can say that attentive observation of men and of the age is not necessary to their being met more perfectly, and, what is greatly to be admired, to their rendering preaching in this respect more christian? for such is the correspondence between the christian religion and humanity, that each, well apprehended, must lead to the other, and so faith and nature approximate each other.

When we speak of the philosophy of christianity, we seem to be speaking of something extraordinary, far remote, accessible to but a few minds; and yet to say that christianity is philosophical, is but saying in other terms, that it agrees with itself, with our nature, that it is human, simple, consistent, practical. Thus we can take no better way to exhibit the philosophy of the gospel, to enter into the spirit of the age, to promote the religious movement, than by making our sermons to abound in the morality which abounds in the gospel itself. The christian pulpit, in this respect, has a position to regain, and until it does regain it, the preacher cannot know what, in such an epoch as ours, may be his authority and his power. Let him examine, then, the book of God, under a new aspect; he will there see morality everywhere prominent, sometimes completing, and sometimes completed by doctrine; he will see these two parts of truth not only in harmony but extending one another. Let him admire this continuity, let him lead his hearers to admire it. Every day he hears the demand from the world, preach morality to us. Let him not repel that demand in contempt of the motives which prompt it; it is founded in right, it deserves to be, at the same time, corrected and met; let the preacher do both; let morality be set at large in his discourses on a solid foundation; with equal care let him show that morality is all doctrine, and doctrine all morality; let the one of these make the other to abound; let this noble science of life and manners, a natural appendage of the preacher, ascend by a severe study to the rank from which it has fallen; let morality, by turns descriptive, speculative, practical, be united in all subjects as intimately as the blood is united to the flesh, fill our discourses with its solid wealth; in a word, let the minister of the Gospel take possession again of his ancient prerogative, that of being the closest confidant of the human heart, the most instructive and the most practical of moralists.

We shall further hearken to the counsels of the times and promote the religious movement, by improving the forms of sacred discourse. The time is past, if it ever existed, in which the pulpit may remain with impunity behind the other branches of the art of writing, in respect of precision and purity of language. It is necessary, at the present day, in order to banish from the threshold of conscience, prejudices which, to certain minds of a fastidious character, may be a lasting hinderance, that evangelical discourse should not be unpolished and rude; it is necessary, that when compared with other products of the understanding, it should not appear chargeable with any kind of inferiority, and that no one should have it to say, with any appearance of reason, that it is only the ears of the vulgar of which it has the command. We approach society, we gain a real authority over it, by striving with it after progress of every kind, by commending to it the only progress in which its zeal is deficient. By expressing truth with precision, with energy, we strengthen the impression which it produces, we render to it its native beauty. And let it not be imagined that the merit of an elaborate composition may be anywhere lost, from its not being everywhere appreciated with the same justice. In all minds true excellence and true beauty find a point where they are felt. Their intimate congruity with all the primitive wants of our soul enables them, at length, to penetrate it; the discernment of just expressions and select forms gradually becomes an instinct with the multitude; and the preacher's care as to the logic of his composition and the texture of his language, gives him a new authority over the people, whereby he becomes not only their spiritual guide, but, in many respects, their law-giver.

The pastor who has always been the principal school-master of each parish, thus becomes so, in a more special manner; the church is the high-school both of adults and little children; religion, in short, is manifestly the centre of all civilizing ideas. For by such an unwonted application to the culture of the entire man, to the provision of pure aliment for each of his faculties, and especially to the establishment of unity and order among them, the secret of effecting which is possessed only by religion, it scatters from the elevation of the pulpit into the furrows of society, the seeds of civilization, which is nothing other than the relative perfection of the state of man. We should beware of engaging in questions which the gospel would neither agitate nor resolve; it is not the part of the gospel to transport itself into the State, rather does it belong to the latter to transport itself to the religious point of view, but it belongs to preaching to open its way to it, by discovering to it, by making visible to it, the sympathy of religion for man, and the cognizance which it takes of all our true interests. In order to do this preaching is under no necessity to forsake its own good part, and, like another Martha, to occupy itself with many different things; let it only understand what "the one thing needful" includes; let it be more consistent with all the characteristics of humanity, and discover no ignorance of the end for which man was made, give him no occasion, by the uniformity of its accent, by a studied dignity, by a factitious asceticism of language, by the affected avoidance of certain details and allusions, in a word, by I know not what excentricity, for the supposition that it dwells in the void, far away from him, and that to begin to be a christian is to cease to be a man. Religion, I think, would appear much more as a real thing, near and necessary, if it were seen as a pure and divine essence, palpitating in the life, and if preaching after showing itself to us as rational, should make us feel that it is a thing of life, that is to say, human.*

If, from a distant date, preaching, with a structure somewhat rigid and forms somewhat arbitrary, has wanted the character of a discourse thoroughly real, and having a business-like purpose, a character which the tribune and the bar have never lost, this is a disadvantage which, in the epoch in which we live, will be much more observable. If anything distinguishes our age it is that positive spirit which restores all the metaphors of life to their proper meaning, which inquires for the value of each sign, the reason of each form, which would have every word to be a fact, every discourse an action, which banishes every arbitrary or unintelligible ceremonial from style as well as from society, and which requires eloquence, especially, to explain its procedures no longer to, I know not what kind of art, what kind of congruities, but to life. Without inquiring whether this tendency is not becoming excessive, we maintain that the traditional form of pulpit discourse, a form which its purpose has never fully authorized, is in this day a real anachronism ; and that in the midst of a movement which tends to transform idea into business, it is most unsuitable to give to the most positive as well as most important business, the deceptive appearance

* See the note at the end of the discourse.

of an idea. Formerly, however, when formality enveloped everything, there was no place for painful comparisons, but from what, in our day, has religious movement to suffer more, than from a parallel which would oblige us to regard it as alone among human interests, dissembling its reality, and, in this respect alone, faithful to the traditions of the past, which thus render it, in spite of itself, a thing of the past, a dead thing ?

We shall not invoke the interest of pulpit dignity in favor of these exceptional forms. Most singular would it be if a form were to be more worthy in proportion as it answers less to its understood purpose ! Unfortunate, indeed, if dignity should exclude naïvete, intimacy, and even good sense (for, from a costume which disfigures every subject, this suffers more than all.) Most certainly we would not have the evangelical word cease to be august in order to be familiar.* Let christianity lose nothing of its majesty ; in an epoch in which respect is disappearing, let it remain the object of a last respect, and restore all other kinds, respect for conscience, for law, for age, for infirmity and misfortune ; but in a positive age, let it show itself yet more positive and more real than everything else ; let us trust to its incomparable dignity to counterbalance the familiarity of forms, and far from fearing that ridicule will connect itself with the simple expressions

* I cannot forbear, here, throwing in a remark. There have been times and places in which preaching became, (almost so, at least,) a serious and familiar colloquy, the pulpit an arm-chair, the church a conventicle ; in some respects this was well, but let us not proceed too far ; let us preserve to preaching that majesty which is connected in part with the idea of a great community, of a confederation of consciences, and of an influence on masses. Let not a stranger who enters a temple, regard as a confidential conversation, a discourse in which he expected a reproduction of the Apostles, the Fathers, and the great orators of the ancient pulpit

of nature, and the vivid colors of reality, let us not forget that to the pulpit only is it permitted to be familiar with impunity, and that nothing more surely exposes it to ridicule than a ceremonious politeness so opposite to the frankness of the prophets, and from a parade of forms so different from the unrestrained pathos and the impetuous logic of the apostles.

There may be no disagreement between artifices intended to disguise the true form of things, and other sorts of eloquence which have to conceal in their purpose, I know not what kind of interior nothing, but christianity, which is essential life and substance, christianity which, among the things which interest us, is the only one absolutely serious and solid, is only a gainer by presenting herself without her veil.

Preachers! your business is a business; yet more than senators and advocates, you are advocates and senators; be both; let your pulpit be to you alternately a tribune and a bar; let your word be an action directed to an immediate object; let not your hearers come to hear a discourse, so much as to receive a message; possess yourselves, possess them of all the advantages which pertain to the subjects of the pulpit; your eloquence has more artless aspects and more vivid tints than that of the senate or the bar; nothing condemns it to abstraction; everything impels it toward sensible facts. Your religion was a history before it became an idea; and to-day, after too long a stagnation, the lake becomes a river again, the idea becomes again a history. What hinders you from adding in the pulpit to the miracles of the past, the marvels of the present, and from recounting, day by day, the history of God? Why may you not mingle with your instructions the glorious news of the kingdom, and make your temples resound with the cries of distress, and the songs of victory, and if it must be so, even with the complaints of the church militant? Why not show in christianity more than a doctrine, but above all, that it is a living fact, perpetually gushing forth, and now, thanks to God, in large and rapid floods. Is the history closed that you relate? Does God sleep? or should his past works be ashamed of his new works? Or, indeed, is all which is done for the glory of God by other than salaried hands, and with other resources than the treasure of the State, without claim to be mentioned in your official pulpits, and before the flock which has been committed to you? And are we still to regard as matter of religious luxury, of christian *dilettantism*, labors which hold the first rank among our duties? And shall we reserve for the conferences of the initiated, the recital of a work which perpetuates that of Peter and Apollos, of Paul and Timothy?

Either, sirs, I am greatly deceived, or the present epoch demands facts from christianity and recitals from the pulpit. Recitals mixed in just proportion with formal and direct in struction, are interesting to all classes of hearers. More than all arguments, they convince the multitude that christianity is living, that religion is a thing for man. I would not surfeit, nor even amuse the imagination. I would not go, of preference, beyond seas and beneath unknown skies, to seek for extraordinary scenes. I would often, so I think, take serious and simple facts from my neighborhood, from the enclosure of our own country and manners; I would select modest, obscure, unobtrusive ones; I would cite, if I might, lives rather than actions; I would only at proper times and at intervals enlarge the horizon of my auditory; I would endeavor by all means gradually to give the religion which I announce, the aspect of a business and an urgent business; I would not fear making it, if needs be, the business of the country, of the commune, of the place; still I would touch discreetly on these aspects of the subject, lest the interest of the individual be merged in that of society, and the eternal in that which is local and transitory.

I have given you, sirs, few ideas and very long details. The subject might have been treated more largely and more briefly. Excuse at the same time my omissions and my expansion. I am impatient to release your wearied attention; but can I do so without, in a few words, relieving a heart which is too full, which until now has been obliged to restrain itself, and which even now would feign repress its emotions, but not by imposing on itself a silence which it cannot maintain ?

One thought has long filled and oppressed my heart, which I would fain express in words; it is that which arises in me when I compare what I am with the chair which has been entrusted to me. But this chair I have at length accepted, and whatever may be the state of my mind and my apprehensions as to my future, I know that henceforth I am not to speak of them to men; an instinct which will be comprehended, from this moment puts a seal on my lips.

But I may, I ought to say thus much:

I enter on my new career with two sentiments, which if God preserve them to me, must impart one direction to my labors, one tenor to my life.

The first of these sentiments is that of the responsibility of my position. I am to succeed a man, whose christian virtues, great experiences, valuable and long-continued services, admirable probity and prudence, gave him an authority to which I shall never aspire. In concert with my honorable colleagues, I am to labor after his example, in giving worthy ministers to the church of Jesus Christ. If the responsibility of ministers is great, what then is ours ? What, in particular, is that of the professor who is charged to give instruction more directly, to candidates for the ministry, in regard to the exercise of their functions, to determine by his lessons the whole character and form of their life. This idea which has taken possession of me, I have retained with a kind of affection; I have not been willing to allow it to escape from me; I have hardly suffered any other that might temper and soften it, to connect itself with it; I have desired to taste without abatement its austerity, and, if I may so express myself, its holy bitterness, and, with a proper distrust of myself, I have repelled, or or at least delayed the outward supports which have been and are presented to me, and which I regard prospectively with gratitude, but which I shall accept only when God shall permit me to do so.

Think not, however, students of this Academy, that my heart refuses the sweet intercourse, to which I doubt not, your friendship will tempt it. This heart, let me assure you, is not reluctant to open itself. It asks but little, in truth, and would not even accept sympathies too much above what it merits; confidence and respect is the mild atmosphere in which I need to live, and apart from which the small abilities I possess are disquieted and vanish. I say nothing of the views with which I come to you; I am afraid to say too much concerning them at a moment in which an intense preoccupation holds the most natural sentiments captive in my heart, and under the weight of this preoccupation, I am also afraid of saying too little. Let us then, sirs, leave the expression of them to time and facts; and rest persuaded, that I regarded you, in accepting my charge, that my predominant thought had relation to you, and that from this moment, the object of your own desires and most serious prayers shall be the first concern of my life.

Be indulgent then, to-day, in your requirements of me. I might speak of my affection for you, and no one would doubt my sincerity. Prefer, however, to hear me on the object of our common affection and on the point of view in which I regard our common vocation. Suffice it that I assure you, that I come in the name and at the call of God, to study with you a human art, which as to its use, and as to its means, has been rendered divine. In particular, be content to know, that the man who offers himself, to aid as far as he can, your meditations and studies in regard to preaching, though firmly resolved to propose to you all the natural resources which give works of art their relative perfection, has the fullest conviction that God alone understands art, that his Spirit alone is eloquent in our discourses, and that in the words of my venerable predecessor, to paint usefully the great things of the everlasting kingdom, "we must dip our pencils in the azure of heaven."

The other sentiment to which I would give utterance is that of gratitude. What a demand has there been upon me for the use, the exercise of this sentiment, the most pure and useful of the human soul! The object of the most touching attentions from the bosom of the honorable and illustrious city in which I have passed in peace the half of my life, I have seen, if I may venture to speak thus, my dear country extending to me her arms; I have seen my native place, after twenty years, acknowledging and again demanding me, and three corporations at once, than which none amongst us are either more respected or more worthy of respect, concurring with one another, in order to bind me anew to my country, by the most honorable ties. To the council of the State, I venture to offer through you, M. Councillor, as their organ, the homage of my respectful gratitude, for the confidence in me which they have shown, and for all the valuable adjuncts with which they have been pleased to surround my function. Be pleased then, as President of the Council of Public Instruction, to assure that authority, the source of so much good and so many useful projects in the midst of us, of my profound desire that the appointment in which it has cordially concurred, may, by the divine blessing, be one day reckoned with the good which it has done. And will you, sir, the Rector, and you gentlemen, members of the Academy, to whom I owe the same sentiment, since you gave the first impulse to that series of actions which have resulted in my as sociation with you in labor, receive with a generosity worthy of you, treat with indulgence, a novice, who perhaps will long remain one ; bear with his inexperience, and pardon him if his health, long since impaired, does not permit him to concur with as much energy as may be desirable, in the various labors in which he is to partake with you. If good-will goes for aught, if in the view of benevolence, it takes the place of positive benefit, the colleague you have just received will cause you no regret. May God, the God of peace and holiness, of equity and love, be always with you and this new colleague ; and may He grant to me that I may not too painfully disappoint your just expectation, that of the honorable government, that of the country. I HAVE DONE.

NOTE REFERRED TO ON PAGE 501.

Is it true that one of the conditions of zeal is a certain narrowness of views, a certain poverty of ideas? Some persons appear so to think, and some facts seem to support their opinion. Many men who are zealous for religion show little jealousy in doing justice to all the faculties of the soul, to all its tendencies, to the whole of human nature. These verses, designed for a wholly different purpose, may be said to apply to them:

De la *limite* rigoureuse,
Où le *cœur* semble reserré,
Il reçoit cette force heureuse
Qui l'elève au plus haut degré.
Telle, dans des canaux pressée,
Avec plus de force élancée,
L'onde s'elève dans les airs.*

A perplexing inconsistency, if it be real; for zeal is not an irregularity, an error; zeal also is a truth; how can it be inconsistent with other truths?—unless, indeed, it be connected with some error, for all error is inconsistent not only with some one particular truth but with all truths taken collectively. But the inconsistency does not exist. It cannot be proved from the nature of things, that one truth can be loved and promoted only at the expense of contemning and opposing other truths; and, then, as there have been men of intelligent and comprehensive views, who were zealous in a given di-

* "From the narrow *limits* within which the heart seems to be confined, it receives a happy force, which increases its elevation; as the wave, by being compressed in its channel, shoots forward with more power, and raises itself on high." —Tr.

rection, the scandal falls of itself. All that we may admit (and this doubtless should be admitted) is that, in our disordered nature, force will always be less uncommon than equilibrium in force, that this equilibrium is more common when there is a mediocrity or indifference of talent, as it is naturally, in the scales of a balance in which there is nothing; that a strong conviction easily disturbs it; man, with all his will for what is true when he has discovered it, for what is good when he has recognized it, has not too much, nor even enough of it. Force in this case throws itself with impetuosity on the important side, or that which has been hitherto neglected, or is in present danger. Be not too severe towards the man of narrow mind; he is narrow only through severity toward himself. Respect his motives while you censure their effects. Prefer anything to indifference, and impute to the narrow, but conscientious man, all the affections which, though he has them not, he yet would have them if his conscience would permit, and will have them as soon as he shall know them to be right and necessary. His time has not yet come. Truth, most certainly is one, and to be in favor of one truth is, at the same time, to be in favor of every one. In principle, in an abstract sense, this is so, and no man unquestionably can be the friend of one truth and intentionally the enemy of any other.

But still it is necessary that this agreement, this unity of truths, be recognized; still must it be perceived how distant and apparently isolated facts are united by invisible links; how, especially, institutions, works, over which vice has spread itself, are yet of divine origin, of divine right, as well as that supreme truth in the light of which they will be one day acknowledged. Let us consider that the actual world puts the zealous christian into some embarrassment, and that to insist that he shall at the first glance admit it into the frame-work of his faith, is most frequently to insist on what is impossible. If you say to him that if his religion be true, it should take a whole world into its enclosure, that the christian ought, if need be, to include the artist, the mechanic, the politician, the philosopher, that all religion which is not coextensive with human nature, is untrue; and that we must either write this nature false, or embrace it fully with all its consequences; perhaps he will not contradict this, but he will be perplexed in making application of it; perhaps, also, he will exclude from human life what he knows he cannot admit into his system, and thus the truth will be, in appearance, a new bed of Procrustes. The truth, however, and the truth alone, so far from excluding anything, receives everything. The gospel alone is as large as life, since it is infinitely large, since, in every sense, "God is greater than our heart;" religion is to life what the horizon of reason is to the horizon of sense; and it is only in its comprehensive bosom that all true things recognize and embrace each other. In the world of the gospel, but in no other, is there a place for everything. A perfect world, in which there is no jar, no discord, is possible only by means of the gospel; and if the appearance be otherwise, it is because the greater part of evangelical men, (I say not the gospel,) cannot at once conceive of the perfect world which the gospel embraces, and have in their view beforehand, as the model of the social world, only that formless mass which actual reality presents to them, and which calls itself the nature of things. These men, in the embarrassment which results to them from this two-fold circumstance, attempt to retain the gospel apart from its developments and applications, apart from human life, apart from the world; to call that mutilated remnant the world and human life which has no longer signification or use; to falsify thus (though without intending it) the gospel itself, and to impress upon it, in the eyes of the multitude, a stamp of narrowness and exclusiveness which does not belong to it. But this error, in sincere and reflecting minds, is not lasting; and even without the aid of reflection, the gospel is so human that of itself it descends towards life, and makes them to descend with it; it quietly proves itself to be in harmony with nature; it silently verifies its relationship to man, while it purifies, corrects, organizes everything, it connects itself with everything; it re-constructs within its own pale a world in which there is scope for all our faculties, food for all our forces, a horizon for all our thoughts, and in an exeellent sense, this world of the gospel or of grace, is the world of man and of nature. Do you ask, where is this world? Where shall we seek it? In no constitution with which I am acquainted, in the morals of no people taken in the mass, but in many an individual, in many a family in whom it is realized with surprising perfection and the sweetest charms.

INDEX.

A.

22*

B.

C.

D.

E.

E.

F.

G.

H.

I.

J.

K.

L.

M.

N.

O.

P.

S.

T.

U.

V.

W.

Z.

WILLSON'S HISTORICAL SERIES.

NOTICES OF WILLSON'S UNITED STATES.

From the Pennsylvania Enquirer.

"We believe it to be by far the most accurate school-history of the United States ever published. The style of the work will be found peculiarly clear and concise and at the same time easy and attractive."

From the Courier and Journal, Albany.

"An improvement upon any history of the United States of the kind that we have met. It is comprehensive enough to give a full idea of the subject, and is brief enough not to be tedious to the pupil. Besides, it is accurate and reliable in its facts."

From the New Jersey Advocate.

"A work superior, in many respects, to all that have preceded it, as a text-book of American History."

Narragansett Fort and Swamp.

From the Poughkeepsie Journal.

"Willson's Historical Works will confer a lasting benefit on our country."

From the Newark Daily Advertiser.

"If the present work is not *all* that we desire, it is, we are persuaded, the nearest approximation to a true standard of School-History that has as yet been made."

From the New York Observer.

"Mr. Willson is favorably known by his United States History, which is distinguished for its accuracy and comprehensiveness."

From the American Journal of Education.

"We know of no other volume of American History which is so accurate, and at the same time so full."

From the Book Committee, Cincinnati.

"The Text-Book Committee having examined Marcius Willson's History of the United States, would hereby recommend it as a suitable book for the use of the Common Schools of the city. We would suggest, that hereafter it should be used in the place of Mrs. Willard's Abridgment. The work now recommended is one of great accuracy, clear and forcible style, and the arrangement of the work is natural. The marginal dates, (new style,) as here arranged, we consider of great importance to a school-book, when dates are taught as a part of Common School Instruction.

On the 22d February, 1847, the Board of Trustees and Visitors of the Common Schools of Cincinnati unanimously adopted the following resolution:—

"*Resolved*, That the United States History, by Marcius Willson, be, and the same is hereby adopted by the Board of Trustees and Visitors, as the text-book to be used in the Common Schools of Cincinnati, in place of the Abridgment, by Mrs. Willard."

WILLSON'S HISTORICAL SERIES.

No. 2.—WILLSON'S HISTORY OF THE UNITED States. 75 cents.

Plan of the Siege of Quebec.

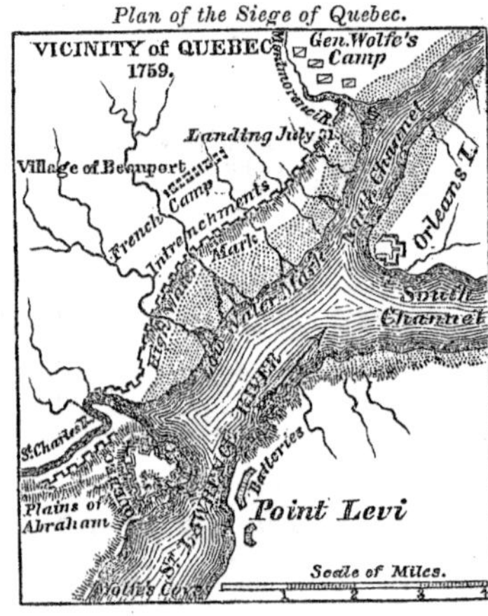

Commencing with the discovery of America, and brought down to the middle of the Nineteenth century. The work presents the following claims to public favor:—1st, superior accuracy; 2d, chronological arrangement of dates, wholly in new style; 3d, illustrative maps and charts, and copious Geographical Notes, exhibiting to the eye, and describing all important localities referred to; 4th, convenient Marginal Arrangement of the Questions. An Appendix contains the Constitution of the United States, with Explanatory Notes, abridged from the author's work on "Civil Polity," or Constitutional Law.

Willson's History of the United States has been introduced into the Public Schools of New York City, the Normal School in Albany, the Public Schools in Newark, Brooklyn, Rochester, Buffalo, Cincinnati and St. Louis, &c., as well as in great numbers of Male and Female Academies and Seminaries in all parts of the country. During the first year of its publication, *fourteen thousand* copies were sold.

From the numerous recommendations and notices of the work, the Publishers select the following:—

Siege of Yorktown.

NOTICES.

"Boston, Dec. 6th, 1845.

"I consider it the best, and in reality the only School History I have ever seen, adapted to the wants of our Common Schools.

"JOSHUA BATES,
"Principal of Brimmer Grammar School."

"Burlington, N. J., 11th mo. 6th, 1845.

"Willson's History of the United States for the use of Schools, I have read through with peculiar satisfaction. If any other book, compiled for the same purpose, equals it in combining brevity with clearness of detail, impartiality with a manly regard for national interests, elevation of style with the simplicity due to youth, and especially geography with history, I am not acquainted with it.

"The writer seems to be imbued with a just perception of the wants of the scholar and the facilities due to the teacher.

"JNO. GRISCOM."

WILLSON'S HISTORICAL SERIES.

FRANKLIN, THE PRINTER'S BOY.

No. 1.—WILLSON'S JUVENILE AMERICAN History. For Primary Schools; on the same general plan as the History of the United States. Embracing the most interesting and morally instructive incidents and events in American History, commencing with the Life of Columbus. Handsomely illustrated. 160 pages. 31 cents.

FRANKLIN, THE PHILOSOPHER.

This work is designed for younger classes in Schools. Many of the lessons are accompanied by judicious pictorial illustrations; allusion is constantly made to the geography of the parts described, and numerous maps associate pictorial events with their localities.

From the Western School Journal.

"Mr. Willson, to avoid the errors of his predecessors, has investigated closely, has faithfully collated and verified his facts and dates, and, as a natural consequence, has produced *a most accurate work*. The narrative is given in a clear, simple style, and the biographical sketches are forcibly and vividly descriptive."

www.ingramcontent.com/pod-product-compliance
Lightning Source LLC
LaVergne TN
LVHW021307110826
845150LV00003B/507

* 9 7 8 1 4 2 5 5 5 9 2 2 9 *